WITHDRAWN

305.896 B631   c.2
BLACKS IN AMERICA;   FV
BIBLIOGRAPHICAL ESSAYS
                                6.45

R BK   305.896   B631
BLACKS IN AMERICA
       1971   6.45 FV
3000 274510 30020
St. Louis Community College

Library

5801 Wilson Avenue
St. Louis, Missouri 63110

JAMES M. MCPHERSON, JAMES M. BANNER, JR., and NANCY J. WEISS teach in the History Department at Princeton University. LAURENCE B. HOLLAND teaches in the English Department at The Johns Hopkins University, and MICHAEL D. BELL teaches in the English Department at Princeton University.

BLACKS IN AMERICA

Bibliographical Essays

by

JAMES M. McPHERSON

LAURENCE B. HOLLAND

JAMES M. BANNER, Jr.

NANCY J. WEISS

MICHAEL D. BELL

ANCHOR BOOKS

Doubleday & Company, Inc.

Garden City, New York

BLACKS IN AMERICA: BIBLIOGRAPHICAL ESSAYS
*was published in a hardcover edition by
Doubleday & Company, Inc. in 1971.*

Anchor Books Edition: 1972

*Copyright © 1971 by The Trustees of Princeton
University for the Program in American
Civilization at Princeton University
All Rights Reserved
Printed in the United States of America*

To
HELEN WRIGHT

ACKNOWLEDGMENTS

We are obligated to several colleagues on the Princeton University faculty and library staff who gave generously of their time and special knowledge to improve many of the topics: Alfred L. Bush, W. Frank Craven, Sheldon Hackney, Robert F. Lyke, Virginia Y. McLaughlin, Charles A. Miller, Gary Orfield, Robert A. Scott, and Peter Wood. A Princeton undergraduate, Andrew Browning, checked most of the citations for accuracy. Students in the American Civilization Program seminar on "The Negro in America" have made numerous constructive suggestions. The ever-patient staff of the Princeton University Library deserve special thanks. The Princeton Library contains close to 90 per cent of the items cited herein; the strength of its holdings and the quality of its staff made our job much easier. The staffs of the following libraries were also helpful: Princeton Theological Seminary; The Johns Hopkins University; Rutgers University; the Enoch Pratt Library in Baltimore; and the New York Public Library. Our editor at Doubleday, Loretta Barrett, has provided invaluable advice and assistance at every stage of this project. The authors owe a debt of gratitude to Mrs. Patricia McPherson, who typed part of the manuscript, made several important suggestions, and checked hundreds of citations for accuracy and for availability in paperback. Most of all we wish to thank Mrs. Helen Wright, whose enthusiasm for this project has been contagious, who typed most of the topics and caught numerous errors, and whose long service as secretary of the Program in American Civilization at Princeton University has made possible the academic setting and format from which this book grew.

J.M.MCP.
L.B.H.
J.M.B.,JR.
N.J.W.
M.D.B.

PREFACE

This book is neither a simple bibliography nor an interpretive survey of the history and culture of black people in the United States. Rather it is an attempt to combine narrative, interpretation, and bibliography in a chronological and topical framework that will provide teachers, students, and interested readers with an up-to-date guide to Afro-American history and culture. Utilizing an interdisciplinary approach, the authors have organized the history of black Americans into 100 topics, from Africa and the slave trade to life-styles in the urban ghettos of 1970. Many of the topics are divided into subtopics, and our aim has been to provide annotated references to the best and most useful literature on the most important aspects of race relations and the black community in the United States.

Each topic is introduced by one or more paragraphs summarizing the factual data and interpretive questions involved in a study of the subject, followed by a discussion of the major books, articles, and printed primary sources relevant to research on the topic. Interwoven with the bibliographical portions of the essays in many cases are further narrative or interpretive commentaries on the subject matter of the topic itself. We have organized more than 4,000 titles into several hundred paragraphs, each paragraph dealing with studies of a specific facet of black history or culture. Each topic or subtopic and in some cases each paragraph provides the basic bibliography for a research paper, seminar discussion, or lecture in a black studies course; the book as a whole forms the basis for one or several courses in black studies at the high school, college, or postgraduate level.

The authors, who collectively have several years of experience teaching college and graduate courses in black history and literature, have tried in this book to make their experience available to others. The book grows out of an undergraduate seminar on "The Negro in America" first offered by the interdepartmental American Civilization Program at Princeton University in 1966 and repeated in 1968 and 1970. All five authors have taught in this seminar. The topical bibliographies that constitute the core of this book were first developed in 1966 as guides for students writing seminar papers; the bibliographies were expanded in 1968, revised and augmented again in 1970, and have been thoroughly updated, expanded, and rewritten for publication in 1971.

In 1968 the American Studies Institute at Lincoln University in Pennsylvania obtained permission from Princeton's American Civilization Program to mimeograph 500 copies of the bibliographies for distribution to individuals and institutions offering black studies courses. The demand was greater than expected, and the supply was soon exhausted. The authors have received dozens of individual requests for copies from colleagues in colleges and high schools around the country. The widespread use of the unpublished bibliographies has persuaded us of the desirability of publishing this revised version of them. The proliferation of programs and courses in black studies has created a need for a comprehensive guide to the subject matter and literature of black history and culture. The number of books and articles on black studies is huge and growing rapidly, so that it has become impossible for the teacher or even the specialist to keep up with the material. Several bibliographies of black history and culture have been published in recent years, but most of them are not annotated and are organized only by very general categories. None of them tries to achieve the combined goals of narration, interpretation, annotation, precise topical organization, and comprehensiveness which we hope will make *Blacks in America* the most useful curricular and bibliographical guide to black studies now available.

We have tried to design these bibliographies so that they are capable of use at several levels. High school teachers and students should find the book useful as a guide to general studies and basic monographs. College instructors can develop lecture-discussion courses or seminars from the format of this book, and college students can use the topics and subtopics as guides to research for seminar reports or term papers. Graduate students should find the bibliographies valuable as an historiographical aid for general examinations and as an introduction to printed sources for research papers or dissertation topics. We hope that even experienced scholars in the field will find here some suggestions or references that might have escaped their attention. At the same time, general readers beyond the classroom who do not wish to pursue extensive research can use the bibliographies both as a general introduction to problems in black history and culture and for direction to the best sources on any given topic.

It must be emphasized, however, that while these bibliographies aim at comprehensiveness, they are nevertheless selective. Indeed, it could not be otherwise. The number of publications on race relations and black people in the United States approaches infinity. In 1928 Monroe N. Work compiled a *Bibliography of the Negro in Africa and America* that contained nearly 10,000 references in the section on the United States; the number has increased vastly since then. The bibliographies in *Blacks in America* represent the authors' distillation of the best or most useful studies on the most important aspects of the black experience in America. Because three of the authors are historians and two are scholars of American literature, this book is strongest in history and literature. But we have made every effort to develop topics and cite relevant works in anthropology, economics, folklore, musicology, psychology, political science, sociology, and other disciplines. We have tried to make this book truly interdisciplinary; we hope it will be useful for students in any of several disciplines.

The topics deal with both major realms of black life in the United States: (1) the attitudes and institutions of the dominant white society that have determined the status of blacks in America and the black response or adjustment to these attitudes and institutions; and (2) the semiautonomous social, cultural, and religious institutions developed by the black community within the segregated society imposed by the white majority. Topics such as "The Atlantic Slave Trade," "The Southern Defense of Slavery," "Black Abolitionists," "The Origins of Jim Crow," "Blacks and the New Deal," or "The Civil Rights Movement" concentrate primarily on the first realm; topics such as those on the black church or black literature and culture deal mainly with the second realm; and many topics, such as those on black nationalism, bridge the two realms. The basic organization of the topics is chronological: Part I presents general bibliography and the concept of racial prejudice and stereotypes; Parts II–VII and Part IX cover social, economic, and political developments to the present and cultural history before the twentieth century; Part VIII deals with blacks in literature and the arts in the twentieth century.

Although each topic constitutes a self-contained interpretive and bibliographical essay, all topics fit together into an integrated whole. Most of the topics are cross-referenced to other topics containing material on related subjects. A student or teacher interested in a specific topic or subject (e.g., black music, black nationalism, or education) can quickly find what he is looking for by reference to the table of contents or to the index; when he consults an individual topic, he will usually find cross references to relevant material in other topics. The index lists names of authors (e.g., Carter G. Woodson, E. Franklin Frazier, Gunnar Myrdal); names of historical figures (e.g., Frederick Douglass, Martin Luther King, Richard Wright); and categories (e.g., the black church, Afro-American spirituals, civil rights legislation). The index, table of contents, and cross references are designed to make this book as useful a reference tool as possible. At the same time the paragraphs introducing each topic and subtopic can be read as a semiconnected narrative of the black experience in America.

In many topics the major schools of interpretation and major differences of viewpoint toward any specific issue are summarized. But these are not critical bibliographies in the sense that the approach or viewpoint of each author is evaluated. Thus, while the major historiographical trends in the study of slavery are carefully set forth, the specific thesis of each and every monograph or article on slavery is not individually treated. The biases or interpretations of path-breaking scholars are discussed (e.g., Ulrich B. Phillips, Kenneth M. Stampp, and Stanley M. Elkins on slavery), but less important scholars and their writings are grouped into paragraphs according to subject matter without specific critical comment in most cases. Books and articles are cited for their relevance to the topic, but such citations do not necessarily indicate our endorsement or approval. The student should be alert to possible author bias in any given study even though these bibliographies do not delineate that bias in every case.

Most of the books cited in these bibliographies are available in good university and college libraries, and the most important titles should be on the shelves of high school and small college libraries. A majority of the articles cited should also be available in university and college libraries. More than 300 articles have been reprinted in the Bobbs-Merrill Reprint Series in Black Studies and can be obtained inexpensively from the Bobbs-Merrill Company in Indianapolis. Bobbs-Merrill reprints are designated by the symbol ** whenever they are cited in these bibliographies. Many of the books cited are available in paperback and are designated by the symbol * following the citation. Many relatively rare and out-of-print books on black history and culture have recently been reprinted in library editions; these are indicated in the citation of the place and date of publication, e.g., (Boston, 1858, reprinted New York, 1969). In most cases, the place and date of the first edition of a book are cited; if a subsequent revised edition has superseded the first edition, the place and date of the revised edition are usually cited. In the case of books available in unrevised paperback editions (even if the paperback has a new preface or introduction), the place and date of the original *hardcover* edition are cited, followed by the symbol * to designate availability in paperback.

We have tried to cite every important work published through 1970 and as many relevant titles published up to the time this book goes to press in early 1971 as possible. Inevitably we will have overlooked a few significant studies. No group of five authors, even when so fortunate as to have received the help of several specialists on various subjects as we have done, can hope to avoid omissions. And despite our best efforts, we have probably cited the titles of some studies erroneously, spelled their authors' names wrong, misstated the place or date of publication, or failed to indicate availability in paperback or hardcover reprint. We have striven for 100 per cent accuracy, but we are realistic enough to know that such a goal is utopian. Moreover, any bibliography is out of date as soon as it appears. Especially is this true in the field of black studies, where new works are published almost every day. We therefore invite readers to inform us of errors and omissions and of new titles published after this book has gone to press. Errors and omissions will be rectified in future editions of *Blacks in America* if, as we hope, the reception of the book justifies future editions.

James M. McPherson
  Department of History
  Princeton University

Laurence B. Holland
  Department of English
  The Johns Hopkins University

James M. Banner, Jr.
  Department of History
  Princeton University

Nancy J. Weiss
  Department of History
  Princeton University

Michael D. Bell
  Department of English
  Princeton University

CONTENTS

GUIDE TO SYMBOLS AND ABBREVIATIONS

Symbols

* after the place and date of a book—e.g. (New York, 1965),*—indicates that the book is available in paperback. In all cases the place and date of publication in parentheses apply to the hardcover edition.

** after the citation of an article indicate that this article has been reprinted in the Bobbs-Merrill Reprint Series in Black Studies. The reprints are available from The Bobbs-Merrill Co., 4300 W. 62nd St., Indianapolis, Indiana 46268.

Abbreviations:

Frequently cited periodicals have been abbreviated as follows:

AHR	*American Historical Review*
AJS	*American Journal of Sociology*
APSR	*American Political Science Review*
AQ	*American Quarterly*
ASR	*American Sociological Review*
Annals	*Annals of the American Academy of Political and Social Science*
CLAJ	*College Language Association Journal*
CWH	*Civil War History*
JAH	*Journal of American History*
JNE	*Journal of Negro Education*
JNH	*Journal of Negro History*
JSH	*Journal of Southern History*
LH	*Labor History*
MVHR	*Mississippi Valley Historical Review*

NCHR	*North Carolina Historical Review*
NHB	*Negro History Bulletin*
PMLA	*Publications of the Modern Language Association*
PSQ	*Political Science Quarterly*
SAQ	*South Atlantic Quarterly*
SF	*Social Forces*
SSQ	*Social Science Quarterly*
WMQ	*William and Mary Quarterly*

BLACKS IN AMERICA: BIBLIOGRAPHICAL ESSAYS

PART I

BASIC BIBLIOGRAPHY AND CATEGORIES

1. General Works

This section lists the most useful general works on black history and culture in the United States: reference works, bibliographies, textbooks, general histories, anthologies of articles, documentary collections, literary criticism, and literary anthologies. These listings are intended as a guide to the literature covering all phases of the black experience in America and as an introduction to the more specifically focused studies cited in the sections that follow. A few of the most important works cited in this introductory section (e.g., Gunnar Myrdal's *An American Dilemma*) are also cited again, where relevant, under specific topics. But for the most part, the items listed in this section are not cited later under individual topics. It is taken for granted that anyone interested in slavery, for example, will consult the chapters on slavery in such general works as John Hope Franklin's *From Slavery to Freedom* or August Meier and Elliott Rudwick's *From Plantation to Ghetto*, even though these titles are not included among the specialized works listed in the topics on slavery.

Many of the articles cited under specific topics have been reprinted in the anthologies listed in this introductory section. But it would be an uneconomical use of space to indicate in each case whether and where a specific article has been anthologized; therefore most citations in the individual topics are to the original publication of articles and essays (with the added provision, as explained in the key to abbreviations and symbols, that articles reprinted in the Bobbs-Merrill Reprint Series in Black Studies are indicated by **). Most anthologies of *original* essays are not listed in this introductory section because it seemed more appropriate and helpful to cite the individual essays where applicable in specific topics.

A. Reference Works

An invaluable compilation is the encyclopedic volume *The American Negro Reference Book*, ed. by John P. Davis (Englewood Cliffs, N.J., 1966), with articles by twenty-four scholars on all aspects of black life in America. Other useful works are *The Negro Handbook*, comp. by the editors of *Ebony* (Chicago, 1966); Harry A. Ploski and Roscoe C. Brown, Jr., eds., *The Negro Almanac* (New York, 1967); and Patricia W. Romero, ed., *In Black America, 1968: The Year of Awakening* (Washington, 1969).* Also of great value, for the years covered, is the series of volumes entitled *Negro Year Book and Annual Encyclopedia of the Negro*, ed. by Monroe N. Work (Tuskegee, Ala., 1912–1952). The first and only volume of an uncompleted project is still a major guide to research and bibliographical resources: W. E. B. Du Bois and Guy B. Johnson, *Encyclopedia of the Negro, Preparatory Volume* (New York, 1945).

A useful guide to factual and biographical data plus basic bibliography is provided by Erwin A. Salk, *A Layman's Guide to Negro History* (Chicago, 1966).* A unique volume describing, state by state, physical landmarks and monuments where important events in black history occurred is Phillip T. Drotning, *A Guide to Negro History in America* (2nd ed., rev., Garden City, N.Y., 1970). Peter M. and Mort N. Bergman, compilers, *The Chronological History of the Negro in America* (New York, 1969),* which includes charts and tables and is thoroughly indexed and cross-referenced, is a valuable reference tool. Three volumes that provide demographic data about black Americans are *Negro Population, 1790–1915* (U. S. Bureau of the Census, Washington, 1918, reprinted New York, 1968); *Negroes in the United States, 1920–1932* (U. S. Bureau of the Census, Washington, 1935); and Clyde V. Kiser, ed., "Demographic Aspects of the Black Community," *The Milbank Memorial Fund Quarterly*, XLVIII (Apr. 1970), pt. 2.

B. Bibliographies and Research Guides

The most complete bibliography of black Americans to the date of its publication is Monroe N. Work, ed., *A Bibliography of the*

Negro in Africa and America (New York, 1928, reprinted New York, 1966). Many additional works are cited in the bibliography of Gunnar Myrdal, *An American Dilemma: The Negro Problem and Modern Democracy* (New York, 1944).* With the growth of interest in black studies during the 1960s, many bibliographies have been published. A good brief introduction to major books is provided by Louis R. Harlan, *The Negro in American History* (Washington, 1965).* More complete, with valuable annotations, is Erwin K. Welsch, *The Negro in the United States: A Research Guide* (Bloomington, Ind., 1965).* A listing of two thousand books dealing with twelve categories of black life is found in Dorothy B. Porter, comp., *A Working Bibliography on the Negro in the United States* (Ann Arbor, 1969), which was reissued in modified form as *The Negro in the United States: A Selected Bibliography* (Washington, 1970). Also helpful are Dorothy R. Homer and Ann M. Swartout, *Books About the Negro: An Annotated Bibliography* (New York, 1966); Elizabeth W. Miller and Mary L. Fisher, comps., *The Negro in America: A Bibliography* (Cambridge, Mass., 1970),* a partially annotated listing of books and articles published from 1954 to 1969; African Bibliographic Center, *Black History Viewpoints: A Selected Bibliographical Guide to Resources for Afro-American and African History* (Westport, Conn., 1969);* and Clara O. Jackson, *A Bibliography of Afro-American and Other American Minorities Represented in Libraries and Library Listings* (New York, 1970). The bimonthly publication of the Negro Bibliographic and Research Center, *Bibliographic Survey: The Negro in Print* (Washington, 1965–), provides continuing and up-to-date references.

Selective bibliographies and curriculum guides aimed at high school and junior high teachers and students include William L. Katz, *Teachers' Guide to American Negro History* (Chicago, 1971);* James A. Banks, *Teaching the Black Experience* (Belmont, Calif., 1970);* Mary W. Cleaves and Alma L. Gray, *A Bibliography of Negro History and Culture for Young Readers* (Pittsburgh, 1968);* New York City Board of Education, *The Negro in American History* (2nd ed., New York, 1967);* and San Francisco Unified School District, *The Negro in American Life and History* (San Francisco, 1967).* All of these publications contain references to audiovisual materials as well as printed sources.

Specialized bibliographies include Juanita B. Fuller, *An Annotated Bibliography of Biographies and Autobiographies of Negroes, 1839–1961* (Assoc. of College and Research Libraries, Microcard, Rochester, N.Y., 1964); S. H. Kessler, "American Negro Literature: A Bibliographical Guide," *Bulletin of Bibliography*, XXI (May–Aug. 1955), 181–85; John S. Lash, "The American Negro and American Literature: A Checklist of Significant Commentaries," *ibid.*, XIX (Sept.–Dec. 1946), 12–15, and (Jan.–Apr. 1947), 33–36; Maxwell Whiteman, *A Century of Fiction by American Negroes, 1853–1952, A Descriptive Bibliography* (Philadelphia, 1955); Dorothy B. Porter, *North American Negro Poets: A Bibliographical Checklist of Their Writings* (Hattiesburg, Miss., 1945, reprinted New York, 1963); Darwin T. Turner, ed., *Afro-American Writers* (New York, 1970),* the best and most comprehensive bibliography listing works by and about black American writers; Nelson R. Burr, "The Negro Church," "Negro Spirituals," and "Negro Religious Literature," respectively pp. 348–81, 839–46, and 938–43 of James Ward Smith and A. Leland Jamison, eds., *Religion in American Life*, vol. IV, *A Critical Bibliography of Religion in America* (Princeton, 1961); and Ethel L. Williams, ed., *Afro-American Religious Studies: A Cumulative Bibliography*, vol. I (Metuchen, N.J., 1971). A guide to a major library collection of books and other materials is New York Public Library, *Dictionary Catalog of the Schomburg Collection of Negro Literature and History*, 9 vols. (Boston, 1962, 2 supp. vols., 1968). Dominique-René de Lerma, ed., *Black Music: A Preliminary Register of the Composers and Their Works* (Bloomington, Ind., 1971), and *The Legacy of Black Music* (Kent, Ohio, 1971), list the works of black composers, plus 10,000 books and articles dealing with black music.

Much of the periodical literature by and about blacks since 1940 has been indexed in the following publications: Albert Prince Marshall, *A Guide to Negro Periodical Literature*, 4 vols. (Jefferson City, Mo., 1941–46); *Index to Selected Periodicals Received in the Hallie Q. Brown Library*, decennial cumulation, 1950–59 (Boston, 1961); *Index to Selected Periodicals*, annual cumulations, vols. 11–16 (Boston, 1962–65); and *Index to Periodical Articles by and about Negroes*, annually (Boston, 1966–). Warren Brown, *Check List of Negro Newspapers in the United*

States (1827–1946) (Jefferson City, Mo., 1946), lists editors' names, dates of founding and expiration, and locations of all known copies of 467 black newspapers. Most of the black newspapers of the period from the 1860s to the 1920s have been microfilmed by the Library of Congress and the American Council of Learned Societies; for a guide, see Armistead Scott Pride, *Negro Newspapers on Microfilm: A Selected List* (Washington, 1953).*

Guides to unpublished materials include Earle H. West, *A Bibliography of Doctoral Research on the Negro, 1933–1966* (Ann Arbor, 1969); Lawrence F. McNamee, *Dissertations in English and American Literature: Theses Accepted by American, British, and German Universities, 1865–1964* (New York, 1968), ch. 32; Paul Lewinson, *A Guide to Documents in the National Archives for Negro Studies* (Washington, 1947); and John McDonough, "Manuscript Sources for the Study of Negro Life and History," *Quarterly Journal of the Library of Congress,* XXVI (July 1969). Walter Schatz, ed., *Directory of Afro-American Resources* (New York, 1971), is a guide to libraries, archives, and other repositories.

Earle E. Thorpe, *Negro Historians in the United States* (Baton Rouge, 1958), and *Black Historians: A Critique* (New York, 1971), identify and discuss every known black historian, professional and amateur.

C. Textbooks and General Histories

Still the most important single survey of race relations in the United States is Gunnar Myrdal, *An American Dilemma: The Negro Problem and Modern Democracy* (New York, 1944),* though much has happened and much has changed in the generation since the research for this massive study was completed. A skillful condensation of *An American Dilemma,* with an introduction summarizing new developments up to 1964, is Arnold Rose, *The Negro in America* (2nd ed., rev., New York, 1964).* For a Marxist critique of *An American Dilemma,* see Herbert Aptheker, *The Negro People in America: A Critique of Gunnar Myrdal's "An American Dilemma"* (New York, 1946).

One of the most successful textbooks for more than forty years at both the college and high school level has been Carter G. Woodson and Charles H. Wesley, *The Negro in Our History* (10th ed., rev., Washington, 1962), now largely superseded by John Hope Franklin, *From Slavery to Freedom: A History of Negro Americans* (3rd ed., rev., New York, 1967).* The best brief interpretive survey, aimed at the college student and general reader, is August Meier and Elliott Rudwick, *From Plantation to Ghetto* (2nd ed., rev., New York, 1970).* Especially valuable for its emphasis on black community institutions and mores is E. Franklin Frazier, *The Negro in the United States* (2nd ed., rev., New York, 1957). One of the earliest historical surveys, useful now primarily as an historiographical example, is George W. Williams, *History of the Negro Race in America from 1619–1880,* 2 vols. (New York, 1883, reprinted New York, 1968).

Additional general histories of value, listed in alphabetical order, are: Lerone Bennett, Jr., *Before the Mayflower: A History of Black America* (4th ed., rev., Chicago, 1969);* Lerone Bennett, Jr., *Confrontation: Black and White* (Chicago, 1965),* an account of freedom movements from the abolitionists to the 1960s; Eli Ginzberg and Alfred S. Eichner, *The Troublesome Presence: American Democracy and the Negro* (New York, 1964);* C. Eric Lincoln, *The Negro Pilgrimage in America* (New York, 1967);* Rayford W. Logan, *The Negro in the United States,* 2 vols., vol. I, to 1945, vol. II (with Michael R. Winston), since 1945 (New York, 1970–71);* Roi Ottley, *Black Odyssey: The Story of the Negro in America* (New York, 1948); Alphonso Pinkney, *Black Americans* (Englewood Cliffs, N.J., 1969);* Benjamin Quarles, *The Negro in the Making of America* (New York, 1964);* J. Saunders Redding, *They Came in Chains: Americans from Africa* (Philadelphia, 1950);* Earle E. Thorpe, *The Mind of the Negro: An Intellectual History of Afro-Americans* (Baton Rouge, 1961); and three volumes by Charles H. Wesley in the International Library of Negro Life and History: (1) *In Freedom's Footsteps: From the African Background to the Civil War* (New York, 1968); (2) *Negro-Americans in the Civil War* (with Patricia W. Romero) (New York, 1967); and (3) *The Quest for Equality: From Civil War to Civil Rights* (New York, 1968).

Marxist perspectives are provided by William Z. Foster, *The Negro People in American History* (New York, 1954),* and Herbert Aptheker, *Afro-American History: The Modern Era* (New York, 1971). A book that emphasizes black contributions to Western culture and technology is Joel A. Rogers, *Africa's Gift to America: The Afro-American in the Making and Saving of the United States* (2nd ed., rev., New York, 1961). Phillip T. Drotning, *Black Heroes in Our Nation's History* (New York, 1969), is a survey of black participants in American wars. An interesting and valuable volume is Langston Hughes and Milton Meltzer, *A Pictorial History of the Negro in America* (3rd ed., rev., New York, 1968).

Textbooks and surveys aimed primarily at high school readers include Carter G. Woodson, *The Story of the Negro Retold* (4th ed., rev., Washington, 1959); Arna Bontemps, *Story of the Negro* (4th ed., New York, 1965); Rayford W. Logan and Irving S. Cohen, *The American Negro: Old World Background and New World Experience* (Boston, 1967);* Kenneth G. Goode, *From Africa to the United States and Then . . . A Concise Afro-American History* (Glenview, Ill., 1969);* and the first two volumes in the *Black Heritage* series edited by John Henrik Clarke and Vincent Harding, *Origins of Afro-Americans* and *Slave Trade and Slavery* (New York, 1970).* The following volumes on black history in Doubleday's Zenith Books series on minority groups designed for slow-reading high school students have been published: Agnes McCarthy and Lawrence Reddick, *Worth Fighting For: The History of the Negro in the United States During the Civil War and Reconstruction* (Garden City, N.Y., 1965);* Carol Drisko and Edgar A. Toppin, *The Unfinished March: The Negro in the United States, Reconstruction to World War I* (Garden City, N.Y., 1967);* Florette Henri, *Bitter Victory: A History of Black Soldiers in World War I* (Garden City, N.Y., 1970);* and Milton Meltzer and August Meier, *Time of Trial, Time of Hope: The Negro in America, 1919–1941* (Garden City, N.Y., 1966).*

D. Collective Biographies

The best introduction to black leaders and achievers in every category from the colonial period to 1959 is Richard Bardolph, *The Negro Vanguard* (New York, 1959),* which is, however, marred by a few mystifying omissions such as Marcus Garvey. *Who's Who of the Colored Race: A General Biographical Dictionary of Men and Women of African Descent* (Chicago, 1915) and the seven editions from 1927 to 1950 of *Who's Who in Colored America: A Biographical Dictionary of Notable Living Persons of African Descent in America* (New York, 1927–50) provide data on thousands of eminent blacks. Other books including forty or more biographical sketches are Russell L. Adams, *Great Negroes, Past and Present* (3rd ed., Chicago, 1969);* Benjamin G. Brawley, *Negro Builders and Heroes* (Chapel Hill, 1937); Walter Christmas, ed., *Negroes in Public Affairs and Government* (Yonkers, N.Y., 1966); John Wesley Cromwell, *The Negro in American History: Men and Women Eminent in the Evolution of the American of African Descent* (Washington, 1914, reprinted New York, 1968); Sylvia G. L. Dannett, *Profiles of Negro Womanhood*, 2 vols. (Yonkers, N.Y., 1964–66); Wilhelmena Robinson, *Historical Negro Biographies* (2nd ed., rev., Washington, 1969); Charlemae Hill Rollins, *They Showed the Way: Forty American Negro Leaders* (New York, 1964); William J. Simmons, *Men of Mark: Eminent, Progressive and Rising* (Cleveland, 1887, reprinted New York, 1968); and Edgar A. Toppin, *A Biographical History of Blacks in America Since 1528* (New York, 1971).*

Collective biographies of fewer than forty persons include Phillip T. Drotning and Wesley W. South, *Up from the Ghetto* (New York, 1970);* Edwin R. Embree, *13 Against the Odds* (New York, 1944); George R. Metcalf, *Black Profiles* (rev. ed., New York, 1970); Lerone Bennett, Jr., *Pioneers in Protest* (Chicago, 1968);* and Mary White Ovington, *Portraits in Color* (New York, 1927). Three interesting specialized treatments are Rebecca Chalmers Barton, *Witnesses for Freedom: Negro Americans in Autobiography* (New York, 1948); Jay David, ed., *Growing Up Black* (New York, 1968),* selections from black autobiographies on the authors' childhoods; and Irving H. Lee, *Negro Medal of Honor Men* (New York, 1967), the stories of forty-five black fighting men from the Civil War to Korea who earned Congressional Medals of Honor. J. Saunders Redding, *The Lonesome Road: The Story of the Negro's Part in America* (Garden City, N.Y., 1958), is a readable popular history of the black American told primarily through the life stories of thirteen outstanding personalities.

Collective biographies intended primarily for younger readers include Arna Bontemps, *100 Years of Negro Freedom* (New York, 1961);* Langston Hughes, *Famous American Negroes* (New York,

1954);* Langston Hughes, *Famous Negro Music Makers* (New York, 1955); and the following volumes in Doubleday's Zenith Books series for junior and senior high school readers: Lavinia Dobler and Edgar A. Toppin, *Pioneers and Patriots: The Lives of Six Negroes of the Revolutionary Era* (Garden City, N.Y., 1965);* Philip Sterling and Rayford W. Logan, *Four Took Freedom: The Lives of Harriet Tubman, Frederick Douglass, Robert Smalls, and Blanche K. Bruce* (Garden City, N.Y., 1967);* and Dorothy Sterling and Benjamin Quarles, *Lift Every Voice: The Lives of B. T. Washington, W. E. B. Du Bois, Mary Church Terrell, and James W. Johnson* (Garden City, N.Y., 1965).*

E. Anthologies of Reprinted Essays and Articles on Black History

Some of the best articles on black history and life have been reprinted in the following anthologies: Melvin Drimmer, ed., *Black History: A Reappraisal* (Garden City, N.Y., 1968);* Eric Foner, ed., *America's Black Past: A Reader in Afro-American History* (New York, 1970);* Sethard Fisher, ed., *Power and the Black Community: A Reader on Racial Subordination in the United States* (New York, 1970);* Dwight W. Hoover, ed., *Understanding Negro History* (Chicago, 1968);* August Meier and Elliott Rudwick, eds., *The Making of Black America*, 2 vols. (New York, 1969);* Peter I. Rose, ed., *Americans from Africa*, 2 vols. (New York, 1970);* Seth M. Scheiner and Tilden Edelstein, eds., *The Black Americans: Interpretive Readings* (New York, 1971);* and Okon E. Uya, ed., *Black Brotherhood: Afro-Americans and Africa* (Lexington, Mass., 1971).* An interdisciplinary collection of original and reprinted articles which concentrates mainly on the 1960s is Norval D. Glenn and Charles M. Bonjean, eds., *Blacks in the United States* (San Francisco, 1969). For an anthology of some of the best recent work in social psychology, see Marcel L. Goldschmid, ed., *Black Americans and White Racism* (New York, 1970).* Anthologies dealing with specific periods of black history are David M. Reimers, ed., *The Black Man in America Since Reconstruction* (New York, 1970);* Allen Weinstein and Frank Otto Gatell, eds., *The Segregation Era, 1863–1954: A Modern Reader* (New York, 1970);* and Charles E. Wynes, ed., *The Negro in the South Since 1865: Selected Essays in American Negro*

History (University, Ala., 1965).* Several of Eugene D. Genovese's interpretive essays are reprinted in his *In Red & Black: Marxian Explorations in Southern and Afro-American History* (New York, 1971). The most valuable teaching and research tool utilizing reprinted articles is the Bobbs-Merrill Reprint Series in Black Studies, which has republished more than 320 articles and excerpts from books dealing with black history, literature, politics, and sociology. A catalogue is available from the Bobbs-Merrill Co., 4300 W. 62nd St., Indianapolis, Ind. 46268.

F. Anthologies of Original Documents

The following volumes contain reprints of contemporary documents on many aspects of race relations and the black community: Alfred E. Cain, ed., *The Winding Road to Freedom: A Documentary Survey of Negro Experiences in America* (Yonkers, N.Y., 1965); Mortimer A. Adler, Charles Van Doren, and George Ducas, eds., *The Negro in American History*, 3 vols. (Chicago, 1969); George Ducas and Charles Van Doren, eds., *Great Documents in Black American History* (New York, 1971);* Thomas R. Frazier, ed., *Afro-American History: Primary Sources* (New York, 1970);* Gilbert Osofsky, ed., *The Burden of Race: A Documentary History of Negro-White Relations in America* (New York, 1967);* Leslie H. Fishel, Jr., and Benjamin Quarles, eds., *The Black American: A Documentary History* (Glenview, Ill., 1970);* Patricia Romero, ed., *I, Too, Am America* (New York, 1968); John H. Bracey, August Meier, and Elliott Rudwick, eds., *The Afro-Americans: Selected Documents*, 2 vols. (Boston, 1970);* and D. D. Anderson and R. L. Wright, eds., *The Dark and Tangled Path: Race in America* (Boston, 1971).* A large number of writings by blacks in the eighteenth and nineteenth centuries, including several full-length slave narratives, are reprinted in Maxwell Whiteman, ed. dir., *Afro-American History Series*, 10 vols. (Wilmington, Del., 1971). Three collections that concentrate on the Afro-American's legal status and on court decisions are Richard Bardolph, ed., *The Civil Rights Record: Black Americans and the Law, 1849–1970* (New York, 1970);* Albert P. Blaustein and Robert L. Zangrando, eds., *Civil Rights and the American Negro: A Documentary History* (New York, 1968);* and Joseph

Tussman, ed., *The Supreme Court on Racial Discrimination* (New York, 1963).* A collection of documents illustrating white racial attitudes is Louis Ruchames, ed., *Racial Thought in America: From the Puritans to Abraham Lincoln* (New York, 1970).* The following volumes emphasize black protest: Herbert Aptheker, ed., *A Documentary History of the Negro People in the United States: From Colonial Times to 1910* (New York, 1951);* Bradford Chambers, ed., *Chronicles of Black Protest* (New York, 1970);* Henry Steele Commager, ed., *The Struggle for Racial Equality: A Documentary Record* (New York, 1967);* Herbert J. Storing, ed., *What Country Have I? Political Writings by Black Americans* (New York, 1970);* Roy L. Hill, ed., *Rhetoric of Racial Revolt* (Denver, 1964); Howard Brotz, ed., *Negro Social and Political Thought, 1850–1920* (New York, 1966);* and August Meier, Elliott Rudwick, and Francis L. Broderick, eds., *Black Protest Thought in the Twentieth Century* (rev. ed., Indianapolis, 1971).* Raymond F. Betts, ed., *The Ideology of Blackness* (Lexington, Mass., 1971),* emphasizes cultural nationalism and negritude. Harvey Wish, ed., *The Negro Since Emancipation* (Englewood Cliffs, N.J., 1964),* and Otto H. Olsen and Abraham S. Eisenstadt, eds., *The Negro Question: From Slavery to Caste, 1863–1910* (New York, 1970),* deal with the periods indicated by the titles.

Documentaries aimed primarily at high school readers include William Loren Katz, *Eyewitness: The Negro in American History* (New York, 1967),* a unique and successful blending of narrative with original documents; Milton Meltzer, ed., *In Their Own Words: A History of the American Negro*, 3 vols. (New York, 1964–67);* and Richard C. Wade, ed., *The Negro in American Life* (Boston, 1965).*

G. Anthologies Combining Documents and Reprinted Articles

Several anthologies interweave contemporary documents with interpretive essays by scholars: Ross K. Baker, ed., *The Afro-American* (New York, 1970),* which emphasizes the themes of black identity and nationalism; William M. Chace and Peter Collier, eds., *Justice Denied: The Black Man in White America* (New York, 1970);* George Ducas, ed., *Black Dialogues: Topics in*

Afro-American History (Chicago, 1970); Henry N. and Cecilia H. Drewry, eds., *Afro-American History: Past to Present* (New York, 1971);* Joanne Grant, ed., *Black Protest: History, Documents, and Analyses, 1619 to the Present* (New York, 1968);* and, on the twentieth century, John Hope Franklin and Isidore Starr, eds., *The Negro in Twentieth Century America* (New York, 1967);* Richard Resh, ed., *Black America: Accommodation and Confrontation in the Twentieth Century* (Lexington, Mass., 1969);* and Gerald Messner, ed., *Another View: To Be Black in America* (New York, 1970).*

H. Black Literature, Music, and Art: Description and Analysis

Two studies of black achievements in the arts and literature are Margaret Just Butcher, *The Negro in American Culture* (New York, 1956); and Benjamin G. Brawley, *The Negro Genius: A New Appraisal of the Achievement of the American Negro in Literature and the Fine Arts* (New York, 1937).* Kenny Jackson Williams, *They Also Spoke* (Nashville, 1970), is a study of the contribution of blacks to American literature from 1787 to 1930, while David Littlejohn, *Black on White: A Critical Survey of Writing by American Negroes* (New York, 1966),* emphasizes the more recent period. Two fine collections of essays are Addison Gayle, Jr., ed., *Black Expression: Essays By and About Black Americans in the Creative Arts* (New York, 1970),* and Jules Chametzky and Sidney Kaplan, eds., *Black and White in American Culture: An Anthology from the Massachusetts Review* (Amherst, Mass., 1970).* Surveys of black poetry include Sterling Brown, *Negro Poetry and Drama* (Washington, 1937);* and J. Saunders Redding, *To Make a Poet Black* (Chapel Hill, 1939). Black fiction of the nineteenth and twentieth centuries is discussed by Hugh M. Gloster, *Negro Voices in American Fiction* (Chapel Hill, 1948); and Robert Bone, *The Negro Novel in America* (rev. ed., New Haven, 1965).* John H. Nelson, *The Negro Character in American Literature* (Lawrence, Kan., 1926, reprinted College Park, Md., 1968), and Sterling Brown, *The Negro in American Fiction* (Washington, 1938),* deal with both black and white authors. Seymour L. Gross and John Edward Hardy, eds., *Image of the Negro in American Literature* (Chicago, 1966),* is a thoughtful collection of essays dealing with both black literature and the treatment of blacks by white writers. Black actors and playwrights and the ways in which blacks have been portrayed by white dramatists are analyzed in Frederick W. Bond, *The Negro and the Drama* (Washington, 1940, reprinted College Park, Md., 1969); Edith J. Isaacs, *The Negro in the American Theatre* (New York, 1947, reprinted College Park, Md., 1969); and Loften Mitchell, *Black Drama: The Story of the American Negro in the Theatre* (New York, 1967).* Interpretive articles are reprinted in Lindsay Patterson, ed., *Anthology of the American Negro in the Theatre: A Critical Approach* (New York, 1967). William R. Reardon and Thomas D. Pawley, *The Black Teacher and the Dramatic Arts* (Westport, Conn., 1971), includes essays about teaching drama in black schools as well as several plays.

A fine collection of essays on all aspects of black music and art is Lindsay Patterson, ed., *The Negro in Music and Art* (New York, 1967). The best general historical and analytical treatments of black music are Maud Cuney Hare, *Negro Musicians and Their Music* (Washington, 1936); Alain L. Locke, *The Negro and His Music* (Washington, 1936, reprinted New York, 1968); Marshall W. Stearns, *The Story of Jazz* (3rd ed., New York, 1956);* LeRoi Jones, *Blues People: Negro Music in White America* (New York, 1963);* and Eileen Southern, *The Music of Black Americans* (New York, 1971).* For black artists in the United States, consult Alain L. Locke, *Negro Art: Past and Present* (Washington, 1936, reprinted New York, 1969); James A. Porter, *Modern Negro Art* (New York, 1943); and Cedric Dover, *American Negro Art* (2nd ed., Greenwich, Conn., 1965). William Schechter, *The History of Negro Humor in America* (New York, 1971), deals with an important folk art.

I. Anthologies of Black Literature, Music, and Art

The best and most complete anthologies of all facets of black literature are Sterling Brown, Arthur Davis, and Ulysses Lee, eds., *The Negro Caravan* (New York, 1941, reprinted New York, 1969); James A. Emanuel and Theodore L. Gross, eds., *Dark Symphony: Negro Literature in America* (New York, 1968);* and Lindsay Patterson, ed., *An Introduction to Black Literature in*

America, From 1746 to the Present (New York, 1968). Other anthologies include Abraham Chapman, ed., *Black Voices: An Anthology of Afro-American Literature* (New York, 1968);* Charles T. Davis and Daniel Walden, eds., *On Being Black: Writings by Afro-Americans from Frederick Douglass to the Present* (New York, 1970);* Robert Hayden, David Burrows, and Frederick Lapides, eds., *Afro-American Literature: A Thematic Reader* (New York, 1971);* Francis E. Kearns, ed., *The Black Experience: An Anthology of American Literature for the 1970's* (New York, 1971);* Bucklin Moon, ed., *Primer for White Folks* (Garden City, N.Y., 1945); and Raman K. Singh and Peter Fellowes, eds., *Black Literature in America: A Casebook* (New York, 1970).* A fine collection for the period it covers is Herbert Hill, ed., *Soon, One Morning: New Writing by American Negroes, 1940–1962* (New York, 1963). Anthologies designed for high school literature courses include Herman Dreer, ed., *American Literature by Negro Authors* (New York, 1950); and Francis E. Kearns, ed., *Black Identity: A Thematic Reader* (New York, 1970).*

Black poetry is anthologized in Langston Hughes and Arna Bontemps, eds., *The Poetry of the Negro, 1746–1970* (Garden City, N.Y., 1970); Arna Bontemps, ed., *American Negro Poetry* (New York, 1963);* and Robert Earl Hayden, ed., *Kaleidoscope: Poems by American Negro Poets* (New York, 1967).* For anthologies of short stories, see John Henrik Clarke, ed., *American Negro Short Stories* (New York, 1966);* and Langston Hughes, ed., *The Best Short Stories by Negro Writers: An Anthology from 1899 to the Present* (Boston, 1967).* Two of the most useful collections of black folklore are Langston Hughes and Arna Bontemps, eds., *The Book of Negro Folklore* (New York, 1958);* and Richard M. Dorson, ed., *Negro Folktales* (New York, 1967).* A fine collection of black wit is Langston Hughes, ed., *The Book of Negro Humor* (New York, 1966).*

The musical contributions of Afro-Americans are treated in Dominique-René de Lerma, *Black Music in Our Culture: Curricular Ideas on the Subjects, Materials and Problems* (Kent, Ohio, 1970). The best of the many collections of spirituals, with words, music, and analysis, are James Weldon Johnson and J. Rosamond Johnson, eds., *The Book of American Negro Spirituals* (New York, 1925), and *The Second Book of Negro Spirituals* (New York,

1926), both reprinted in one vol., *The Books of American Negro Spirituals* (New York, 1956).* For the words and music of the most famous blues songs, consult W. C. Handy, *A Treasury of the Blues* (New York, 1949), and Samuel Charters, *The Poetry of the Blues* (New York, 1963).* Many of the works cited in Part VIII, topic 11, "Soul Music: Blues, Jazz, and Variations," contain examples of the words and music of these genres.

Alain L. Locke, *The Negro in Art* (Washington, 1940), is a pictorial history of the black artist and of black themes in American art.

J. Periodicals

The following are selected current and recent periodicals that deal with black life and race relations:

Afro-American Studies: An Interdisciplinary Journal. 1970–. Quarterly.

A.M.E. Church Review. 1884–. Quarterly.

Amistad: Writings on Black History and Culture. 1970–. Semiannually.

Black Arts Magazine. 1968–. Quarterly.

Black Enterprise. 1970–. Monthly.

Black Lives: A Journal of Black Studies. 1970–. Quarterly.

Black Orpheus: A Journal of African and Afro-American Literature. 1957–. Irregularly.

The Black Panther. 1966–. Weekly.

The Black Politician. 1969–. Quarterly.

Black Review. 1971–. Semiannually.

The Black Scholar. 1969–. Monthly.

Black World (formerly *Negro Digest*). 1942–51, 1961–. Monthly.

CLA Journal. (Official Publication of the College Language Association, black counterpart of the Modern Language Association.) 1945–. Quarterly.

CORE. (Publication of the Congress of Racial Equality.) 1969–. Monthly.

CORElator. 1959–65. Monthly.

Crisis. 1910–. Monthly.

Ebony. 1945–. Monthly.

Freedomways: A Quarterly Review of the Negro Freedom Movement. 1961–. Quarterly.

Harvard Journal of Negro Affairs. 1967–. Semiannually.

Integrated Education. 1963–. Bimonthly.

Interracial Review. 1928–. Monthly.

Jet. 1951–. Weekly.

Journal of African History. 1960–. Quarterly.

Journal of Black Poetry. 1967–. Quarterly.

Journal of Black Studies. 1970–. Quarterly.

Journal of Human Relations. 1952–. Quarterly.

Journal of Intergroup Relations. 1959–. Quarterly.

Journal of Negro Education. 1932–. Quarterly.

Journal of Negro History. 1916–. Quarterly.

Journal of Religious Thought. (Published by the Howard University School of Religion.) 1943–. Semiannually.

Journal of the National Medical Association. (The NMA is the black counterpart of the AMA.) 1909–. Bimonthly.

Liberator. 1961–. Monthly.

Midwest Journal. (Published at Lincoln University, Jefferson City, Mo.) 1948–56. Quarterly.

Muhammed Speaks. 1961–. Weekly.

Negro Educational Review. 1950–. Quarterly.

Negro Heritage. 1961–. Monthly.

Negro History Bulletin. 1937–. Monthly.

New South. (Publication of the Southern Regional Council.) 1946–. Quarterly.

Opportunity: A Journal of Negro Life. (Organ of the National Urban League.) 1923–49. Monthly.

Phylon: The Atlanta University Review of Race and Culture. 1940–. Quarterly.

Quarterly Review of Higher Education Among Negroes. 1933–. Quarterly.

Race Relations Law Reporter. 1956–67. Quarterly.

Rights and Reviews. 1966–. Irregularly.

Sepia. 1952–. Monthly.

Southern Patriot. (Published by the Southern Conference Educational Fund.) 1942–. Monthly.

Southern School News. 1954–. Monthly.

2. Black and Negro as Image, Category, and Stereotype

Language and the human mind being what they are, the very words "black," "Afro-American," and "Negro" as well as "white" and "Caucasian" strongly affect those who hear and read them. These terms name their subjects and fix attention to them by separating "blacks" or "whites" from other people, identifying them as constituting a particular category and labeling them by reference to the ostensible color of their skin—of which there are innumerable varieties in all races. Like most categories or images, the terms threaten to dehumanize their subjects by hardening into stereotypes.

Furthermore, the terms "black" and "Negro" or "white" and "Caucasian" come freighted with connotations—explicit and implicit, conscious and unconscious. The terms are compounds of cultural traditions, fictions, categories, stereotypes, and brands. Thus our experiences and prejudices (whatever the hues of our skins) may affect the connotations that the terms "black" and "white" carry in any particular instance of our using them. This pertains to personal biases, whether of Alabama sheriff or Black Panther, white radical or black conservative. And it pertains also to the assumptions and methods used in the serious study of black Americans.

For an introduction to the problems of bias and stereotype, see Gordon W. Allport, *The Nature of Prejudice* (Cambridge, Mass., 1954),* chs. 1–3, 7, 11–13, and 20–24. Problems of racial identity and mechanisms of racial antagonism are described by Everett V. Stonequist, *The Marginal Man: A Study in Personality and Culture Conflict* (New York, 1937), chs. 1, 4, 7, and 11. Bruno Bettelheim and Morris Janowitz, *Social Change and Prejudice* (New York, 1967), especially ch. 2, links racial prejudice to social mobility. Other studies dealing with the typology of prejudice are Theodore W. Adorno, Else Frenkel-Brunswik, Daniel J. Levinson, R. Nevitt Sanford, et. al., *The Authoritarian Personality* (New York, 1950);* Bruno Bettelheim and Morris Janowitz,

Dynamics of Prejudice: A Psychological and Social Study of Veterans (New York, 1950); and Martin Deutsch, Irwin Katz, and Arthur Jensen, eds., *Social Class, Race, and Psychological Development* (New York, 1968). For a provocative discussion of the way images and stereotypes affect perceptions and attitudes, see Kenneth E. Boulding, *The Image: Knowledge in Life and Society* (Ann Arbor, 1956).*

There are numerous studies of the effects of discrimination and oppression on both the oppressed and the oppressor. Many of these are based on experimental work, and many deal with anti-black bias in the context of larger patterns of prejudice and racial stereotyping. The best guides to work on the psychology and sociology of stereotypes are the bibliography and the notes to chs. 1–3 and 5 of Thomas Pettigrew, *A Profile of the Negro American* (Princeton, 1964).* Chs. 3 and 18 of John Dollard, *Caste and Class in a Southern Town* (New York, 1937),* contain an analysis of bias and loaded image at work in one community. "White Woman, Black Man," pt. IV of Eldridge Cleaver's *Soul on Ice* (New York, 1968),* is a provocative approach to the problems of repression and stereotype. For historical treatments of these problems, see David Brion Davis, *The Problem of Slavery in Western Culture* (Ithaca, N.Y., 1966),* ch. 15; Winthrop D. Jordan, *White over Black: American Attitudes Toward the Negro, 1550–1812* (Chapel Hill, 1968),* especially chs. 1, 4, 6, 12, and 13; and Stanley M. Elkins, *Slavery: A Problem in American Institutional and Intellectual Life* (Chicago, 1959, rev. ed., 1968),* pt. III, "Slavery and Personality," an attempt to understand the effects of slavery in terms of modern theories of personality. For references to criticisms of Elkins, see Part III, topic 1, "Plantation Slavery in the Antebellum South."

The classic studies of the impact of stereotypes and prejudice on black personality patterns are Abram Kardiner and Lionel Ovesey, *The Mark of Oppression: A Psychosocial Study of the American Negro* (New York, 1951),* and Thomas Pettigrew, *A Profile of the Negro American,* cited above. Two black psychiatrists examine the impact of discrimination on their patients in Charles Grier and Price M. Cobbs, *Black Rage* (New York, 1968).* Marcel L. Goldschmid, ed., *Black Americans and White Racism* (New York, 1970),* is a fine anthology of articles in social psychology.

The essays in John Hope Franklin, ed., *Color and Race* (Boston, 1968),* examine comparatively the psychosocial functions of skin color in several societies. Four articles provide insights on the psychological functions of prejudice: Ira N. Brophy, "The Luxury of Anti-Negro Prejudice," *Public Opinion Quarterly*, IX (Winter 1945–46), 456–66; and three articles by J. Kenneth Morland: "Racial Recognition by Nursery School Children in Lynchburg, Virginia," *SF*, XXXVII (Dec. 1958), 132–37; "Racial Acceptance and Preference of Nursery School Children in a Southern City," *Merrill-Palmer Quarterly*, III, no. 4 (1962), 271–80; and "A Comparison of Race Awareness in Northern and Southern Children," *American Journal of Orthopsychiatry*, XXXVI, no. 1 (1966), 22–31. Judith D. R. Porter, *Black Child, White Child* (Cambridge, Mass., 1971), is a study of the way in which young children acquire racial attitudes. A provocative Freudian view of racial stereotypes is presented by Joel Kovel, *White Racism: A Psychohistory* (New York, 1970).* See also Calvin Hernton, *Sex and Racism in America* (New York, 1966).* A more broadly conceived social-psychological interpretation is found in Roger Daniels and Harry H. L. Kitano, *American Racism: Exploration of the Nature of Prejudice* (Englewood Cliffs, N.J., 1970).*

For nearly two decades after World War II most students of racial categories tended to assume that such categories promoted prejudice and that the purpose of studying them was to overcome them. Many today still hold this view. But in recent years, proponents of a more or less distinct black American culture have championed racial categorization, and even certain kinds of racial stereotypes, as positive means for black self-identification. (See Part IX, topic 14, "Black Life-Styles in the Ghetto," and the section on the "Black Aesthetic" in Part VIII, topic 6, "After Protest: Black Writers in the 1950s and 1960s.") One result of this new attitude toward "black" as a category has been the establishment in many universities, colleges, and secondary schools of black studies programs, some of them in separate and autonomous departments. The viability of black studies as a separate discipline, the question whether white teachers and students should participate in such programs, and the whole nature and purpose of black studies have provoked heated debate. Most of the major issues are outlined and discussed in Armstead L. Robinson, Craig C. Foster, and Donald H. Ogilvie, eds., *Black Studies in the University: A Symposium* (New Haven, 1969);* John W. Blassingame, ed., *New Perspectives on Black Studies* (Urbana, Ill., 1971); and Rose W. Levy, ed., *Black Studies in Schools* (Washington, 1970).* See also ch. 10, "Black Studies," in Theodore Draper, *The Rediscovery of Black Nationalism* (New York, 1970).* The Autumn 1969 (vol. XXXVIII) issue of *American Scholar* contains several articles on black studies. Considerable skepticism about the racial chauvinism of some black studies programs is expressed by the essays in Bayard Rustin, ed., *Black Studies: Myths and Realities* (New York, 1969).* Testimony on a bill to create a national commission on black history and culture is reprinted in Howard N. Meyer, ed., *Integrating America's Heritage: A Congressional Hearing to Establish a National Commission on Negro History and Culture* (New York, 1970). Robert Starobin, "The Negro: A Central Theme in American History," *Journal of Contemporary History*, III (Apr. 1968), 37–53, and Otto Lindenmeyer, *Of Black America: Black History: Lost, Stolen, or Strayed* (New York, 1970),* urge the recognition of black contributions to America's past. Nathan I. Huggins dissects "Afro-American History: Myths, Heroes, Reality," in Huggins, Martin Kilson, and Daniel M. Fox, eds., *Key Issues in the Afro-American Experience*, 2 vols. (New York, 1971),* vol. I, pp. 5–19. The best definition of the differences between the old-style "Negro history" and the new directions of "black history" is provided by Vincent Harding, "Beyond Chaos: Black History and the Search for the New Land," in John A. Williams and Charles F. Harris, eds., *Amistad 1: Writings on Black History and Culture* (New York, 1970),* pp. 267–92. Sterling Stuckey, "Twilight of Our Past: Reflections on the Origins of Black History," *Amistad 2* (New York, 1971),* pp. 261–96, urges a reinterpretation of black history from a black perspective. Several interesting essays on black history and historiography are contained in Earle E. Thorpe, *The Central Theme of Black History* (Durham, N.C., 1969).

PART II

FROM AFRICA TO THE
NEW WORLD, 1500–1800

1. The African Background

Previous generations of Western historians described Africa as the "Dark Continent," full of savage tribes and devoid of any attributes of civilization before the coming of the white man. According to this view, slaves brought to America came from a primitive, barbarous culture, and their experience of slavery in the New World was actually a great benefit because it brought them into contact with progressive white civilization. In the words of Ulrich B. Phillips, slavery was a "school" in which the black man learned the superior ways of the white man. Without the schooling of slavery (and the later impact of Western imperialism in Africa) blacks would have remained illiterate, naked savages and Africa would have remained a backward, benighted continent. For an expression of these views, see Joseph A. Tillinghast, *The Negro in Africa and America* (New York, 1902, reprinted New York, 1968); Jerome Dowd, *The Negro Races: A Sociological Study* (New York, 1907); and Ulrich B. Phillips, *American Negro Slavery* (New York, 1918),* ch. 1.

Black historians strove to correct this view, but made little impact on culture-bound white scholarship until the 1940s and 1950s, when new studies in archaeology, anthropology, and history began to confirm black assertions that Africa had enjoyed a rich and complex cultural heritage before Europeans came to exploit the continent. For early black efforts to rehabilitate the image of Africa, see W. E. B. Du Bois, *The Negro* (New York, 1915),* chs. 1–8, and *Black Folk: Then and Now* (New York, 1939), chs. 1–7; and Carter G. Woodson, *The African Background Outlined* (Washington, 1936, reprinted Westport, Conn., 1970). Appreciative and stimulating essays on recent and contemporary African history and culture are published in John A. Davis, ed., *Africa from the Point of View of American Negro Scholars* (Paris, 1958).* A classic revisionist study was Melville J. Herskovits, *The*

Myth of the Negro Past (New York, 1941),* especially ch. 3. Two recent works that summarize and elaborate upon the historiography of the past three decades are Philip D. Curtin, *African History* (Washington, 1964),* and Robert O. Collins, ed., *Problems in African History* (Englewood Cliffs, N.J., 1968).*

One of the most prolific historians of Africa is Basil Davidson, whose following three books provide broad surveys of sub-Saharan African development: *The Lost Cities of Africa* (Boston, 1959);* *The Growth of African Civilisation: West Africa 1000–1800* (London, 1965, rev. ed., 1967, American paperback ed. New York, 1966, under the title *A History of West Africa to the Nineteenth Century*);* and *The African Genius: An Introduction to African Social and Cultural History* (Boston, 1970).* Other important books and articles include Robert W. July, *A History of the African People* (New York, 1970); John D. Fage, *A History of West Africa* (4th ed., London, 1969);* Edward W. Bovill, *The Golden Trade of the Moors* (London, 1958); Joseph Greenberg, "The Negro Kingdoms of the Sudan," *Transactions of the New York Academy of Sciences*, ser. II, vol. II (1949), 126–35;** John D. Fage, "Slavery and the Slave Trade in the Context of West African History," *Journal of African History*, X (1969), 393–404;** and Walter Rodney, "Upper Guinea and the Significance of the Origins of Africans Enslaved in the New World," *JNH*, LIV (Oct. 1969), 327–45. For a comparison of labor and agricultural systems in Africa and the antebellum American South, see Eugene D. Genovese, *The Political Economy of Slavery* (New York, 1965),* ch. 3.

2. *The Figure of the Black in English Renaissance Drama*

"Attitudes"—including racial attitudes—are complex "postures" that are both psychological and social. They operate simultaneously on many levels of personality (conscious and subconscious, deliberate and habitual) and in many sectors of social behavior (institutions and mores, formulated policies and unwritten codes, cultural traditions and tacit conventions). Literary works, because they respond to both psychological and social realities, can reveal attitudes in all their integral complexity. Moreover they can function, intentionally and unintentionally, to modify such attitudes or to transmit them from generation to generation.

The great age of Elizabethan and Jacobean drama almost exactly coincided with the settlement of the English colonies and the beginnings of slavery in the New World, and accordingly the treatment of blacks in English Renaissance drama has particular relevance for students of the origins of slavery. The dramatists' portrayal of sixteenth- and seventeenth-century blacks was of course not accurate. Few writers or playgoers knew much at firsthand about blacks, and plays are after all imaginative works that exaggerate and dramatize the attitudes they express or scrutinize. The exaggerations may originate in racial attitudes; even when they originate in aesthetic, rhetorical, or theatrical motives, however, they may significantly affect the image of blacks presented in the plays. The drama either reveals or forges connections between skin color, social behavior, intellectual capacities, and moral values, and it shows us a great deal about attitudes that were familiar to writers and audiences at the time Jamestown and Plymouth were settled. The patterns that the plays reveal—which are displayed not only in the behavior of black characters but also in the behavior of whites toward them and in such things as the imagery of light and dark—comprise the "set" or structure of expectations regarding blacks that English Renaissance culture presented to ensuing generations.

The dramatic material most relevant to this topic (each is available in numerous editions) includes Ben Jonson's *The Masque of Blacknesse*, John Webster's *The White Devil*, and William Shakespeare's *Titus Andronicus* and *Othello*. (Those interested in Shakespeare should also pay attention to the treatment of the Prince of Morocco, one of Portia's suitors, in *The Merchant of Venice*.)

Important background material will be found in David Brion Davis, *The Problem of Slavery in Western Culture* (Ithaca, N.Y., 1966),* especially chs. 3–4, 6–7; and in Winthrop D. Jordan, *White over Black: American Attitudes Toward the Negro, 1550–*

1812 (Chapel Hill, 1968),* particularly ch. 1. Eldred Jones'
*Othello's Countrymen: The African in English Renaissance
Drama* (London, 1965) very briefly surveys the material and some
of the issues it raises in connection with attitudes toward blacks,
including the question of distinctions between Moors and blacks
in Renaissance culture, and problems of costuming and staging.
The quantity of secondary material on sixteenth- and seventeenth-
century English plays is enormous, but several items are particularly useful in leading into some of the complexities of the
problem: B. J. Layman, "The Equilibrium of Opposites in *The
White Devil,*" *PMLA,* LXXIV (1959), 336–47; the remarks on
Othello's color in A. C. Bradley, *Shakespearean Tragedy* (London, 1904),* ch. 5; Kenneth Burke, "*Othello:* An Essay to Illustrate a Method," *Hudson Review,* IV (Summer 1951), 165–203;
Lily B. Campbell, *Shakespeare's Tragic Heroes* (Cambridge, Eng.,
1930),* ch. 13, which emphasizes Othello's blackness as a token
of hotheadedness and lust; Arthur Sewell, *Character and Society
in Shakespeare* (Oxford, Eng., 1951), in which Othello is viewed
more as a Noble Savage; Bernard Spivack, *Shakespeare and the Allegory of Evil* (New York, 1958), especially ch. 12, which discusses
the way in which older moral stereotypes are grafted onto more
plausible individualized characters to form a "hybrid image" in
Shakespeare's dramas; and the heated exchange in the *APSR,* LIV
(Mar. 1960), 130–67, which opens with Allan D. Bloom's "Cos-
mopolitan Man and the Political Community: An Interpretation
of *Othello*" and includes Sigurd Burckhardt's reply, "English
Bards and APSR Reviewers." There is also relevant material in
Philip Mason, *Prospero's Magic: Some Thoughts on Class and
Race* (London, 1962), ch. 3.

The most recent controversy over the question of Othello's
color and the interpretation of his character was provoked by
Laurence Olivier's production in London, which was released on
film in 1966. For comment on his "Jamaican" performance, see
reviews, comment, and letters in the New York *Times,* Apr. 22,
1965, p. 56; Feb. 2, 1966, p. 24; Feb. 13, 1966, Sect. II, p. 1; Feb.
20, 1966, Sect. II, p. 9. See also the account in *Newsweek,* LXVII
(Jan. 17, 1966), 85; and N. Kallet, "Olivier and the Moor," *Holiday,* XXXIX (Apr. 1966), 143–44.

3. The Atlantic Slave Trade

One of the most starkly brutal features of slavery was the slave trade from Africa to the Western Hemisphere, a brutality for which Westerners were chiefly responsible but in which Africans had a share. The chief precipitant of the trade was the opening of the New World and the development by whites of a new economy based upon the production of staple crops. The white merchants and sea captains who transported Africans to the New World were actuated by their desire for profit and by the insatiable demand for cheap labor on the part of plantation capitalism. The Africans who captured and sold slaves for the European traders were responding to vast social and economic changes taking place elsewhere; those whom they sold away to American slavery were sometimes the captives taken in the course of African wars, but as time passed the victims were increasingly the hapless pawns seized specifically for a corrupting exchange involving irresistible Western guns and goods. In the end, at least nine million people were brought forcibly from Africa to the plantations of the Western Hemisphere, a total which excludes the uncounted millions more who died on the long march to the slave barracoons of Africa, on the awful Middle Passage across the Atlantic, or during the "seasoning" process in the New World.

Two vivid and anecdotal histories of the trade are of considerable value, despite some defects and inaccuracies: Daniel P. Mannix and Malcolm Cowley, *Black Cargoes: A History of the Atlantic Slave Trade, 1518–1865* (New York, 1962);* and James Pope-Hennessy, *Sins of the Fathers: A Study of the Atlantic Slave Traders, 1441–1807* (New York, 1968).* A moving story of the impact of the trade on African society is Basil Davidson, *Black Mother: The Years of the African Slave Trade* (Boston, 1961, retitled in the paperback edition *The African Slave Trade*).* Two older studies, which include accounts of the efforts to suppress the trade in the nineteenth century, are W. E. B. Du Bois, *Suppression of the African Slave Trade to the United States, 1638–1870* (New York, 1896),* and John R. Spears, *The Ameri-*

can Slave Trade: An Account of Its Origin, Growth and Suppression (New York, 1900). For examinations of British attempts to end the illegal slave trade in the nineteenth century, see W. E. F. Ward, *The Royal Navy and the Slavers* (London, 1969),* and Christopher Lloyd, *The Navy and the Slave Trade: The Suppression of the African Slave Trade in the Nineteenth Century* (London, 1949). The standard study of British enterprise in slaves is Kenneth G. Davies, *The Royal African Company* (London, 1957).*

Two recent monographs on the American role in the trade, legal and illegal, are Peter Duignan and Clarence Clendenen, *The United States and the African Slave Trade, 1619–1862* (Stanford, 1963); and Warren S. Howard, *American Slavers and the Federal Law, 1837–1862* (Berkeley, 1963). The basic source material for a study of the slave trade is contained in the four volumes edited by Elizabeth Donnan, *Documents Illustrative of the History of the Slave Trade to America* (Washington, 1930–35). Another important collection of primary sources is Philip D. Curtin, ed., *Africa Remembered: Narratives by West Africans from the Era of the Slave Trade* (Madison, 1967).* An important new study which contains the most thorough and reliable estimates of the numbers, origins, and destinations of African slaves is Philip D. Curtin, *The Atlantic Slave Trade: A Census* (Madison, 1969). See also Curtin's article, "Epidemiology and the Slave Trade," *PSQ*, LXXXIII (June 1968), 190–216;** W. Robert Higgins, "The Geographical Origins of Negro Slaves in Colonial South Carolina," *SAQ*, LXX (Winter 1971), 34–47; and, concerning a later period, Herbert S. Klein, "North American Competition and the Characteristics of the African Slave Trade to Cuba, 1790 to 1794," *WMQ*, Ser. 3, XXVIII (Jan. 1971), 86–102.

Eric Williams, *Capitalism and Slavery* (Chapel Hill, 1944),* assesses from a Marxist perspective the effect of the British West Indian slave trade upon the rise of English industry and offers some provocative hypotheses about the interrelationships of the trade, profits, and abolition. Significant articles on different aspects of the slave trade are: Walter Rodney, "African Slavery and Other Forms of Social Oppression on the Upper Guinea Coast in the Context of the Atlantic Slave Trade," *Journal of African*

History, VII (1966), 219–46;** Elizabeth Donnan, "The New England Slave Trade After the Revolution," *New England Quarterly*, III (Apr. 1930), 251–78; Simon Rottenberg, "The Business of Slave Trading," *SAQ*, LXVI (Summer 1967), 402–23;** Harvey Wish, "The Revival of the African Slave Trade in the United States, 1856–1860," *MVHR*, XXVII (Mar. 1941), 569–88;** and Barton J. Bernstein, "Southern Politics and Attempts to Reopen the African Slave Trade," *JNH*, LI (Jan. 1966), 16–35. Three recent essays on the slave trade are published in vol. I, pp. 39–93, of Nathan D. Huggins, Martin Kilson, and Daniel M. Fox, eds., *Key Issues in the Afro-American Experience*, 2 vols. (New York, 1971):* Marion Kilson, "West African Society and the Atlantic Slave Trade, 1441–1865"; Basil Davidson, "Slaves or Captives? Some Notes on Fantasy and Fact"; and Philip D. Curtin, "The Slave Trade and the Atlantic Basin: Intercontinental Perspectives." Another useful essay is C. L. R. James, "The Atlantic Slave Trade and Slavery: Some Interpretations of Their Significance in the Development of the United States and the Western World," *Amistad 1: Writings on Black History and Culture* (New York, 1970),* 119–64. A full-scale treatment of the efforts to reopen the trade to the United States in the 1850s is found in Ronald Takaki, *A Proslavery Crusade: The Agitation to Reopen the African Slave Trade* (New York, 1971).* An interesting monograph on one of the last illegal slave-trading voyages to the United States (in 1858) is Tom Henderson Wells, *The Slave Ship Wanderer* (Athens, Ga., 1967).

The horrors of the Middle Passage are treated in a narrative poem by Louis O. Coxe, *The Middle Passage* (Chicago, 1960).

Many slaves imported to the American colonies did not come directly from Africa but from the West Indies, where they had gone through a process of "seasoning" before being purchased by mainland planters. Many of the studies cited above discuss this process. For comparative perspectives on slavery in the West Indies and the United States, see Part II, topic 5, "Slavery in the United States and Latin America: Comparative Analyses."

4. African Cultural Survivals Among Black Americans

For several decades a debate has flourished among anthropologists, sociologists, historians, and folklorists over the extent of African cultural survivals among Afro-Americans. The most comprehensive argument in favor of significant African survivals is the classic study by anthropologist Melville J. Herskovits, *The Myth of the Negro Past* (New York, 1941).* See also Herskovits' article "On the Provenience of New World Negroes," *SF*, XII (Dec. 1933), 247–62,** and the posthumous collection of his articles entitled *The New World Negro* (Bloomington, Ind., 1966). A similar thesis is expressed by Lorenzo D. Turner, "African Survivals in the New World with Special Emphasis on the Arts," in John A. Davis, ed., *Africa from the Point of View of American Negro Scholars* (Paris, 1958),* pp. 101–16. Though conceding that African influences were greater among blacks in South America and the Caribbean, Herskovits claimed that folktales, superstitions, dances, songs, religion, family structure, and certain social practices among blacks in the United States bore signs of African origins, especially in southern counties with heavy concentrations of black population. The chief critic of Herskovits' thesis was sociologist E. Franklin Frazier, who maintained that the experience of slavery and minority status in an Anglo-Saxon culture had almost completely obliterated the Afro-American's African culture and substituted for it a Jim Crow imitation of the religion, mores, and values of white society. See the first chapter in each of three books by Frazier: *The Negro in the United States* (rev. ed., New York, 1957); *The Negro Family in the United States* (Chicago, 1939, abridged paperback ed., Chicago, 1966);* and *The Negro Church in America* (New York, 1964).* Two earlier articles that also maintained that the Afro-American lost most of his native culture in the United States were Robert E. Park, "The Conflict and Fusion of Cultures with Special Reference to the Negro," *JNH*, IV (Apr. 1919), 111–33; and

Gold Refined Wilson, "The Religion of the American Slave: His Attitude Towards Life and Death," *ibid.*, VIII (Jan. 1923), 41–71. Balanced appraisals that try to sort out African and American influences are William Bascom, "Acculturation Among the Gullah Negroes," *American Anthropologist*, XLIII (Jan.–Mar. 1941), 43–50; Kenneth M. Stampp, *The Peculiar Institution: Slavery in the Ante-Bellum South* (New York, 1956),* pp. 361–77; and August Meier and Elliott Rudwick, *From Plantation to Ghetto* (rev. ed., New York, 1970),* pp. 17–24. In recent years the growth of cultural nationalism among black Americans and the increasing interest of anthropologists in the life of black urban communities have produced an emphasis on indigenous Afro-American cultural patterns and their linkages with African culture. (Part IX, topic 14, "Black Life-Styles in the Ghetto.") Some evidence of Afro-American and African similarities in religion and family patterns as well as in music and folklore has been uncovered, but it remains true that the similarities to Africa are greater in the Caribbean and South America than in the United States. The essays in Norman E. Whitten, Jr., and John F. Szwed, eds., *Afro-American Anthropology: Contemporary Perspectives* (New York, 1970),* provide full and varied discussions. See also Roger Bastide, *Les Amériques Noires: Les Civilisations Africaines dans le Nouveau Monde* (Paris, 1967).

African cultural survivals seem to have been strongest in black folklore and music, especially in the spirituals and their secular successors, the blues and jazz. Yet even on these subjects there has been much disagreement among scholars. On one matter most commentators are agreed: the haunting melodies and moving lyrics of the spirituals, the syncopation and harmonies of the blues and jazz are among the few original contributions the United States has made to the world's music. But the controversial problem of tracing the roots of this music has engendered a vast outpouring of books and articles, only the most important of which can be mentioned here. The historiography of this controversy is summarized in Donald K. Wilgus, *Anglo-American Folksong Scholarship Since 1898* (New Brunswick, N.J., 1959), pp. 345–64. See also Bruce Jackson, ed., *The Negro and His Folklore in Nineteenth-Century Periodicals* (Austin, Tex., 1967).

The spirituals were "discovered" by northern white teachers

and missionaries among the freedmen during and after the Civil
War and popularized by the Fisk University Jubilee Singers in
the 1870s. The first and basic collection of spirituals was published
by three of these missionaries in 1867: William Francis Allen,
Charles P. Ware, and Lucy McKim Garrison, *Slave Songs of the
United States* (New York, 1867, reprinted several times, most
recently New York, 1965). Black folklore was popularized by the
appearance of Joel Chandler Harris' first book of "Uncle Remus"
stories in 1880. In those years it was widely assumed that the animal stories of Uncle Remus were derived from African folktales;
in a long introduction to the second collection of stories, *Nights
with Uncle Remus* (Boston, 1883), Harris pointed out many ana-
logues with African and Indian animal tales. The African roots
of the *music* of the spirituals (though not their words or concepts, which grew largely out of Christianity as molded by slavery)
were also generally assumed: see, for example, Jeannette Robinson Murphy, "The Survival of African Music in America," *Popular Science Monthly*, LV (Sept. 1899), 660–72.** But in the
1890s a German musicologist sweepingly asserted that black music
was imitative of Western music: see Richard Wallaschek, *Primitive Music: An Inquiry into the Origin and Development of the
Music, Songs, Instruments, Dances and Pantomimes of Savage
Races* (London, 1893), especially pp. 60–62. Though this argument gained considerable acceptance among whites who doubted
the ability of black people to create anything original, it was
sharply rebutted by several scholars, among whom the foremost
was the music critic of the New York *Tribune*, Henry Edward
Krehbiel, whose *Afro-American Folk Songs: A Study in Racial
and National Music* (New York, 1914), esp. ch. 2, analyzed parallels between African and Afro-American music.

The debate over the origins of black music and folklore, particularly the former, intensified from the 1920s through the 1940s
as a generation of southern-born white anthropologists and folklorists proclaimed the essentially European roots of black folk
culture, and a generation of blacks and largely northern-born
white scholars countered with assertions of the African or pluralist origins of black music and folklore. An influential 1926 study,
Newell N. Puckett, *Folk Beliefs of the Southern Negro* (Chapel
Hill, 1926),* analyzed the mixed African and European roots of

black superstitions and folklore, but in an article five years later, "Religious Folk-Beliefs of Whites and Negroes," *JNH*, XVI (Jan. 1931), 9–35, Puckett emphasized more strongly the importance of European origins. Newman I. White, *American Negro Folk Songs* (Cambridge, Mass., 1928), acknowledged that some of the music of black folk songs was African in origin, but contended that the concepts and words of the spirituals were almost entirely derived from white hymns and camp-meeting songs. The anthropologist Guy B. Johnson investigated black communities on the South Carolina Sea Islands and elsewhere and advanced the thesis that most aspects of the spirituals and of folkways, even the Gullah dialect, were largely survivals of earlier white culture: see Johnson's *Folk Culture on St. Helena Island, South Carolina* (Chapel Hill, 1930, reprinted Hatboro, Pa., 1968), and two of his essays: "The Negro Spiritual, A Problem in Anthropology," *American Anthropologist*, XXXIII (Apr.–June 1931), 157–71, and "Negro Folk-Songs in the South," in W. T. Couch, ed., *Culture in the South* (Chapel Hill, 1934), pp. 547–69. The most thoroughgoing advocate of white origins for both words and music of black spirituals was George Pullen Jackson, whose "The Genesis of the Negro Spiritual," *American Mercury*, XXVI (June 1932), 243–48; *White Spirituals in the Southern Uplands* (Chapel Hill, 1933);* and *White and Negro Spirituals, Their Life Span and Kinship* (New York, 1943), carefully traced the similarities of the spirituals to earlier Methodist, Baptist, and camp-meeting hymns.

Johnson and Jackson made a strong case for the basically white roots of the spirituals. But several black writers countered with the persuasive argument that all folk music is the product of borrowing and adaptation, and that the spirituals grew from a blending of Christian concepts and hymns with African musical forms and expression to produce a unique and original musical genre. See Sterling Brown, *Negro Poetry and Drama* (Washington, 1937),* ch. 2, and Brown's essay, "Spirituals," in Langston Hughes and Arna Bontemps, eds., *The Book of Negro Folklore* (New York, 1958),* pp. 279–88. In 1925 the African-born Nicholas G. J. Ballanta published a collection entitled *Saint Helena Island Spirituals* (New York, 1925), in which he found many parallels to African songs. Two of the most important collections of spirituals were James Weldon Johnson and J. Rosa-

mond Johnson, eds., *The Book of American Negro Spirituals*
(New York, 1925), and *The Second Book of Negro Spirituals*
(New York, 1926), both reprinted in one vol., *The Books of
American Negro Spirituals* (New York, 1956).* In a long preface
to the first volume, Johnson asserted that the spirituals were a
creative fusion of the black's musical genius and evangelical
Christianity. A similar point was made by John Wesley Work,
who maintained in the introductory chapters to his *American
Negro Songs: A Comprehensive Collection of 230 Folk Songs,
Religious and Secular* (New York, 1940), that the slaves did not
merely *imitate* white hymns, but *reassembled* them into something
richer and deeper growing out of the blending of African musical
forms and the slave experience. Another appraisal of the pluralistic
origins of black music and folk poetry is Margaret Just Butcher,
The Negro in American Culture (New York, 1956), chs. 2, 3, and
5.

In addition to Herskovits, several scholars in the 1930s and
1940s emphasized the African origins of many facets of Afro-
American folk culture. Mason Crum, *Gullah: Negro Life in the
Carolina Sea Islands* (Durham, N.C., 1940, reprinted New York,
1969); Lydia Parrish, *Slave Songs of the Georgia Sea Islands*
(New York, 1942, reprinted Hatboro, Pa., 1965); and Lorenzo D.
Turner, *Africanisms in the Gullah Dialect* (Chicago, 1949), re-
butted Guy B. Johnson's hypothesis of white origins for the music
and dialect of Sea Island blacks. A volume by the Savannah,
Georgia, unit of the Federal Writers Project, *Drums and Shadows:
Survival Studies Among the Georgia Coastal Negroes* (Athens,
Ga., 1940), contains much evidence of African survivals, though
Guy B. Johnson's preface tries to deny their significance. An informative brief analysis is Robert A. Hall, Jr., "African Substra-
tum in Negro English," *American Speech*, XXV (Feb. 1950),
51–54. A study of black church sermons in Macon County,
Georgia, in the 1940s found significant Africanisms in the imagery
and cadence of these sermons: see William H. Pipes, *Say Amen,
Brother! Old-Time Negro Preaching: A Study in American Frustration* (New York, 1951), especially ch. 3. (But Arthur Huff
Fauset, *Black Gods of the Metropolis: Negro Religious Cults of
the Urban North* [Philadelphia, 1944],* pp. 101–06, denied the existence of African survivals among black Holiness churches in the

cities.) Three discussions of Voodoo cults emphasized the survival of African religio-magic practices in some parts of the United States: Zora Neale Hurston, *Mules and Men* (Philadelphia, 1935),* pt. 2; Robert Tallant, *Voodoo in New Orleans* (New York, 1946);* and Norman E. Whitten, Jr., "Contemporary Patterns of Malign Occultism Among Negroes in North Carolina," *Journal of American Folklore*, LXXV (Oct.–Dec. 1962), 311–25. The most forthright exponent of African origins and the persistence of African allusions in the spirituals is Miles Mark Fisher, *Negro Slave Songs in the United States* (Ithaca, N.Y., 1953, based on a 1945 doctoral diss.),* a book whose thesis is weakened by undocumented assertions that defy common sense.

In the 1950s and 1960s the debate has continued in studies of greater sophistication based on a larger knowledge of contemporary and historical African culture than earlier works. While this knowledge has produced increasing evidence of significant African survivals in black music, it has caused a leading folklorist, Richard M. Dorson, to reach the opposite conclusion about black folktales, whose assumed African origins had previously been relatively uncontroversial (except for the Puckett studies, cited above, which had pointed out many European roots). Dorson asserts flatly that the beliefs and folktales of black Americans, even including the Uncle Remus stories and other animal tales, "are in large part directly traceable to Europe and England"; see his *American Folklore* (Chicago, 1959),* ch. 5, and *American Negro Folktales* (Greenwich, Conn., 1967).* A fascinating study of the Uncle Remus stories, Bernard Wolfe, "Uncle Remus and the Malevolent Rabbit," *Commentary*, VIII (July 1949), 31–41, analyzes Br'er Rabbit's triumphs over Br'er Fox and the other larger animals as an allegory of the slave's effort to alleviate his lot by winning tricks from the master; these famous tales, suggests Wolfe, were therefore a product of American slavery, not African folklore. But J. Mason Brewer, ed., *American Negro Folklore* (Chicago, 1968), maintains the pre-eminence of African roots of much black folk culture. See also Daniel J. Crowley, "Negro Folklore: An Africanist's View," *Texas Quarterly*, V (Autumn 1962), 65–71, and Richard A. Waterman and William R. Bascom, "African and New World Negro Folklore," in Maria Leach, ed., *Dictionary of Folklore, Mythology, and Legend* (New York, 1949).

In musicology, recent studies have asserted the pluralist origins of Afro-American music, placing varying degrees of emphasis on the importance of African roots. Richard A. Waterman, "African Influences on the Music of the Americas," in Sol Tax, ed., *Acculturation in the Americas* (Chicago, 1952), pp. 207–18, declares that the similarities between African and Western music made it easy for slaves to adapt white hymns and tunes to their own musical forms. LeRoi Jones' excellent *Blues People: Negro Music in White America* (New York, 1963),* especially chs. 1–4, argues that the major roots of Afro-American music are African. Harold Courlander, *Negro Folk Music, U.S.A.* (New York, 1963),* adopts a pluralist approach, but finds strong evidence of African survivals in spirituals despite their Christian origins, and even greater survivals in black secular folk music. Lawrence W. Levine, "Slave Songs and Slave Consciousness: An Exploration in Neglected Sources," in Tamara K. Hareven, ed., *Anonymous Americans: Explorations in 19th Century Social History* (Englewood Cliffs, N.J., 1971),* pp. 99–130, provides a balanced appraisal of the mixed origins of the spirituals. Alan Lomax, "The Homogeneity of African–Afro-American Musical Style," in Norman E. Whitten, Jr., and John F. Szwed, eds., *Afro-American Anthropology* (New York, 1970),* pp. 181–201, uses a computer-aided technique of analysis called "cantometrics" to demonstrate the similarity of African and Afro-American music. Marshall Stearns, *The Story of Jazz* (New York, 1956),* describes jazz as a blending of African rhythms, Euro-African melodies, and European harmony, but Gunther Schuller, *Early Jazz: Its Roots and Musical Development* (New York, 1968), asserts that harmonic and melodic as well as rhythmic patterns in jazz correspond more closely to those of African music than earlier musicologists had believed. Schuller's book is the most detailed technical analysis of jazz yet published. John F. Szwed, "Afro-American Musical Adaptation," in Whitten and Szwed, eds., *Afro-American Anthropology*, cited above, pp. 219–28, finds Africanisms to be an important component of "soul" music. Eileen Southern, *The Music of Black Americans: A History* (New York, 1971),* esp. chs. 1–2, discusses the African roots of many aspects of Afro-American music. For additional references to relevant studies of black music, see Part VIII, topic 11, "Soul Music: Blues, Jazz, and Variations."

Robert Farris Thompson, "African Influence on the Art of the United States," in Armstead L. Robinson, Craig C. Foster, and Donald H. Ogilvie, eds., *Black Studies in the University* (New Haven, 1969),* pp. 122–70, demonstrates the survival of African forms of wood sculpture, ceramics, and basketry among Afro-Americans and their diffusion among southern whites as well.

5. The Origins of Slavery in the British Colonies of North America

One might think that tracing the origins of the Afro-American's legal status as a slave in the American colonies would be a relatively simple matter. But the process by which the black man or woman moved from an uncertain servant status, somewhat similar in condition to the white servant in the early seventeenth century, to a chattel slave by the 1660s is shrouded in uncertainty and controversy. And it remains so despite its being one of the most critical problems in the whole of Afro-American history. For a summary of the historiography of this question through 1960, consult Winthrop D. Jordan, "Modern Tensions and the Origins of American Slavery," *JSH*, XXVIII (Feb. 1962), 18–30.**

The controversy, which has important implications for contemporary race relations, centers on the cause-effect relationship between white Americans' prejudice against blacks and the reduction of black servants from indentured status to chattelhood. Ultimately, of course, slavery was a result of the power, possessed and enforced, of one group over another. But what caused this power to be exploited and applied as it was? Was it due, initially and basically, to race prejudice or to economic and social pressures? And were there, at any time, alternative arrangements besides slavery to the association of blacks and whites? For the argument that slavery at once preceded and intensified race prejudice, see Oscar and Mary F. Handlin, "Origins of the Southern Labor System," *WMQ*, Ser. 3, VII (Apr. 1950), 199–222** (reprinted in Oscar Handlin, *Race and Nationality in American Life* [Boston,

1957],* ch. 1). For a statement that slavery was fundamentally a product of the white man's prejudice against the African as a member of a different, pagan, and "inferior" race, see Carl N. Degler, "Slavery and the Genesis of American Race Prejudice," *Comparative Studies in Society and History,* II (Oct. 1959), 49–66.** There is a pointed exchange of letters on the matter between Degler and the Handlins, *ibid.* (July 1960), 488–95. In ch. 2 of *White over Black: American Attitudes Toward the Negro, 1550–1812* (Chapel Hill, 1968),* Winthrop D. Jordan provides a balanced account of the origins of American slavery, which in essence confirms the Degler interpretation, as does Wesley Frank Craven, *The Colonies in Transition, 1660–1713* (New York, 1968),* pp. 294–300. An important essay on the same matter is George M. Frederickson, "Toward a Social Interpretation of the Development of American Racism," in Nathan I. Huggins, Martin Kilson, and Daniel M. Fox, eds., *Key Issues in the Afro-American Experience,* 2 vols. (New York, 1971),* vol. I, pp. 240–54. Another related study is Paul C. Palmer, "Servant into Slave: The Evolution of the Legal Status of the Negro Laborer in Colonial Virginia," SAQ, LXV (Summer 1966), 355–70. See also Winthrop D. Jordan, "The Influence of the West Indies on the Origin of New England Slavery," WMQ, Ser. 3, XVIII (Apr. 1961), 243–50,** and Jonathan L. Alpert, "The Origin of Slavery in the United States: The Maryland Precedent," *American Journal of Legal History,* XIV (July 1970), 189–221.

Additional understanding of this complex subject can be gained by comparing black-white relations with the early history of Indian-white relations. Slavery and its approximations were at times the fate of red men as well as black men during the colonial era; and the attitudes and institutions that gave rise to Indian enslavement, the treatment of Indian slaves, and the ultimate failure of Indian slavery are important subjects of investigation—to which scholars are only now beginning to devote the attention they deserve. Moreover, a comparison of the enslavement of the native populations of Latin America with the bondage of both Afro-Americans and American Indians should yield still further insights; on this subject, some suggestions can be found in the works cited in Part III, topic 5, "Slavery in the United States and Latin America: Comparative Analyses."

For basic materials on the differences between African and Indian enslavement, consult David Brion Davis, *The Problem of Slavery in Western Culture* (Ithaca, N.Y., 1966),* chs. 4 and 6; Gary B. Nash, "Red, White, and Black: The Origins of Racism in Colonial America," in Gary B. Nash and Richard Weiss, eds., *The Great Fear: Race in the Mind of America* (New York, 1970),* pp. 1–26; William S. Willis, "Divide and Rule: Red, White, and Black in the Southeast," *JNH*, XLVIII (July 1963), 157–76;** and Almon W. Lauber, *Indian Slavery in Colonial Times Within the Present Limits of the United States* (New York, 1913), esp. ch. 12. Four books which examine the idea of the Indian in the Western mind are Lewis Hanke, *Aristotle and the American Indian: A Study in Race Prejudice in the Modern World* (London, 1959);* Hoxie N. Fairchild, *The Noble Savage: A Study in Romantic Naturalism* (New York, 1928); Roy Harvey Pearce, *The Savages of America: A Study of the Indian and the Idea of Civilization* (Baltimore, 1953);* and Howard Mumford Jones, *O Strange New World: American Culture, the Formative Years* (New York, 1964),* chs. 1–2 and 12. The bases for some comparisons between black and Indian slavery are found in Wilcomb E. Washburn, "The Moral and Legal Justification for Dispossessing the Indians," in James Morton Smith, ed., *17th-Century America: Essays in Colonial History* (Chapel Hill, 1959),* pp. 15–32; Nancy Oestreich Lurie, "Indian Cultural Adjustment to European Civilization," *ibid.*, pp. 33–60; and Bernard W. Sheehan, "Indian-White Relations in Early America: A Review Essay," *WMQ*, Ser. 3, XXVI (Apr. 1969), 267–86. Indian-black relations are treated in Carter G. Woodson, "The Relations of Negroes and Indians in Massachusetts," *JNH*, IV (Jan. 1920), 44–58; and Laurence Foster, *Negro-Indian Relationships in the Southeast* (Philadelphia, 1935). On Indians who owned black slaves, see Annie H. Abel, *The American Indian as Slaveholder and Secessionist* (Cleveland, 1915).

Finally, a full understanding of the origins of Afro-American slavery can be gained only by comparing them with the origins and character of white servitude and labor during the colonial period. For an introduction to this question, consult Abbot Emerson Smith, *Colonists in Bondage: White Servitude and Convict Labor in America, 1607–1776* (Chapel Hill, 1947); Marcus

W. Jernegan, *Laboring and Dependent Classes in Colonial America, 1607–1783* (Chicago, 1931); Richard B. Morris, *Government and Labor in Early America* (New York, 1946);* and Warren B. Smith, *White Servitude in Colonial South Carolina* (Columbia, S.C., 1961).*

6. Slaves and Free Blacks in the Colonial South

The question of the blacks' status and life in the new societies of the colonial South introduces the critical problem of explaining the similarities of and differences between the "peculiar institution" in each of the colonies and raises once again the persistent matter of alternatives open to blacks and whites alike in their relationships with each other. Furthermore, only by understanding the development of eighteenth-century chattel slavery is it possible fully to come to grips with changes in the lot of Afro-Americans, both slave and free, in the decades from the Revolution to the Civil War.

Despite the racism and paternalism of its viewpoint, Ulrich B. Phillips, *American Negro Slavery* (New York, 1918),* chs. 4–5, provides the only general introduction to slavery in the colonial South; it should be used with care, as indicated in Part III, topic 1, "Plantation Slavery in the Antebellum South." Chs. 2–6 of Winthrop D. Jordan, *White over Black: American Attitudes Toward the Negro, 1550–1812* (Chapel Hill, 1968),* survey white attitudes toward Afro-Americans to 1755 and contain a great deal of information on the status of free and enslaved black people (in the North as well as the South), as does Jordan's "American Chiaroscuro: The Status and Definition of Mulattoes in the British Colonies," *WMQ*, Ser. 3, XIX (Apr. 1962), 183–200.**

There are many monographs of varying quality on blacks in the southern colonies. For Virginia: James C. Ballagh, *A History of Slavery in Virginia* (Baltimore, 1902, reprinted Chicago, 1969); John H. Russell, *The Free Negro in Virginia, 1619–1865* (Baltimore, 1913); Philip A. Bruce, *Economic History of Virginia in the Seventeenth Century*, 2 vols. (New York, 1907), vol. II, pp. 57–

130; James H. Brewer, "Negro Property Owners in Seventeenth-Century Virginia," WMQ, Ser. 3, XII (Oct. 1955), 575–80;** ch. 3 of Robert E. Brown and B. Katherine Brown, Virginia, 1705–1786: Democracy or Aristocracy? (E. Lansing, Mich., 1964); Thad W. Tate, Jr., The Negro in Eighteenth-Century Williamsburg (Charlottesville, Va., 1965);* and Adele Hast, "The Legal Status of the Negro in Virginia, 1705–1765," JNH, LIV (July 1969), 217–39. For Maryland: Jeffrey R. Brackett, The Negro in Maryland: A Study of the Institution of Slavery (Baltimore, 1889); and James M. Wright, The Free Negro in Maryland, 1634–1860 (New York, 1921, reprinted New York, 1969). For North Carolina: John Spencer Bassett, Slavery and Servitude in the Colony of North Carolina (Baltimore, 1896); Rosser H. Taylor, Slaveholding in North Carolina: An Economic View (Chapel Hill, 1926); and J. A. Padgett, "The Status of Slaves in Colonial North Carolina," JNH, XIV (July 1929), 300–27. For South Carolina: Frank J. Klingberg, An Appraisal of the Negro in Colonial South Carolina: A Study in Americanization (Washington, 1941); M. Eugene Sirmans, "The Legal Status of the Slave in South Carolina, 1670–1740," JSH, XXVIII (Nov. 1962), 462–73; Howell M. Henry, The Police Control of the Slave in South Carolina (Emory, Va., 1914); E. Horace Fitchett, "The Origin and Growth of the Free Negro Population of Charleston, South Carolina," JNH, XXVI (Oct. 1941), 421–37;** and, also by Fletcher, "The Traditions of the Free Negro in Charleston, South Carolina," ibid., XXV (Apr. 1940), 139–52. For Georgia: Asa H. Gordon, The Georgia Negro: A History (Ann Arbor, 1937); Darold D. Wax, "Georgia and the Negro Before the American Revolution," Georgia Historical Quarterly, LI (Mar. 1967), 63–77; Willard Range, "The Agricultural Revolution in Royal Georgia, 1752–1775," Agricultural History, XXI (Oct. 1947), 250–55; Ralph B. Flanders, Plantation Slavery in Georgia (Chapel Hill, 1930); and, by the same author, "The Free Negro in Ante-Bellum Georgia," NCHR, IX (July 1932), 250–72. For Florida: Wilbur H. Siebert, "Slavery and White Servitude in East Florida, 1726–1776," Florida Historical Society Quarterly, X (July 1931), 3–23, and, by the same author, "Slavery in East Florida, 1776–1785," ibid., X (Jan. 1932), 139–61. On Louisiana blacks through the 1790s, see Alice Dunbar-Nelson, "People of Color in Louisiana:

Part I," *JNH*, I (Oct. 1916), 361–76. And finally, on the important frontier aspects of Afro-American life in the early South, consult Laurence Foster, *Negro-Indian Relationships in the Southeast* (Philadelphia, 1935); Kenneth W. Porter, "Negroes on the Southern Frontier, 1670–1763," *JNH*, XXXIII (Jan. 1948), 53–78; and William S. Willis, "Divide and Rule: Red, White, and Black in the Southeast," *ibid.*, XLVIII (July 1963), 157–76.

7. Slaves and Black Freemen in the Northern Colonies

Although slaves were neither so numerous nor important economically in the northern colonies as in the southern, the blacks nevertheless played a significant role in colonial life north of the Mason-Dixon line. Slavery was abolished by the northern states in the generation after 1775, but before the Revolution the institution existed in all of the northern colonies. Ch. 6 of Ulrich B. Phillips, *American Negro Slavery* (New York, 1918),* and chs. 2–6 of Winthrop D. Jordan, *White over Black: American Attitudes Toward the Negro, 1550–1812* (Chapel Hill, 1968),* contain background information on slavery and free blacks in the colonial North. The standard study for New England is Lorenzo J. Greene, *The Negro in Colonial New England* (New York, 1942).* New England slavery and free blacks are also the subject of Robert C. Twombly and Richard H. Moore, "Black Puritan: The Negro in Seventeenth-Century Massachusetts," *WMQ*, Ser. 3, XXIV (Apr. 1967), 224–42;** Lorenzo J. Greene, "Slave-Holding New England and its Awakening," *JNH*, XIII (Oct. 1928), 492–533, and, by the same author, "The New England Negro as Seen in Advertisements for Runaway Slaves," *ibid.*, XXIX (Apr. 1944), 125–46; Carter G. Woodson, "The Relations of Negroes and Indians in Massachusetts," *ibid.*, IV (Jan. 1920), 44–58; George H. Moore, *Notes on the History of Slavery in Massachusetts* (New York, 1866);* William D. Johnston, *Slavery in Rhode Island, 1755–1776* (Providence, 1894); Bernard C.

Steiner, *History of Slavery in Connecticut* (Baltimore, 1893);
Ralph F. Weld, *Slavery in Connecticut* (New Haven, 1935);
Mary H. Mitchell, "Slavery in Connecticut and Especially in
New Haven," New Haven Colony Historical Society, *Papers*, X
(1951), 286–312; and William C. Fowler, "The Historical Status
of the Negro in Connecticut," *Yearbook, City of Charleston,
S.C., 1900* (Charleston, 1901), app., pp. 3–64. On middle-
colony slavery, see Edgar J. McManus, *A History of Negro Slav-
ery in New York* (New York, 1966); Samuel McKee, *Labor in
Colonial New York, 1664–1776* (New York, 1935), ch. 4; Ken-
neth Scott, "The Slave Insurrection in New York in 1712," *New
York Historical Society Quarterly*, XLV (Jan. 1961), 43–74;**
Henry S. Cooley, *A Study of Slavery in New Jersey* (Baltimore,
1896); Marion T. Wright, *The Education of Negroes in New
Jersey* (New York, 1941), chs. 1–5; Edward R. Turner, *The
Negro in Pennsylvania, Slavery-Servitude-Freedom, 1639–1861*
(Washington, 1911), chs. 1–7; Frank J. Klingberg, "The African
Immigrant in Colonial Pennsylvania and Delaware," *Historical
Magazine of the Protestant Episcopal Church*, XI (Mar. 1952),
126–53; and three essays by Darold D. Wax: "Quaker Merchants
and the Slave Trade in Colonial Pennsylvania," *Pennsylvania
Magazine of History and Biography*, LXXXVI (Apr. 1962),
143–59; "Negro Imports into Pennsylvania," *Pennsylvania His-
tory*, XXXII (July 1965), 254–87; and "The Demand for Slave
Labor in Colonial Pennsylvania," *ibid.*, XXXIV (Oct. 1967),
331–45. The attitudes of Quakers, principally of those in Pennsylvania, towards blacks both slave and free are treated in Sydney
V. James, *A People Among Peoples: Quaker Benevolence in
Eighteenth-Century America* (Cambridge, Mass., 1963), chs. 7,
12, 15.

8. *Afro-Americans in the Revolutionary Era*

Black Americans participated in the American Revolution in two
ways: as contributors and as beneficiaries. As contributors, blacks
played a part as laborers and soldiers. Thousands of slaves escaped to the British lines and thereby won their freedom; some

of them served with the British forces against their erstwhile masters. The colonies, in contrast, were at first reluctant to enlist blacks as soldiers, both because of the common assumption of their inferiority and because of the threat that their enlistment would pose to the institution of slavery. But the colonists' manpower needs eventually overcame this reluctance, and before the conflict was over at least 5,000 blacks had entered the fray as soldiers on the American side. The standard work on the Afro-American in the Revolution is Benjamin Quarles, *The Negro in the American Revolution* (Chapel Hill, 1961).* See also Herbert Aptheker, *The Negro in the American Revolution* (New York, 1940); George H. Moore, *Historical Notes on the Employment of Negroes in the American Army of the Revolution* (New York, 1862); William C. Nell, *Colored Patriots of the American Revolution* (Boston, 1855, reprinted New York, 1968); Lorenzo J. Greene, "Some Observations on the Black Regiment of Rhode Island in the American Revolution," *JNH*, XXXVII (Apr. 1952), 142–72; Luther P. Jackson, "Virginia Negro Soldiers and Seamen in the American Revolution," *ibid.*, XXVII (July 1942), 242–87; and W. B. Hartgrove, "The Negro Soldier in the American Revolution," *ibid.*, I (Apr. 1916), 110–32.

The libertarian ideology of the Revolution also sparked the impulse in the northern states for the abolition of slavery, one of the great achievements of the era. At the same time, however, the spread of republican and abolitionist sentiments throughout the North created sectional problems which were only temporarily shelved by the constitutional compromises of 1787. With a few exceptions, therefore, it was only the relatively few black slaves in the North who benefited at all directly by the separation of the colonies from Britain. For a solid account of the process of northern abolition, see Arthur Zilversmit, *The First Emancipation: The Abolition of Slavery in the North* (Chicago, 1967).* Also useful are Zilversmit, "Quok Walker, Mumbet, and the Abolition of Slavery in Massachusetts," *WMQ*, Ser. 3, XXV (Oct. 1968), 614–24; John D. Cushing, "The Cushing Court and the Abolition of Slavery in Massachusetts: More Notes on the 'Quok Walker Case,'" *American Journal of Legal History*, V (Apr. 1961), 118–44; William O'Brien, "Did the Jennison Case Outlaw Slavery in Massachusetts?" *WMQ*, Ser. 3, XVII (Apr. 1960),

219-41; and Gwendolyn Evans Logan, "The Slave in Connecticut During the Revolution," *Connecticut Historical Society Bulletin,* XXX (July 1965), 73–80.

Antislavery sentiment reached a high point among southern and national leaders in the decade prior to the Constitutional Convention of 1787, and some contemporaries hoped that the impetus of libertarian ideas would result in the total abolition of slavery in the new republic. But the vested interests of southern planters and the limitations in the emancipationist sentiments of many of the Founding Fathers prevented significant action against slavery in the South, even before the invention of the cotton gin in 1793 entrenched the peculiar institution still more firmly. For a detailed and perceptive discussion of white attitudes toward slavery and Afro-Americans during the Revolutionary and post-Revolutionary eras, see Winthrop D. Jordan, *White over Black: American Attitudes Toward the Negro, 1550–1812* (Chapel Hill, 1968),* chs. 7–15. A recent study which examines at length the link between slavery and politics is Donald L. Robinson, *Slavery in the Structure of American Politics, 1765–1820* (New York, 1971), esp. chs. 1–6. A pertinent related study is John C. Greene, "American Debate on the Negro's Place in Nature, 1780–1815," *Journal of the History of Ideas,* XV (June 1954), 384–96. Two useful compilations of documents on both northern and southern attitudes toward slavery are George Livermore, *An Historical Research Respecting the Opinions of the Founders of the Republic on Negroes, as Slaves, as Citizens, and as Soldiers* (Boston, 1862, reprinted New York, 1969); and Matthew T. Mellon, ed., *Early American Views on Negro Slavery* (Boston, 1934).* For critical analyses of the limitations of the Founding Fathers' antislavery sentiments and of the Constitution's proslavery compromises, see Melvin Drimmer, "Was Slavery Dying Before the Cotton Gin?" and Staughton Lynd, "Slavery and the Founding Fathers," in Melvin Drimmer, ed., *Black History: A Reappraisal* (Garden City, N.Y., 1968),* pp. 96–131; and Staughton Lynd, *Class Conflict, Slavery, and the United States Constitution* (Indianapolis, 1967),* chs. 7–8. A more sympathetic interpretation of the most prominent Founding Father is Walter H. Mazyck, *George Washington and the Negro* (Washington, 1932).

A slaveowner who disliked the institution but emancipated only a few of his own slaves, Thomas Jefferson presents the case of an enlightened statesman who felt deeply the impact of contradictory attitudes toward black Americans that prevailed at the turn of the eighteenth and nineteenth centuries. Jefferson's libertarianism ran afoul of his belief in black inferiority, and more than any other man of his times he wrestled with the problems created by this conflict. In the end, Jefferson's abolitionism succumbed to his racial prejudice; his personal experience was a microcosm of the failures of his generation. Critical examinations of Jefferson's attitudes are ch. 12 of Winthrop D. Jordan's *White over Black*, cited above, and David Brion Davis, *Was Thomas Jefferson an Authentic Enemy of Slavery?* (Oxford, Eng., 1970).* See also William Cohen, "Thomas Jefferson and the Problem of Slavery," *JAH*, LVI (Dec. 1968), 503–26; and Daniel J. Boorstin, *The Lost World of Thomas Jefferson* (New York, 1948),* chs. 2 and 4. One should also examine some of Jefferson's writings at first hand, particularly in his *Notes on the State of Virginia* (Paris, 1784),* Queries 6, 8, 11, 14, and 18. A critical analysis of Jefferson and his contemporaries is Robert McColley, *Slavery and Jeffersonian Virginia* (Urbana, Ill., 1964). Frederick M. Binder, *The Color Problem in Early National America, As Viewed by John Adams, Jefferson, and Jackson* (The Hague, 1968), examines the attitudes of three Presidents toward Afro-Americans and Indians.

PART III

SLAVERY AND RACE IN THE ANTEBELLUM SOUTH

1. Plantation Slavery in the Antebellum South

The nature and effect of slavery is probably the most controversial subject in the historical literature on black Americans. It is also the most filled with implications for the current debate over the situation and future of Afro-Americans in the United States. Three subdivisions of the literature on this subject stand out: the slaves' own recorded responses to bondage, the general interpretations of antebellum slavery, and the debate over the effect of servitude on the bond servant himself.

For accounts of slavery by the slaves, the narratives of the fugitive and ex-slaves should be consulted. The most comprehensive collection of reprinted slave narratives, with scholarly introductions and interpretations, is George P. Rawick's multivolume *The American Slave: A Composite Autobiography* (Westport, Conn., 1971–). A useful brief analysis of and selections from the narratives can be found in Charles H. Nichols, *Many Thousand Gone: The Ex-Slaves' Account of Their Bondage and Freedom* (Leiden, Netherlands, 1963).* Some of the best slave autobiographies have been reprinted in modern anthologies: Gilbert Osofsky, ed., *Puttin' on Ole Massa: The Slave Narratives of Henry Bibb, William Wells Brown, and Solomon Northup* (New York, 1969);* Arna Bontemps, ed., *Great Slave Narratives* (Boston, 1969);* *Five Slave Narratives: A Compendium* (New York, 1968); John F. Bayliss, ed., *Black Slave Narratives* (New York, 1970);* Julius Lester, ed., *To Be a Slave* (New York, 1968);* and vols. 2, 7, and 8 of Maxwell Whiteman, ed., *Afro-American History Series*, 10 vols. (Wilmington, Del., 1970). The best single autobiography by an ex-slave is Frederick Douglass, *A Narrative of the Life of Frederick Douglass, an American Slave, Written by Himself* (Boston, 1845),* which was expanded ten years later into *My Bondage and My Freedom* (New York, 1855).* Others include *An Autobiography of the Reverend Josiah Henson*, Robin W.

Winks, ed. (Reading, Mass., 1969);* *Austin Steward: Twenty-Two Years a Slave and Forty Years a Freeman,* Jane H. and William H. Pease, eds. (Reading, Mass., 1969);* *The Refugee: A North-Side View of Slavery by Benjamin Drew,* Tilden G. Edelstein, ed. (Reading, Mass., 1969).* During the New Deal a Federal Writers Project interviewed scores of aged ex-slaves; the verbatim accounts of many of them are collected in Benjamin A. Botkin, ed., *Lay My Burden Down: A Folk History of Slavery* (Chicago, 1945);* and Norman R. Yetman, ed., *Life Under the "Peculiar Institution": Selections from the Slave Narrative Collection* (New York, 1970).* See also Stanley Feldstein, ed., *Once a Slave: The Slaves' View of Slavery* (New York, 1971).* Scholars at Fisk University interviewed surviving ex-slaves in the 1920s and 1930s and published two valuable volumes of their reminiscences: *Unwritten History of Slavery: Autobiographical Accounts of Negro Ex-Slaves* (Nashville, 1945, reprinted Washington, 1968); and *God Struck Me Dead, Religious Conversion Experiences and Autobiographies of Negro Ex-Slaves* (Nashville, 1945, reprinted in paperback, ed. by Clifton Johnson, Philadelphia, 1969).* A useful compilation of contemporary descriptions of slavery by both blacks and whites is Harvey Wish, ed., *Slavery in the South* (New York, 1964).* One of the most readable contemporary appraisals of slavery, by a critical northerner, is Frederick Law Olmsted, *The Cotton Kingdom,* ed. by Arthur M. Schlesinger (New York, 1953).

Much of the slaves' feeling about their life in bondage was expressed in folklore and song. For a brief interpretation of these materials, see Sterling Stuckey, "Through the Prism of Folklore: The Black Ethos in Slavery," *Massachusetts Review,* IX (Summer 1968), 417–37. The most helpful interpretations and collections of spirituals are Lawrence W. Levine, "Slave Songs and Slave Consciousness," in Tamara K. Hareven, ed., *Anonymous Americans: Explorations in 19th Century Social History* (Englewood Cliffs, N.J., 1971),* pp. 99–130; Howard Thurman, *Deep River: Reflections on the Religious Insight of Certain of the Negro Spirituals* (rev. ed., New York, 1955); and, by the same author, *The Negro Spiritual Speaks of Life and Death* (New York, 1947); James Weldon Johnson and J. Rosamond Johnson, eds., *The Book of American Negro Spirituals* (New York, 1925), and *The Second*

Book of Negro Spirituals (New York, 1926), both reprinted in one vol., *The Books of American Negro Spirituals* (New York, 1956);* and Bernard Katz, ed., *The Social Implications of Early Negro Music in the United States* (New York, 1969).* Miles Mark Fisher, *Negro Slave Songs in the United States* (Ithaca, N.Y., 1953),* overstates the case for the survival of African symbols and practices in slave music and ideology. An interpretation of slave spirituals, folklore, and sermons which denies the existence of African influences is Gold Refined Wilson, "The Religion of the American Negro Slave: His Attitude Toward Life and Death," *JNH*, VIII (Jan. 1923), 41–71. Additional references on these subjects will be found in Part II, topic 4, "African Cultural Survivals Among Black Americans," and Part VIII, topic 11, "Soul Music: Blues, Jazz, and Variations."

Scholarly studies of slavery necessarily build upon such individual testimonies, from both blacks and whites, of the slave system. These studies, growing in sophistication and number during the twentieth century, have failed, however, to establish a consensus among historians. Two good summaries of the historiography of slavery are Stanley Elkins, *Slavery: A Problem in American Institutional and Intellectual Life* (Chicago, 1959, rev. ed., 1968),* pt. I, and Bennett H. Wall, "African Slavery," in Arthur S. Link and Rembert W. Patrick, eds., *Writing Southern History: Essays in Historiography in Honor of Fletcher M. Green* (Baton Rouge, 1965),* pp. 175–97. Three recent anthologies of interpretations are Allen Weinstein and Frank O. Gatell, eds., *American Negro Slavery: A Modern Reader* (New York, 1968);* Richard D. Brown, ed., *Slavery in American Society* (Lexington, Mass., 1969);* and Irwin Unger and David Reimers, eds., *The Slavery Experience in the United States* (New York, 1970).* The two classic and sharply opposed studies are Ulrich B. Phillips, *American Negro Slavery* (New York, 1918),* which portrays slavery as an essentially benign institution that conferred many benefits upon a backward race; and Kenneth M. Stampp, *The Peculiar Institution: Slavery in the Ante-Bellum South* (New York, 1956),* which depicts slavery as primarily a harsh, repressive system for the exploitation of cheap labor. Phillips' interpretation is also presented in briefer compass in his *Life and Labor in the Old South* (Boston, 1929),* chs. 9–11, and his *The Slave Econ-*

omy of the Old South: Selected Essays in Economic and Social History, ed. by Eugene D. Genovese (Baton Rouge, 1968);* and Stampp's in "The Daily Life of the Southern Slave," in Nathan I. Huggins, Martin Kilson, and Daniel M. Fox, eds., *Key Issues in the Afro-American Experience,* 2 vols. (New York, 1971),* vol. I, pp. 116–37. Two of the best studies of slavery in individual states (though tainted by the Phillips viewpoint) are Charles S. Sydnor, *Slavery in Mississippi* (New York, 1933);* and James B. Sellers, *Slavery in Alabama* (University, Ala., 1950). On the subject of plantation management, see William K. Scarborough, *The Overseer: Plantation Management in the Old South* (Baton Rouge, 1966). Another useful monograph is William D. Postell, *The Health of Slaves on Southern Plantations* (Baton Rouge, 1951). For further information and suggestions about the vital statistics, diseases, and health of slaves, see Richard H. Shryock, "Medical Sources and the Social Historian," *AHR,* XLI (Apr. 1936), 458–73, reprinted in Shryock, *Medicine in America: Historical Essays* (Baltimore, 1966), pp. 275–97.

For critiques of Ulrich B. Phillips' viewpoint and research techniques, see Richard Hofstadter, "U. B. Phillips and the Plantation Legend," *JNH,* XXIX (Apr. 1944), 109–124,** and Kenneth M. Stampp, "The Historian and Southern Negro Slavery," *AHR,* LVII (Apr. 1952), 613–24.** For a qualified defense of Phillips, see Eugene D. Genovese's introduction to the 1966 reissue of *American Negro Slavery* (Baton Rouge, 1966).* Genovese's *The Political Economy of Slavery: Studies in the Economy and Society of the Slave South* (New York, 1965)* is a provocative study that accepts, rejects, and modifies portions of both the Phillips and Stampp interpretations. Genovese has also written an important brief analysis of the behavior and attitude of slaves in "American Slaves and Their History," *New York Review of Books,* XV (Dec. 3, 1970), 34–43. A balanced and informative portrayal of slavery that should be consulted is Allan Nevins, *Ordeal of the Union,* 2 vols. (New York, 1947–50), vol. I, pp. 412–62.

The complex question whether or not slavery was a profitable economic enterprise has generated a large and somewhat confusing scholarly literature of its own. Good anthologies of primary and secondary writings on this issue are Harold D. Woodman, ed., *Slavery and the Southern Economy* (New York, 1966),* and Hugh G. J. Aitken, ed., *Did Slavery Pay? Readings in the Economics of Black Slavery in the U.S.* (Boston, 1971).* Summaries of the economic historiography of slavery can be found in Eugene D. Genovese, "Recent Contributions to the Economic Historiography of the Slave South," *Science and Society*, XXIV (Winter 1960), 53–66;** Harold D. Woodman, "The Profitability of Slavery: A Historical Perennial," *JSH*, XXIX (Nov. 1963), 303–25;** and Stanley L. Engerman, "The Effects of Slavery Upon the Southern Economy: A Review of the Recent Debate," *Explorations in Entrepreneurial History*, Ser. 2, IV (Winter 1967), 71–97. Recent compendia of various viewpoints are Alfred H. Conrad et al., "Slavery as an Obstacle to Economic Growth in the United States; a Panel Discussion," *Journal of Economic History*, XXVII (Dec. 1967), 518–60;** and William N. Parker, ed., *The Structure of the Cotton Economy of the Antebellum South* (Washington, 1970). An important recent study utilizing advanced methods of econometric analysis is Robert W. Fogel and Stanley L. Engerman, "The Economics of Slavery," in Fogel and Engerman, eds., *The Reinterpretation of American Economic History* (New York, 1971), pp. 311–41.

More important for the student of black history than the question of slavery's profitability is the impact of the institution upon its victims, individually and collectively. The marks of servitude on the slaves were undeniably profound. But whereas much is known regarding such matters as the immediate consequences of the loss of liberty, the poverty of the slaves' homes, and the penalties of flight, much less is known about the longer and more permanent effects of slavery upon the personality and institutions of black Americans. Not surprisingly, Americans of all races have debated the subject from divergent perspectives for three centuries, but in the last decade the debate has taken on a new focus and intensity with the publication of Stanley Elkins' controversial *Slavery: A Problem in American Institutional and Intellectual Life* (Chicago, 1959, rev. ed., 1968),* of which pt. III and pp. 238–45 relate to the question of slavery's effects on the slave. Elkins argues that in the United States the institution of slavery was more psychologically repressive than in other slave societies and that this "closed" system reduced Negroes to fawning, dependent, childlike "Samboes," a personality syndrome from which black

Americans have struggled for more than a century to escape. Elkins uses the analogy of Nazi concentration camps to demonstrate the possibility of the infantilization of an adult personality.
His thesis has met heavy criticism from the start, most of the outlines of which are found in "The Question of Sambo," *Newberry
Library Bulletin*, V (Dec. 1958), 14–40. Other discussions that
directly or indirectly challenge Elkins' major contentions are
Earle E. Thorpe, "Chattel Slavery and Concentration Camps,"
NHB, XXV (May 1962), 171–76; Eugene D. Genovese, "Rebelliousness and Docility in the Negro Slave: A Critique of the Elkins Thesis," *CWH*, XIII (Dec. 1967), 293–314;** George M.
Fredrickson and Christopher Lasch, "Resistance to Slavery,"
ibid., 315–29;** Mary A. Lewis, "Slavery and Personality: A
Further Comment," *AQ*, XIX (Spring 1967), 114–21; Joseph
Logsdon, "Diary of a Slave: Recollection and Prophecy," in William G. Shade and Roy C. Herrenkohl, eds., *Seven on Black: Reflections on the Negro Experience in America* (Philadelphia,
1969),* pp. 25–48; Henry Allen Bullock, "A Hidden Passage in
the Slave Regime," in James C. Curtis and Lewis L. Gould, eds.,
The Black Experience in America: Selected Essays (Austin, Tex.,
1970),* pp. 3–32; Mina Davis Caulfield, "Slavery and the Origins
of Black Culture," in Peter I. Rose, ed., *Americans from Africa*,
vol. I: *Slavery and Its Aftermath* (New York, 1970),* pp. 171–93;
and the essay by Sterling Stuckey, "Through the Prism of Folklore," cited above. Much of the debate about the Elkins thesis is
presented in Ann Lane, ed., *The Debate over Slavery: Stanley
Elkins and His Critics* (Urbana, Ill., 1971).* See also Elkins, "The
Social Consequences of Slavery," in Huggins, Kilson, and Fox,
eds., *Key Issues in the Afro-American Experience* cited above,
vol. I, pp. 138–53. Another aspect of this debate, concerning slave
revolts, is dealt with separately in this Part under topic 4, "Slave
Revolts."

2. Slavery in an Urban and Industrial Environment

Slavery was a cruel institution whether on the plantation or in
the town and city, whether for the field hand or for the skilled

black artisan. Yet there were noteworthy variations in the life and treatment of the bond servant from plantation to plantation and also striking differences in the lot of farm and city slaves. It is clear that slavery underwent significant alterations when it moved to the city, and although scholars of the subject may still differ on many matters, there is no denying the implications of these alterations when examining the critical issues of the future and adaptability of slavery, the causes of the Civil War, the origins of segregation, and the history of black urban communities.

The standard study of urban slavery is Richard C. Wade, *Slavery in the Cities: The South, 1820–1860* (New York, 1964),* which argues persuasively that the institution tended to break down in an urban environment. See also ch. 20, "Town Life," in Ulrich B. Phillips, *American Negro Slavery* (New York, 1918).* The best single study of slavery in southern industries is Robert S. Starobin, *Industrial Slavery in the Old South* (New York, 1970),* an aspect of which is also dealt with in Starobin, "The Economics of Industrial Slavery in the Old South," *Business History Review*, XLIV (Summer 1970), 131–74. Also useful are the following monographs and articles on southern industries: Kathleen Bruce, *Virginia Iron Manufacture in the Slave Era* (New York, 1931); Charles B. Dew, *Ironmaker to the Confederacy: Joseph R. Anderson and the Tredegar Iron Works* (New Haven, 1966); Joseph Clarke Robert, *The Tobacco Kingdom: Plantation, Market, and Factory in Virginia and North Carolina, 1800–1860* (Durham, N.C., 1938); James F. Hopkins, *A History of the Hemp Industry in Kentucky* (Lexington, Ky., 1951); Kathleen Bruce, "Slave Labor in the Virginia Iron Industry," *WMQ*, Ser. 2, VII (Jan. 1927), 21–31; S. Sydney Bradford, "The Negro Ironworker in Ante Bellum Virginia," *JSH*, XXV (May 1959), 194–206;** E. M. Lander, "Slave Labor in South Carolina Cotton Mills," *JNH*, XXXVIII (Apr. 1953), 161–73; John H. Moore, "Simon Gray, Riverman: A Slave Who Was Almost Free," *MVHR*, XLIX (Dec. 1962), 472–84;** and Robert S. Starobin, "Disciplining Industrial Slaves in the Old South," *JNH*, LIII (Apr. 1968), 111–28.** An important feature of urban slavery was the leasing of slaves, which released them from the immediate control of their owners and enabled them to save part of the wages they earned toward purchase of their own freedom: see Clement Eaton,

"Slave-Hiring in the Upper South: A Step Toward Freedom," *MVHR*, XLVI (Mar. 1960), 663–78.

Slavery in the deep South's largest city is analyzed by John S. Kendall, "New Orleans' 'Peculiar Institution,'" *Louisiana Historical Quarterly*, XXIII (July 1940), 864–86, and Robert C. Reinders, "Slavery in New Orleans in the Decade Before the Civil War," *Mid-America*, XLIV (Oct. 1962), 211–21. Bondage in the nation's capital is described in Constance M. Green, *The Secret City: A History of Race Relations in the Nation's Capital* (Princeton, 1967),* chs. 1–2. The following studies of slavery in southern states with the largest urban populations are also useful: Jeffrey R. Brackett, *The Negro in Maryland: A Study of the Institution of Slavery* (Baltimore, 1889); J. Winston Coleman, *Slavery Times in Kentucky* (Chapel Hill, 1940); Ivan E. Mc-Dougle, *Slavery in Kentucky, 1792–1865* (Worcester, Mass., 1918); Harrison A. Trexler, *Slavery in Missouri, 1804–1865* (Baltimore, 1914); Chase C. Mooney, *Slavery in Tennessee* (Bloomington, Ind., 1957); and Joe Gray Taylor, *Negro Slavery in Louisiana* (Baton Rouge, 1963).

3. The Internal Slave Trade

Besides the day-to-day life of the slave, the worst feature of the peculiar institution was the internal slave trade. It promised for the slave the hardships of coffle, chains, and cross-country marches; it aroused deep fears and anxieties about new and unknown masters to whom the slave had been sold; and, worst of all, it required the separation of slave families. In all, roughly 700,000 slaves were sold from the upper South into the deep South from 1830 to the Civil War. Many thousands more exchanged masters before then or moved within the intrastate trade during the same period.

Because students of slavery have generally treated the internal slave trade as just one dimension of the larger problem of bond servitude, most monographs on slavery contain some useful material on the forced migration of the black population. But not surprisingly, the most vivid and moving accounts of the domestic slave trade are to be found in the testimonies of the ex-slaves themselves. These monographs and slave narratives are cited in this Part under topic 1, "Plantation Slavery in the Antebellum South," and topic 2, "Slavery in an Urban and Industrial Environment."

There still does not exist, however, an examination of the internal slave trade which places the institution in its broadest context: which, for example, compares the rate and effect of the forced migration of blacks to the voluntary migration of whites; which compares the lot of the slave taken along by a migrating plantation owner to that of the bond servant sold off to a new owner; which evaluates the capacities for endurance and drastic change shown by different slaves under different circumstances in the slave trading system; or which takes up the function of the slave trader, not simply as an economic middleman, but also, when depicted as an obnoxious figure in southern literature, as a scapegoat for those Southerners unable easily in other ways to release any guilt about slavery which they may have felt.

The standard studies of the internal slave trade are Winfield H. Collins, *The Domestic Slave Trade of the Southern States* (New York, 1904), and Frederick Bancroft, *Slave Trading in the Old South* (Baltimore, 1931).* Other works that illuminate specific facets of the trade are Alrutheus A. Taylor, "The Movement of Negroes from the East to the Gulf States from 1830 to 1850," *JNH*, VIII (Oct. 1923), 367–83; Charles H. Wesley, "Manifests of Slave Shipments Along the Waterways, 1808–1864," *ibid.*, XXVII (Apr. 1942), 155–74; William T. Laprade, "The Domestic Slave Trade in the District of Columbia," *ibid.*, XI (Jan. 1926), 17–34; Thomas D. Clark, "The Slave Trade between Kentucky and the Cotton Kingdom," *MVHR*, XXI (Dec. 1934), 331–42; and Wendell H. Stephenson, *Isaac Franklin, Slave Trader and Planter of the Old South* (University, Ala., 1938). The famous Confederate general Nathan Bedford Forrest had been a slave trader; some information on that aspect of his career can be found in Robert S. Henry, *"First with the Most" Forrest* (Indianapolis, 1944), ch. 2.

4. Slave Revolts

The subject of slave rebellions in the United States is not only an important historical issue but also a matter of current and emotional debate. Nobody denies that unrest among black slaves occurred everywhere and that small-scale outbreaks of violence against masters and overseers, not to mention malingering, daily sabotage, flight, and other kinds of opposition, were common in the antebellum South. But the difficult questions concern how slave rebellions are to be defined, how many revolts actually took place, under what conditions they broke out, and finally how frequently the revolts occurred in comparison with rebellions elsewhere. What is at stake in such matters is nothing less than the validity of claims to a revolutionary black tradition, the success or failure of the entire chattel system, and, once again, the effect of slavery upon the Afro-American himself. Regarding this last question, see the items cited in this Part under topic 1, "Plantation Slavery in the Antebellum South."

The classic study of slave rebellions in the United States is Herbert Aptheker, *American Negro Slave Revolts* (New York, 1943),* which tends to overemphasize slave rebelliousness. See also Aptheker, "Slave Resistance in the United States," in Nathan I. Huggins, Martin Kilson, and Daniel M. Fox, eds., *Key Issues in the Afro-American Experience*, 2 vols. (New York, 1971),* vol. I, pp. 161–73. Eugene D. Genovese, among other scholars, has recently been raising some new questions about the older formulations of the problem, including Aptheker's; for a sharp exchange between Genovese and Aptheker, plus the comments of two other scholars on this and other subjects, see "The Legacy of Slavery and the Roots of Black Nationalism," in *Studies on the Left*, VI (Nov.–Dec. 1966), 3–65. The issues raised by Genovese, which concern the relative absence of militancy among slaves in the United States, are further debated by George Rawick, "The Historical Roots of Black Liberation," *Radical America*, II (July–Aug. 1968), 1–13, and Robert S. Starobin and Dale Tomich, "Black Liberation Historiography," *ibid.* (Sept.–Oct. 1968), 24–28. Slave unrest and resistance is also a central theme of the introduction and selections in the volumes of George P. Rawick, *The American Slave: A Composite Autobiography* (Westport, Conn., 1971–). Two valuable articles that treat the incidence and motivation of slave revolts are Marion D. DeB. Kilson, "Towards Freedom: An Analysis of Slave Revolts in the United States," *Phylon*, XXV (Summer 1964), 175–87,** and Vincent Harding, "Religion and Resistance among Antebellum Negroes, 1800–1861," in August Meier and Elliott Rudwick, eds., *The Making of Black America*, 2 vols. (New York, 1969),* vol. I, pp. 179–97.

For a description of three slave revolts in the United States and two in Latin America, see Thomas Wentworth Higginson, *Black Rebellion*, ed. by James M. McPherson (New York, 1969).* The greatest slave revolt in the Western Hemisphere was the Haitian uprising of the 1790s and early 1800s led by Toussaint L'Ouverture. C. L. R. James, *The Black Jacobins: Toussaint L'Ouverture and the San Domingo Revolution* (rev. ed., New York, 1963),* should be consulted to place the slave revolts in the United States in perspective. Winthrop D. Jordan, *White over Black: American Attitudes Toward the Negro, 1550–1812* (Chapel Hill, 1968),* ch. 10, analyzes the impact of foreign and domestic rebellions in the 1790s upon the American mind. Other studies comparing slavery, and in some cases slave revolts, in Latin America and the United States are cited in the topic that follows, "Slavery in the United States and Latin America: Comparative Analyses."

A balanced and readable study of slave uprisings in the United States is Nicholas Halasz, *The Rattling Chains: Slave Unrest and Revolt in the Antebellum South* (New York, 1966). William F. Cheek, ed., *Black Resistance Before the Civil War* (Beverly Hills, Calif., 1970),* is a good collection of documents. Monographs and articles of value include Joseph S. Carroll, *Slave Insurrections in the United States, 1800–1865* (Boston, 1938);* Harvey Wish, "American Slave Insurrections before 1861," *JNH*, XXII (July 1937), 299–320;** Wendell G. Addington, "Slave Insurrections in Texas," *ibid.*, XXXV (Oct. 1950), 408–34; Davidson B. McKibben, "Negro Slave Insurrections in Mississippi, 1800–1865," *ibid.*, XXXIV (Jan. 1949), 73–90; Edwin A. Miles, "The Mississippi

Slave Insurrection Scare of 1835," *ibid.*, XLII (Jan. 1957), 48–60; R. H. Taylor, "Slave Conspiracies in North Carolina," *NCHR*, V (Jan. 1928), 20–34; and William W. White, "The Texas Slave Insurrection of 1860," *Southwestern Historical Quarterly*, LII (Jan. 1949), 259–85.

Some slaves escaped to black "maroon" colonies in the swamps or backwoods of the South, where they lived an independent existence and periodically raided the plantations for supplies or recruits. These maroons are treated in two articles by Herbert Aptheker: "Maroons Within the Present Limits of the United States," *JNH*, XXIV (Apr. 1939), 167–84,** and "Slave Guerrilla Warfare," in *To Be Free: Studies in American Negro History* (New York, 1948),* pp. 11–30. Fugitive slaves in Florida joined the Seminole Indians in a sporadic war against the United States Army; for an account of this affair, see two articles by Kenneth W. Porter: "Florida Slaves and Free Negroes in the Seminole War, 1835–1842," *JNH*, XXVIII (Oct. 1943), 390–421,** and "Negroes and the Seminole War, 1835–1842," *JSH*, XXX (Nov. 1964), 427–50. Most escaped slaves, however, traveled to the North on the Underground Railroad; for studies of this form of resistance to slavery, see Part IV, topic 9, "The Underground Railroad."

Another form of resistance involved neither escape nor rebellion, but rather the conscious or subconscious sabotage of the system through malingering, destruction of tools and implements, inefficient working habits, and the like. For a discussion of such tactics, see Raymond A. and Alice H. Bauer, "Day-to-Day Resistance to Slavery," *JNH*, XXVII (Oct. 1942), 388–419.** The white Southerner's precautions against insurrections, proof of the fear, if not of the reality, of slave rebelliousness, are documented in John Hope Franklin, "Slavery and the Martial South," *ibid.*, XXXVII (Jan. 1952), 36–53;** Marion J. Russell, "American Slave Discontent in Records of the High Courts," *ibid.*, XXXI (Oct. 1946), 411–34; and Howell M. Henry, *The Police Control of the Slave in South Carolina* (Emory, Va., 1914).

Some slave revolts took place before enslaved Africans set foot on American soil. For an account of insurrections on slave ships, see Lorenzo J. Greene, "Mutiny on the Slave Ships," *Phylon*, V (4th Quarter 1944), 346–54.** The story of the successful *Amistad* mutineers and their leader Joseph Cinque, defended before the U. S. Supreme Court by John Quincy Adams, is told by

William A. Owens, *Slave Mutiny: The Revolt on the Schooner Amistad* (New York, 1953, retitled in paperback *Black Mutiny*);* Christopher Martin, *The Amistad Affair* (New York, 1970); and Mary Cable, *Black Odyssey* (New York, 1971).

There is a considerable literature on individual slave rebellions on the mainland United States. Winthrop D. Jordan, *White over Black*, cited above, pp. 110–22, discusses uprisings in the colonial period. The revolt of 1712 in New York City and the suspected plot of 1741 are treated by Kenneth Scott, "The Slave Insurrection in New York in 1712," *New York Historical Society Quarterly*, XLV (Jan. 1961), 43–74,** and T. Wood Clarke, "Negro Plot, 1741," *New York History*, XXV (Apr. 1944), 167–81. The Gabriel Prosser conspiracy in Virginia in 1800 is analyzed by Gerald W. Mullin, "Gabriel's Insurrection," in Peter I. Rose, ed., *Americans from Africa*, vol. II: *Old Memories, New Moods* (New York, 1970),* pp. 53–73, and is the subject of Arna Bontemps' novel *Black Thunder* (New York, 1936).* Another major slave conspiracy was the Denmark Vesey plot in Charleston in 1822; for a full-length study see John W. Lofton, *Insurrection in South Carolina: The Turbulent World of Denmark Vesey* (Yellow Springs, Ohio, 1964). But Richard C. Wade has questioned whether a real conspiracy existed in his "The Vesey Plot: A Reconsideration," *JSH*, XXX (May 1964), 143–61. Sterling Stuckey has written a rebuttal of the Wade essay entitled "Remembering Denmark Vesey," *Negro Digest*, XV (Feb. 1966), 28–41. An assessment of the effects of the Vesey plot scare in South Carolina will be found in William W. Freehling, *Prelude to Civil War: The Nullification Controversy in South Carolina, 1816–1836* (New York, 1966),* pp. 53–65. A good collection of contemporary documents and historical accounts of the revolt can be found in Robert S. Starobin, ed., *Denmark Vesey: The Slave Conspiracy of 1822* (Englewood Cliffs, N.J., 1970).* The complete official report of Vesey's trial is reprinted in John Oliver Killens, ed., *The Trial Record of Denmark Vesey* (Boston, 1970).*

Finally, there is the agitated matter of the Nat Turner rebellion. Two sharply contrasting viewpoints on the revolt can be found in William S. Drewry, *Slave Insurrections in the United States* (Washington, 1900), and Herbert Aptheker, *Nat Turner's Slave Rebellion* (New York, 1966).* See also F. Roy Johnson, *The Nat Turner Slave Insurrection* (Murfreesboro,

N.C., 1966). The current controversy centers around William Styron's "meditation on history," *The Confessions of Nat Turner* (New York, 1966),* whose novelistic treatment and racial attitudes are sharply assailed by the contributors to John Hendrik Clarke, ed., *William Styron's Nat Turner: Ten Black Writers Respond* (Boston, 1968).* The issue has also been taken up by white critics, whose following reviews and comments should be consulted: Eugene D. Genovese, "The Nat Turner Case," a review of *Ten Black Writers Respond*, in the *New York Review of Books*, XI (Sept. 12, 1968), 34–37; Martin Duberman, "Historical Fictions," a review of the same book in the *New York Times Book Review*, Aug. 11, 1968, pp. 1, 26–27; Herbert Aptheker, "A Note on the History," *Nation*, CCV (Oct. 16, 1967), 375–76; and Aptheker and Styron, "Truth and Nat Turner: An Exchange," *Nation*, CCVI (Apr. 22, 1968), 543–47. Since the black reaction to Styron's book is almost as much against the favorable white "liberal" reviews of the book as against the book itself, it is useful to read some friendly reviews, such as C. Vann Woodward, "Confessions of a Rebel: 1831," *New Republic*, CLVII (Oct. 7, 1967), 25–28; Richard Gilman, "Nat Turner Revisited," *ibid.*, CLVIII (Apr. 27, 1968), 23–32; and Wilfred Sheed, "The Slave Who Became a Man," *New York Times Book Review*, Oct. 8, 1967, pp. 1–3. Styron discusses the novel in an interview with C. Vann Woodward and R. W. B. Lewis published in *The Yale Alumni Magazine*, Nov. 1967, 33–39. A valuable anthology containing contemporary documents, historical analyses, and material on Styron's novel is John B. Duff and Peter M. Mitchell, eds., *The Nat Turner Rebellion: The Historical Event and the Modern Controversy* (New York, 1971).*

5. Slavery in the United States and Latin America: Comparative Analyses

Some of the most fruitful and provocative insights about slavery have resulted from comparative analyses of the institution in different societies, especially the United States and Latin America.

There are two basic schools of historiography on this issue, the first developed by Frank Tannenbaum in his classic study, *Slave and Citizen: The Negro in the Americas* (New York, 1947),* and amplified by Stanley M. Elkins, *Slavery: A Problem in American Institutional and Intellectual Life* (Chicago, 1959, rev. ed., 1968),* esp. pt. II and pp. 245–53; and Herbert S. Klein, *Slavery in the Americas: A Comparative Study of Cuba and Virginia* (Chicago, 1967).* These scholars maintain that in Latin America the legal slave code deriving from ancient Greece and Rome, the institutional role of the state and the Roman Catholic Church, and the traditionally more tolerant attitude of Latin peoples toward a dark skin resulted in a form of slavery that was less harsh, less destructive of the black man's personality, and more open to manumission and assimilation of the manumitted slave than slavery in British America, where most of these institutional safeguards to protect the Afro-American against "the dynamics of unopposed capitalism" were absent and where white racial attitudes were much less tolerant of black people, especially if they were free. But recent research has found that slavery in many parts of Latin America was extremely brutal and that the emancipated slave did not always find it easy to assimilate into a society committed to white supremacy, while slavery in the United States is now being portrayed by some scholars as less exploitative and more tolerant of the integrity of the black man's personality than the Tannenbaum-Elkins school had allowed. Moreover, there is now no doubt that the physical conditions of slavery in the United States were less harsh than nearly everywhere else, especially in the nineteenth century. For example, the mortality rate of slaves was far lower in the United States than in any other part of the Western Hemisphere. For startling evidence on this point, see Philip D. Curtin, *The Atlantic Slave Trade: A Census* (Madison, 1969), esp. pp. 89–93.

The best starting point for research on this topic is an excellent anthology of scholarship on comparative slavery: Laura Foner and Eugene D. Genovese, eds., *Slavery in the New World: A Reader in Comparative History* (Englewood Cliffs, N.J., 1969),* which contains excerpts from some of the books cited for this topic, plus several important articles and reviews; its selective bibliography is also very useful. The Tannenbaum, Elkins, and Klein volumes mentioned above present one viewpoint; for revisions and modifications of their interpretations, see David Brion Davis, *The Problem of Slavery in Western Culture* (Ithaca, N.Y., 1966),* chs. 8–9; Eugene D. Genovese, "Rebelliousness and Docility in the Negro Slave: A Critique of the Elkins Thesis," *CWH*, XIII (Dec. 1967), 293–314;** Marvin Harris, *Patterns of Race in the Americas* (New York, 1964);* Eugene D. Genovese, *The World the Slaveholders Made* (New York, 1969),* pt. 1; Carl N. Degler, "Slavery in Brazil and the United States: An Essay in Comparative History," *AHR*, LXXV (Apr. 1970), 1004–28; Degler, *Neither Black Nor White: Slavery and Race Relations in Brazil and the United States* (New York, 1971);* plus the essays by Sidney W. Mintz, David Brion Davis, Arnold A. Sio, Elsa V. Goveia, and Eugene D. Genovese, in Foner and Genovese, eds., *Slavery in the New World*, cited above. Other pertinent essays are David Brion Davis, "Slavery," in C. Vann Woodward, ed., *The Comparative Approach to American History* (New York, 1968),* pp. 121–34, and two studies by Woodward, "Protestant Slavery in a Catholic World" and "Southern Slaves in the World of Thomas Malthus," in his *American Counterpoint: Slavery and Race in the North-South Dialogue* (Boston, 1971),* pp. 47–77, 78–106.

A student of comparative slavery should also consult some of the studies of slavery in Latin-American societies. The foremost advocate of the relatively benign nature of slavery in a Latin-American country is Gilberto Freyre; his most comprehensive work is *The Masters and the Slaves: A Study in the Development of Brazilian Civilization* (New York, 1946).* Studies that portray a much harsher slave regime include Charles R. Boxer, *The Golden Age of Brazil, 1695–1750: Growing Pains of a Colonial Society* (Berkeley, 1964),* and his *Race Relations in the Portuguese Colonial Empire, 1415–1825* (Oxford, Eng., 1963); John V. Lombardi, *The Decline and Abolition of Slavery in Venezuela, 1820–1854* (Westport, Conn., 1971); Stanley J. Stein, *Vassouras: A Brazilian Coffee County, 1850–1900* (Cambridge, Eng., 1957);* and Franklin W. Knight, *Slave Society in Cuba During the Nineteenth Century* (Madison, 1970). Also useful is Magnus Moerner, *Race Mixture in the History of Latin America* (Boston, 1967).*

A recent study useful for comparisons is Robin W. Winks, *The Blacks in Canada: A History* (New Haven, 1971).

6. The Southern Defense of Slavery

The slavery system did not go without its defenders, but their defense took the form of an argument rather than a genuine theory. The result was often a significant combination of special pleading, rationalization, and early sociological inquiry. The Bible, ancient political theory, American constitutional principles, science, pseudoscience, and socialist thought then current in Europe were all brought to bear on the task of demonstrating that slavery was expedient and just.

The standard work on the subject is William Sumner Jenkins, *Pro-Slavery Thought in the Old South* (Chapel Hill, 1935, reprinted Gloucester, Mass., 1960). Chs. 3–4, 6–7 of David Brion Davis, *The Problem of Slavery in Western Culture* (Ithaca, N.Y., 1966),* analyze the more venerable cultural and intellectual origins of the proslavery argument, as do many portions of Winthrop D. Jordan, *White over Black: American Attitudes Toward the Negro, 1550–1812* (Chapel Hill, 1968).* See also George M. Fredrickson, "Toward a Social Interpretation of the Development of American Racism," in Nathan I. Huggins, Martin Kilson, and Daniel M. Fox, eds., *Key Issues in the Afro-American Experience*, 2 vols. (New York, 1971),* vol. 1, pp. 240–54; Arthur Young Lloyd, *The Slavery Controversy, 1831–1860* (Chapel Hill, 1939); Clement Eaton, *Freedom of Thought in the Old South* (Durham, N.C., 1940);* and Jesse T. Carpenter, *The South as a Conscious Minority, 1789–1861; A Study in Political Thought* (New York, 1930). Ronald Takaki, "The Black Child-Savage in Ante-Bellum America," in Gary B. Nash and Richard Weiss, eds., *The Great Fear: Race in the Mind of America* (New York, 1970),* pp. 27–44, describes popular images of blacks which whites used to bolster slavery and white supremacy. The scientific argument in favor of black racial inferiority and unsuitability for freedom is carefully summarized and analyzed by William Stanton, *The Leopard's Spots: Scientific Attitudes Toward Race in America, 1815–1859* (Chicago, 1960).* A useful and well-edited compilation of proslavery arguments is Eric L. McKitrick, ed.,

Slavery Defended: The Views of the Old South (Englewood Cliffs, N.J., 1963).*

The foremost proslavery advocate was George Fitzhugh, who has been the subject of much historical writing. See especially Harvey Wish, *George Fitzhugh: Propagandist of the Old South* (Baton Rouge, 1943), and Eugene D. Genovese, *The World the Slaveholders Made* (New York, 1969),* pt. 2. Harvey Wish has edited and reprinted Fitzhugh's two most famous proslavery writings, *Sociology for the South* and *Cannibals All, or Slaves Without Masters*, in a volume entitled *Ante-Bellum: Writings of George Fitzhugh and Hinton Rowan Helper on Slavery* (New York, 1960).*

The incompatibility of slavery with Christian ethics and democratic ideology produced moral schizophrenia and guilt feelings in the hearts and minds of many Southerners, including slaveholders. A recent essay has tried to come to grips with this schizophrenia; see James M. McPherson, "Slavery and Race," *Perspectives in American History*, III (1969), 460–73. The clearest exposition of the guilt thesis is Charles G. Sellers, "The Travail of Slavery," in Charles G. Sellers, ed., *The Southerner as American* (Chapel Hill, 1960),* pp. 40–71.** See also Kenneth M. Stampp, "The Southern Road to Appomattox," *Cotton Memorial Papers*, no. 4 (El Paso, Tex., 1969). Two outstanding treatments of the intricate and profound impact of slavery on the southern mind, politics, and world view are William W. Freehling, *Prelude to Civil War: The Nullification Controversy in South Carolina, 1816–1836* (New York, 1966),* and Steven A. Channing, *Crisis of Fear: Secession in South Carolina* (New York, 1970). The climax and decline of southern antislavery sentiment was marked by the 1832 debate over slavery in the Virginia legislature, which is treated in Joseph C. Robert, *The Road from Monticello: A Study of the Virginia Slavery Debate of 1832* (Durham, N.C., 1941). An important analysis of the white view of black Americans is George M. Fredrickson, *The Black Image in the White Mind: The Debate on Afro-American Character and Destiny, 1817–1914* (New York, 1971), esp. chs. 2 and 3.

7. Free Blacks in the Antebellum South

Free blacks were anomalies in a society that equated a black skin with slavery. The free blacks of the South were not slaves, but neither were most of them wholly free. Subjected to discrimination and restrictions, possessing few rights which white men were bound to respect, these Afro-Americans nevertheless carved out a niche for themselves in the South, and in some places, such as New Orleans, Mobile, Charleston, and Baltimore, light-skinned "free people of color" achieved a respectable level of prosperity, education, and culture. These people, the descendants of unions between white men and slave women, frequently formed a separate caste distinct from both whites and blacks. They became the basis of the "Negro aristocracy" and the black bourgeoisie that developed in the generations after the Civil War.

There is no general history of free blacks in the South, but Ulrich B. Phillips, *American Negro Slavery* (New York, 1918),* ch. 21, provides a general overview from his own conservative and patronizing perspective. Wilbur Zelinsky, "The Population Geography of the Free Negro in *Ante-Bellum* America," *Population Studies*, III (Mar. 1950), 386–401, provides useful demographic data. The best monograph on free blacks is John Hope Franklin, *The Free Negro in North Carolina, 1790–1860* (Chapel Hill, 1943).* Other useful monographs and articles include James M. Wright, *The Free Negro in Maryland, 1634–1860* (New York, 1921, reprinted New York, 1969); John H. Russell, *The Free Negro in Virginia, 1619–1865* (Baltimore, 1913);* Luther P. Jackson, *Free Negro Labor and Property Holding in Virginia, 1830–1860* (New York, 1942); James H. Johnston, *Race Relations in Virginia and Miscegenation in the South, 1776–1860* (Amherst, Mass., 1970); Ralph B. Flanders, "The Free Negro in Ante-Bellum Georgia," *NCHR*, IX (July 1932), 250–72; David Y. Thomas, "The Free Negro in Florida before 1965," *SAQ*, X (Oct. 1911), 335–45; J. Merton England, "The Free Negro in Ante-Bellum Tennessee," *JSH*, IX (Feb. 1943), 37–58;** Charles S. Sydnor, "The Free Negro in Mississippi before the Civil War," *AHR*, XXXII (July 1927), 769–88;** Alice D. Nelson, "People of Color in Louisiana,"

JNH, I (Oct. 1916), 359–74, and II (Jan. 1917), 51–78; Annie L. W. Stahl, "The Free Negro in Ante-Bellum Louisiana," *Louisiana Historical Quarterly*, XXV (Apr. 1942), 300–96; and Harold Schoen, "The Free Negro in the Republic of Texas," *Southwestern Historical Quarterly*, XXXIX (Apr. 1936), 292–308, XL (July 1936), 26–34, (Oct. 1936), 85–113, (Jan. 1937), 169–99, (Apr. 1937), 267–89, XLI (July 1937), 83–108. Enterprising and successful free Negroes are described by John Hope Franklin, "James Boon, Free Negro Artisan," *JNH*, XXX (Apr. 1945), 150–80;** and Edwin A. Davis and William R. Hogan, *The Barber of Natchez* (Baton Rouge, 1954).

Most free blacks lived in cities and towns. There is information on the urban freemen scattered through Richard C. Wade, *Slavery in the Cities: The South, 1820–1860* (Chicago, 1964),* esp. pp. 249–52. See also Constance M. Green, *The Secret City: A History of Race Relations in the Nation's Capital* (Princeton, 1967),* chs. 2–3; E. Horace Fitchett, "The Origin and Growth of the Free Negro Population of Charleston, South Carolina," *JNH*, XXVI (Oct. 1941), 421–37;** and James E. Winston, "The Free Negro in New Orleans, 1803–1861," *Louisiana Historical Quarterly*, XXI (Oct. 1938), 1075–85.

Ironically, several free blacks owned slaves; some free quadroons in Louisiana were wealthy planters. A sizable number of black slaveholders, however, used the legal fiction of ownership only to buy the *de facto* freedom of their families as a means of circumventing the restrictive manumission laws of some states. For information on this subject, consult Carter G. Woodson, *Free Negro Owners of Slaves in the United States in 1830* (Washington, 1925, reprinted New York, 1968); John H. Russell, "Colored Freemen as Slave Owners in Virginia," *JNH*, I (July 1916), 233–42; and Calvin D. Wilson, "Negroes Who Owned Slaves," *Popular Science Monthly*, LXXXI (Nov. 1912), 483–94. The free black family is analyzed by E. Franklin Frazier, *The Free Negro Family* (Nashville, 1932); and Carter G. Woodson, *Free Negro Heads of Families in the United States in 1830* (Washington, 1925). For studies of the major social institution among free blacks, see the references cited in Part IV, topic 4, "The Antebellum Black Church." A rare and special aspect of the free black's legal status is treated in Roger W. Shugg, "Negro Voting in the Ante-Bellum South," *JNH*, XXI (Oct. 1936), 357–64.

PART IV

THE BLACK COMMUNITY AND THE ANTISLAVERY MOVEMENT, 1800–1861

1. Afro-Americans and the Law, 1619–1861

Although slavery was defended frequently on philosophical, theological, anthropological, social, or economic grounds, the institution in the final analysis rested primarily on law backed by the power of the state. During the centuries after the first importation of blacks into Virginia, the legislatures and courts of the colonies, states, and federal government gradually developed legal codes to define and enforce chattel slavery. These codes were based on two millennia of European precedents as modified by New World conditions. For the legal evolution of slavery and of the rights of freed slaves down to the adoption of the Constitution in 1789, see David Brion Davis, *The Problem of Slavery in Western Culture* (Ithaca, N.Y., 1966),* pts. I–II; Winthrop D. Jordan, *White over Black: American Attitudes Toward the Negro, 1550–1812* (Chapel Hill, 1968),* chs. 2–3; and the relevant titles cited in Part I, topics 5–8: "The Origins of Slavery in the British Colonies of North America"; "Slaves and Free Blacks in the Colonial South"; "Slaves and Black Freemen in the Northern Colonies"; and "Afro-Americans in the Revolutionary Era."

Good brief introductions to the laws and decisions governing bondage from 1789 to the Civil War are provided by Loren Miller, *The Petitioners: The Story of the Supreme Court of the United States and the Negro* (New York, 1966),* chs. 2–6, and M. Eugene Sirmans, "The Legal Status of the Slave in South Carolina, 1670–1740," *JSH*, XXVIII (Nov. 1962), 462–73. An exhaustive collection, with annotations, of court cases on slavery and Afro-Americans is Helen T. Catterall, ed., *Judicial Cases Concerning American Slavery and the Negro*, 5 vols. (Washington, 1926–37, reprinted New York, 1968). Also useful is John C. Hurd, *The Law of Freedom and Bondage in the United States*, 2 vols. (Boston, 1858–63, reprinted New York, 1968). For briefer, selective collections of legal documents, consult Barnett Hollander, *Slavery in America: Its Legal History* (New York, 1963); Albert P. Blaustein and Robert L. Zangrando, eds., *Civil Rights and the American Negro: A Documentary History* (New York, 1968),* pts. 1–3; and Richard Bardolph, ed., *The Civil Rights Record: Black Americans and the Law, 1849–1970* (New York, 1970),* pt. 1. One of the most readily comparable criteria of slavery in different societies was the legal status of slaves and free blacks. Nearly all of the works cited in Part III, topic 5, "Slavery in the United States and Latin America: Comparative Analyses," most notably Frank Tannenbaum, *Slave and Citizen: The Negro in the Americas* (New York, 1947),* contain discussions of legal codes.

The issue of slavery in the territories was one of the most explosive political questions in the United States from the Missouri Compromise of 1820 to the Civil War. For cogent discussions of this issue see Loren Miller, *The Petitioners*, cited above, chs. 3–5; and Alfred H. Kelly and Winfred A. Harbison, *The American Constitution* (3rd ed., New York, 1963), chs. 10, 14–15. The antebellum climax to the law of slavery was the notorious Dred Scott decision of 1857, which ostensibly nullified the power of Congress and of the inhabitants of a United States territory to prohibit slavery in a territory and therefore opened the legal possibility of the spread of slavery beyond its existing confines. The majority of the Supreme Court, led by Chief Justice Roger B. Taney, hoped that a decision on Dred Scott's status would quiet the increasingly violent and divisive slavery and sectional controversies; yet the decision provoked them to still higher pitch, especially in the North. Moreover, because it was enunciated by a court from which further judicial appeal was impossible, the decision cast these inflammable issues irrevocably into the conflicting currents of party politics. There, appeal might only be had to the voters—or to guns.

The decision itself, including the confusing medley of concurring and dissenting opinions, is to be found in the official *Reports of the United States Supreme Court*, as *Dred Scott* v. *Sandford*, 19 Howard 393. The standard history of the case is Vincent C. Hopkins, *Dred Scott's Case* (New York, 1951),* which should be supplemented by Bruce Catton's illuminating brief essay, "The Dred Scott Case," in John A. Garraty, ed., *Quarrels That Have*

Shaped the Constitution (New York, 1962),* pp. 77–89. A master-ful examination of the case, including an investigation of the political context of the decision and of the roles played by in-dividual justices, is Allan Nevins, *The Emergence of Lincoln*, 2 vols. (New York, 1950),* vol. I, ch. 4, and the essential supple-ment in vol. II, app. 1. Stanley I. Kutler, ed., *The Dred Scott De-cision: Law or Politics?* (Boston, 1967),* brings together some contemporary speeches and press comments about the decision, plus subsequent analyses by legal historians. Additional articles of importance are Frederick S. Allis, Jr., "The Dred Scott Laby-rinth," in H. Stuart Hughes, ed., *Teachers of History: Essays in Honor of Lawrence Bradford Packard* (Ithaca, N.Y., 1954), pp. 341–68; Carl B. Swisher, "Dred Scott One Hundred Years After," *Journal of Politics*, XIX (May 1957), 167–83; and Walter Ehrlich, "Was the Dred Scott Case Valid?" *JAH*, LV (Sept. 1968), 256–65.

Chief Justice Taney ruled in the Dred Scott decision that blacks —free or slave—were not United States citizens. This ruling was not constitutionally overturned until the adoption of the Four-teenth Amendment in 1868, though the events of the Civil War had meanwhile partly revoked it in practice. Taney's statement on Afro-American citizenship, far from instituting a new policy, was but a ratification of the second-class legal status of free blacks in most states, North as well as South. Only New England's tiny black population enjoyed anything approaching equal citizen-ship, and even there black people suffered considerable discrimina-tion. Nearly all of the monographs cited in Part III, topic 7, and this Part, topic 2, "Free Blacks in the Antebellum South" and "Free Blacks North of Slavery," discuss the legal status of free blacks. Especially relevant is Leon F. Litwack, *North of Slavery: The Negro in the Free States, 1790–1860* (Chicago, 1961),* esp. chs. 1–4. See also Henry W. Farnham, *Chapters in the History of Social Legislation in the United States to 1860* (Washington, 1938), especially the appendix, for laws and court decisions pertaining to black Americans. For an account of the precedent-setting decision by the Massachusetts Supreme Court in 1849 up-holding Boston's right to maintain segregated schools, see Leonard W. Levy and Harlan B. Phillips, "The *Roberts* Case: Source of the 'Separate but Equal' Doctrine," *AHR*, LVI (Apr. 1951), 510–18.** The Massachusetts legislature subsequently outlawed

segregated schools, but the "separate but equal" principle established by the court returned later to haunt American race relations.

2. Free Blacks North of Slavery

"The North" was the goal of the fugitive slave, a land where
bondage did not exist and where, it was hoped, a black man could
have a white man's chance in life. But as the standard study of
this subject demonstrates, most northern blacks had nothing like
a white man's chance or a white man's rights before the Civil
War: see Leon F. Litwack, *North of Slavery: The Negro in the
Free States*, 1790–1860 (Chicago, 1961).* A monograph that pin-
points sharply the antiblack discrimination of the western states
in the generation before the war is Eugene H. Berwanger, *The
Frontier Against Slavery: Western Anti-Negro Prejudice and the
Slavery Extension Controversy* (Urbana, Ill., 1967).* A recent
study by James A. Rawley, *Race and Politics: "Bleeding Kansas"
and the Coming of the Civil War* (Philadelphia, 1969),* argues
that the real issue in Kansas was not so much slavery as the desire
to keep blacks, free or slave, out of the territory. Eric Foner, *Free
Soil, Free Labor, Free Men: The Ideology of the Republican
Party Before the Civil War* (New York, 1970),* ch. 8, sensitively
explores the paradoxes of racial attitudes in the Free Soil and
Republican parties. Foner's authoritative bibliography lists other
works dealing with northern attitudes toward race. These studies
partly confirm Alexis de Tocqueville's observation in the 1830s
that "the prejudice of race appears to be stronger in the states
that have abolished slavery than in those where it still exists; and
nowhere is it so intolerant as in those states where servitude has
never been known"; see Tocqueville's *Democracy in America*, ed.
by Phillips Bradley, 2 vols. (New York, 1945),* vol. I, ch. 18.

Other useful monographs on the condition of antebellum
northern blacks include Emma Lou Thornbrough, *The Negro in
Indiana: A Study of a Minority* (Indianapolis, 1957), chs. 1–7;
Charles T. Hickok, *The Negro in Ohio*, 1802–70 (Cleveland,

1896); Edward R. Turner, *The Negro in Pennsylvania: Slavery-Servitude-Freedom, 1639–1861* (Washington, 1911), chs. 8–13; Leo H. Hirsch, Jr., "The Negro and New York, 1783 to 1865," *JNH*, XVI (Oct. 1931), 382–473; Robert Ernst, "The Economic Status of New York City Negroes, 1850–1863," *NHB*, XII (Mar. 1944), 131–32, 139–43; Carter G. Woodson, "The Negroes of Cincinnati prior to the Civil War," *JNH*, I (Jan. 1916), 1–22;** Richard C. Wade, "The Negro in Cincinnati, 1800–1830," *ibid.*, XXXIX (Jan. 1957), 43–57; and Simeon F. Moss, "The Persistence of Slavery and Involuntary Servitude in a Free State (1685–1866)," *ibid.*, XXV (July 1950), 289–314. Demographic data is provided by Wilbur Zelinsky, "The Population Geography of the Free Negro in *Ante-Bellum* America," *Population Studies*, III (Mar. 1950), 386–401.

Despite their disabilities, black Americans north of the Mason-Dixon line could organize and agitate for education, equal rights, and self-improvement, and the beginnings of organized black protest in this country date from the antebellum period. See especially Howard H. Bell, *A Survey of the Negro Convention Movement, 1830–1861* (New York, 1969); and William H. and Jane H. Pease, "The Negro Convention Movement," in Nathan I. Huggins, Martin Kilson, and Daniel M. Fox, eds., *Key Issues in the Afro-American Experience*, 2 vols. (New York, 1971),* vol. I, pp. 191–205. Also relevant are Dixon Ryan Fox, "The Negro Vote in Old New York," *PSQ*, XXXII (June 1917), 252–75;** Marion T. Wright, "Negro Suffrage in New Jersey, 1776–1875," *JNH*, XXXII (Apr. 1948), 168–224; Louis Ruchames, "Jim Crow Railroads in Massachusetts," *AQ*, VIII (Spring 1956), 61–75,** "Race and Education in Massachusetts," *NHB*, XIII (Dec. 1949), 53–59, 71, and "Race, Marriage, and Abolitionism in Massachusetts," *JNH*, XL (July 1955), 250–73; and J. Reuben Sheeler, "The Struggle of the Negro in Ohio for Freedom," *ibid.*, XXXI (Apr. 1946), 208–26. An interesting article on cultural and self-improvement activities is Dorothy Porter, "The Organized Educational Activities of Negro Literary Societies, 1828–1846," *JNE*, V (Oct. 1936), 556–66. Dorothy Porter has also edited a collection of antebellum protest pamphlets under the title of *Negro Protest Pamphlets: A Compendium* (New York, 1969). Many newspaper selections are reprinted in Martin E. Dann, ed., *The Black Press, 1827–*

1890: *The Quest for National Identity* (New York, 1971). One important difference between the position of free blacks in the North and in the South was the availability of greater educational opportunities in the North; see Carter G. Woodson, *The Education of the Negro Prior to 1861* (New York, 1915, reprinted New York, 1968). Also pertinent is Donald M. Jacobs, "The Nineteenth Century Struggle over Segregated Education in the Boston Schools," *JNE*, XXXIX (Winter 1970), 76–85. A specialized work on a little-known subject is William H. and Jane H. Pease, *Black Utopia: Negro Communal Experiments in America* (Madison, 1963).

References to additional studies relevant to northern blacks can be found in Part IV, topics 4, 8, 12, and 13: "The Antebellum Black Church"; "Black Abolitionists"; "Black Literature Before the Civil War"; and "Black Nationalism Before the Civil War."

3. American Churches and Slavery

The role of the white church in race relations has always been characterized by ambivalence. On the one hand, churches have reflected the generally racist attitudes of their membership; before the Civil War most of the major denominations countenanced slavery, or at least failed to come out unequivocally for emancipation. On the other hand, much of the abolitionist and equalitarian sentiment in antebellum America grew from Quaker and evangelical origins, and significant minorities within all denominations crusaded for emancipation and for the treatment of black people as equals in the sight of man just as their souls were equal in the sight of God. The issue of slavery played a key role in splitting the foremost Protestant denominations into northern and southern factions and in furthering the sectional divisiveness that led to the Civil War. Some of the antislavery churches welcomed black members; others, however, equivocated on this issue or encouraged the formation of segregated churches. In white churches, blacks were a patronized, powerless, and often segregated minority; black Christians therefore preferred black churches under black leadership. This combination of white prejudice and black desire for control of the major institution in black life led to the formation of separate and independent black churches (see the following topic, "The Antebellum Black Church").

The best general treatments of white churches and the Afro-American before the Civil War are Willis D. Weatherford, *American Churches and the Negro* (Boston, 1957), chs. 1–8; David M. Reimers, *White Protestantism and the Negro* (New York, 1965), ch. 1; and Ralph L. Moellering, *Christian Conscience and Negro Emancipation* (Philadelphia, 1965), chs. 1–6. Colonial churches were confronted with a conflict between their desire to convert the pagan slaves to Christianity and the slaveowners' fear that conversion would mean emancipation—for how could a Christian hold a fellow-Christian as a slave? The fears proved groundless when the church rationalized the enslavement of black Christians. But by the early 1700s many Quakers and prominent individuals in other denominations began denouncing slavery and moving to purge their own membership of the institution. Only the Quakers succeeded in eliminating slaveholders from their denomination, but the early Christian antislavery movement, which reached a climax in the 1780s, did provide a basis and inspiration for the abolitionist crusade of the nineteenth century. The churches and slavery in the seventeenth and eighteenth centuries are discussed in David Brion Davis, *The Problem of Slavery in Western Culture* (Ithaca, N.Y., 1966),* chs. 6–7, 10; Winthrop D. Jordan, *White over Black: American Attitudes Toward the Negro, 1550–1812* (Chapel Hill, 1968),* chs. 5, 9; Marcus W. Jernegan, "Slavery and Conversion in the American Colonies," AHR, XXI (Apr. 1916), 504–27;** and Lorenzo J. Greene, *The Negro in Colonial New England* (New York, 1942),* ch. 10. The early missionary efforts of the Anglican church among slaves are treated by Faith Vibert, "The Society for the Propagation of the Gospel in Foreign Parts: Its Work for the Negroes of North America before 1783," JNH, XVIII (Apr. 1933), 171–212; and George F. Bragg, *History of the Afro-American Group of the Episcopal Church* (Baltimore, 1922, reprinted New York, 1968), chs. 1–2. Though the Quakers deserved their antislavery reputation, many Friends were conservative on the issue and some Quaker societies were reluctant to admit blacks to membership; see Stephen B.

Weeks, *Southern Quakers and Slavery: A Study in Institutional History* (Baltimore, 1896); Thomas E. Drake, *Quakers and Slavery in America* (New Haven, 1950); Herbert Aptheker, "The Quakers and Negro Slavery," *JNH*, XXV (July 1940), 331–62; and Henry J. Cadbury, "Negro Membership in the Society of Friends," *ibid.*, XXI (Apr. 1936), 151–213. The Methodist Church came close to prohibiting slaveholding by its membership in the 1780s, but soon receded from this position. The increasing divergence between proslavery southern Methodists and their moderately antislavery northern brethren finally led to a formal separation of this largest of American denominations in 1844; see Donald G. Mathews, *Slavery and Methodism: A Chapter in American Morality, 1780–1845* (Princeton, 1965); Charles Swaney, *Episcopal Methodism and Slavery* (Boston, 1926); and James B. F. Shaw, *The Negro in the History of Methodism* (Nashville, 1954), chs. 1–2. Even after the schism of 1844, however, many border state congregations with slaveholding members remained in the northern Methodist Church, and not until 1864 did the northern church take an unequivocal stand against slavery. Many Methodist abolitionists left the church in protest against this conservatism and formed separate, abolitionist denominations; for an account of the most important of these radical churches, see Ira Ford McLeister and Roy S. Nicholson, *History of the Wesleyan Methodist Church of America* (3rd ed., Marion, Ind., 1959), chs. 3–8.

The rise of militant abolitionism in the 1830s grew partly out of a fundamental reorientation of Calvinism and a revival movement that led to greater social concern and radicalism in northern churches, especially among Congregationalists and Presbyterians. For treatments of these developments, see Gilbert Hobbs Barnes, *The Anti-Slavery Impulse, 1830–1844* (New York, 1933);* Charles C. Cole, *The Social Ideas of the Northern Evangelists, 1826–1860* (New York, 1954), ch. 7; John Bodo, *The Protestant Clergy and Public Issues, 1812–1848* (Princeton, 1954), ch. 5; Timothy L. Smith, *Revivalism and Social Reform in Mid-Nineteenth-Century America* (New York, 1957),* chs. 12–13; and Bertram Wyatt-Brown, *Lewis Tappan and the Evangelical War Against Slavery* (Cleveland, 1969),* esp. chs. 5–7 and 14–16. A critical study of the Presbyterian Church is Andrew E. Murray, *Presbyterians and*

the Negro—A History (Philadelphia, 1966), chs. 1–4. Congrega-
tionalist abolitionists founded the American Missionary Associa-
tion in 1846, which became one of the foremost agencies of
Christian abolitionism in the decade before the Civil War and a
leader in black education after the war. For the founding and early
years of this association, see Wyatt-Brown, *Lewis Tappan and the
Evangelical War Against Slavery*, ch. 15, and Augustus F. Beard,
*A Crusade of Brotherhood: A History of the American Missionary
Association* (Boston, 1909, reprinted New York, 1969), chs. 1–6.
The wholesale conversion of northern denominations to aboli-
tionism during the war is described in Chester F. Dunham, *The
Attitude of the Northern Clergy Toward the South, 1860–1865*
(Toledo, Ohio, 1942).

4. The Antebellum Black Church

Historically the black church has been the social and cultural as
well as religious center of the black community and one of the
few institutions in that community largely led and controlled by
blacks themselves. The church afforded opportunities for training
in leadership and independence, and in turn the black clergy provided much of the leadership in the black community at large.
The pathos and beauty of Afro-American spirituals and the powerful imagery of black sermons have immeasurably enriched the
American cultural heritage and have added a valuable extra dimension to the meaning of Christianity.

The Christianization of black Americans began with slavery in
the seventeenth century, but independent black churches did not
develop until the late eighteenth and early nineteenth centuries
among free blacks and until after the Civil War among freed
slaves. For a brief summary of the historiography of the black
church, see Robert T. Handy, "Negro Christianity and American
Church Historiography," in Jerald C. Brauer, ed., *Reinterpretation in American Church History* (Chicago, 1968), pp. 91–112.
The following are the most useful general narrative and interpretive accounts of black religion before 1865: Carter G. Woodson,

The History of the Negro Church (2nd ed., Washington, 1945), chs. 1–9; E. Franklin Frazier, *The Negro Church in America* (New York, 1964),* chs. 1–2; Leonard Haynes, *The Negro Community Within American Protestantism, 1619–1844* (Boston, 1953); and Joseph R. Washington, *Black Religion: The Negro and Christianity in the United States* (Boston, 1964),* pp. 163–220.

The early missionaries of the Anglican and other denominations made some efforts to Christianize the slaves, but not until the Great Awakening of the mid-eighteenth century did large numbers of blacks, slave and free, become converted. The democratic fervor of the Baptist and Methodist denominations appealed strongly to the lower classes of both races, and most blacks became members of these two denominations. Among the slaves an "invisible institution" of informal congregations evolved into semi-independent institutions of considerable power and influence in the slave community. Composed largely of illiterate members and leaving almost no written records, the slaves' church is one of the least understood but perhaps most important institutions in the black experience. Much of what we do know about this invisible institution comes from spirituals, folklore, and slave narratives. For an analysis based on these materials, see Gold Refined Wilson, "The Religion of the American Negro Slave: His Attitude Toward Life and Death," *JNH*, VIII (Jan. 1923), 41–71. Other brief treatments are found in Frazier, *The Negro Church in America*, cited above, ch. 1; Daniel Boorstin, *The Americans: The National Experience* (New York, 1965),* ch. 24; and Luther P. Jackson, "Religious Development of the Negro in Virginia from 1760–1860," *JNH*, XVI (Apr. 1931), 168–239.** For a biography of the most famous of the slave preachers, see William E. Hatcher, *John Jasper, the Unmatched Negro Philosopher and Preacher* (New York, 1908).

A considerable amount of information about slave religion has survived in the oral tradition of ex-slaves; for a valuable sample, see the collection of reminiscences entitled *God Struck Me Dead, Religious Conversion Experiences and Autobiographies of Negro Ex-Slaves* (Nashville, 1945, reprinted in paperback, ed. by Clifton Johnson, Philadelphia, 1969).* There is also material on the slaves' religious experiences scattered among the narratives collected from ex-slaves by the Federal Writers Project in the 1930s: see Benjamin A. Botkin, ed., *Lay My Burden Down: A Folk His-*

tory of Slavery (Chicago, 1945),* and Norman R. Yetman, ed., *Life Under the "Peculiar Institution": Selections from the Slave Narrative Collection* (New York, 1970).* Additional information can be found in some of the collections of fugitive slave autobiographies cited in Part III, topic 1, "Plantation Slavery in the Antebellum South." All of the numerous collections and interpretations of spirituals contain insights on the nature of the slave's religion as reflected in his songs. Perhaps the most useful volumes are Howard Thurman, *Deep River: Reflections on the Religious Insight of Certain of the Negro Spirituals* (New York, 1955), and *The Negro Spiritual Speaks of Life and Death* (New York, 1947); James Weldon Johnson and J. Rosamond Johnson, eds., *The Book of American Negro Spirituals* (New York, 1925), and *The Second Book of Negro Spirituals* (New York, 1926), both reprinted in one vol., *The Books of American Negro Spirituals* (New York, 1956);* and John Wesley Work, ed., *American Negro Songs and Spirituals* (New York, 1940).

Formally organized independent black churches first emerged among the Baptists in the South during the Revolution, with mixed slave and free congregations. For the origins and antebellum history of black Baptists in both North and South, see John W. Davis, "George Liele and Andrew Bryan, Pioneer Negro Baptist Preachers," *JNH*, III (Apr. 1918), 119–27; Walter H. Brooks, "The Evolution of the Negro Baptist Church," *ibid.*, VII (Jan. 1922), 11–22; Owen D. Pelt and Ralph L. Smith, *The Story of the National Baptists* (New York, 1960), chs. 2–4; and James D. Tyms, *The Rise of Religious Education Among Negro Baptists: A Historical Case Study* (New York, 1965), chs. 4–6. Though some slaves belonged to independent black congregations, most masters wished to maintain surveillance over their slaves' religious activities and frowned upon unregulated black churches, especially churches with free black members, who were presumed to have a dangerous influence on the slaves. For the efforts by southern white denominations from 1830 to 1850 to control their slave membership, see Haven Perkins, "Religion for Slaves: Difficulties and Methods," *Church History*, X (Sept. 1941), 228–45. The independent black churches were located primarily in the North and in southern and border state cities. For the black church in southern cities, see Richard C. Wade, *Slavery in the Cities* (New York, 1964),* pp. 160–72. For the North, which was

84 THE BLACK COMMUNITY

the real center of the institutional black church before the Civil War, the best brief treatment is Leon F. Litwack, *North of Slavery: The Negro in the Free States, 1790–1860* (Chicago, 1961),* ch. 6.

Though less numerous than the Baptists, black Methodists exercised a more powerful impact in many communities because of their centralized organizational structure, in contrast to the local autonomy of Baptist congregations, and have left a more complete historical record. The two most important independent black Methodist denominations were the African Methodist Episcopal (A.M.E.) and the African Methodist Episcopal Zion (A.M.E. Zion) churches, which were confined to the northern and border states before the war. James B. F. Shaw, *The Negro in the History of Methodism* (Nashville, 1954), chs. 3, 5, provides a general treatment of both denominations. The best biography of the founder of the A.M.E. Church is Charles H. Wesley, *Richard Allen, Apostle of Freedom* (Washington, 1935). One of the most prominent bishops in the A.M.E. Church was Daniel A. Payne, who recorded the church's antebellum history in chs. 1–17 of his *Recollections of Seventy Years* (Nashville, 1888, reprinted New York, 1968), and in his *History of the African Methodist Episcopal Church* (Nashville, 1891). A modern biography of Payne, who established Wilberforce University as the first independent black college, is Josephus Roosevelt Coan, *Daniel Alexander Payne, Christian Educator* (Philadelphia, 1935). Another useful account of the antebellum A.M.E. Church is George A. Singleton, *The Romance of African Methodism: A Study of the African Methodist Episcopal Church* (New York, 1951), chs. 1–6. The history of the A.M.E. Zion denomination is chronicled by James W. Hood, *One Hundred Years of the African Methodist Episcopal Zion Church* (New York, 1895), and by David Henry Bradley, *A History of the A.M.E. Zion Church, 1796–1872* (Nashville, 1956).

For treatments of separate black congregations in white churches (and in a few cases of integrated congregations), see Andrew E. Murray, *Presbyterians and the Negro—A History* (Philadelphia, 1966), chs. 1–4; George F. Bragg, *History of the Afro-American Group of the Episcopal Church* (Baltimore, 1922, reprinted New York, 1968), chs. 3–12, 23; and John T. Gillard,

The Catholic Church and the Negro (Baltimore, 1929, reprinted New York, 1968), ch. 2.

Religion is a two-edged sword, and this was especially true of slave religion. On the one hand it was potentially an "opiate" for the slave, concentrating his attention on the joys of heaven and blunting the edge of discontent with his existence on earth. Certainly many masters saw Christianity, when properly taught under white auspices ("Servants, obey your masters," etc.), as a means of social control. On the other hand, Christianity carries a messianic, equalitarian, revolutionary message, and in the hands of clever slave preachers it could become a means of inciting insurrection. Secret "prayer meetings" could and did become strategy sessions for planning rebellions. Gabriel Prosser and Nat Turner were slave preachers, and the black Methodist church in Charleston, South Carolina, of which Denmark Vesey was a prominent member, was a breeding ground for the Vesey plot of 1822. For a suggestive article that defines the role of religion in the modern protest movement and by implication points the way to historical inquiry about the comparable role of slave religion, see Gary T. Marx, "Religion: Opiate or Inspiration of Civil Rights Militancy Among Negroes?" *ASR*, XXXII (Feb. 1967), 64–72.**

Many of the works cited in the preceding paragraphs touch upon the question whether religion was an opiate or a call to militancy for antebellum blacks; especially relevant are Gold Refined Wilson, "The Religion of the American Negro Slave"; E. Franklin Frazier, *The Negro Church in America*, ch. 1; and Daniel Boorstin, *The Americans: The National Experience*, ch. 24. A valuable study which emphasizes the accommodating function of religion is Benjamin Mays, *The Negro's God as Reflected in His Literature* (Boston, 1938),* chs. 2–3. Two provocative articles advance the opposing interpretation: John Lovell, "The Social Implications of the Negro Spiritual," *JNE*, VIII (Oct. 1939), 634–43, which argues that the slaves' religion, as expressed in spirituals, inspired discontent and escape; and Vincent Harding, "Religion and Resistance Among Antebellum Negroes, 1800–1860," in August Meier and Elliott Rudwick. eds., *The Making of Black America*, 2 vols. (New York, 1969),* vol. I, pp. 179–97, which discusses the role of Christianity in fomenting slave uprisings. See also Carleton L. Lee, "Religious Roots of the Negro Protest," in Arnold Rose, ed., *Assuring Freedom to the Free: A Century of Emancipation in the USA* (Detroit, 1964), pp. 45–71. In the North there is no question but that religion was a major driving force in black abolitionism, as it was among white abolitionists, and many prominent black abolitionists were ministers; see Benjamin Quarles, *Black Abolitionists* (New York, 1969),* ch. 4. At the same time, however, many northern black churches were conservative; see Litwack, *North of Slavery*, cited above, ch. 6, which treats both the accommodating and militant function of the church.

5. *The Antislavery Movement Before Garrison*

The movement to free the slaves, which in the early 1830s was transformed from a relatively low-keyed campaign of evolutionary gradualism to a militant crusade, originated in the early colonial period, and by 1820 the "impulse," as it has been called, was clearly channeled in several directions that sought in different ways to alter profoundly the situation of Afro-Americans in the United States. The movement has had great consequences in establishing the identity of the American community and redefining and extending the principles of democratic society.

One of the origins of the pre-1830 antislavery movement was the doctrine and polity of Protestant churches in the United States, including most notably the Quaker denomination whose members during and after the Revolution became leaders in antislavery organizations. Another origin was the ideology of the Declaration of Independence and the newly aroused sense of national purpose that followed 1789. The reformers utilized pulpit, pamphlet, and political pressure, and they founded newspapers and voluntary organizations, with the result that their efforts and objectives complicated national political life from the Convention of 1787 through such political crises as the Missouri Compromise and the Virginia debate of 1831–32. The objectives of the various groups were not identical and did not always envision the conferring of full rights or citizenship on black Americans. One aim was the voluntary emancipation of slaves by their owners. Another was the abolition of the slave trade. A third was the containment of the slavery system within the area where it prevailed already. A fourth was the project to purge the nation of blacks by deporting them to Africa.

Chs. 10–15 of David Brion Davis, *The Problem of Slavery in Western Culture* (Ithaca, N.Y., 1966),* provide excellent background on the evolution of antislavery thought in the eighteenth century. Additional information and analysis can be found in Winthrop D. Jordan, *White over Black: American Attitudes Toward the Negro, 1550–1812* (Chapel Hill, 1968),* chs. 5, 7, 9, 12, 15. Chs. 1–17 of Dwight L. Dumond, *Antislavery: The Crusade for Freedom in America* (Ann Arbor, 1961),* are a factual introduction to early antislavery movements, which are treated in more detail in the following monographs: Mary S. Locke, *Anti-Slavery in America: From the Introduction of African Slaves to the Prohibition of the Slave Trade, 1619–1808* (Boston, 1901); Alice D. Adams, *The Neglected Period of Anti-Slavery in America, 1808–1831* (Boston, 1908); Thomas E. Drake, *Quakers and Slavery in America* (New Haven, 1950); Sydney V. James, *A People Among Peoples: Quaker Benevolence in Eighteenth-Century America* (Cambridge, Mass., 1963), esp. chs. 5, 7–8, 12; and Donald G. Mathews, *Slavery and Methodism: A Chapter in American Morality, 1780–1845* (Princeton, 1965). Antislavery sentiment in the North and South during the Revolutionary generation is treated in Arthur Zilversmit, *The First Emancipation: The Abolition of Slavery in the North* (Chicago, 1967);* Robert McColley, *Slavery and Jeffersonian Virginia* (Urbana, Ill., 1964); and Ruth Scarborough, *The Opposition to Slavery in Georgia Prior to 1860* (Nashville, 1933). For an introduction to some northern, especially Federalist, attitudes toward slavery and the slave, consult James M. Banner, Jr., *To the Hartford Convention: The Federalists and the Origins of Party Politics in Massachusetts, 1789–1815* (New York, 1970), pp. 99–109, and Linda K. Kerber, *Federalists in Dissent: Imagery and Ideology in Jeffersonian America* (Ithaca, N.Y., 1970), ch. 2. On the tangled relationships between slavery and politics before 1820, see Donald L. Robinson, *Slavery in the Structure of American Politics, 1765–1820* (New York, 1971), esp. chs. 7–11. A useful compilation of the Founding Fathers' views on slavery is Matthew T. Mellon, ed., *Early American Views on Negro Slavery* (Boston, 1934).* The efforts to abolish the slave trade are treated in the relevant chapters of the volumes by Mannix and Cowley, Du Bois, and Spears, cited in Part II, topic 3, "The Atlantic Slave Trade." The movement for colonization of freed blacks in Africa is analyzed in P. J. Staudenraus, *The African Colonization Movement, 1816–1865* (New York, 1961), and Early Lee Fox, *The American Colonization Society, 1817–1840* (Baltimore, 1919). The tortuous course of southern antislavery thought is treated in McColley's book, cited above, and in Joseph C. Robert, *The Road from Monticello, A Study of the Virginia Slavery Debate of 1832* (Durham, N.C., 1941).

6. Colonization as a Proposed Solution to the Race Problem

From the beginning of the republic, there were many white leaders who could see no solution to the combined problems of slavery and race short of getting rid of the problem by getting rid of the blacks themselves. Thus originated many proposals for the emigration (induced or forced) of free blacks to Africa or the Caribbean. Thomas Jefferson was one of the earliest and most prominent exponents of colonization; for a good introduction to Jefferson's ambivalent racial ideas and the related issue of emigration, see Winthrop D. Jordan, *White over Black: American Attitudes Toward the Negro, 1550–1812* (Chapel Hill, 1968),* chs. 12, 15.

There are several general studies of the colonization movement: Early L. Fox, *The American Colonization Society, 1817–1840* (Baltimore, 1919); P. J. Staudenraus, *The African Colonization Movement, 1816–1865* (New York, 1961); Penelope Campbell, *Maryland in Africa: The Maryland State Colonization Society, 1831–1857* (Urbana, Ill., 1971); the essays on colonization by Frederic Bancroft in Jacob E. Cooke, *Frederic Bancroft, Historian* (Norman, Okla., 1957); Brainerd Dyer, "The Persistence of the Idea of Negro Colonization," *Pacific Historical Review*, XII (1943), 53–67;** Walter L. Fleming, "Deportation and Colonization: An Attempted Solution of the Race Problem," in *Studies in Southern History . . . Inscribed to William Archibald Dunning* (New York, 1914), pp. 3–30; Henry N. Sherwood, "Early Negro Deportation Projects," *MVHR*, II (Mar. 1916), 484–508; Andrew N. Cleven, "Some Plans for Colonizing Liberated Negro Slaves in Hispanic America," *JNH*, XI (Jan. 1926), 35–49; and Charles I. Foster, "The Colonization of Free Negroes in Liberia," *ibid.*, XXXVIII (Jan. 1953), 41–66. Most free blacks were opposed to the effort to colonize them (though for the recurring waves of black nationalism and emigrationism before the Civil War, see this Part under topic 13, "Black Nationalism Before the Civil War"). For the responses of Afro-Americans to colonization and emigration projects, see Leon F. Litwack, *North of Slavery: The Negro in the Free States, 1790–1860* (Chicago, 1961),* pp. 20–27, 252–62, 272–78; Louis R. Mehlinger, "The Attitude of the Free Negro toward Colonization," *JNH*, I (July 1916), 276–301, and relevant titles under the topic cited above.

Abraham Lincoln was basically a colonizationist and sponsored two efforts during the Civil War to promote emigration of freed slaves to the Caribbean and Central America; for the story of colonization efforts during the war, see James M. McPherson, ed., *The Negro's Civil War; How American Negroes Felt and Acted During the War for the Union* (New York, 1965),* ch. 6; Charles H. Wesley, "Lincoln's Plan for Colonizing the Emancipated Negroes," *JNH*, IV (Jan. 1919), 7–21; Willis D. Boyd, "James Redpath and American Negro Colonization in Haiti, 1860–1862," *The Americas*, XII (Oct. 1955), 169–182; Warren A. Beck, "Lincoln and Negro Colonization in Central America," *Abraham Lincoln Quarterly*, VI (Sept. 1950), 162–83; and Paul J. Scheips, "Lincoln and the Chiriqui Colonization Project," *JNH*, XXXVII (Oct. 1952), 418–53.

7. The Abolitionist Movement, 1830–1865

Though the abolitionists were a small minority of the northern people their writings and activities are among the most significant in American social and intellectual history. Current interest in the abolitionists and their literature has centered on three issues. The first is the relation between emotional fervor or psychological tensions and the intellectual commitment to ideas and values in the abolitionists' program. Were the abolitionists rational reformers or fanatics? Why were they concerned about the plight of the blacks? A second issue is the ways in which religious traditions affected the movement, accounting for differences in programs and policies among the reformers. How did Quaker traditions or Protestant evangelicalism affect the movement? Were the abolitionists more interested in Christian duties and in purging themselves of guilt than in the Afro-Americans' legal and social position? Finally, a matter of debate is the adequacy of the abolitionists' intellectual position and political strategies. Did they channel American thought into slogans or abstractions instead of developing a full and coherent political philosophy or a detailed remedy for the situation of black people? Did they arouse the North to a genuine moral commitment, stimulate broad-based movements for social reform, and devise astute political methods? Or did they siphon off such energies into abolitionism alone and ignore important questions about the blacks' status and about reform tactics?

Good starting points for an understanding of the abolitionist movement are Arthur Zilversmit, "The Abolitionists: From Patience to Militance," in James C. Curtis and Lewis L. Gould, eds., *The Black Experience in America* (Austin, Tex., 1970),* pp. 51–67, which contrasts the moderate antislavery movement of the late eighteenth century with the militancy of the post-1830 reformers; Lewis A. Coser, *Men of Ideas: A Sociologist's View* (New York, 1965),* pp. 207–15; David Donald, "Toward a Reconsideration of Abolitionists," in Donald, *Lincoln Reconsidered: Essays on the Civil War Era* (New York, 1956),* pp. 19–36; Robert A. Skotheim, "A Note on Historical Method: David Donald's 'Toward a Reconsideration of Abolitionists,'" *JSH*, XXV (Aug. 1959), 356–65; the essays by Dwight L. Dumond, Martin Duberman, and Stanley Elkins in Hugh Hawkins, ed., *The Abolitionists: Immediatism and the Question of Means* (Boston, 1964);* the critique of Elkins by Aileen S. Kraditor, "A Note on Elkins and the Abolitionists," *CWH*, XIII (Dec. 1967), 330–39; the essays by Larry Gara, John L. Thomas, Sylvan S. Tomkins, Martin Duberman, and Howard Zinn, in Martin Duberman, ed., *The Antislavery Vanguard: New Essays on the Abolitionists* (Princeton, 1965);* Donald G. Mathews, "The Abolitionists on Slavery: The Critique Behind the Social Movement," *JSH*, XXXIII (May 1967), 163–82; Bertram Wyatt-Brown, "Abolitionism: Its Meaning for Contemporary American Reform," *Midwest Quarterly*, VIII (Autumn 1966), 41–55; and Richard Hofstadter's essay on Wendell Phillips in Hofstadter, *The American Political Tradition and the Men Who Made It* (New York, 1948),* pp. 135–61. For a good review of recent historiography on the abolitionists, see Merton L. Dillon, "The Abolitionists: A Decade of Historiography, 1959–1969," *JSH*, XXXV (Nov. 1969), 500–22. Useful collections of primary material are Louis Ruchames, ed., *The Abolitionists: A Collection of Their Writings* (New York, 1963);* Truman Nelson, ed., *Documents of Upheaval: Selections from . . . Garrison's The Liberator, 1831–1865* (New York, 1966);* and William H. and Jane H. Pease, eds., *The Antislavery Argument* (Indianapolis, 1965).* A good collection of primary sources and interpretive essays is Richard O. Curry, ed., *The Abolitionists: Reformers or Fanatics?* (New York, 1965).*

There are several important monographs on the abolitionist movement. One of the best and most recent is Aileen Kraditor, *Means and Ends in American Abolitionism: Garrison and His Critics on Strategy and Tactics, 1834–1850* (New York, 1969).* Four other standard studies are Gilbert Hobbs Barnes, *The Anti-Slavery Impulse, 1830–1844* (New York, 1933);* Louis Filler, *The Crusade Against Slavery, 1830–1860* (New York, 1960);* Dwight L. Dumond, *Antislavery: The Crusade for Freedom in America* (Ann Arbor, 1961),* which is marred by an excessive anti-Garrison bias; and Lawrence Lader, *The Bold Brahmins: New England's War Against Slavery, 1831–1863* (New York, 1961). The impact of the movement on civil liberties is treated by Russel B. Nye, *Fettered Freedom: Civil Liberties and the Slavery Controversy, 1830–1860* (East Lansing, Mich., 1949). A survey of abolitionism and non-violence is Carleton Mabee, *Black Freedom: The Nonviolent Abolitionists from 1830 through the Civil War* (New York, 1970). A study of antiabolitionist mob violence which contains important information and insights on the abolitionists as well is Leonard L. Richards, *"Gentlemen of Property and Standing": Anti-Abolition Mobs in Jacksonian*

America (New York, 1970).* Related works are Linda K. Kerber, "Abolitionists and Amalgamators: The New York City Race Riots of 1834," *New York History,* XLVIII (Jan. 1967), 28–39, and Edmund Fuller, *Prudence Crandall: An Incident of Racism in Nineteenth-Century Connecticut* (Middletown, Conn., 1971). An important study of the social and psychological dynamics of the conflict between abolitionists and southern extremists is David Brion Davis, *The Slave Power Conspiracy and the Paranoid Style* (Baton Rouge, 1969). James M. McPherson, *The Struggle for Equality: Abolitionists and the Negro in the Civil War and Reconstruction* (Princeton, 1964),* traces the role of the abolitionists after 1860. The best of the many biographies of abolitionists are John L. Thomas, *The Liberator: William Lloyd Garrison* (Boston, 1963); Irving H. Bartlett, *Wendell Phillips, Brahmin Radical* (Boston, 1961); Benjamin P. Thomas, *Theodore Weld, Crusader for Freedom* (New Brunswick, N.J., 1950); Benjamin Quarles, *Frederick Douglass* (Washington, 1948);* and Stephen B. Oates, *To Purge This Land with Blood: A Biography of John Brown* (New York, 1970). A provocative study of a figure long associated with the antislavery cause is David Donald's two volumes, *Charles Sumner and the Coming of the Civil War* (New York, 1960), and *Charles Sumner and the Rights of Man* (New York, 1970).

Several of the titles cited in this Part under topics 3 and 5, "American Churches and Slavery" and "The Antislavery Movement Before Garrison," also contain information relevant to this topic.

8. Black Abolitionists

Not all northern blacks were active abolitionists, for most of them had to spend their time and effort in the struggle to make a living and had no energy left for reform activities. Nevertheless a number of prominent northern blacks became active in the abolitionist movement, and they contributed a vitality and in many cases a direct testimony to the conditions of slavery that added an important dimension to the antislavery movement.

There is a considerable literature on the black abolitionists; the best and most recent general study, which is indispensable for this topic, is Benjamin Quarles, *Black Abolitionists* (New York, 1969).* In addition, consult Quarles' "Freedom's Black Vanguard," in Nathan I. Huggins, Martin Kilson, and Daniel M. Fox, eds., *Key Issues in the Afro-American Experience*, 2 vols. (New York, 1971),* vol. I, pp. 174–90. Also important is Howard H. Bell, *A Survey of the Negro Convention Movement, 1830–1861* (New York, 1969), which treats the organized black protest and self-improvement movements. In addition, see Herbert Aptheker, *The Negro in the Abolitionist Movement* (New York, 1941);* and three articles by Charles H. Wesley: "The Negro in the Organization of Abolition," *Phylon*, II (Autumn 1941), 223–35; "The Negroes of New York in the Emancipation Movement," *JNH*, XXIV (Jan. 1939), 65–103;** and "The Participation of Negroes in Anti-Slavery Political Parties," *ibid.*, XXIX (Jan. 1944), 32–74.**

Relations between white and black abolitionists were sometimes marred by friction, racial and otherwise; for discussions of these tensions within the antislavery movement see, in addition to Quarles' discussion of the question in *Black Abolitionists*, Leon F. Litwack, *North of Slavery: The Negro in the Free States, 1790–1860* (Chicago, 1961),* ch. 7, and "The Emancipation of the Negro Abolitionist,"** in Martin Duberman, ed., *The Antislavery Vanguard: New Essays on the Abolitionists* (Princeton, 1965),* pp. 137–55; Benjamin Quarles, "The Breach between Douglass and Garrison," *JNH*, XXIII (Apr. 1938), 144–54; William H. and Jane H. Pease, "Antislavery Ambivalence: Immediatism, Expediency, Race," *AQ*, XVII (Winter 1965), 682–95;** William H. and Jane H. Pease, "Boston Garrisonians and the Problem of Frederick Douglass," *Canadian Journal of History*, II (Sept. 1967), 29–48; and Jane H. and William H. Pease, "Black Power—The Debate in 1840," *Phylon*, XXIX (Spring 1968), 19–26.

Letters, articles, editorials, and speeches by black abolitionists can be found in Carter G. Woodson, ed., *The Mind of the Negro as Reflected in Letters during the Crisis, 1800–1860* (Washington, 1926),* and *Negro Orators and Their Orations* (Washington, 1925), chs. 1–6; and Herbert Aptheker, ed., *A Documentary History of the Negro People in the United States* (New York, 1951),* pp. 82–458. The most famous black abolitionist was Frederick

Douglass, and the best biography of this remarkable man is Benjamin Quarles, *Frederick Douglass* (Washington, 1948).* Much valuable biographical material on Douglass and all of his important writings and speeches can be found in Philip S. Foner, *The Life and Writings of Frederick Douglass*, 4 vols. (New York, 1950–55).* See also August Meier, "Frederick Douglass' Vision for America," in Harold M. Hyman and Leonard W. Levy, eds., *Freedom and Reform* (New York, 1967), pp. 127–48; and Benjamin Quarles, ed., *Frederick Douglass* (Englewood Cliffs, N.J., 1968).* Information on other black abolitionists is contained in William E. Farrison, *William Wells Brown: Author and Reformer* (Chicago, 1969); Earl Conrad, *Harriet Tubman* (Washington, 1935);* Arthur H. Fauset, *Sojourner Truth, God's Faithful Pilgrim* (Chapel Hill, 1938); Herbert Aptheker, ed., *One Continual Cry: David Walker's Appeal to the Colored Citizens of the World, 1829–1830* (New York, 1965);* Dorothy Porter, "David M. Ruggles, an Apostle of Human Rights," *JNH*, XXVIII (Jan. 1943), 23–50; Monroe N. Work, "The Life of Charles B. Ray," *ibid.*, IV (Oct. 1919), 361–71; William Brewer, "Henry Highland Garnet," *ibid.*, XIII (Jan. 1928), 36–52; William Brewer, "John B. Russwurm," *ibid.*, XIII (Oct. 1928), 413–22; Ray Allen Billington, "James Forten: Forgotten Abolitionist," *NHB*, XIII (Nov. 1949), 31–36, 45; and William F. Cheek, "John Mercer Langston: Black Protest Leader and Abolitionist," *CWH*, XVI (June 1970), 101–20. A useful collection of articles is John H. Bracey, August Meier, and Elliott Rudwick, eds., *Blacks in the Abolitionist Movement* (Belmont, Calif., 1971).*

Several of the titles cited in this Part under topics 2 and 7, "Free Blacks North of Slavery" and "The Abolitionist Movement, 1830–1865," also contain material on black abolitionism.

9. The Underground Railroad

The most common form of overt resistance to slavery was escape. An average of perhaps 1,000 slaves per year followed the North Star to freedom; many times that number tried and failed. Organized efforts to help slaves find freedom in the free states or the settlements of Ontario, Canada, began among the Quakers in the eighteenth century. After 1850, when Congress passed the Fugitive Slave Act and many northern state governments enacted personal liberty laws to prevent its enforcement, the adventure became more desperate. Recent scholarship has centered on the question whether white organizations or the initiative and ingenuity of blacks were more significant in sustaining the Underground Railroad. Most of the older works on the subject were based on the reminiscences of aged white abolitionists whose memories easily magnified the heroism and sacrifices of their own roles. A good example is Wilbur H. Siebert, *The Underground Railroad from Slavery to Freedom* (New York, 1898, reprinted New York, 1968). Two more recent works reflect a similar viewpoint: Henrietta Buckmaster, *Let My People Go: The Story of the Underground Railroad and the Growth of the Abolition Movement* (New York, 1941),* and William A. Breyfogle, *Make Free: The Story of the Underground Railroad* (Philadelphia, 1958).

But Larry Gara, *The Liberty Line: The Legend of the Underground Railroad* (Lexington, Ky., 1961),* is a valuable corrective to earlier studies. Gara argues that the network of Underground Railroad "stations" in the North was not nearly so widespread nor as well organized in fact as it became in legend, and that more credit for initiative and daring belongs to the blacks who found their way, often unaided, to the North than to the white abolitionists who helped them once they arrived. Though Gara probably carries his revisionism too far, his book is the most important single source for this topic. George Rawick, "The Historical Roots of Black Liberation," *Radical America*, II (July–Aug. 1968), 1–13, and Robert S. Starobin and Dale Tomich, "Black Liberation Historiography," *ibid.* (Sept.–Oct. 1968), 24–28, discuss the function of escape and the Underground Railroad as an important form of resistance to slavery. Many of the slave narratives cited in Part III, topic 1, "Plantation Slavery in the Antebellum South," contain explicit accounts of their authors' escapes from bondage; most of them give more credit to white "conductors" on the Underground Railroad than does Gara. A black abolitionist who organized the network of underground stations in Philadelphia later published a book based on his own experiences and research: William Still, *The Underground Railroad* (Philadelphia, 1872, reprinted New York, 1968). Levi Coffin, a Cincinnati Quaker, was the reputed "president" of the Underground Railroad; for his account of the work, see Levi Coffin, *Reminiscences of Levi Coffin* (Cincinnati, 1876, reprinted New York, 1968). Horatio T. Strother, *The Underground Railroad in Connecticut* (Middletown, Conn., 1962),* is a modern presentation of the Railroad in one state as an organized and efficient institution. Efforts to derail the Underground Railroad by enforcement of the Fugitive Slave Law are treated in Stanley W. Campbell, *The Slave Catchers: Enforcement of the Fugitive Slave Law, 1850–1860* (Chapel Hill, 1970). On an early and bloody fugitive slave case under the Fugitive Slave Act of 1850, see Roderick W. Nash, "The Christiana Riot: An Evaluation of its National Significance," *Journal of the Lancaster County Historical Society*, LXV (Spring 1961), 65–91, and Richard Grau, "The Christiana Riot of 1851: A Reappraisal," *ibid.*, LXVIII (Michaelmas 1964), 147–63. The story of one slave's attempts to escape the South is Robert Brent Toplin, "Peter Still Versus the Peculiar Institution," *CWH*, XIII (Dec. 1967), 340–49.**

10. White Abolitionist Writers

A. Harriet Beecher Stowe

Mark Twain thought that Sir Walter Scott caused the Civil War, but Lincoln, in a moment of high charm, attributed the national holocaust to the most famous novel of Harriet Beecher Stowe: "So you're the little lady," he said on meeting her, "who made this big war." Although she claimed that "God wrote it," most scholars credit Mrs. Stowe with the authorship of *Uncle Tom's Cabin* (1852),* along with *Dred: A Tale of the Great Dismal Swamp* (1856), an attack on the slave-owning South for which she never claimed divine assistance. Recent interest in her works has centered on the way she fixes black stereotypes (especially that of the "Uncle Tom") while enlisting them in the service of abolitionism, and in the way she channeled Christian piety into moral or social reform. A recent critical study of Mrs. Stowe's fiction is Alice Crozier, *The Novels of Harriet Beecher Stowe* (New York, 1969). Illuminating essays on her career and writings include Constance Rourke's in *Trumpets of Jubilee* (New York, 1927), pp. 87–148; Tremaine McDowell's "The Use of Negro Dialect by Harriet Beecher Stowe," *American Speech*, VI (June 1931), 322–26; John W. Ward's Afterword to the Signet edition of *Uncle Tom's Cabin* (New York, 1966);* Edmund Wilson's "Harriet Beecher Stowe" in *Patriotic Gore: Studies in the Literature of the American Civil War* (New York, 1962),* pp. 3–58; and Ellen Moers' "Mrs. Stowe's Vengeance," *New York Review of Books*, XV (Sept. 3, 1970), 25–32. Other useful studies include Harry Birdoff, *The World's Greatest Hit: Uncle Tom's Cabin* (New York, 1947); Charles H. Foster, *The Rungless Ladder: Harriet Beecher Stowe and New England Puritanism* (Durham, N.C., 1954); Joseph C. Furnas, *Goodbye to Uncle Tom* (New York, 1956);* and Forrest Wilson's biography, *Crusader in Crinoline* (Philadelphia, 1941). Among the proslavery counterstatements provoked by Mrs. Stowe's work are Edward J. Stearns, *Notes on Uncle Tom's Cabin* (Philadelphia, 1853), and A. Woodward, *A Review of Uncle Tom's Cabin* (Cincinnati, 1853). Mrs. Stowe documented the authenticity of scenes described in *Uncle Tom's Cabin* in *The Key to Uncle Tom's Cabin* (Boston, 1854, reprinted New York, 1968).

B. John Greenleaf Whittier and James Russell Lowell

John Greenleaf Whittier, a New England Quaker, and James Russell Lowell, scion of an old Boston family, are two writers who devoted their talents as editors, essayists, and poets to the cause of blacks and of abolition. Their writings provide an opportunity to study the extent to which the issues raised by the abolitionist movement were expressed in their prose and poetry, the ways in which they portrayed blacks and/or southern slaveowners, and the extent to which their antislavery poetry gained or suffered in quality because of the issues it treated or the wide audience to which it was addressed. One may study their writings, finally, in an effort to understand the motivation behind the outpouring of abolitionist sentiment in New England.

Both poets are treated in "The Literature of Conflict," in *The Literary History of the United States*, ed. by Robert E. Spiller, Willard Thorp, et al., 2 vols. (New York, 1948; rev. eds., 1963, 1969); in Roy Harvey Pearce, *The Continuity of American Poetry* (Princeton, 1961),* pp. 192–97, 246–52, 214–20, 226–33, where he discusses them in relation to the position of the popular poet and the predilections of the common reader; and in Vernon L. Parrington, *Main Currents in American Thought*, 3 vols. (New York, 1927–30),* vol. II, pp. 467–72. Considerations of Lowell's career and achievement include Warren G. Jenkins, "Lowell's Criteria of Political Values," *New England Quarterly*, VII (Mar. 1934), 115–41; Leon Howard, *Victorian Knight-Errant: A Study of the Early Literary Career of James Russell Lowell* (Berkeley, 1952); and Martin Duberman's important study, *James Russell Lowell* (Boston, 1966).* Studies of Whittier include John A. Pollard, *John Greenleaf Whittier, Friend of Man* (Boston, 1949); Osborn T. Smallwood, "The Historical Significance of Whittier's Anti-Slavery Poems . . . ," *JNH*, XXXV (Jan. 1950), 53–68; Cecil B. Williams, "Whittier's Relation to Garrison and the 'Liberator,'" *New England Quarterly*, XXV (June 1952), 248–54; and the biography by Edward Wagenknecht, *John Greenleaf Whittier: A Portrait in Paradox* (New York, 1967).

Editions of Whittier's and Lowell's works include Harry H. Clark and Norman Foerster, eds., *James Russell Lowell: Representative Selections* (New York, 1947); *The Biglow Papers*, First Series (Boston, 1848), Second Series (Boston, 1867); *The Anti-Slavery Papers of James Russell Lowell*, 2 vols. (Boston, 1902); Whittier's *Justice and Expediency* (Boston, 1833); the section "Anti-Slavery Poems" in his *Poetical Works* (Riverside ed., Boston, 1888), vol. III; the section "The Conflict with Slavery" in his *Prose Works* (Riverside ed., Boston, 1889), vol. III; Harry H. Clark, ed., *John Greenleaf Whittier: Representative Selections* (New York, 1935); and Louis Untermeyer, ed., *The Poems of John Greenleaf Whittier* (New York, 1945).

11. Racial Themes in the Writings of Poe and Melville

The years from the 1830s into the 1850s are among the most impressive in American literary history. Washington Irving and James Fenimore Cooper did much of their writing during this period. Walt Whitman began his career toward the end of it. And this period saw the appearance of the major works of three of our greatest writers of fiction, Edgar Allan Poe, Nathaniel Hawthorne, and Herman Melville. This is also the period, of course, during which the issues of slavery and race were helping to push the nation into civil war. What, then, were the connections between this literary "renaissance" and the growing explosiveness of racial issues in the United States?

Racial themes clearly dominate the work of the abolitionist writers, and Harriet Beecher Stowe's *Uncle Tom's Cabin* is one of the major novels of the period (see the previous topic, "White Abolitionist Writers"). And yet there is relatively little direct treatment of black characters and racial themes in the works of the principal writers of the so-called "American Renaissance." Irving and Cooper treat black figures, when they treat them at all, as happy, mindless "Sambos" (although Cooper did express fears about apocalyptic racial violence in ch. 38 of *The American Democrat* [New York, 1838]*). Hawthorne seems almost deliberately to have avoided presenting black characters. Of the major writers of the period only Melville dealt consistently and directly with black figures, hence his inclusion here. Poe, finally, presents a special case, for although there is little *direct* treatment of racial themes in his fiction certain of his tales reveal an *indirect*, but nonetheless powerful, concern with America's racial guilt and terror.

A. Edgar Allan Poe

Edgar Allan Poe is more often associated with Gothic horror fiction than with the social issues of nineteenth-century America.

But Poe was a Southerner, at least by upbringing, writing in the years before the Civil War (he died in 1849). As a magazine editor he linked himself with the Whig and southern opposition to abolitionism. Even Poe's Gothic symbolism has peculiarly American connotations—the symbolic white, red, and black of the Gothic palette reflecting the racial composition (and antagonisms) of the United States.

Poe's racial fears usually appear in his fiction (when they appear at all) in disguised or sublimated forms—as in the appearance of violent and sinister orangutans in such stories as "The Murders in the Rue Morgue," "The System of Doctor Tarr and Professor Fether" and "Hop-Frog." Lest the association of these tales with Poe's racial fears seem forced, one might note that the latter two stories are clearly intended as commentaries on (or satires of) American democracy. And blacks enter directly into some of Poe's stories. There is, for instance, the black valet in another of Poe's political satires, "The Man That Was Used Up." Most importantly, there are a number of black characters (including the entire population of the mysterious kingdom of Tsalal) in Poe's only novel, *The Narrative of Arthur Gordon Pym* (1838).

An excellent general study of Poe is Edward H. Davidson, *Poe: A Critical Study* (Cambridge, Mass., 1957). More directly relevant to this topic are Harry Levin, *The Power of Blackness; Hawthorne, Poe, and Melville* (New York, 1958),* esp. ch. 4; and Leslie Fiedler, *Love and Death in the American Novel* (New York, 1960),* pp. 370–82 (in a more general sense, all of Fiedler's ch. 11 is relevant). See also Killis Campbell, "Poe's Treatment of the Negro and Negro Dialect," *Texas Studies in Literature and Language*, XVI (1936), 107–14. The relation between Poe's activities as a magazine editor and his antiabolitionist politics is touched on in Bette Weidman, "A Casualty of Abolition Politics," *Bulletin of the New York Public Library*, LXXIII (Feb. 1969), 94–113. A treatment of Poe's political satire is William Whipple, "Poe's Political Satire," *University of Texas Studies in English*, XXXV (1956), 81–95. There are numerous critical studies of *The Narrative of Arthur Gordon Pym*. Of particular relevance to this topic (in addition to the material on *Pym* in the books by Levin and Fiedler) are Pascal Covici, Jr., "Toward a Reading of Poe's *Narrative of A. Gordon Pym*," *Mississippi Quar-*

terly, XXI (Spring 1968), 111–18, and Sidney Kaplan's introduction to his edition of *The Narrative of Arthur Gordon Pym* (New York, 1960).*

B. Herman Melville

In 1856, at the height of the slavery controversy, Herman Melville published a stunning short tale, "Benito Cereno." In it a New England sea captain, Amasa Delano, comes upon a slave ship commanded by a Spaniard, Don Benito Cereno. Although Delano senses that something is wrong, his fears are allayed by his own optimism and by the gentle officiousness of a slave named Babo. It turns out, however, that there has been a brutal mutiny on board the ship, led by Babo, and that the slaves are in control. Babo's servility is only a mask. At the close, Cereno is rescued, and some slaves are slaughtered, others captured and brutally punished. Melville treats this story with such force and subtlety that it continues to puzzle and agitate critics and cultural historians. Some have accused Melville of racism, of undermining the stereotype of the docile "Sambo" only to replace it, in the figure of Babo, with a stereotype of black maliciousness. Others have found it an exposure of the deadness of white society. Some have interpreted it as a philosophical study of evil with only an incidental interest in slavery or the race question.

Interpretation of the story is complicated by two matters that require attention. One is that Melville's symbolic forms are notoriously complicated in what they mean or symbolize while being drawn from Gothic literary conventions that abound in typed and stereotyped characters. Critics have disagreed over the extent to which Melville's Gothic stereotypes are racial stereotypes as well. And they have disagreed over whether Melville's use of stereotypes to present characters means that his conception of those characters is stereotyped. This question applies as much to the two white captains as to Babo. The second matter has to do with Melville's themes. In "Benito Cereno" he is clearly concerned with the viability of rebelliousness, the vitality of the subconscious, the enervation of established institutions and forms, and the "power of blackness"—the validity even of "evil" and its interconnections with "good." What has been less clear is what relationship these

themes have, in "Benito Cereno," with the central struggle between black and white characters.

Critical works on "Benito Cereno" that attach importance to
the issues of race, racism, and slavery include Jean F. Yellin's indispensable "Black Masks: Melville's 'Benito Cereno,' " AQ, XXII
(Fall 1970), 678–89; Joseph Schiffman, "Critical Problems in
Benito Cereno," Modern Language Quarterly, XI (Sept. 1950),
317–24; Sidney Kaplan, "Herman Melville and the American National Sin: The Meaning of Benito Cereno," JNH, XLII (Jan.
1957), 11–37; Robert Forrey, "Herman Melville and the Negro
Question," Mainstream, XV (Feb. 1962), 23–32; Eleanor E.
Simpson, "Melville and the Negro: From Typee to 'Benito
Cereno,' " American Literature, XLI (1969), 19–38; and Warren
D'Avezedo, "Revolt on the San Dominick," Phylon, XVII (2nd
Quarter 1956), 129–40. Complications in Melville's attitude toward the Negro are illuminated by Priscilla Allen Zirker, "Evidence of the Slavery Dilemma in White Jacket," AQ, XVIII (Fall
1966), 477–92. Brief but provocative comments are in F. O. Ma-
thiessen, American Renaissance (New York, 1941),* especially
p. 508, and Leslie Fiedler, Love and Death in the American Novel
(New York, 1960),* pp. 382–83.

Other useful articles that place less emphasis on race but illumi-
nate the racial and social significance of the tale include Allen
Guttman, "The Enduring Innocence of Captain Amasa Delano,"
Boston University Studies in English, V (Summer 1961), 35–45;
John Bernstein, "Benito Cereno and the Spanish Inquisition,"
Nineteenth Century Fiction, XVI (Mar. 1962), 345–49; Max
Putzel, "The Source and the Symbols of Melville's Benito Cereno,"
American Literature, XXXIV (May 1962), 191–206; H. Bruce
Franklin, " 'Apparent Symbol of Despotic Command': Mel-
ville's Benito Cereno," New England Quarterly, XXXIV (Dec.
1961), 462–77; G. A. Knox, "Lost Command: Benito Cereno
Reconsidered," Person, XL (Summer 1962), 188–97; Richard H.
Fogle, "The Monk and the Bachelor: Melville's Benito Cereno,"
Tulane Studies in English, III (1952), 155–78; William Stein,
"The Moral Axis of Benito Cereno," Accent, XV (Summer 1955),
221–23.

A recent dramatization of "Benito Cereno" that is itself a commentary on Melville's tale is Robert Lowell, *The Old Glory* (New York, 1965),* pp. 135–214.

12. Black Literature Before the Civil War

There was little formal literature by blacks in the United States before the 1890s. Only three known black novels were published before 1892, all of them in the 1850s. Several early poets, among them Phillis Wheatley and George Moses Horton, grace the anthologies of black literature; most of their poems are only of historical interest today. But nineteenth-century black Americans produced an impressive body of informal literature—spirituals, folklore, sermons, slave narratives, editorials, essays and speeches against slavery and racism—which is more enduring and moving than nearly all the writings of antebellum black poets and novelists. A detailed survey and analysis of all forms of black literature before the Civil War, including the press, is Vernon Loggins, *The Negro Author, His Development in America to 1900* (New York, 1931, reprinted New York, 1964), chs. 1–6, 9. The most complete anthology of antebellum black writers, with critical evaluations of each, is Benjamin Brawley, ed., *Early Negro American Writers* (Chapel Hill, 1935). Other valuable surveys, anthologies, and bibliographies are Margaret Just Butcher, *The Negro in American Culture* (New York, 1956), chs. 5–7; Sterling Brown, Arthur Davis, and Ulysses Lee, eds., *The Negro Caravan: Writings by American Negroes* (New York, 1941, reprinted New York, 1969), pp. 138–61, 247–97, 415–52, 703–28; Benjamin Brawley, *The Negro Genius: A New Appraisal of the Achievement of the American Negro in Literature and the Fine Arts* (New York, 1937),* chs. 1–3; and Dorothy B. Porter, "Early American Negro Writings: A Bibliographical Study," *The Papers of the Bibliographical Society of America*, XXXIX (3rd Quarter 1945), 192–268.

Although little formal antebellum black literature has much claim to literary merit, it can be of great interest to the student of American history and culture. It offers the possibility to study the ways in which black writers tried to adapt the modes of the dominant white culture to their own experience (in much the same way that that culture was trying to adapt the modes of European literature to *its* own experience). How, in short, did black writers modify the conventions they borrowed? Also, literature—even when it is conventional and imitative—can provide insight into the emotional complexity and intensity of black reactions to black culture, slave or free, and to white racism. As for informal antebellum black literature, especially oratory and spirituals, it can speak for itself.

Poetry. The first black American poet was Jupiter Hammon, a slave on Long Island who began publishing religious poems in 1760. Better known and a better poet was Phillis Wheatley, a remarkably precocious Boston slave whose first poem was printed in 1770; her work soon attracted the favorable attention of prominent Americans, including George Washington. A useful brief survey of antebellum black poetry is Sterling Brown, *Negro Poetry and Drama* (Washington, 1937),* ch. 1. Dorothy B. Porter, *North American Negro Poets: A Bibliographical Check List of Their Writings* (1760–1944) (Hattiesburg, Miss., 1944), provides a complete bibliography. A fine anthology of antebellum poetry is William Robinson, ed., *Early Black American Poets* (Dubuque, Iowa, 1970). Jupiter Hammon's life and poems are treated by Oscar Wegelin, *Jupiter Hammon, American Negro Poet* (New York, 1915).* A good anthology and analysis of Phillis Wheatley's poems is Julian D. Mason, ed., *The Poems of Phillis Wheatley* (Chapel Hill, 1966). Another black poet and author of some merit was Frances Ellen Watkins Harper; for her early poems, see Frances E. W. Harper, *Poems on Miscellaneous Subjects* (1st ed., Philadelphia, 1854, 20th ed., Philadelphia, 1874).

Fiction. Brief discussions of the three black novelists of the 1850s can be found in Sterling Brown, *The Negro in American Fiction* (Washington, 1937),* pp. 39–41; Hugh M. Gloster, *Negro Voices in American Fiction* (Chapel Hill, 1948), pp. 25–29; and Robert A. Bone, *The Negro Novel in America* (rev. ed., New Haven, 1965),* pp. 29–32. One of the most prolific black writers in the nineteenth century was William Wells Brown, an escaped slave, who tried his hand at autobiography, biography, history, travel literature, essays, poetry, songs, drama, and the novel. His *Clotel; or, the President's Daughter* (London, 1853, reprinted

New York, 1969),* was the first novel by a black author. The best description of Brown's literary and other careers is William E. Farrison, *William Wells Brown: Author and Reformer* (Chicago, 1969). The other two black novels of the 1850s have been reprinted in modern editions: Frank J. Webb, *The Garies and Their Friends* (London, 1857, reprinted New York, 1969); and Martin R. Delany, *Blake, or The Huts of America* (serialized in the *Anglo-African Magazine*, 1859 and 1861–62, reprinted Boston, 1970, ed. by Floyd J. Miller).*

The Theater. In the nineteenth century the Afro-American was usually portrayed on the stage by burnt-cork minstrels. The few black companies that tried to present serious plays collapsed or were suppressed, and the one black man who achieved fame as a Shakespearean actor in the generation before the Civil War, Ira Aldridge, spent his entire career in Europe and never returned to his native land after he became a star. For minstrelsy and blacks in the antebellum theater, see Loften Mitchell, *Black Drama: The Story of the American Negro in the Theatre* (New York, 1967),* chs. 1–2. A fine biography of Aldridge is Herbert Marshall and Mildred Stock, *Ira Aldridge, the Negro Tragedian* (New York, 1958).*

Oratory, Journalism, and Letters. One form of literature in which blacks excelled was oratory. For two anthologies of black speeches during this period, see Carter G. Woodson, *Negro Orators and Their Orations* (Washington, 1925, reprinted New York, 1970), chs. 1–6; and Alice Moore Dunbar, ed., *Masterpieces of Negro Eloquence: The Best Speeches Delivered by the Negro from the Days of Slavery to the Present Time* (New York, 1914, reprinted New York, 1970). Many poems, essays, speeches, and letters as well as news articles and editorials were published in the black press, and much of this writing was related to the abolitionist movement. For the black press and other literary aspects of black abolitionism, see Leon F. Litwack, *North of Slavery: The Negro in the Free States, 1790–1860* (Chicago, 1961),* ch. 7, and Benjamin Quarles, *Black Abolitionists* (New York, 1969),* esp. ch. 4. Many unpublished and published letters from blacks, some of genuine literary value, were unearthed and reprinted by Carter G. Woodson, ed., *The Mind of the Negro as Reflected in Letters Written During the Crisis, 1800–1860* (Washington, 1926).* The foremost black editor and orator, of course, was Frederick Douglass, whose major antebellum writings have been published in Philip S. Foner, ed., *The Life and Writings of Frederick Douglass*, 4 vols. (New York, 1950–55),* vols. I, II.

Religious Literature and Spirituals. Religion was a major theme in much of antebellum black literature, including poetry, autobiography, and essays as well as sermons and spirituals. For an analysis of this literature, see Benjamin Mays, *The Negro's God as Reflected in His Literature* (New York, 1938),* chs. 1–2. The spirituals may well have been the most meaningful literature produced by black people before the war. Four brief evaluations of them are W. E. B. Du Bois, "The Sorrow Songs,"** ch. 14 of *The Souls of Black Folk* (New York, 1903);* Alain L. Locke, "The Negro Spirituals," in Locke, *The New Negro* (New York, 1925),* pp. 199–213;** Sterling Brown, *Negro Poetry and Drama* (Washington, 1937),* ch. 2; and Wayman B. McLaughlin, "Symbolism and Mysticism in the Spirituals," *Phylon*, XXIV (Spring 1963), 69–77. Additional references to the spirituals and religious literature can be found in Part II, topic 4, "African Cultural Survivals Among Black Americans," and in this Part, topic 4, "The Antebellum Black Church."

Slave Narratives. Another significant form of black literature was the fugitive slave narrative. Many escaped or emancipated slaves fed the curiosity of the northern public by writing (or having ghostwritten) accounts of their experiences. Scores of slave narratives made their way into print, ranging in quality from outright trash to superlative literature and in truthfulness from outright fabrication to authentic autobiography. They were used as propaganda by the abolitionist movement, which sometimes detracted from their literary value. But the best of them are moving human documents and contain a great deal of information about the nature of slavery, the slave personality, the strategy and tactics of escape, and the role of black men and women in the abolitionist movement. The most comprehensive analysis and sample of slave narratives is George P. Rawick, ed., *The American Slave: A Composite Autobiography*, 8 vols. (Westport, Conn., 1971–). A useful interpretation is Charles H. Nichols, *Many Thousand Gone: The Ex-Slaves' Account of Their Bondage and Freedom* (Leiden, Netherlands, 1963).* The most famous fugitive slave was Frederick Douglass, and his *Narrative of the Life of Frederick Douglass* (Boston, 1845)* is one of the best examples of the genre. One of the most useful anthologies of slave narratives is Gilbert Osofsky, ed., *Puttin' On Ole Massa: The Slave Narratives of Henry Bibb, William Wells Brown, and Solomon Northup* (New York, 1969).* For other anthologies, see Part III, topic 1, "Plantation Slavery in the Antebellum South."

13. Black Nationalism Before the Civil War

A persistent theme in the response of black Americans to racism and discrimination has been disillusionment with the prospect for pluralism, integration, or assimilation in the United States and a consequent emphasis on race pride and solidarity, all-black organizations (such as churches), cultural nationalism, and emigration to Africa or the Caribbean where blacks might build a strong republic and prove their capacity for self-government and achievement. Black nationalism has been strongest during periods of reaction following the failure of equalitarian movements. Two periods of reaction occurred before the Civil War, the first in the generation after 1790, when the antislavery hopes of the Revolutionary era began to fade and slavery fastened itself ever more tightly upon the South, and the second in the 1850s, when the Fugitive Slave Law, the Kansas-Nebraska Act, and the Dred Scott decision seemed to foreshadow a determined southern effort to cripple the abolitionist movement, rob free blacks of the few rights they possessed, and impose the peculiar institution on all new territories. The forms and rhetoric of antebellum black nationalism bear considerable resemblance to the themes of nationalism and black power in the 1960s.

The best place to start a study of antebellum black nationalism is with the introduction and Pts. 1 and 2 of John H. Bracey, Jr., August Meier, and Elliott Rudwick, eds., *Black Nationalism in America* (Indianapolis, 1970).* Leon F. Litwack, *North of Slavery: The Negro in the Free States, 1790–1860* (Chicago, 1961),* esp. chs. 6 and 8, treats some of the manifestations of nationalism, including the evolution of the black church and the emigration movement in the 1850s. Good articles dealing with antebellum nationalism are Hollis R. Lynch, "Pan-Negro Nationalism in the

New World, Before 1862," in *Boston University Papers on Africa*, vol. II, *African History* (Boston, 1966), pp. 149–79; August Meier, "The Emergence of Negro Nationalism (A Study in Ideologies)," *Midwest Journal*, IV (Winter 1951–52), 96–104;** and Howard H. Bell, "The Negro Emigration Movement, 1849–1854: A Phase of Negro Nationalism," *Phylon*, IX (Summer 1959), 132–42, and "Negro Nationalism: A Factor in Emigration Projects, 1858–1861," *JNH*, XLVII (Jan. 1962), 42–53. Prominent individual nationalists are discussed in H. N. Sherwood, "Paul Cuffe," *ibid.*, VIII (Apr. 1923), 153–232; Mike M. Fisher, "Lott Cary, the Colonizing Missionary," *ibid.*, VII (Oct. 1922), 380–418; and Kathleen O'Mara Wahle, "Alexander Crummell: Black Evangelist and Pan-Negro Nationalist," *Phylon*, XXIX (Winter 1968), 388–95. Two black advocates of emigration to Haiti present their arguments in James Theodore Holly and J. Dennis Harris, *Black Separatism and the Caribbean*, 1860, ed. by Howard H. Bell (Ann Arbor, 1970). The foremost nationalist in the 1850s was Martin R. Delany, who along with Robert Campbell visited the Niger River Valley in Africa to explore the possibility of building a new nation there. For background information on Delany and on this exploratory trip, see A. H. M. Kirk-Greene, "America in the Niger Valley: A Colonization Centenary," *Phylon*, XXII (Autumn 1962), 225–39, and Howard H. Bell, ed., *Search for a Place: Black Separatism and Africa*, 1860 (Ann Arbor, 1969).* A militant pro-emigration publication of 1852 worth consulting is Martin R. Delany, *The Condition, Elevation, Emigration, and Destiny of the Colored People of the United States* (New York, 1852, reprinted New York, 1968). A provocative interpretation of Delany and other early nationalists can be found in Theodore Draper, *The Rediscovery of Black Nationalism* (New York, 1970),* chs. 1–2. Two recent biographies of Delany are Victor Ullman, *Martin R. Delany: The Beginnings of Black Nationalism* (Boston, 1971), and, intended for young readers, Dorothy Sterling, *The Making of an Afro-American: Martin Robison Delany, 1812–1885* (Garden City, N.Y., 1971).* An interesting aspect of black separatism is treated in William H. and Jane H. Pease, *Black Utopia: Negro Communal Experiments in America* (Madison, 1963).

PART V

THE CIVIL WAR AND RECONSTRUCTION

1. An Abortive Revolution of Equality: The Civil War and Reconstruction

The decade of the 1860s, like that of the 1960s, was a period of rapid and apparently revolutionary racial change. In less than ten years, four million slaves were emancipated by the force of arms, enfranchised by the national government, and granted equal civil and political rights by the United States Constitution; their leaders were elected to high office in southern states and their children admitted to missionary and public schools for the first time. But this was an abortive revolution; the promise of racial equality was never fully implemented even during Reconstruction, and after 1870 black Americans were gradually robbed of many of the hard-won rights of the 1860s.

For brief treatments of these themes of promise and betrayal, consult August Meier, "Negroes in the First and Second Reconstruction of the South," CWH, XIII (June 1967), 114–30; James M. McPherson, "The Civil War and Reconstruction: A Revolution of Racial Equality?" in William G. Shade and Roy C. Herrenkohl, eds., *Seven on Black: Reflections on the Negro Experience in America* (Philadelphia, 1969),* pp. 49–72; and Larry Kincaid, "Two Steps Forward, One Step Back: Racial Attitudes During the Civil War and Reconstruction," in Gary B. Nash and Richard Weiss, eds., *The Great Fear: Race in the Mind of America* (New York, 1970),* pp. 45–70. Some of the most penetrating essays on the equalitarian triumph and tragedy during the Civil War and Reconstruction have been written by C. Vann Woodward. See his "Equality: The Deferred Commitment," and "The Political Legacy of Reconstruction," in *The Burden of Southern History* (Baton Rouge, 1960),* pp. 69–108, and "Seeds of Failure in Radical Race Policy," in Harold M. Hyman, ed., *New Frontiers of the American Reconstruction* (Urbana, Ill., 1966), pp. 125–47.

For a book-length study that reviews the war and Reconstruction as a potential revolution of freedom and equality from the vantage point of the abolitionists, see James M. McPherson, *The Struggle for Equality: Abolitionists and the Negro in the Civil War and Reconstruction* (Princeton, 1964).* Other volumes that deal with this theme during the war include Charles H. Wesley and Patricia Romero, *Negro Americans in the Civil War: From Slavery to Citizenship* (2nd ed., rev., New York, 1969), chs. 2, 5, 7; James M. McPherson, ed., *The Negro's Civil War* (New York, 1969),* chs. 1–5, 18–22; and two works by Benjamin Quarles: *The Negro in the Civil War* (Boston, 1953),* chs. 3–8, 11, 13–15, and *Lincoln and the Negro* (New York, 1962), chs. 4–6, 8–10. A carefully documented monograph on the coming of freedom in one state is Charles L. Wagandt, *The Mighty Revolution: Negro Emancipation in Maryland, 1862–1864* (Baltimore, 1964). The progress of the revolution at the national level can be traced by a series of proclamations, legislative enactments, and constitutional amendments; for studies of these developments, see John Hope Franklin, *The Emancipation Proclamation* (Garden City, N.Y., 1963);* Harry V. Jaffa, "The Emancipation Proclamation," in Robert A. Goldwin, ed., *100 Years of Emancipation* (Chicago, 1963),* pp. 1–24; Jacobus ten Broek, *The Antislavery Origins of the Fourteenth Amendment* (Berkeley, 1951, reprinted in a paperback ed., New York, 1965, under the title *Equal Under Law*);* Joseph B. James, *The Framing of the Fourteenth Amendment* (Urbana, Ill., 1956);* and William Gillette, *The Right to Vote: Politics and the Passage of the Fifteenth Amendment* (Baltimore, 1965).* Also of value for the Civil War and especially for the Reconstruction period are Hans Trefousse, *The Radical Republicans: Lincoln's Vanguard for Racial Justice* (New York, 1969); Kenneth M. Stampp, *The Era of Reconstruction, 1865–1877* (New York, 1965);* John Hope Franklin, *Reconstruction After the Civil War* (Chicago, 1961);* LaWanda Cox and John H. Cox, *Politics, Principle, & Prejudice, 1865–66: Dilemma of Reconstruction America* (New York, 1963);* William R. Brock, *An American Crisis: Congress and Reconstruction, 1865–1867* (New York, 1963);* and Eric L. McKitrick, *Andrew Johnson and Reconstruction* (Chicago, 1960).*

The persistence of northern racism was a serious hindrance to the real achievement of equal rights. Two fine monographs deal with this issue: Forrest G. Wood, *Black Scare: The Racist Response to Emancipation and Reconstruction* (Berkeley, 1968);* and V. Jacque Voegeli, *Free But Not Equal: The Midwest and the Negro During the Civil War* (Chicago, 1967).* The antiblack actions of white workingmen are described in Williston H. Lofton, "Northern Labor and the Negro During the Civil War," *JNH*, XXXIV (July 1949), 251–73. The New York draft riots were the most violent manifestation of antiblack sentiment during the war; for a recent (though exaggerated) account of the riots, consult James McCague, *The Second Rebellion: The Story of the New York City Draft Riots of 1863* (New York, 1968). Eyewitness accounts of wartime race riots in Detroit and New York are reprinted in James M. McPherson, ed., *Anti-Negro Riots in the North* (New York, 1969). The ambivalent or negative racial attitudes of Presidents Abraham Lincoln, Andrew Johnson, and Ulysses S. Grant are treated in George Sinkler, *The Racial Attitudes of American Presidents: From Abraham Lincoln to Theodore Roosevelt* (Garden City, N.Y., 1971), chs. 2–4.

The counterrevolutionary violence of southern whites during Reconstruction was a major factor in the overthrow of Republican regimes and the destruction of black political power. This violence was carried out by armed paramilitary organizations, the most important and best known of which was the Ku Klux Klan. Stanley F. Horn, *Invisible Empire: The Story of the Ku Klux Klan, 1866–1871* (Boston, 1939), has been superseded by Allen W. Trelease's vividly detailed *White Terror: The Ku Klux Klan Conspiracy and Southern Reconstruction* (New York, 1971). The monographs on Reconstruction in particular states cited in this Part, topics 8 and 9, "Blacks in Southern Reconstruction: South Carolina and Mississippi," and "Blacks in Southern Reconstruction: Virginia, Tennessee, and North Carolina," also discuss the operation of the Klan and similar organizations.

2. Blacks in the Confederacy

Though at least half a million of the Confederacy's 3,500,000 slaves came within Union lines during the war, and many of these fought or worked for the North, the majority of slaves remained in the fields and factories of the South, where their labor was vital to the Confederate war effort. Slaves (and some free blacks) were also employed as cooks, servants, teamsters, and laborers for the Confederate army. Blacks constituted more than one third of the Confederacy's population; without black labor the South would not have been able to wage war.

But slavery was also the Achilles' heel of the Confederacy. Though there were no major insurrections during the war and most slaves remained quietly at work, many blacks were well aware that by 1863 the North was fighting for their freedom while the South was fighting to keep them in slavery. News of the Emancipation Proclamation traveled rapidly via the slaves' grapevine telegraph. Slave restlessness increasingly threatened the South's internal security. Thousands of bondsmen ran away to Union lines whenever they got the chance, where many of them enlisted in the Yankee armies to help deliver the blows that crippled and destroyed the Confederacy.

The best place to begin a study of Confederate blacks, despite its slightly condescending viewpoint, is Bell I. Wiley, *Southern Negroes, 1861–1865* (New Haven, 1938).* The home front and military contributions of blacks in the major theater of war are described by James H. Brewer, *The Confederate Negro: Virginia's Craftsmen and Military Laborers, 1861–1865* (Durham, N.C., 1969). A fine monograph that portrays the important role of slaves in the Confederate arms industry is Charles B. Dew, *Ironmaker to the Confederacy: Joseph R. Anderson and the Tredegar Iron Works* (New Haven, 1966). Several revealing vignettes are provided by aged ex-slaves' recollections of their Civil War experiences recorded by the Federal Writers Project in the 1930s. The best of these recollections have been published in Benjamin A. Botkin, ed., *Lay My Burden Down: A Folk History of Slavery* (Chicago, 1945),* esp. pts. 4 and 5, and Norman R. Yetman, ed., *Life Under the "Peculiar Institution": Selections from the Slave Narrative Collection* (New York, 1970).* Chs. 2 and 12 of Benjamin Quarles, *The Negro in the Civil War* (Boston, 1953),* also contain relevant information.

Several articles are of importance for this topic. Harvey Wish, "Slave Disloyalty under the Confederacy," *JNH*, XXIII (Oct.

1938), 435–50, and Herbert Aptheker, "Notes on Slave Conspiracies in Confederate Mississippi," *ibid.*, XXIX (Jan. 1944), 75–79, document the restlessness of slaves. Bernard H. Nelson, "Legislative Control of the Southern Free Negro, 1861–1865," *Catholic Historical Review*, XXXII (Apr. 1946), 28–46, describes the tightened discipline and control imposed on free blacks during the crisis. For the impressment of black workers for the war effort, see Tinsley Lee Spraggins, "Mobilization of Negro Labor for the Department of Virginia and North Carolina, 1861–1865," *NCHR*, XXIV (Apr. 1947), 160–97. For accounts of the abortive efforts in the final months of the war to raise black regiments for the Confederate army, consult Nathaniel W. Stephenson, "The Question of Arming the Slaves," *AHR*, XVIII (Jan. 1913), 295–308; Charles H. Wesley, "The Employment of Negroes as Soldiers in the Confederate Army," *JNH*, IV (July 1919), 239–53; and ch. 9 of Wiley's *Southern Negroes, 1861–1865*, cited above.

3. Black Soldiers in the Union Army

Nearly 180,000 blacks fought in the Union army and another 25,000 served in the navy. In addition, thousands of freedmen worked as teamsters, cooks, laborers, scouts, and spies for the northern forces. The black fighting men, most of them former slaves, made significant contributions to Union victory, and without question their performance played an important part not only in the achievement of emancipation, but in making equal rights a cornerstone of the Republican Reconstruction policy. It was hard to justify the continued denial of first-class citizenship to a race that had furnished nearly 10 per cent of the Union armed forces and had helped to win the biggest war in the nation's history. Twenty-one blacks received Congressional Medals of Honor, and this fact, coupled with the general performance of black troopers, converted many white skeptics into supporters of racial equality.

The basic study of black soldiers in the Civil War is Dudley T. Cornish, *The Sable Arm: Negro Troops in the Union Army,*

1861–1865 (New York, 1956).* For additional and supplemental information, including accounts by black soldiers and their white officers of combat experiences, see James M. McPherson, ed., *The Negro's Civil War* (New York, 1965),* chs. 10–17. Other studies of value include Benjamin Quarles, *The Negro in the Civil War* (Boston, 1953),* chs. 1–2, 9–10, 13; Benjamin Quarles, *Lincoln and the Negro* (New York, 1962), ch. 7; and Charles H. Wesley and Patricia Romero, *Negro Americans in the Civil War: From Slavery to Citizenship* (2nd ed., rev., New York, 1969), chs. 3–4. Four articles should not be overlooked: Herbert Aptheker, "Negro Casualties in the Civil War," *JNH*, XXXII (Jan. 1947), 10–80, and "The Negro in the Union Navy," *ibid.* (Apr. 1947), 169–200;** Fred Shannon, "The Federal Government and the Negro Soldier, 1861–1865," *ibid.*, XI (Oct. 1926), 563–83; and Albert E. Cowdrey, "Slave into Soldier, The Enlistment by the North of Runaway Slaves," *History Today*, XX (Oct. 1970), 704–15. A classic account of black troops by a white abolitionist officer, well worth reading, is Thomas Wentworth Higginson, *Army Life in a Black Regiment* (Boston, 1869).* Two black veterans of the Union army produced bulky volumes on the contribution of black troopers to the Union cause: George W. Williams, *A History of the Negro Troops in the War of the Rebellion, 1861–1865* (New York, 1888, reprinted New York, 1969), and Joseph T. Wilson, *The Black Phalanx: A History of the Negro Soldiers of the United States in the Wars of 1775–1812 and 1861–65* (Hartford, 1888, reprinted New York, 1968).

The fine record of black troops in the Civil War caused the War Department to incorporate two black infantry regiments and two black cavalry regiments into the twenty-five regiments of the regular army after the war. These black units saw extensive service in the Indian wars of the post-bellum generation. Two good studies of black soldiers in the regular army (whom the Indians called "buffalo soldiers" because of their woolly hair) are William H. Leckie, *The Buffalo Soldiers, A Narrative of the Negro Cavalry in the West* (Norman, Okla., 1967), and Arlen L. Fowler, *The Black Infantry in the West, 1869–1891* (Westport, Conn., 1971).

4. The Black Freedmen

How did southern blacks react to freedom? What were their hopes, their fears, their aspirations? How did they behave? What were the immediate effects of freedom? What adjustments had to be made by both races? What were the long-range implications of emancipation for the masses of blacks? For the South? For the outcome of the Civil War and the forging of a Reconstruction policy? These and many other questions have been raised by the following works, but the answers are still ambiguous, contradictory, or incomplete.

The standard study of the southern blacks as slaves and freedmen during the war, marred by some condescension toward them, is Bell I. Wiley, *Southern Negroes, 1861–1865* (New Haven, 1938);* chs. 1 and 11–15 are especially relevant for this topic. A monograph suffering from a quasi-racist bias is Henderson Donald, *The Negro Freedman: Life Conditions of the American Negro in the Early Years after Emancipation* (New York, 1952). The origins and impact of the "black codes" passed by southern states after the war to control the freedmen are treated in Theodore B. Wilson, *The Black Codes of the South* (University, Ala., 1965). A superb case study of the coming of freedom to the ten thousand slaves on the South Carolina Sea Islands is Willie Lee Rose, *Rehearsal for Reconstruction: The Port Royal Experiment* (Indianapolis, 1964).* Five books on federal administration of freedmen's affairs are important for this topic: John Eaton, *Grant, Lincoln and the Freedmen* (New York, 1907);* George R. Bentley, *A History of the Freedmen's Bureau* (Philadelphia, 1955); William S. McFeely, *Yankee Stepfather: General O. O. Howard and the Freedmen* (New Haven, 1968);* Martin Abbott, *The Freedmen's Bureau in South Carolina, 1865–1872* (Chapel Hill, 1967); and Howard Ashley White, *The Freedmen's Bureau in Louisiana* (Baton Rouge, 1970). See also McFeely's "The Hidden Freedmen: Five Myths in the Reconstruction Era," in James C. Curtis and Lewis L. Gould, eds., *The Black Experience in America: Selected Essays* (Austin, Tex., 1970),* pp. 68–86, and "Unfinished Business: The Freedmen's Bureau and Federal Action in Race Relations," in Nathan I. Huggins, Martin Kilson, and Daniel M. Fox, eds., *Key Issues in the Afro-American Experience*, 2 vols. (New York, 1971),* vol. II, pp. 5–25. John William De Forest, *A Union Officer in the Reconstruction*, ed. by James H. Croushore and David M. Potter (New Haven, 1948), reprints a series of 1868–69 articles by an observant and sometimes unsympathetic official of the Freedmen's Bureau.

The letters, diaries, and memoirs of black and white Yankee teachers who went South to establish schools for the freedmen contain penetrating descriptions of the attitudes of ex-slaves. See especially Ray Allen Billington, ed., *The Journal of Charlotte L. Forten* (New York, 1953),* chs. 5–7; Rupert S. Holland, ed., *Letters and Diary of Laura M. Towne, Written from the Sea Islands of South Carolina, 1862–84* (Cambridge, Mass., 1912, reprinted Westport, Conn., 1970); Elizabeth Ware Pearson, ed., *Letters from Port Royal Written at the Time of the Civil War* (Boston, 1906, reprinted New York, 1969);* Elizabeth Hyde Botume, *First Days Amongst the Contrabands* (Boston, 1893, reprinted New York, 1968); and Henry L. Swint, ed., *Dear Ones at Home: Letters from Contraband Camps* (Nashville, 1966). Pauli Murray, *Proud Shoes: The Story of an American Family* (New York, 1956), based on the diary of a northern black who went south as a teacher of the freedmen, provides some interesting insights on postemancipation black communities in Virginia and North Carolina. A revealing memoir by a young slave who escaped to Union lines early in the war and became a teacher of the freedmen is Susie King Taylor, *Reminiscences of My Life in Camp with the 33rd United States Colored Troops* (Boston, 1902, reprinted New York, 1968). Interviews with ex-slaves by the Federal Writers Project in the 1930s produced many fascinating accounts of how freedom came to the slaves; see Benjamin A. Botkin, ed., *Lay My Burden Down: A Folk History of Slavery* (Chicago, 1945),* esp. pts. 4 and 5, and Norman R. Yetman, ed., *Life Under the "Peculiar Institution": Selections from the Slave Narrative Collection* (New York, 1970).* Analyses of the coming of freedom in three key states are provided by Vernon L. Wharton, *The Negro in Mississippi, 1865–1890* (Chapel Hill, 1947),* chs. 1–2; Joel Williamson, *After Slavery: The Negro in*

South Carolina During Reconstruction, 1861–1877 (Chapel Hill, 1965),* chs. 1–3; and Joe M. Richardson, *The Negro in the Reconstruction of Florida, 1865–1877* (Tallahassee, Fla., 1965), chs. 2–6. See also James M. McPherson, ed., *The Negro's Civil War* (New York, 1965),* chs. 4, 8, 9, 20, and 22; Benjamin Quarles, *The Negro in the Civil War* (Boston, 1953),* chs. 3–5, 14; Joel Williamson, "Black Self-Assertion Before and After Emancipation," in Huggins, Kilson, and Fox, eds., *Key Issues in the Afro-American Experience*, vol. I, pp. 213–39, cited above; Robert H. Abzug, "The Black Family During Reconstruction," *ibid.*, vol. II, pp. 26–41; and Leon F. Litwack, "Free at Last," in Tamara K. Hareven, ed., *Anonymous Americans: Explorations in 19th Century Social History* (Englewood Cliffs, N.J., 1971),* pp. 131–71.

5. Freedmen's Education During the Civil War and Reconstruction

Slaves and free blacks in the South had made some efforts to educate themselves before the Civil War (see Carter G. Woodson, *The Education of the Negro Prior to 1861* [New York, 1915, reprinted New York, 1968]), but because of laws against the teaching of slaves (and in some states free blacks) to read and write, at least half of the free blacks and 90 per cent of the slaves were illiterate in 1861. During and after the war, dozens of freedmen's aid and missionary societies were organized in the North to found schools and send teachers to the freed slaves. This outpouring of missionary idealism constituted an early version of the Peace Corps and VISTA combined and was one of the most heroic stories of the Civil War era. Out of these freedmen's schools (financed by northern philanthropy, the Freedmen's Bureau, and the painfully accumulated savings of blacks themselves) grew the South's public school system for blacks and the best black colleges, headed by Howard, Fisk, and Atlanta universities. While the accomplishments of the freedmen's education movement were impressive, the federal government and the southern states never committed enough resources to carry through the crash program that was needed, and after nearly two decades of effort, 70 per cent of the southern blacks were still illiterate in 1880. Moreover, the freedmen's aid societies often became embroiled in denominational and bureaucratic rivalries that diminished their effectiveness. Nevertheless the schools founded by northern missionaries educated the black leaders of future generations and laid the foundations for Negro education in the South.

A compact factual history of the beginnings of freedmen's education can be found in Julius H. Parmelee, "Freedmen's Aid Societies, 1861–1871," in *Negro Education: A Study of the Private and Higher Schools for Colored People in the United States,* ed. by Thomas Jesse Jones for the Bureau of Education, *Bulletin* no. 38 (1916), 2 vols. (Washington, 1917, reprinted in 1 vol., New York, 1969), vol. I, pp. 268–95. James M. McPherson, *The Struggle for Equality: Abolitionists and the Negro in the Civil War and Reconstruction* (Princeton, 1964),* chs. 7, 14, treats the role of abolitionists in freedmen's education, and his *The Negro's Civil War* (New York, 1965),* chs. 8–9, emphasizes the enterprise of blacks themselves. An important monograph, tinged with a prosouthern bias, is Henry L. Swint, *The Northern Teacher in the South, 1862–1870* (Nashville, 1941). Augustus F. Beard, *A Crusade of Brotherhood: A History of the American Missionary Association* (Boston, 1909, reprinted New York, 1969), is a eulogistic account of the most important of the religious educational associations. George R. Bentley, *A History of the Freedmen's Bureau* (Philadelphia, 1955), esp. chs. 12–14, analyzes the bureau's important role in freedmen's education. Bell I. Wiley, *Southern Negroes, 1861–1865* (New Haven, 1938),* ch. 14, describes wartime education of the freedmen. Two articles of importance for this topic are Ira V. Brown, "Lyman Abbott and Freedmen's Aid, 1865–1869," *JSH,* XV (Feb. 1949), 22–38, and Richard B. Drake, "Freedmen's Aid Societies and Sectional Compromise," *ibid.,* XXIX (May 1963), 175–86.

The most intensive and best-documented effort to educate the freedmen was carried out on the South Carolina Sea Islands. A fine study of this enterprise is Willie Lee Rose, *Rehearsal for Reconstruction: The Port Royal Experiment* (Indianapolis, 1964).* See also the memoirs or journals of Botume, Forten, Towne, and Pearson plus the books by Swint and Murray, cited in the previous topic, "The Black Freedmen." A compact description of the origins of public education for blacks in the South can be found in ch. 15 of W. E. B. Du Bois, *Black Reconstruction . . . in America, 1860–1880* (New York, 1935).* Horace Mann Bond, *The Education of the Negro in the American Social Order* (2nd ed., rev., New York, 1966), chs. 1–4, treats the freedmen's aid movement and the rise of public education during the war and Reconstruction, as does Henry Allen Bullock, *A History of Negro Education in the South* (Cambridge, Mass., 1967),* chs. 1, 2. The beginnings of higher education for blacks during this period are described by Dwight O. W. Holmes, *The Evolution of the Negro College* (New York, 1934, reprinted New York, 1969), esp. chs. 3–5, and Willard Range, *The Rise and Progress of Negro Colleges in Georgia, 1865–1949* (Athens, Ga., 1951), ch. 1.

The missionary freedmen's schools were open to both races, though in practice only a handful of whites ever attended them; the public schools, outside of a few in New Orleans during the 1870s, were segregated from the beginning in the South. For three articles on this subject, see John Hope Franklin, "Jim Crow Goes to School: The Genesis of Legal Segregation in Southern Schools," SAQ, LVIII (Spring 1959), 225–35; Alfred H. Kelly, "The Congressional Controversy over School Segregation, 1867–1875," AHR, LXIV (Apr. 1959), 537–63;** and Louis R. Harlan, "Desegregation in New Orleans Public Schools During Reconstruction," *ibid.*, LXVII (Apr. 1962), 663–75.**

6. "40 Acres and a Mule": The Failure of Land Reform

Most emancipated slaves owned little more than the clothes on their backs when freedom came. Unless they received some kind of massive economic assistance it was clear they would remain an economically subordinate class, dependent on whites for employment. Several black leaders, radical Republicans, and abolitionists urged the confiscation of plantations owned by "rebels" and their redistribution in 40-acre plots among the freedmen.

This was the origin of the freed slaves' hope for "40 acres and a mule," which was no delusion of ignorant minds, but a concrete proposal for agrarian reform. The Freedmen's Bureau was charged with the responsibility for settling emancipated slaves on abandoned or confiscated plantations. Several thousand families were settled on such land, but in the end most of the property was returned to its Confederate owners; the blacks were evicted and forced to become sharecroppers or wage earners. Congress did adopt piecemeal legislation designed to facilitate the freedmen's acquisition of land, but these provisions were far too little and too late. There was no major program of agrarian reform. Most blacks became wage earners, sharecroppers, or tenant farmers, rather than independent, landowning farmers. The South was not reconstructed economically, and consequently political reconstruction rested on an unstable foundation.

The best introduction to the land question is LaWanda Cox, "The Promise of Land for the Freedmen," MVHR, XLV (Dec. 1958), 413–40.** Additional background and information is provided by James M. McPherson, The Struggle for Equality: Abolitionists and the Negro in the Civil War and Reconstruction (Princeton, 1964),* pp. 246–59, 407–16. For the role of the Freedmen's Bureau in this matter, see William S. McFeely, Yankee Stepfather: General O. O. Howard and the Freedmen (New Haven, 1968),* esp. chs. 4–8, and Martin Abbott, "Free Land, Free Labor, and the Freedmen's Bureau," Agricultural History, XXX (Oct. 1956), 150–56.** Christie Farnham Pope, "Southern Homesteads for Negroes," ibid., XLIV (Apr. 1970), 201–12, chronicles the failure of the Southern Homestead Act of 1866 to provide freedmen with good land.

The triumph and tragedy of agrarian reform were best illustrated by the events on the South Carolina Sea Islands during and after the war; for this story, see Edwin D. Hoffman, "From Slavery to Self-Reliance," JNH, XLI (Jan. 1956), 8–42; Willie Lee Rose, Rehearsal for Reconstruction: The Port Royal Experiment (Indianapolis, 1964),* chs. 7, 10, 11; and Joel Williamson, After Slavery: The Negro in South Carolina During Reconstruction, 1861–1877 (Chapel Hill, 1965),* ch. 2. In South Carolina the Reconstruction government created a land commission to help the freedmen obtain property. For the ill-starred career of this commission, see ch. 5 of Williamson's study, cited above, plus Carol K. Rothrock Bleser, *The Promised Land: The History of the South Carolina Land Commission, 1869–1890* (Columbia, S.C., 1969).

Marxist historians have strongly emphasized the importance of the failure of agrarian reform. For some examples, see Manuel Gottlieb, "The Land Question in Georgia During Reconstruction," *Science and Society*, III (Summer 1939), 356–88; James S. Allen, *Reconstruction: The Battle for Democracy 1865–1876* (New York, 1937),* ch. 2; and W. E. B. Du Bois, *Black Reconstruction . . . in America, 1860–1880* (New York, 1935),* esp. chs. 8–10, 14.

7. Origins of Legal Equality: The Fourteenth and Fifteenth Amendments

The Fourteenth Amendment conferred equal citizenship upon the freedmen; the Fifteenth Amendment prohibited states from denying blacks the right to vote. These two Reconstruction amendments were more laxly enforced and widely evaded than any other part of the Constitution for three quarters of a century, but in the 1950s and 1960s they have become the basis for Supreme Court decisions and civil rights/voting rights legislation that have laid the basis for the black revolution of our own times. The processes by which these amendments were adopted afford fascinating glimpses into the complexities of political history during Reconstruction, with its cross-pressures of idealism, partisanship, and expediency. The rights of the freedmen often became the pawn of factional political battles and the Fourteenth and Fifteenth Amendments were weaker than the sweeping commitment to civil and political equality demanded by radicals, but these amendments were nevertheless major achievements in the struggle for black rights. The works cited in this topic deal with the origins, passage, and enforcement of the amendments during Reconstruction; for the legal interpretations of the amendments in subsequent decades, see Part VI, topic 5, "The Supreme Court and Negro Rights, 1873–1915."

The principles of the Fourteenth and Fifteenth Amendments were rooted in the ideology of the abolitionist movement and of radical Republicanism. The following studies treat the background as well as the adoption of the amendments: Jacobus ten Broek, *The Antislavery Origins of the Fourteenth Amendment* (Berkeley, 1951, retitled in paperback ed. *Equal Under Law*, New York, 1965);* Robert J. Harris, *The Quest for Equality: The Constitution, Congress and the Supreme Court* (Baton Rouge, 1960), chs. 1–2; James M. McPherson, *The Struggle for Equality: Abolitionists and the Negro in the Civil War and Reconstruction* (Princeton, 1964),* esp. chs. 10, 14–15, 18; and Hans L. Trefousse, *The Radical Republicans: Lincoln's Vanguard for Racial Justice* (New York, 1969), esp. chs. 10–13. Two important monographs are Joseph B. James, *The Framing of the Fourteenth Amendment* (Urbana, Ill., 1956),* and William Gillette, *The Right to Vote: Politics and the Passage of the Fifteenth Amendment* (Baltimore, 1965).* See also Eric McKitrick, *Andrew Johnson and Reconstruction* (Chicago, 1960),* ch. 11, and William R. Brock, *An American Crisis: Congress and Reconstruction, 1865–1867* (New York, 1963),* chs. 5–8.

For a sophisticated analysis of the political problems involved in the congressional passage of the amendments, consult LaWanda and John Cox, "Negro Suffrage and Republican Politics: The Problem of Motivation in Reconstruction Historiography," *JSH*, XXXIII (Aug. 1967), 303–30.** The opposition of many northern whites to Negro suffrage in their own states was an important stumbling block to adoption of the Fifteenth Amendment; for a discussion, see Leslie H. Fishel, Jr., "Northern Prejudice and Negro Suffrage, 1865–1870," *JNH*, XXXIX (Jan. 1954), 8–26. Two articles on the enforcement of the Fifteenth Amendment in the South are of value: Everette Swinney, "Enforcing the Fifteenth Amendment, 1870–1877," *JSH*, XXVIII (May 1964), 202–18,** and William Gillette, "Anatomy of a Failure: Federal Enforcement of the Right to Vote in the Border States During Reconstruction," in Richard O. Curry, ed., *Radicalism, Racism, and Party Realignment: The Border States During Reconstruction* (Baltimore, 1969), pp. 265–304.

The question whether the "equal protection" and "privileges and immunities" clauses of the Fourteenth Amendment were intended to prohibit segregation in public facilities, especially schools, was much debated in the 1870s and the 1950s. The federal Civil Rights Act of 1875 (declared unconstitutional in 1883) was based on the Fourteenth Amendment; for the background and passage of this act, see Alfred H. Kelly, "The Congressional Controversy over School Segregation, 1867–1875," AHR, LXIV (Apr. 1959), 537–63,** and James M. McPherson, "Abolitionists and the Civil Rights Act of 1875," JAH, LII (Dec. 1965), 493–510.** When the question of public school segregation came before the Supreme Court in the 1950s, legal historians tried to discover the original intent and understanding of the Fourteenth Amendment on this matter; for a sample of the literature, see J. D. Hyman, "Segregation and the Fourteenth Amendment," Vanderbilt Law Review, IV (Apr. 1951), 555–73; Howard J. Graham, "The 14th Amendment and School Segregation," Buffalo Law Review, III (1953), 1–24; Alexander M. Bickel, "The Original Understanding and the Segregation Decision," Harvard Law Review, LXIX (July 1955), 1–65; Alfred H. Kelly, "The Fourteenth Amendment Reconsidered: The Segregation Question," Michigan Law Review, LIV (June 1956), 1049–86; and John P. Frank and Robert Mauro, "The Original Understanding of 'Equal Protection of the Law,'" Columbia Law Review, L (Jan. 1950), 131–69. Howard Graham has reprinted his important articles on the origins and interpretation of the Fourteenth Amendment in a volume entitled Everyman's Constitution: Historical Essays on the Fourteenth Amendment, the "Conspiracy Theory," and American Constitutionalism (Madison, 1968).

8. Blacks in Southern Reconstruction: South Carolina and Mississippi

What was the Afro-American's role in Reconstruction? Did blacks play an active leadership part in Reconstruction politics or were they merely the passive pawns of white politicians? Were black politicians corrupt and incompetent? Were black voters ignorant and easily exploited? What was the nature of the Republican administrations in southern states during Reconstruction? What changes in the black man's status in the South were wrought by the Reconstruction experience? Tentative answers to some of these questions, plus an outline of problems that require further research, are suggested by John Hope Franklin, "Reconstruction and the Negro," and August Meier, "Comment on John Hope Franklin's Paper," in Harold M. Hyman, ed., *New Frontiers of the American Reconstruction* (Urbana, Ill., 1966), pp. 59–86. An important basic study is Robert Cruden, *The Negro in Reconstruction* (Englewood Cliffs, N.J., 1969).*

South Carolina and Mississippi were the only two states with significant black voting majorities during Reconstruction; not surprisingly, these states produced the most active and aggressive black political leadership. Two valuable monographs are Joel Williamson, *After Slavery: The Negro in South Carolina During Reconstruction, 1861–1877* (Chapel Hill, 1965),* and Vernon Lane Wharton, *The Negro in Mississippi, 1865–1890* (Chapel Hill, 1947).* Wharton's study is marred by a slightly condescending view toward blacks and by a residue of southern hostility to Reconstruction. A calm and fact-filled account of South Carolina by a black scholar is provided by Alrutheus A. Taylor, *The Negro in South Carolina During the Reconstruction* (Washington, 1924, reprinted New York, 1970). Two specialized monographs of value are Martin Abbott, *The Freedmen's Bureau in South Carolina, 1865–1872* (Chapel Hill, 1967), and Otis Singletary, *Negro Militia and Reconstruction* (Austin, Tex., 1957),* esp. chs. 3, 6, and 9. One of the leading black politicians in South Carolina was Robert Smalls, who is treated in Okon E. Uya, *From Slavery to Public Service: Robert Smalls, 1839–1915* (New York, 1971).*

For the classic indictment of "corruption and misgovernment" in South Carolina, see James Shepherd Pike, *The Prostrate State: South Carolina Under Negro Government* (New York, 1874),* which should be read in conjunction with Robert Durden, *James Shepherd Pike: Republicanism and the American Negro, 1850–1882* (Durham, N.C., 1957). An interesting defense of Reconstruction by a black man who had served as speaker of the Mississippi House of Representatives and as a member of Congress in the 1870s is John R. Lynch, *The Facts of Reconstruction* (New York, 1913).* See also Lynch's autobiography, ed. by John Hope Franklin, *Reminiscences of an Active Life* (Chicago, 1970). A vivid and dramatic (sometimes melodramatic) account of Reconstruction by Lerone Bennett, *Black Power U.S.A.: The Human Side of Reconstruction, 1867–1877* (Chicago, 1967),* concentrates on South Carolina and Mississippi; see esp. chs. 3–4 and 7–9.

South Carolina sent six black congressmen to Washington (more than any other state), and Mississippi elected one black congressman and the only two black senators from the South. A detailed study of blacks in Congress is Samuel Denny Smith, *The Negro in Congress, 1870–1901* (Chapel Hill, 1940), which is blemished by an anti-Reconstruction bias. A more sympathetic interpretation is found in Alrutheus A. Taylor, "Negro Congressmen a Generation After," *JNH*, VII (Apr. 1922), 127–71. For material on blacks who served in active political capacities, see Monroe N. Work, "Some Negro Members of Reconstruction Conventions and Legislatures and Members of Congress," *JNH*, V (Jan. 1920), 63–119. Other articles of interest include Herbert Aptheker, "South Carolina Negro Conventions, 1865," *ibid.*, XXXI (Jan. 1946), 91–97; Robert H. Woody, "Jonathan J. Wright, Associate Justice of the Supreme Court of South Carolina," *ibid.*, XVIII (Apr. 1933), 114–31; and Edward F. Sweat, "Francis L. Cardozo: Profile of Integrity in Reconstruction Politics," *ibid.*, XLVI (Oct. 1961), 217–32.**

9. Blacks in Southern Reconstruction: Virginia, Tennessee, and North Carolina

How did blacks fare during Reconstruction in three states of the upper South with substantial white majorities? How did these states compare with the predominantly black states, South Carolina and Mississippi, which were covered in the previous topic? Did the early restoration of the three upper South states to white

Democratic rule reduce violence and corruption? Was the black man the ultimate gainer or loser by being quickly shut out of substantial political power in these three states, while he retained some measure of power in the deep South several years longer?

For general background and comparison, see the titles cited in the first paragraph of the previous topic, plus Lerone Bennett, *Black Power U.S.A.: The Human Side of Reconstruction, 1867–1877* (Chicago, 1967),* ch. 6. The basic monograph on Virginia is Alrutheus A. Taylor, *The Negro in the Reconstruction of Virginia* (Washington, 1926, reprinted New York, 1970). The conservative white viewpoint is reflected in Hamilton J. Eckenrode, *The Political History of Virginia During the Reconstruction* (Baltimore, 1904). Luther P. Jackson, *Negro Officeholders in Virginia, 1865–1895* (Norfolk, Va., 1946), contains information on black political leaders. For the aftermath of Reconstruction, see Charles E. Wynes, *Race Relations in Virginia, 1870–1902* (Charlottesville, Va., 1961). The most useful study of Tennessee is Alrutheus A. Taylor, *The Negro in Tennessee, 1865–1880* (Washington, 1941). Thomas B. Alexander's *Political Reconstruction in Tennessee* (Nashville, 1950) should also be consulted.

The old-fashioned, anti-Negro interpretation of Reconstruction in North Carolina is set forth by J. G. de Roulhac Hamilton, *Reconstruction in North Carolina* (Raleigh, N.C., 1906). For a revisionist corrective, with emphasis on the role of the black man and his white allies, see Otto H. Olsen, *Carpetbagger's Crusade: The Life of Albion Winegar Tourgée* (Baltimore, 1965), chs. 3–17. A fine study of Wilmington, North Carolina, and the surrounding area is William McKee Evans, *Ballots and Fence Rails: Reconstruction on the Lower Cape Fear* (Chapel Hill, 1967). For post-Reconstruction developments in North Carolina, consult Frenise Logan, *The Negro in North Carolina, 1876–1894* (Chapel Hill, 1964). See also Leonard Bernstein, "The Participation of Negro Delegates in the Constitutional Convention of 1868 in North Carolina," *JNH*, XXV (Oct. 1940), 391–409.

For black political leaders from these three states, see the items by Alrutheus A. Taylor, Monroe Work, and Samuel D. Smith cited in the preceding topic, "Blacks in Southern Reconstruction: South Carolina and Mississippi."

10. The Abandonment and Aftermath of Reconstruction

In 1877 a Republican administration withdrew the last federal troops from the South, virtually bringing to an end the national government's effort to enforce the hard-won gains of Reconstruction. Republican governments had been overthrown in one southern state after another, until by 1877 there were only two Republican governors still in office in the South, and they were driven out after the troops were withdrawn. Promises were extracted from southern leaders that the freedmen's rights would be respected by white Democrats in the South, and President Rutherford B. Hayes, who withdrew the troops, did not believe his action to be an abandonment of the freedmen. But in effect it was precisely that, and during the next generation southern blacks were gradually deprived of their right to vote, subjected to the humiliations of "Jim Crow" laws, and reduced to second-class citizenship. The Republicans controlled the presidency during most of this period, and there was considerable debate within the party over the southern policy it should pursue. Some Republicans urged a partial return to the Reconstruction methods of enforcing black rights, but in the end they were able to do little more than "wave the bloody shirt" occasionally at election time. Northern public opinion, the Supreme Court, and most political leaders were opposed to a revival of Reconstruction, which was widely believed to have been a failure. (For a review of the literature on the Supreme Court, see Part VI, topic 5, "The Supreme Court and Negro Rights, 1873–1915.")

The Reconstruction governments in the South were overturned by a combination of intimidation, violence, and the weakness and poor leadership of the governments themselves. For a concise account, see Robert Cruden, *The Negro in Reconstruction* (Englewood Cliffs, N.J., 1969),* chs. 5–6. Lerone Bennett, *Black Power U.S.A.: The Human Side of Reconstruction, 1867–1877* (Chicago, 1967),* chs. 8–9, presents a vivid description of the overthrow and abandonment of Reconstruction. More sober treatments of three key states can be found in Vernon Lane Wharton, *The Negro in Mississippi, 1865–1890* (Chapel Hill, 1947),* chs. 13–14; Joel Williamson, *After Slavery: The Negro in South Carolina During Reconstruction* (Chapel Hill, 1965),* ch. 13; George B. Tindall, *South Carolina Negroes, 1877–1900* (Columbia, S.C., 1952),* chs. 2–3; and Joe M. Richardson, *The Negro in the Reconstruction of Florida, 1865–1877* (Tallahassee, 1965), ch. 16.

The two basic studies of the northern (and particularly the Republican) retreat from Reconstruction are Vincent De Santis, *Republicans Face the Southern Question, 1877–1897* (Baltimore, 1959), and Stanley P. Hirshson, *Farewell to the Bloody Shirt: Northern Republicans and the Southern Negro, 1877–1893* (Bloomington, Ind., 1962).* See also Patrick W. Riddleberger, "The Radicals' Abandonment of the Negro During Reconstruction," *JNH*, XLV (Apr. 1960), 88–102.** The disputed election of 1876 and the Compromise of 1877 that resolved the dispute played a key part in the Republican abandonment of Reconstruction; for an intricate account of the 1877 compromise, which perhaps overemphasizes economic factors, see C. Vann Woodward, *Reunion and Reaction: The Compromise of 1877 and the End of Reconstruction* (Boston, 1951).* Paul Buck, *The Road to Reunion, 1865–1900* (Boston, 1937),* traces the growing sentiment of reconciliation between North and South which also played a part in the retreat from Reconstruction. Another book that discusses the increasingly indifferent or hostile attitude of political parties and public opinion toward the black man during this period is Rayford W. Logan, *The Negro in American Life and Thought: The Nadir, 1877–1901* (New York, 1954), which was published in a revised and enlarged paperback edition under the title *The Betrayal of the Negro: From Rutherford B. Hayes to Woodrow Wilson* (New York, 1965).* A study of the racial attitudes of the Presidents during the generation after Reconstruction is George Sinkler, *The Racial Attitudes of American Presidents: From Abraham Lincoln to Theodore Roosevelt* (Garden City, N.Y., 1971), chs. 5–8.

Three articles dealing with facets of the Compromise of 1877, its aftermath, and the attempt to pass a voting rights act in 1890 are James M. McPherson, "Coercion or Conciliation: Abolitionists Debate President Hayes's Southern Policy," *New England Quarterly*, XXXIX (Dec. 1966), 474–97, and "The Antislavery Legacy: From Reconstruction to the NAACP," in Barton J. Bernstein, ed., *Towards a New Past* (New York, 1968),* pp. 126–57; and Richard E. Welch, Jr., "The Federal Elections Bill of 1890: Postscripts and Prelude," *JAH*, LII (Dec. 1965), 511–26.

11. Marxist Historians on Blacks in the Civil War and Reconstruction

As America's most submerged proletariat, the black man has received much attention from Marxist historians. The potentially revolutionary upheaval of Civil War, emancipation, and Reconstruction is a natural for Marxian analysis. Three classic accounts are Herbert Aptheker's brief *The Negro in the Civil War* (New York, 1938); James S. Allen's tightly organized *Reconstruction: The Battle for Democracy 1865–1876* (New York, 1937);* and W. E. B. Du Bois's sprawling *Black Reconstruction . . . in America, 1860–1880* (New York, 1935).* See also George O. Virtue, "Marxian Interpretations of the Civil War," *Nebraska History*, XXX (Mar. 1949), 19–50. The closest thing to an official American Communist interpretation can be found in William Z. Foster, *The Negro People in American History* (New York, 1954),* chs. 20–32. A Marxian political sociologist, Barrington Moore, Jr., has provided a somewhat different interpretation in his *Social Origins of Dictatorship and Democracy: Lord and Peasant in the Making of the Modern World* (Boston, 1966),* ch. 3, "The American Civil War: The Last Capitalist Revolution."

Karl Marx and Friedrich Engels followed the American Civil War from Europe with close attention and wrote many articles on the subject for the New York *Tribune* and the Vienna *Presse*. These articles and their personal correspondence, which included many references to blacks and emancipation, have been reprinted in Richard Enmale, ed., *The Civil War in the United States* (New York, 1937).* For a collection of documents (with commentaries) on black people in the Civil War and Reconstruction years edited by a prominent Marxist historian, see Herbert Aptheker, ed., *A Documentary History of the Negro People in the United States* (New York, 1951),* pp. 459–644.

For a fascinating debate between Marxists with sharply differing interpretations of black history and of the role of blacks in the Civil War and Reconstruction, see Eugene D. Genovese, "The Legacy of Slavery and the Roots of Black Nationalism," with comments by Herbert Aptheker, C. Vann Woodward, Frank Kofsky, and a reply by Genovese, in *Studies on the Left*, VI (Nov.–Dec. 1966), 3–65. The key pages for the war and Reconstruction are 11–14, 32–33, 40, 63–64.

Marxist historians have viewed the frustration of efforts for land reform in the South as the greatest failure of Reconstruction. For Marxian and non-Marxian discussions of this issue, see the works cited in this Part under topic 6, "40 Acres and a Mule: The Failure of Land Reform." Also of value, for those who read Russian, is a fascinating study by a Soviet historian, Robert F. Ivanov, *The Struggles of Negroes for Land and Freedom in the Southern U.S.A., 1865–1877* (Moscow, 1958). Finally, for those who can read Italian, the Marxist historian Raimondo Luraghi has written a massive study of the American Civil War, *Storia della guerra civile Americana* (Turin, 1966), which contains analyses of slavery and emancipation, esp. pt. 3, ch. 16.

PART VI

YEARS OF REACTION AND ADJUSTMENT, 1877–1915

1. Nullification of the Fifteenth Amendment: The Disfranchisement Movement

In recent years it has been common to read newspaper stories stating that Georgia (or Mississippi, Alabama, North Carolina, etc.) has just elected its first black representative to the state legislature (or sheriff, city councilman, etc.) since Reconstruction. The assumption prevails that the end of Reconstruction brought an abrupt and complete termination of black participation in southern politics. Such an assumption is misleading. While it is true that there was a distinct decline in black voting and officeholding after 1877, especially in the deep South where whites took desperate steps to cripple or destroy the political power of the black majority, blacks continued to vote in substantial numbers and even to hold office in many parts of the South for two decades after Reconstruction. As C. Vann Woodward points out in *The Strange Career of Jim Crow* (New York, 1955, rev. ed., 1966),* chs. 2–3, the elimination of blacks from southern politics took place gradually, by fits and starts, in the last quarter of the century, reaching its climax in the disfranchisement movement of the late 1890s and early 1900s.

Between 1890 and 1908, seven southern states disfranchised all but a handful of black voters by means of literacy or property qualifications (coupled with "understanding" and "grandfather" clauses to enable illiterate, propertyless whites to retain the ballot), poll taxes, and the white primary, while four additional states disfranchised most of their black voters by the poll tax and the white primary. The meaning of "disfranchisement" can be understood by a glance at the registration statistics of Louisiana: Before the adoption of its new constitution in 1898, there were 130,444 registered black voters; after the constitution went into effect, black voters numbered 5,320.

Disfranchisement was produced by the crosscurrents of many

pressures, which sometimes conflicted with each other, and it is unsafe to generalize about the South as a whole, for the pressures were often different in each state. In some states the leaders of the "redneck" whites took the lead in depriving blacks of voting rights; in other states, old-regime conservatives favored the imposition of restrictions that would limit the suffrage to the propertied and the educated. In some states the Populists, who sought black political allies, resisted disfranchisement; in others, they welcomed it, partly because the black vote had been used against them. Whatever the immediate motives or causes, it is safe to say that the overriding rationale for the disfranchisement movement was the desire to reduce the black man to political impotency and to eliminate blacks as an active issue in politics.

For useful brief summaries of disfranchisement, consult the following: C. Vann Woodward, *Origins of the New South, 1877–1913* (Baton Rouge, 1951),* ch. 12, and *The Strange Career of Jim Crow,* ch. 3; Paul Lewinson, *Race, Class, and Party: A History of Negro Suffrage and White Politics in the South* (New York, 1932),* chs. 4–6; William F. Nowlin, *The Negro in American National Politics* (Boston, 1931), chs. 1, 3–6; Claude H. Nolen, *The Negro's Image in the South: The Anatomy of White Supremacy* (Lexington, Ky., 1967),* chs. 6–7; and V. O. Key, *Southern Politics in State and Nation* (New York, 1949),* pt. 5.

The following state studies deal with black voting after Reconstruction and with the accomplishment of disfranchisement: Vernon Lane Wharton, *The Negro in Mississippi, 1865–1890* (Chapel Hill, 1947),* ch. 14; Albert D. Kirwan, *Revolt of the Rednecks, Mississippi Politics, 1876–1925* (Lexington, Ky., 1951),* chs. 6–7; William A. Mabry, "Disfranchisement of the Negro in Mississippi," *JSH,* IV (Aug. 1938), 318–33; George B. Tindall, "The Campaign for the Disfranchisement of Negroes in South Carolina," *ibid.,* XV (May 1949), 212–34,** "The Question of Race in the South Carolina Constitutional Convention of 1895," *JNH,* XXXVII (July 1952), 277–303, and *South Carolina Negroes, 1877–1900* (Columbia, S.C., 1952),* chs. 4–5; William A. Mabry, "Ben Tillman Disfranchised the Negro," *SAQ,* XXXVII (Apr. 1938), 170–83; Francis B. Simkins, *Pitchfork Ben Tillman: South Carolinian* (Baton Rouge, 1944),* ch. 20; William Ivy Hair, *Bourbonism and Agrarian Protest: Louisiana Poli-*

tics, 1877–1900 (Baton Rouge, 1970); William A. Mabry, "Louisiana Politics and the Grandfather Clause," *NCHR*, XIII (Oct. 1936), 290–310, *The Negro in North Carolina Politics Since Reconstruction* (Durham, N.C., 1940), and "Negro Suffrage and Fusion Rule in North Carolina," *NCHR*, XII (Apr. 1935), 79–102; Frenise Logan, *The Negro in North Carolina, 1876–1894* (Chapel Hill, 1964), pt. 1; Helen G. Edmonds, *The Negro and Fusion Politics in North Carolina, 1894–1901* (Chapel Hill, 1951); Sheldon Hackney, *Populism to Progressivism in Alabama* (Princeton, 1969), chs. 8–10; Charles E. Wynes, *Race Relations in Virginia, 1870–1902* (Charlottesville, Va., 1961), chs. 1–4; and Lawrence D. Rice, *The Negro in Texas, 1874–1900* (Baton Rouge, 1971). One state in which the Democratic party tried but failed to disfranchise blacks was Maryland; there the black vote was an important element in sustaining a Republican party that was strong enough to defeat disfranchisement. For the Maryland story, see Margaret Law Callcott, *The Negro in Maryland Politics, 1870–1912* (Baltimore, 1969).

For the ambivalent role of the Populists in the disfranchisement movement, see, in addition to the studies by Woodward, Edmonds, and Hackney cited above, the following: C. Vann Woodward, "Tom Watson and the Negro in Agrarian Politics," *JSH*, IV (Feb. 1938), 14–33; Jack Abramowitz, "The Negro and the Populist Movement," *JNH*, XXXVIII (July 1953), 257–89,** and "The Negro in the Agrarian Revolt," *Agricultural History*, XXIV (Apr. 1950), 89–95; J. H. Taylor, "Populism and Disfranchisement in Alabama," *JNH*, XXXIV (Oct. 1949), 410–27; Herbert Shapiro, "The Populists and the Negro: A Reconsideration," in August Meier and Elliott Rudwick, eds., *The Making of Black America*, 2 vols. (New York, 1969),* vol. II, pp. 27–36;** Robert Saunders, "Southern Populists and the Negro, 1893–1905," *JNH*, LIV (July 1969), 240–61, and "The Transformation of Tom Watson, 1894–95," *Georgia Historical Quarterly*, LIV (Fall 1970), 339–54; and William W. Rogers, *The One-Gallused Rebellion: Agrarianism in Alabama, 1865–1896* (Baton Rouge, 1970).

2. The Origins of Jim Crow

As in the case of disfranchisement, legalized segregation in southern public facilities came in the 1890s and early 1900s rather than immediately after Reconstruction. But the nature and extent of segregation before the 1890s has become a subject of disagreement among historians. In his classic study, *The Strange Career of Jim Crow* (New York, 1955, rev. ed., 1966),* esp. chs. 1–3, C. Vann Woodward argues that during the 1870s and 1880s there was flexibility in race relations, that some public facilities (especially trains and streetcars) in some parts of the South were integrated, and that not until the two decades after 1890 did racial caste lines become rigid and universally enforced. Several historians have taken issue with Woodward's thesis. The most outspoken critic has been Joel Williamson; see his *After Slavery: The Negro in South Carolina During Reconstruction, 1861–1877* (Chapel Hill, 1965),* ch. 10, and the introduction to the anthology he edited, *The Origins of Segregation* (Boston, 1968).* Williamson argues that the segregation of nearly all facilities was widespread from the beginning of Reconstruction and that exceptions were too insignificant to matter. For Williamson, the Jim Crow legislation of the late nineteenth and early twentieth centuries merely codified a system of attitudes and customs that had always existed in the South.

As usual, the truth is ambiguous and difficult to determine. Most historians who have written on the subject agree with Woodward that there was a definite hardening of white attitudes and a corresponding intensification of discrimination and segregation after 1890 (which was accompanied by a high lynching rate and constitutional disfranchisement); at the same time it is clear that integrated public facilities or social relationships were the exception rather than the rule before 1890. Several points of view and a considerable amount of factual information are presented in Williamson's anthology. The books by George B. Tindall, Vernon Lane Wharton, and Charles E. Wynes from which excerpts are published in the anthology should also be consulted.

Woodward has refined his argument and suggested new ways of looking at the problem in an essay entitled "The Strange Career of a Historical Controversy," in his *American Counterpoint: Slavery and Race in the North-South Dialogue* (Boston, 1971),* pp. 234–60. Other studies of value are Frenise Logan, *The Negro in North Carolina, 1876–1894* (Chapel Hill, 1964), intro. and ch. 17; Claude F. Nolen, *The Negro's Image in the South: The Anatomy of White Supremacy* (Lexington, Ky., 1967);* Lawrence J. Friedman, *The White Savage: Racial Fantasies in the Postbellum South* (Englewood Cliffs, N.J., 1970);* Clarence A. Bacote, "Some Aspects of Negro Life in Georgia, 1880–1908," *JNH*, XLIII (July 1958), 186–213;** Bacote, "Negro Proscriptions, Protests, and Proposed Solutions in Georgia, 1880–1908," *JSH*, XXV (Nov. 1959), 471–98;** Roger A. Fischer, "Racial Segregation in Ante Bellum New Orleans," *AHR*, LXXIV (Feb. 1969), 926–37; John Hope Franklin, "History of Racial Segregation in the United States," *Annals*, CCCIV (Mar. 1956), 1–9;** Henry C. Dethloff and Robert P. Jones, "Race Relations in Louisiana, 1877–1898," *Louisiana History*, IX (Fall 1968), 301–23; August Meier and Elliott Rudwick, "A Strange Chapter in the Career of 'Jim Crow,'" in Meier and Rudwick, eds., *The Making of Black America*, 2 vols. (New York, 1969),* vol. II, pp. 14–19; Guion Griffis Johnson, "Southern Paternalism Toward Negroes after Emancipation," *JSH*, XXIII (Nov. 1957), 483–509; James M. McPherson, "The Antislavery Legacy: From Reconstruction to the NAACP," in Barton J. Bernstein, ed., *Towards a New Past* (New York, 1968),* pp. 126–57; and Otey M. Scruggs, "The Economic and Racial Components of Jim Crow," in Nathan I. Huggins, Martin Kilson, and Daniel M. Fox, eds., *Key Issues in the Afro-American Experience*, 2 vols. (New York, 1971),* vol. II, pp. 70–87. For compilations and descriptions of Jim Crow laws, see Gilbert T. Stephenson, *Race Distinctions in American Law* (New York, 1910); Franklin Johnson, *The Development of State Legislation Concerning the Free Negro* (New York, 1919); Pauli Murray, *State Laws on Race and Color* (Cincinnati, 1951), and Roger L. Rice, "Residential Segregation by Law, 1910–1917," *JSH*, XXXIV (May 1968), 179–99.** An interesting study of black response to streetcar segregation is August Meier and Elliott Rudwick, "The Boycott Movement Against Jim Crow Streetcars in the South, 1900–

1906," *JAH*, LI (Mar. 1969), 756–75.** The mixed record of the North on segregation in public accommodations is treated in Valeria W. Weaver, "The Failure of Civil Rights 1875–1883 and Its Repercussions," *JNH*, LIV (Oct. 1969), 368–82.

In *The Strange Career of Jim Crow*, C. Vann Woodward maintains that the Populists represented an equalitarian alternative to segregation and exploitation of blacks, but that the defeat of the Populist movement and the subsequent racism of many Populists who made the black a scapegoat for their failure accelerated the pace of segregation after 1896. Other historians are skeptical of Populist professions of racial liberalism in the first place. For the pros and cons of the Populists and the blacks, see the books and articles cited in the last paragraph of topic 1 of this Part, "Nullification of the Fifteenth Amendment: The Disfranchisement Movement."

3. Racial Violence: Lynching and Riots

Without question, the high rate of lynching in the United States from 1885 to 1915 comprises the ugliest episode in our national history. Nearly 3,000 known lynchings of black men and women took place during that period. The frenzy of mob psychology, the barbarism of primitive blood lust, the tendency to consider blacks as merely animals, the complete disregard of legal and judicial processes, and the atavistic practices of torture all characterized the lynch mobs of those years. The actual *number* of lynchings declined after 1892, but the *percentage* of black victims increased, the practice of lynching became more and more a public spectacle, sometimes with hundreds or even thousands of witnesses, and lynchings increasingly included torture, dismemberment, and burning at the stake. Lynching was the ultimate manifestation of the post-Reconstruction deterioration in the Afro-American's status, and the decade with the highest lynching rate (the 1890s) also saw the beginnings of disfranchisement and Jim Crow.

Historical surveys of lynching include James Elbert Cutler, *Lynch Law: An Investigation into the History of Lynching in* the United States (New York, 1905); NAACP, Thirty Years of Lynching in the United States, 1889–1918 (New York, 1919, reprinted Westport, Conn., 1969); Walter F. White, Rope and Faggot: A Biography of Judge Lynch (New York, 1929, reprinted New York, 1969); and Frank Shay, Judge Lynch, His First Hundred Years (New York, 1938). An excellent brief summary of lynching and race riots is found in Gunnar Myrdal, An American Dilemma (New York, 1944),* ch. 27. A useful contemporary account by a northern journalist is Ray Stannard Baker, Following the Color Line (New York, 1908),* ch. 9. Three pamphlets by the black antilynching crusader of the 1890s and 1900s Ida Wells-Barnett have been reprinted in a modern edition, Ida Wells-Barnett, On Lynchings (New York, 1969).* Mrs. Wells-Barnett's autobiography, Crusade for Justice: The Autobiography of Ida B. Wells, ed. by Alfreda M. Duster (Chicago, 1970), recounts her anti-lynching activities. Arthur Raper, The Tragedy of Lynching (Chapel Hill, 1933),* concentrates primarily on the 1920s and 1930s, but includes some useful historical background. Two essays on the social psychology of lynch mobs should not be overlooked: Hadley Cantril, "The Lynching Mob," in his The Psychology of Social Movements (New York, 1941),* and Earl F. Young, "Relation of Lynching to the Size of Political Areas," Sociology and Social Research, XII (Mar.–Apr. 1928), 348–53. For the early years of the NAACP's efforts against lynching, see Charles Flint Kellogg, NAACP: A History of the National Association for the Advancement of Colored People, vol. I: 1909–1920 (Baltimore, 1967), ch. 10.

The decade beginning with the Wilmington, N.C., race riot of 1898 and ending with the Springfield, Ill., race riot of 1908 witnessed several riots in which white mobs beat and killed blacks in the streets, invaded black neighborhoods, and destroyed black property; in most cases blacks fought back and there were many casualties on both sides, though most of the dead were black. The Wilmington riot is described in Helen G. Edmonds, The Negro and Fusion Politics in North Carolina, 1894–1901 (Chapel Hill, 1951), ch. 11. The worst riot occurred in Atlanta in 1906; for a contemporary account, see Ray Stannard Baker, Following the Color Line, ch. 1; for an historian's analysis, consult Charles Crowe, "Racial Violence and Social Reform—Origins of the Atlanta Riot of 1906," *JNH*, LIII (July 1968), 234–56, and "Racial Massacre in Atlanta September 22, 1906," *ibid.*, LIV (Apr. 1969), 150–73. The best study of the Springfield riot is James L. Crouthamel, "The Springfield Race Riot of 1908," *ibid.*, XLV (July 1960), 164–81. Contemporary accounts of the Wilmington and Atlanta riots are reprinted in Richard Hofstadter and Michael Wallace, eds., *American Violence: A Documentary History* (New York, 1970),* pp. 230–40.

4. *Theories of Race in the Late Nineteenth and Early Twentieth Centuries*

From at least as early as the seventeenth century, scientific and pseudoscientific ideas on race were used to justify slavery and the exploitation of African peoples. Theories that placed the black man on the bottom of the racial scale were particularly widespread in the nineteenth and early twentieth centuries and became a major bulwark of white supremacy. The rapid acceptance of Darwinism in the decades after 1860 provided a new and scientifically potent basis for ranking races along an evolutionary scale—with blacks still at the bottom. The development of IQ tests in the twentieth century and their widespread use to measure the "intelligence" of American soldiers in World War I provided even more "proof" of the black man's inferiority for those who were looking for such proof.

The best over-all survey of American racial attitudes is Thomas F. Gossett, *Race: The History of an Idea in America* (Dallas, 1963).* Chs. 4, 7, 8, 11, and 14 deal with racial theories about the Negro in the nineteenth and early twentieth centuries. The pre-Civil War background is best treated by William B. Stanton, *The Leopard's Spots: Scientific Attitudes Toward Race in America, 1815–1859* (Chicago, 1960);* the best monographs on the late nineteenth and early twentieth centuries are John S. Haller, Jr., *Outcasts from Evolution: Scientific Attitudes of Racial Inferiority, 1859–1900* (Urbana, Ill., 1971), and Idus A. Newby, *Jim Crow's Defense: Anti-Negro Thought in America, 1900–1930*

(Baton Rouge, 1965).* Two other useful discussions are Guion Griffis Johnson, "The Ideology of White Supremacy, 1876–1910," in Fletcher Green, ed., *Essays in Southern History* (Chapel Hill, 1949), ch. 8; Claude H. Nolen, *The Negro's Image in the South: The Anatomy of White Supremacy* (Lexington, Ky., 1967),* pt. 1; and Lawrence J. Friedman, *The White Savage: Racial Fantasies in the Postbellum South* (Englewood Cliffs, N.J., 1970).* For the impact of Darwinism, see Theodosius Dobzhansky, "The Genetic Nature of Differences Among Men," in Stow Persons, ed., *Evolutionary Thought in America* (New Haven, 1950), ch. 3, and Richard Hofstadter, *Social Darwinism in American Thought* (Philadelphia, 1944),* ch. 9. See also George M. Fredrickson, *The Black Image in the White Mind: The Debate on Afro-American Character and Destiny, 1817–1914* (New York, 1971), chs. 8–10.

The flavor of racial thought can perhaps best be understood by sampling the writings of some turn-of-the-century theorists. A useful anthology of racist writings is Idus A. Newby, ed., *The Development of Segregationist Thought* (Homewood, Ill., 1968).* Books asserting the black's congenital inferiority include Robert W. Shufeldt, *The Negro: A Menace to American Civilization* (Boston, 1907), and *America's Greatest Problem: The Negro* (Philadelphia, 1915); and Howard W. Odum, *Social and Mental Traits of the Negro* (New York, 1910). Thomas P. Bailey, *Race Orthodoxy in the South* (New York, 1914, reprinted New York, 1969), examines the southern white viewpoint. Racism was the central theme of Thomas Dixon's popular novels, especially *The Leopard's Spots: A Romance of the White Man's Burden* (New York, 1902), and *The Clansman: An Historical Romance of the Ku Klux Klan* (New York, 1905),* which was the basis for the film *The Birth of a Nation*. Contemporary writings that attack racism and deny the innate inequality of the Negro and other "backward" races include the influential work by Franz Boas, *The Mind of Primitive Man* (New York, 1911);* two addresses at the founding meeting of the NAACP in 1909 (see *Proceedings of the National Negro Conference* [New York, 1909, reprinted New York, 1969], pp. 14–66); and a book by a black author, Charles V. Roman, *American Civilization and the Negro* (Philadelphia, 1916).

5. The Supreme Court and Negro Rights, 1873–1915

The Fourteenth and Fifteenth Amendments, particularly the former, have given rise to more litigation before the Supreme Court than the rest of the Constitution combined, and much of this litigation has concerned Negro rights, especially in recent years. These two amendments were intended to provide the black man with equal citizenship and the ballot, but beginning with the *Slaughterhouse Cases* in 1873 the Supreme Court over the next forty years gradually whittled down the scope and meaning of the amendments insofar as they applied to black people, while it enlarged the scope of the Fourteenth Amendment's "due process" clause to protect business enterprise against state regulation. The Court's interpretation of the Fourteenth and Fifteenth Amendments and of Reconstruction legislation designed to protect the rights of blacks was a classic example of Mr. Dooley's remark that the Supreme Court follows the election returns, for the Court retreated with the tide of public opinion in its attitude toward blacks in the period from 1873 to 1915.

Background, context, and specific information on judicial decisions can be found in Alfred H. Kelly and Winfred A. Harbison, *The American Constitution* (3rd ed., New York, 1963), chs. 18–19, and Charles Warren, *The Supreme Court in United States History*, 3 vols. (Boston, 1923), vol. III, chs. 32–34. A fine book by a black California judge whose father was born a slave provides an excellent account of the Court's interpretation of the Reconstruction amendments and legislation: Loren Miller, *The Petitioners: The Story of the Supreme Court of the United States and the Negro* (New York, 1966),* pts. 2–3. Robert J. Harris, *The Quest for Equality: The Constitution, Congress and the Supreme Court* (Baton Rouge, 1960), chs. 3–4, is the most useful and concise account of the judicial interpretation of the Fourteenth Amendment during this period. Edward F. Waite, "The Negro in the Supreme Court," *Minnesota Law Review*, XXX (Mar. 1946), 219–304; Morroe Berger, *Equality by Statute* (New York,

1952, rev. ed., 1967),* ch. 2; and Rayford W. Logan, *The Negro in American Life and Thought: The Nadir, 1877–1901* (New York, 1954, rev. paperback ed. 1965, under the title *The Betrayal of the Negro, from Rutherford B. Hayes to Woodrow Wilson*),* ch. 6, contain succinct summaries of the Court's role in upholding white supremacy. See also the relevant portions of Leon Friedman and Fred L. Israel, comps., *The Justices of the United States Supreme Court, 1789–1961*, 4 vols. (New York, 1969), vols. II–III. Texts of the most important Supreme Court decisions on blacks in this period are reprinted in Richard Bardolph, ed., *The Civil Rights Record: Black Americans and the Law, 1849–1970* (New York, 1970),* pts. 2–3.

Two of the Court's key decisions were the *Civil Rights Cases* in 1883 and *Plessy* v. *Ferguson* in 1896; for readable accounts of the background and meaning of these decisions, consult the essays by Alan F. Westin and C. Vann Woodward in John A. Garraty, ed., *Quarrels That Have Shaped the Constitution* (New York, 1964).* Detailed analyses and documentations of *Plessy* v. *Ferguson* are contained in Barton J. Bernstein, "*Plessy* v. *Ferguson*: Conservative Sociological Jurisprudence," *JNH*, XLVIII (July 1963), 196–205, and "Case Law in *Plessy* v. *Ferguson*," *ibid.*, XLVII (July 1962), 192–98; and Otto H. Olsen, ed., *The Thin Disguise: The Turning Point in Negro History*, Plessy *v.* Ferguson (New York, 1968).

The lone and eloquent dissenter from the Court's conservative decisions on the rights of blacks from 1877 to 1911 was Justice John Marshall Harlan; two useful studies of Harlan's career and dissents are Alan F. Westin, "John Marshall Harlan and the Constitutional Rights of Negroes: The Transformation of a Southerner," *Yale Law Journal*, LXVI (Apr. 1957), 637–710, and Frank B. Latham, *The Great Dissenter: John Marshall Harlan, 1833–1911* (New York, 1970). The NAACP challenged racial discrimination in the courts from the beginning of its existence; for the major cases it fought (and won) before 1920, see chs. 9 and 10 of Charles Flint Kellogg, *NAACP: A History of the National Association for the Advancement of Colored People*, vol. I: 1909–1920 (Baltimore, 1967).

6. Progressivism and Race

The progressive movement had a mixed and largely negative record on the issue of race. Progressivism in the South was, for the most part, "for whites only" (this is C. Vann Woodward's phrase in ch. 14 of his *Origins of the New South, 1877–1913* [Baton Rouge, 1951]*). Most northern progressives shared, to some degree, the racial assumptions of their generation, and the black man benefited less from the standard progressive reforms than any other group in society. For a brief evaluation, critical of progressivism, see Dewey W. Grantham, "The Progressive Movement and the Negro," SAQ, LIV (Oct. 1955), 461–77. A short and superficial study, useful despite its limitations, which indicts most progressives as racists, is David W. Southern, *The Malignant Heritage: Yankee Progressives and the Negro Question, 1901–1914* (Chicago, 1968). A number of northern progressives, however, particularly in Boston and New York, were actively concerned about civil rights and took the lead in founding the Urban League and the NAACP. For excellent brief surveys of these "social justice" progressives, see Allen F. Davis, *Spearheads for Reform: The Social Settlements and the Progressive Movement, 1890–1914* (New York, 1967),* ch. 5, and Gilbert Osofsky, "Progressivism and the Negro: New York, 1900–1915," AQ, XVI (Summer 1964), 153–68.**

The federal government under Republican Presidents Theodore Roosevelt and William Howard Taft pursued a wavering course—it wavered generally downwards—toward blacks. At first it appeared that Roosevelt meant to include blacks in his "Square Deal," and he spoke out strongly against lynching, consulted Booker T. Washington about southern appointments, and resisted efforts by southern whites to force him to rescind appointments of black officeholders. But during his second term Roosevelt alienated much of the black community by certain actions, especially his summary discharge of three companies of black infantry who refused to inform on their fellows who had allegedly shot up the town of Brownsville, Texas. Several black leaders denounced Roosevelt and the Republican party, and supported the Democrats, despite the latter's white supremacy stance, in the 1908 presidential elections. Black alienation from Roosevelt became stronger when the Progressive party refused to seat black delegates from the South in its 1912 convention or to consider an equal rights plank drafted by W. E. B. Du Bois. President Taft in 1912 was not a particularly attractive candidate from a black point of view; while he had named a few black men to government posts, he more often abided by his inaugural promise not to appoint to federal office anyone whom white southerners found objectionable. Although most black votes went to the Progressives and the Republicans, the election of 1912 saw the surprising development of important support among black leaders for the Democratic candidate Woodrow Wilson, the first native of the South to win the presidency since the Civil War. Wilson received more black votes than any previous Democratic presidential candidate, but the Wilson administration dashed the hopes and expectations of its black supporters by severely cutting already meager black patronage and by instituting a policy of officially sanctioned Jim Crow in the Treasury and Post Office Departments, among others. Despite extensive protest from the NAACP and other sources against Wilsonian segregation policies, the President maintained that the Jim Crow arrangements were "to their [blacks'] advantage," and in the election of 1916 disillusioned black voters, in the words of Henry Lee Moon, apparently "returned en masse to the party of liberation."

A good starting point for a study of the federal government and the fluctuating political allegiance of blacks during this period is chs. 16–17 of Rayford W. Logan, *The Betrayal of the Negro* (New York, 1965).* There is useful background material in John B. Wiseman, "Racism in Democratic Politics, 1904–1912," *Mid-America*, LI (Jan. 1969), 38–58; August Meier, "The Negro and the Democratic Party, 1875–1915," *Phylon*, XVII (Summer 1956), 173–91; and August Meier and Elliott Rudwick, "The Rise of Segregation in the Federal Bureaucracy, 1900–1930," *ibid.*, XXVIII (Summer 1967), 178–84. On the Roosevelt administration, see Seth M. Scheiner, "President Theodore Roosevelt and the Negro, 1901–1908," *JNH*, XLVII (July 1962), 169–82; J. A. Tinsley, "Roosevelt, Foraker, and the Brownsville Foray," *ibid.*, XLI (Jan. 1965), 43–65; Emma Lou Thornbrough, "The Brownsville Episode and the Negro Vote," *MVHR*, XLIV (Dec. 1957), 469–83; Willard B. Gatewood, "Theodore Roosevelt and the Indianola Affair," *JNH*, LIII (Jan. 1968), 48–69, which also appears as one of three essays on Roosevelt and the race problem in Willard B. Gatewood, Jr., *Theodore Roosevelt and the Art of Controversy: Episodes of the White House Years* (Baton Rouge, 1970); John D. Weaver, *The Brownsville Raid* (New York, 1970); and George Sinkler, *The Racial Attitudes of American Presidents: From Abraham Lincoln to Theodore Roosevelt* (Garden City, N.Y., 1971), chs. 9–10. On blacks and the Socialist party during the Roosevelt and Taft administrations, see R. Laurence Moore, "Flawed Fraternity—American Socialist Response to the Negro, 1901–1912," *Historian*, XXXII (Nov. 1969), 1–18. For the 1912 campaign, consult George E. Mowry, "The South and the Progressive Lily White Party of 1912," *JSH*, VI (May 1940), 237–47; and Arthur S. Link, "The Negro as a Factor in the Campaign of 1912," *JNH*, XXXII (Jan. 1947), 81–99.

There is an extensive literature on various aspects of the Wilson administration's policy toward blacks, especially the segregation of civil service employees. See Nancy J. Weiss, "The Negro and the New Freedom: Fighting Wilsonian Segregation," *PSQ*, LXXXIV (Mar. 1969), 61–79; Henry Blumenthal, "Woodrow Wilson and the Race Question," *JNH*, XLVI (Jan. 1963), 1–22; George C. Osborn, "The Problem of the Negro in Government: 1913," *Historian*, XXIII (May 1961), 330–48; Kathleen L. Wolgemuth, "Woodrow Wilson and Federal Segregation," *JNH*, XLIV (Apr. 1959), 158–73, and her "Woodrow Wilson's Appointment Policy and the Negro," *JSH*, XXIV (Nov. 1958), 457–71; and Arthur S. Link, *Wilson: The New Freedom* (Princeton, 1956),* pp. 243–54. Although Link and Wolgemuth suggest that the protests against discrimination were successful, there is little concrete evidence of any real reversal of the segregation policies; see the Meier and Rudwick article cited above. For accounts of the NAACP's activities, see Charles Flint Kellogg, *NAACP: A History of the National Association for the Advancement of Colored People*, vol. I: 1909–1920 (Baltimore, 1967), ch. 8, and Constance McLaughlin Green, *The Secret City: A History of Race Relations in the Nation's Capital* (Princeton, 1967),* ch. 8. Other articles relevant to the relationship between blacks and the

Wilson administration include Richard M. Abrams, "Woodrow Wilson and the Southern Congressmen, 1913–1916," *JSH*, XXII (Nov. 1956), 417–38; and Jane Lang Scheiber and Harry N. Scheiber, "The Wilson Administration and the Wartime Mobilization of Black Americans, 1917–18," *LH*, X (Summer 1969), 433–58, which also appears as ch. 5 of Milton Cantor, ed., *Black Labor in America* (Westport, Conn., 1970).

7. Accommodation and Protest in Black Thought

Since the inception of the modern civil rights revolution, "black thought" has commonly been identified with protest, with the tradition of agitation for equal rights, accomplished either through legislation or by direct action, whether non-violent or violent. But there is another tradition in the United States of black adaptation to a predominantly white world, a tradition of accommodation, of resigned (but not always passive) acceptance of the black man's subordinate place in society, coupled with gradual, non-political efforts to improve the race's condition within the existing framework. From 1890 to 1915, when the black man's legal, political, and social status was at its lowest point since emancipation, the foremost spokesman of accommodation, Booker T. Washington, rose to leadership of the black community. Yet a militant minority of blacks, most of them living in the North where they received support from a small band of white liberals, refused to accept the leadership of the Tuskegee educator and forged a protest movement that led to the founding of the NAACP in 1909–10. These years witnessed the classic conflict between accommodation and protest in the black community, a conflict that is best analyzed in August Meier's excellent *Negro Thought in America, 1880–1915: Racial Ideologies in the Age of Booker T. Washington* (Ann Arbor, 1963).* Robert L. Factor, *The Black Response to America: Men, Ideals, and Organizations from Frederick Douglass to the NAACP* (Reading, Mass., 1970),* pts. 2–4, is an important study of changes in black leadership. See also Francis L. Broderick, "The Gnawing Dilemma: Separatism and

Integration, 1865–1925," in Nathan I. Huggins, Martin Kilson, and Daniel M. Fox, eds., *Key Issues in the Afro-American Experience*, 2 vols. (New York, 1971),* vol. II, pp. 93–106. Francis L. Broderick and August Meier, eds., *Negro Protest Thought in the Twentieth Century* (Indianapolis, 1965),* pt. 1, which corresponds to pt. 1 of August Meier, Elliott Rudwick, and Francis L. Broderick, eds., *Black Protest Thought in the Twentieth Century* (rev. ed., Indianapolis, 1971),* and Howard Brotz, ed., *Negro Social and Political Thought, 1850–1920* (New York, 1966),* pp. 351–463, 483–549, are both useful anthologies of representative documents. Kelly Miller, *Radicals and Conservatives, and Other Essays on the Negro in America*, ed. with intro. by Philip Reiff (New York, 1968),* is a collection of essays by a black intellectual whose ideas blended strains of both accommodation and protest.

A. Accommodation: Booker T. Washington

The strategy of accommodation coincides, to an extraordinary extent, with the career of Booker T. Washington. Washington's ideas and style are best displayed in his own writings, especially E. Davidson Washington, ed., *Selected Speeches of Booker T. Washington* (New York, 1932), and several books by Washington: *The Future of the American Negro* (Boston, 1899, reprinted Westport, Conn., 1970);* *The Story of My Life and Work* (Naperville, Ill., 1900, reprinted Westport, Conn., 1970); *Up From Slavery* (New York, 1901);* and *My Larger Education* (New York, 1911).* In later years, some of Washington's published articles were noticeably less accommodating in tone than his major books; see, for example, "Is the Negro Having a Fair Chance?" *Century*, LXXXV (Nov. 1912), 46–55, and "My View of Segregation Laws," *New Republic*, V (Dec. 4, 1915), 113–15. The first volume of a projected 15-vol. collection of Washington's writings and correspondence has recently been published; see Louis R. Harlan, ed., *The Booker T. Washington Papers*, vol. I (Urbana, Ill., 1971).

Louis R. Harlan, *A Biography of Booker T. Washington* (forthcoming, 1972) is the fullest and most incisive study of Washington's life and career. The following brief biographies are notably laudatory or sympathetic toward Washington: Emmett J. Scott and Lyman Beecher Stowe, *Booker T. Washington: Builder of a Civilization* (New York, 1916), which Washington commissioned before his death in 1915; Basil Mathews, *Booker T. Washington, Educator and Interracial Interpreter* (Cambridge, Mass., 1948), the first attempt at a scholarly biography; and Samuel R. Spencer, Jr., *Booker T. Washington and the Negro's Place in American Life* (Boston, 1955),* the best of the three. The following articles about Washington, some favorable and some antagonistic, should also be consulted: two studies by Jack Abramowitz, "Crossroads of Negro Thought, 1890–1915," *Social Education*, XVIII (Mar. 1954), 117–20, and "The Emergence of Booker T. Washington as a National Negro Leader," *ibid.*, XXXII (May 1968), 445–51; J. Donald Calista, "Booker T. Washington: Another Look," *JNH*, XLIX (Oct. 1964), 240–55; Oliver C. Cox, "The Leadership of Booker T. Washington," *SF*, XXX (Oct. 1951), 91–97; W. Edward Farrison, "Booker T. Washington: A Study in Educational Leadership," *SAQ*, XLI (July 1942), 313–19; Charles S. Johnson, "The Social Philosophy of Booker T. Washington," *Opportunity*, VI (Apr. 1928), 102–05, 115; three essays by Louis R. Harlan, "Booker T. Washington and the White Man's Burden," *AHR*, LXXI (Jan. 1966), 441–67,** "Booker T. Washington in Biographical Perspective," *ibid.*, LXXV (Oct. 1970), 1581–99, and "The Secret Life of Booker T. Washington," *JSH*, XXXVII (Aug. 1971), 393–416; August Meier, "Toward a Reinterpretation of Booker T. Washington," *ibid.*, XXIII (May 1957), 220–27; and Herbert J. Storing, "The School of Slavery: A Reconsideration of Booker T. Washington," in Robert A. Goldwin, ed., *100 Years of Emancipation* (Chicago, 1963),* 47–79. There is also a chapter on Washington in Merle E. Curti's *The Social Ideas of American Educators* (New York, 1935). Hugh C. Bailey, *Liberalism in the New South: Southern Social Reformers and the Progressive Movement* (Coral Gables, Fla., 1969), ch. 3, is a succinct interpretation of Booker T. Washington and T. Thomas Fortune. Finally, there are two good brief anthologies of writings by and about Washington: Hugh Hawkins, ed., *Booker T. Washington and His Critics: The Problem of Negro Leadership* (Boston, 1962),* and Emma Lou Thornbrough, ed., *Booker T.*

Washington (Englewood Cliffs, N.J., 1969),* the more valuable of the two.

B. Protest: W. E. B. Du Bois

Dissatisfied not only with the demonstrable lack of progress toward the achievement of black rights under the accommodationist formula set forth by Washington, but also with the formidable personal power Washington wielded, a group of northern black intellectuals began after the turn of the century to criticize the Tuskegeean and to propose alternate strategies. Although it was William Monroe Trotter, the militant editor of the Boston *Guardian,* who actually launched the public attack on Washington's leadership, it was W. E. B. Du Bois who became the most prominent black spokesman for agitation to realize the legal rights of the race. By 1905 Du Bois had emerged as the leader of the "anti-Bookerites," who banded together in a meeting at Niagara Falls, Canada, to inaugurate an organized program of public agitation for black rights. In 1909–10 Du Bois and other black veterans of the Niagara Movement joined with white liberals to found the NAACP, and Du Bois became the editor of its journal, *The Crisis.* On the Niagara Movement and the NAACP, see Part VII, topic 5, "The Origins of Modern Protest and Reform: The NAACP and the National Urban League." Two other useful articles on the emerging split between advocates of accommodation and protest are Daniel Walden, "The Contemporary Opposition to the Political and Educational Ideals of Booker T. Washington," *JNH,* XLV (Apr. 1960), 103–15, and Elliott M. Rudwick, "Race Leadership Struggle: Background of the Boston Riot of 1903," *JNE,* XXXI (Winter 1962), 16–24.

For an account of the career of William Monroe Trotter, the sharpest black critic of Booker T. Washington, see Stephen R. Fox, *The Guardian of Boston: William Monroe Trotter* (New York, 1970),* and Charles W. Puttkammer and Ruth Worthy, "William Monroe Trotter, 1872–1934," *JNH,* XLIII (Oct. 1958), 298–316.

Du Bois' commitments can be examined in his famous *The Souls of Black Folk* (Chicago, 1903),* *Darkwater: Voices from Within the Veil* (New York, 1920),* and two autobiographies that reflect the substantial changes in his thinking as he grew older: *Dusk of Dawn: An Essay Toward an Autobiography of a Race Concept* (New York, 1940),* and *The Autobiography of W. E. B. Du Bois: A Soliloquy on Viewing My Life from the Last Decade of Its First Century* (New York, 1968).* A broad selection from Du Bois' shorter writings is Meyer Weinberg, ed., *W. E. B. Du Bois: A Reader* (New York, 1970).* Philip S. Foner, ed., *W. E. B. Du Bois Speaks*, 2 vols. (New York, 1970), is a collection of speeches and addresses from the 1890s through 1963. Herbert Aptheker, ed., *The Correspondence of W. E. B. Du Bois*, vol. I: 1883–1934 (forthcoming, 1972), includes letters to and from Du Bois, with the exception of purely personal correspondence.

There are two good biographies of Du Bois: Francis L. Broderick, *W. E. B. Du Bois: Negro Leader in a Time of Crisis* (Stanford, 1959),* and Elliott M. Rudwick, *W. E. B. Du Bois: A Study in Minority Group Leadership* (Philadelphia, 1960).* Rayford W. Logan, ed., *W. E. B. Du Bois: A Profile* (New York, 1971),* includes appraisals by various scholars. S. P. Fullinwider, *The Mind and Mood of Black America: 20th Century Thought* (Homewood, Ill., 1969),* ch. 3, treats Du Bois as an intellectual leader. The W. E. B. Du Bois Memorial Issue of *Freedomways*, V (Winter 1965), also contains valuable commentary and analysis. The editors of *Freedomways* have put together a volume of Du Bois' writings and of interpretations by scholars and current black leaders entitled *Black Titan: W. E. B. Du Bois* (Boston, 1970).*

8. The Black Church, 1865–1915

A major result of emancipation was the freeing of the quasi-independent "invisible institution" of the slaves' church from the surveillance of the master class. All over the South in the years immediately after 1865, black Baptists and Methodists left their masters' churches and formed their own congregations. Nearly three fifths of the black church members in the United States by

1900 were Baptists, more than one third belonged to the Methodist denominations, and the remaining 5 per cent were scattered among the Presbyterian, Congregational, and other predominantly white churches. As among whites, black church membership tended to reflect social class, with the tiny upper and upper-middle classes often members of the Episcopal, Congregational, and Presbyterian churches, the middle and lower-middle classes primarily Methodists, and the masses of lower-class blacks faithful to the free-wheeling, loosely organized Baptist churches.

The postwar black church became the central social, economic, and moral institution in black life and provided much of the order, structure, and cohesion that existed in the black community. Despite frequent complaints about the ignorance, venality, or immorality of some black ministers, much of the race's educational, political, and business leadership was recruited from the ranks of the clergy. Along with the fraternal and mutual benefit societies (see the next topic, "Social Welfare Organizations and Fraternal Societies"), the church was an institution controlled almost entirely by the black community. The drive for separatism from white churches was fueled by this desire for control of a major community institution, as well as by the preferences of both whites and blacks for their own social centers. Thus the black church represented, in part, an accommodation to Jim Crow. But at the same time the churches, especially those affiliated with the black middle and upper classes, furnished much of the leadership in protest movements and several prominent black ministers were among the founders of the Niagara Movement and the NAACP.

A brief summary of the status of scholarship on the black church is provided by Robert T. Handy, "Negro Christianity and American Church Historiography," in Jerald C. Brauer, ed., *Reinterpretation in American Church History* (Chicago, 1968), pp. 91–112. The best general treatments of all aspects of black religion during this period are Carter G. Woodson, *The History of the Negro Church* (2nd ed., Washington, 1945), chs. 10–15; E. Franklin Frazier, *The Negro Church in America* (New York, 1964),* ch. 3; W. E. B. Du Bois, *The Negro Church* (Atlanta University Studies #8, Atlanta, 1903, reprinted New York, 1968), and "Of the Faith of the Fathers," ch. 10 of *The Souls of Black Folk* (New York, 1903);* and Benjamin E. Mays, *The Negro's God as Re-*

flected in His Literature (Boston, 1938),* chs. 2, 4. For the role of the clergy in providing leadership for both accommodation to the existing order and protest against it, see August Meier, *Negro Thought in America, 1880–1915* (Ann Arbor, 1963),* pp. 130–33, 218–24; and S. P. Fullinwider, *The Mind and Mood of Black America* (Homewood, Ill., 1969),* ch. 2. The social and mission work of the black church is discussed by Booker T. Washington, *The Story of the Negro* (New York, 1909), vol. II, ch. 13, and by Richard R. Wright, Jr., "Social Work and Influence of the Negro Church," *Annals*, XXX (Nov. 1907), 509–21.

Most of the monographs on blacks in southern states and northern cities during this period contain helpful discussions of the black church: see Alrutheus A. Taylor, *The Negro in the Reconstruction of Virginia* (Washington, 1926, reprinted New York, 1970), ch. 10, *The Negro in Tennessee, 1865–1880* (Washington, 1941), ch. 11, and *The Negro in South Carolina During Reconstruction* (Washington, 1924, reprinted New York, 1970), ch. 7; Joel Williamson, *After Slavery: The Negro in South Carolina During Reconstruction, 1861–1877* (Chapel Hill, 1965),* ch. 7; George B. Tindall, *South Carolina Negroes, 1877–1900* (Columbia, S.C., 1952),* ch. 10; Vernon Lane Wharton, *The Negro in Mississippi, 1865–1890* (Chapel Hill, 1947),* ch. 18; Joe M. Richardson, *The Negro in the Reconstruction of Florida, 1865–1877* (Tallahassee, Fla., 1965), ch. 8; Frenise Logan, *The Negro in North Carolina, 1876–1894* (Chapel Hill, 1964), ch. 16; W. E. B. Du Bois, *The Philadelphia Negro* (Philadelphia, 1899),* ch. 12; Seth M. Scheiner, *Negro Mecca: A History of the Negro in New York City, 1865–1920* (New York, 1965),* ch. 4; and Allan H. Spear, *Black Chicago: The Making of a Negro Ghetto, 1890–1920* (Chicago, 1967),* chs. 5, 9.

The growth of individual denominations is discussed in several works. For the Baptists, consult Owen D. Pelt and Ralph L. Smith, *The Story of the National Baptists* (New York, 1960), chs. 5–8, and A. W. Pegues, *Our Baptist Ministers and Schools* (Springfield, Mass., 1892). The A.M.E. and A.M.E. Zion churches are treated in J. Beverly F. Shaw, *The Negro in the History of Methodism* (Nashville, 1954), chs. 4–9; George A. Singleton, *The Romance of African Methodism, A Study of the African Methodist Episcopal Church* (New York, 1951), chs. 8–11;

Charles S. Smith, A *History of the African Methodist Episcopal Church . . . from 1856 to 1922* (Philadelphia, 1922, reprinted New York, 1969); and David Henry Bradley, A *History of the A.M.E. Zion Church, 1872–1968* (Nashville, 1970). The origins and development of the Colored Methodist Episcopal Church are described in the autobiography of its leading bishop during the period: Isaac Lane, *Autobiography . . . with a Short History of the Colored Methodist Episcopal Church in America and of Methodism* (Nashville, 1916). See also Horace C. Savage, *The Life and Times of Bishop Isaac Lane* (Nashville, 1958).

For the attitudes of predominantly white churches and the role of the small black membership of these denominations, the best general treatment is David M. Reimers, *White Protestantism and the Negro* (New York, 1965), chs. 2–3. Individual denominations are treated in Joseph C. Hartzell, "Methodism and the Negro in the United States," *JNH*, VIII (July 1923), 301–15; Andrew E. Murray, *Presbyterians and the Negro—A History* (Philadelphia, 1966), chs. 5–6; Matthew Anderson, *Presbyterianism—Its Relation to the Negro* (Philadelphia, 1897); George F. Bragg, *History of the Afro-American Group of the Episcopal Church* (Baltimore, 1922), chs. 13–38; John T. Gillard, *The Catholic Church and the Negro* (Baltimore, 1929, reprinted New York, 1968), ch. 3; and Albert S. Foley, *God's Men of Color: The Colored Catholic Priests of the United States, 1854–1954* (New York, 1955), chs. 1–10.

Several biographies and autobiographies of individual black clergymen provide valuable insights into the role of the Negro church. William E. Hatcher, *John Jasper, The Unmatched Negro Philosopher and Preacher* (New York, 1908), is an account of the famous slave preacher who continued his career for many years after emancipation. Much information on the A.M.E. Church can be found in Theophilus Gould Steward, *Fifty Years in the Gospel Ministry* (Philadelphia, 1922). J. Minton Batten, "Henry M. Turner, Negro Bishop Extraordinary," *Church History*, VII (Sept. 1938), 231–46, analyzes the militant A.M.E. bishop and black nationalist leader. For an autobiography and a biography of one of the most prominent A.M.E. educators and bishops, see Daniel A. Payne, *Recollections of Seventy Years* (Nashville, 1888, reprinted New York, 1968); and Josephus Roosevelt Coan, *Daniel Alexan-*

der Payne, Christian Educator (Philadelphia, 1935). Alexander Walters was an outstanding bishop of the A.M.E. Zion Church, a race leader, and a founder of the NAACP; for his career, see Alexander Walters, *My Life and Work* (New York, 1917). Another prominent protest leader and pastor of the Fifteenth Street Presbyterian Church in Washington was Francis J. Grimké; his activities and ideas are documented in Carter G. Woodson, ed., *The Works of Francis James Grimké*, 4 vols. (Washington, 1942).

White and black churches were the foremost agencies of black higher education during this period. Several of the works cited in the preceding paragraphs contain material on Negro education. See also the studies cited in this Part, topic 11, "Black Education, 1877–1915." In addition, the following works are important for the church and Negro education during this period: James D. Tyms, *The Rise of Religious Education Among Negro Baptists: A Historical Case Study* (New York, 1965), chs. 7–9; Jay S. Stowell, *Methodist Adventures in Negro Education* (New York, 1922); and William A. Daniel, *The Education of Negro Ministers* (New York, 1925, reprinted Westport, Conn., 1970).

9. *Social Welfare Organizations and Fraternal Societies*

The last third of the nineteenth century witnessed a proliferation among blacks of social clubs, professional and literary associations, and mutual benefit and fraternal societies as the race emerged painfully from slavery and organized itself for freedom. As in the case of the church, the Jim Crow policies of white institutions and the preferences of many blacks themselves for a race-centered social life led to the creation of separate organizations that imitated or paralleled those of white society. For brief discussions of fraternal, professional, and social welfare organizations, including the important National Association of Colored Women, see August Meier, *Negro Thought in America, 1880–1915* (Ann Arbor, 1963),* ch. 8; Robert L. Factor, *The Black Response to America: Men, Ideals, and Organizations from Frederick Douglass to the*

NAACP (Reading, Mass., 1970),* chs. 9–10; Booker T. Washington, *The Story of the Negro* (New York, 1909), vol. II, chs. 6, 12; and B. F. Lee, Jr., "Negro Organizations," *Annals,* XLIX (Sept. 1913), 129–37. Three of the Atlanta University Studies by W. E. B. Du Bois surveyed the various black social welfare and cooperative associations: *Some Efforts of American Negroes for Their Own Social Betterment* (Atlanta, 1898); *Economic Co-operation Among Negro Americans* (Atlanta, 1907); and *Efforts for Social Betterment Among Negro Americans* (Atlanta, 1909).

Next to the church, the fraternal and mutual benefit societies were the most important social institutions in the black community during this period (some of the societies were organized by ministers and closely connected with the church). The earliest black secret society, the Masons, had been founded by Prince Hall in Massachusetts in 1787. A few other black fraternal societies were organized by free blacks before the Civil War, but the period of their greatest growth came in the half century after Reconstruction. By the first decade of the twentieth century there were at least twenty national black fraternal or mutual benefit societies and scores of local or regional associations with a total membership of more than a million. Several of the black lodges, including the Masons, Odd Fellows, and Elks, paralleled white organizations of the same name which refused to admit blacks and in some cases refused even to recognize the existence of the black societies. The ceremonial and good-fellowship functions of these societies were important, but even more significant was their role as mutual benefit and insurance associations. Most of them provided sickness and death benefits for their members, and some established banks and invested in business or real estate. The black insurance companies emerged primarily out of these societies (see the next topic, "Black Capitalism in the Age of Booker T. Washington"). Most of the works cited in the preceding paragraph deal in part with the fraternal and mutual benefit associations. Two other brief surveys are Edward N. Palmer, "Negro Secret Societies," *SF,* XXIII (Dec. 1944), 207–12, which is sympathetic; and Charles W. Ferguson, *Fifty Million Brothers: A Panorama of American Lodges and Clubs* (New York, 1937), ch. 13, which is patronizing.

Many of the following books are laudatory official histories of individual societies and are out of print and rare. The Masons are the best chronicled society: see William Upton, *Negro Masonry* (Cambridge, Mass., 1902); William H. Grimshaw, *Official History of Freemasonry Among the Colored People of North America* (Montreal, 1903); George W. Crawford, *Prince Hall and His Followers; Being a Monograph on the Legitimacy of Negro Masonry* (New York, 1914, reprinted New York, 1969); Harry A. Williamson, *Negroes and Freemasonry* (Brooklyn, 1920); Harold Van Buren Voorhis, *Negro Masonry in the United States* (New York, 1940); and Charles H. Wesley, *The History of the Prince Hall Grand Lodge of Free and Accepted Masons of the State of Ohio, 1849–1960* (Wilberforce, Ohio, 1961). For a discussion of the largest black lodge, see Charles H. Brooks, *A History and Manual of the Grand United Order of Odd Fellows in America* (Philadelphia, 1902). Other societies are treated in W. P. Burrell and D. E. Johnson, *Twenty-five Years History of the Grand Fountain of the United Order of True Reformers* (Richmond, Va., 1909); Charles H. Wesley, *History of the Improved Benevolent and Protective Order of Elks of the World, 1898–1954* (Washington, 1955); Howard H. Turner, *Turner's History of the Independent Order of Good Samaritans and Daughters of Samaria* (Washington, 1881); and E. A. Williams, *History and Manual of the Colored Knights of Pythias* (Nashville, 1917). An account of the earliest and largest black college fraternity is Charles H. Wesley, *The History of the Alpha Phi Alpha* (Washington, 1935), while a leading sorority is treated in Mary Elizabeth Vroman, *Shaped to Its Purpose: Delta Sigma Theta—The First Fifty Years* (New York, 1965).

10. *Black Capitalism in the Age of Booker T. Washington*

A leading formula for racial progress, urged especially by Booker T. Washington and his associates, was black ownership of property and business enterprises. There had long been black entrepreneurs in the United States, of course, but in the 1880s and

1890s business ownership became almost a panacea among some elements of the black community at the same time that the nature of black entrepreneurship was changing and expanding. The most successful black businessmen in the earlier period had owned restaurants, barbershops, catering services, and similar enterprises that attracted mostly white customers. But with the growing urbanization of the black population and the intensifying racial discrimination in the late nineteenth century that brought about increased economic segregation, a new generation of black entrepreneurs began establishing funeral parlors, cosmetics firms, insurance companies, and other businesses to serve almost exclusively the black community. For this important change, and for background information on the theory and practice of black business, see August Meier, *Negro Thought in America, 1880–1915* (Ann Arbor, 1963),* esp. ch. 9.

The foremost advocate of black capitalism as a means for the race to lift itself by its bootstraps was Booker T. Washington, who founded the National Negro Business League in 1900. For an excellent brief analysis of Washington and the league, see Louis R. Harlan, "Booker T. Washington and the National Negro Business League," in William G. Shade and Roy C. Herrenkohl, eds., *Seven on Black: Reflections on the Negro Experience in America* (Philadelphia, 1969),* pp. 73–91. Washington's book, *The Negro in Business* (New York, 1907, reprinted Chicago, 1970), is a laudatory account of black entrepreneurs and the league. Two Atlanta University Studies by W. E. B. Du Bois document the scope and nature of black capitalism: *The Negro in Business* (Atlanta, 1899, reprinted New York, 1968), and *Economic Co-operation Among Negro Americans* (Atlanta, 1907). Two monographs contain perceptive analyses of the growth of black business in the late nineteenth and early twentieth centuries: Abram L. Harris, *The Negro as Capitalist: a Study of Banking and Business Among American Negroes* (Philadelphia, 1936, reprinted College Park, Md., 1969); and John Henry Harmon, Arnett G. Lindsay, and Carter G. Woodson, *The Negro as a Business Man* (Washington, 1929, reprinted College Park, Md., 1969). Some of the largest black businesses were insurance companies. Three accounts of these enterprises are Merah S. Stuart, *An Economic Detour: A History of Insurance in the Lives of*

American Negroes (New York, 1940, reprinted College Park, Md., 1969); William J. Trent, *Development of Negro Life Insurance Enterprises* (Philadelphia, 1932); and James B. Browning, "The Beginnings of Insurance Enterprise Among Negroes," *JNH*, XXII (Oct. 1937), 417–52. For a sharply critical appraisal of the achievements of black business and the values of the middle class, see E. Franklin Frazier, *Black Bourgeoisie* (Glencoe, Ill., 1957).*

Most of the new black capitalists of the 1890s and early 1900s were located in the South, but with increasing black migration to northern cities there emerged a number of successful northern businessmen. For New York City, where the operations of a black realtor helped to transform Harlem from a white to black neighborhood, see Gilbert Osofsky, *Harlem: The Making of a Ghetto; Negro New York, 1890–1930* (New York, 1966),* esp. ch. 7; and Seth M. Scheiner, *Negro Mecca: A History of the Negro in New York City, 1865–1920* (New York, 1965),* esp. chs. 1, 3. A useful account of black businessmen in Chicago is contained in Allan H. Spear, *Black Chicago: The Making of a Negro Ghetto, 1890–1920* (Chicago, 1967),* esp. chs. 4, 6, 10.

A major black business enterprise was the press. An extraordinarily large number of black newspapers, most of them short-lived, existed during this period. Although there is no satisfactory study of the black press in the 1875–1915 period, considerable information can be obtained from I. Garland Penn, *The Afro-American Press and its Editors* (Springfield, Mass., 1891); and Frederick G. Detweiler, *The Negro Press in the United States* (Chicago, 1922, reprinted College Park, Md., 1968). See also the relevant portions of Martin E. Dann, ed., *The Black Press, 1827–1890: The Quest for National Identity* (New York, 1971). During Booker T. Washington's ascendancy, much of the press lined up for or against the Tuskegean, and Washington subtly subsidized several newspapers to keep them on his side. See August Meier, *Negro Thought in America, 1880–1915,* cited above, pp. 224–36; August Meier, "Booker T. Washington and the Negro Press, with Special Reference to the *Colored American Magazine*," *JNH,* XXXVIII (Jan. 1953), 68–82;** and Emma Lou Thornbrough, "More Light on Booker T. Washington and the New York *Age*," *ibid.,* XLIII (Jan. 1958), 34–49. Washington's most bitter critic was William Monroe Trotter, founder and editor of the Boston *Guardian.*

For accounts of Trotter's career, see Charles W. Puttkammer and Ruth Worthy, "William Monroe Trotter, 1872–1934," *ibid.*, XLIII (Oct. 1958), 298–318, and Stephen R. Fox, *The Guardian of Boston: William Monroe Trotter* (New York, 1970).* The greatest black journalist of the era was Robert Abbott, who founded the Chicago *Defender* in 1905. A fine biography of Abbott is Roi Ottley, *The Lonely Warrior: The Life and Times of Robert S. Abbott* (Chicago, 1955).

11. Black Education, 1877–1915

During and after the Civil War, freedmen's education societies and Protestant missionary bodies founded hundreds of schools for freedmen in the South (see Part V, topic 5, "Freedmen's Education During the Civil War and Reconstruction"). Most of these evolved during Reconstruction into public elementary schools for blacks; some continued as private elementary schools; about a hundred became secondary schools and colleges, still supported primarily by northern philanthropy. Out of these schools have grown the best institutions of higher education for blacks in the South and border states, including Fisk, Atlanta, and Howard universities, Morehouse, Spelman, and Tougaloo colleges, and many others. Several schools founded by black leaders themselves, notably Tuskegee, also flourished during this period. Under the prodding of the Morrill Act of 1890, southern states also established land-grant agricultural and mechanical (A. & M.) colleges for blacks, which were at first little more than elementary and secondary vocational schools. Most high school education for blacks in the South until well into the twentieth century, however, was provided by the private, northern-supported colleges and academies, since southern school districts were slow to build public high schools for blacks—Atlanta, for example, had no black public high school until 1924.

Several interrelated issues complicated the development of black education during the half century after the war. One was the debate, among blacks as well as whites, about the aims of black education: should the full range of training, from elementary to graduate and professional education, be made available to black people, or should the main emphasis be on a smattering of basic elementary education and vocational or agricultural training for a people who were mostly farmers and workers, and who, in the opinion of many whites, were not capable of higher education? Another issue was the quality and scope of public schools for blacks in the South: every southern state appropriated less per student for black schools than for white, and the disparity grew greater in the first two decades of the twentieth century. Still another issue in some of the black colleges supported by northern whites was a black power controversy: blacks desired more faculty positions and greater control of the schools, and this led to continuing debate and occasional disruption in several institutions.

General overviews of black education during this period, with particular emphasis on the debate over the goals of such education, are provided by Horace Mann Bond, *The Education of the Negro in the American Social Order* (New York, 1934, reprinted New York, 1966), chs. 5–7; Henry A. Bullock, *A History of Negro Education in the South* (Cambridge, Mass., 1967),* chs. 2–7; and August Meier, *Negro Thought in America, 1880–1915* (Ann Arbor, 1963),* chs. 6, 10. For the theory and practice of industrial education, see August Meier, "The Beginning of Industrial Education in Negro Schools," *Midwest Journal*, VII (Spring, Fall 1955), 21–44, 241–66.** The inspiration and examples for industrial education came primarily from Hampton and Tuskegee institutes, and in particular from Samuel C. Armstrong and Booker T. Washington. Consult Francis Greenwood Peabody, *Education for Life: The Story of Hampton Institute* (Garden City, N.Y., 1919); Booker T. Washington, *Up From Slavery* (New York, 1901);* Washington et al., *The Negro Problem* (New York, 1901, reprinted New York, 1969), ch. 1; Washington, ed., *Tuskegee and Its People: Their Ideals and Achievements* (New York, 1905, reprinted Westport, Conn., 1970); Washington, *My Larger Education* (New York, 1911), esp. chs. 1–2, 7, 11–12; Merle Curti, *The Social Ideas of American Educators* (New York, 1935), ch. 8; and William H. Hughes and F. D. Patterson, eds., *Robert Russa Moton of Hampton and Tuskegee* (Chapel Hill, 1956).

W. E. B. Du Bois was the foremost spokesman for black higher education, and the colleges founded by the American Missionary Association and other northern mission societies were its main practitioners. Some of Du Bois' essays on education can be found in his *The Souls of Black Folk* (New York, 1903),* ch. 6; his "The Talented Tenth," in Booker T. Washington et al., *The Negro Problem*, ch. 2; his *Dusk of Dawn: An Essay Toward an Autobiography of a Race Concept* (New York, 1940),* ch. 3; and in Meyer Weinberg, ed., *W. E. B. Du Bois: A Reader* (New York, 1970),* pt. 5. For the growth of black higher education, see Dwight O. W. Holmes, *The Evolution of the Negro College* (New York, 1934, reprinted New York, 1969); Willard Range, *The Rise and Progress of Negro Colleges in Georgia* (Athens, Ga., 1951); W. E. B. Du Bois, *The College-Bred Negro* (Atlanta University Studies, #5, Atlanta, 1900); and W. E. B. Du Bois and Augustus G. Dill, *The College-Bred Negro American* (Atlanta University Studies, #15, Atlanta, 1910, reprinted New York, 1968). An indispensable statistical and historical compilation whose interpretations are often slanted in favor of industrial education and against higher education, is Thomas Jesse Jones, ed., *Negro Education: A Study of the Private and Higher Schools for Colored People in the United States* (Bureau of Education, Bulletin #38, 1916, 2 vols., Washington, 1917, reprinted in 1 vol., New York, 1969). Among the many histories of individual colleges, the following are the most useful: Rayford W. Logan, *Howard University, 1867–1967* (New York, 1969); Frederick A. McGinnis, *A History and an Interpretation of Wilberforce University* (Wilberforce, Ohio, 1941); Edward A. Jones, *A Candle in the Dark: A History of Morehouse College* (Valley Forge, Pa., 1967); and Clarence A. Bacote, *The Story of Atlanta University: A Century of Service, 1865–1965* (Atlanta, 1969). A fine biography of one of the earliest black college presidents is Ridgely Torrence, *The Story of John Hope* (New York, 1948). The black power issue in higher education is treated by James M. McPherson, "White Liberals and Black Power in Negro Education, 1865–1915," *AHR*, LXXV (June 1970), 1357–86.

A general survey of public education in the South from the white viewpoint is Edgar W. Knight, *Public Education in the South* (New York, 1922). Monographs that contain specific information on black public schools as well as (in some cases) higher education, are W. E. B. Du Bois, *The Negro Common School* (Atlanta University Studies, #6, Atlanta, 1901); W. E. B. Du Bois and Augustus G. Dill, *The Common School and the Negro American* (Atlanta University Studies, #16, Atlanta, 1911, reprinted New York, 1968); Louis R. Harlan, *Separate and Unequal: Public School Campaigns and Racism in the Southern Seaboard States, 1901–1915* (Chapel Hill, 1958);* Horace Mann Bond, *Negro Education in Alabama: A Study in Cotton and Steel* (Washington, 1939),* esp. chs. 10–17; Vernon Lane Wharton, *The Negro in Mississippi, 1865–1890* (Chapel Hill, 1947),* ch. 17; George B. Tindall, *South Carolina Negroes, 1877–1900* (Columbia, S.C., 1952),* ch. 11; Frenise Logan, *The Negro in North Carolina, 1876–1894* (Chapel Hill, 1964), chs. 14–15; and Lillian Gertrude Dabney, *The History of Schools for Negroes in the District of Columbia, 1807–1947* (Washington, 1949). A good brief account of the unsuccessful effort in the 1880s to obtain legislation granting federal aid to public schools in the South is Daniel W. Crofts, "The Black Response to the Blair Education Bill," *JSH*, XXXVII (Feb. 1971), 41–65.

The roles of the most important missionary society and of northern philanthropy in black education are treated in Augustus Beard, *A Crusade of Brotherhood: A History of the American Missionary Association* (New York, 1909, reprinted New York, 1968); Lura Beam, *He Called Them by the Lightning: A Teacher's Odyssey in the Negro South, 1908–1919* (Indianapolis, 1967); Ullin W. Leavell, *Philanthropy in Negro Education* (Nashville, 1930, reprinted Westport, Conn., 1970); Louis D. Rubin, *Teach the Freeman: The Correspondence of Rutherford B. Hayes and the Slater Fund*, 2 vols. (Baton Rouge, 1959); Jabez L. M. Curry, *A Brief Sketch of George Peabody and a History of the Peabody Education Fund* (Cambridge, Mass., 1898, reprinted Westport, Conn., 1970); and in Louis R. Harlan's study, cited above.

Two important studies that critically evaluate the development of black education from the vantage point of the shortcomings of black schools and colleges in the 1930s and 1960s are Carter G. Woodson, *The Mis-Education of the Negro* (Washington, 1933);* and ch. 10 of Christopher Jencks and David Riesman, *The Academic Revolution* (Garden City, N.Y., 1968).*

12. Black Farmers in the New South

Lynching, disfranchisement, racial violence, Jim Crow, and black protest movements were the most dramatic aspects of race relations in the New South. But the central fact of life for most black people was the day-to-day struggle to make a living and to get ahead in the world, or at least to keep from falling farther behind. Most blacks in the post-Reconstruction generation lived and worked on the land—usually land owned by white men. Without some knowledge of the black man as an independent farmer, a tenant farmer, a sharecropper, and an agricultural laborer, one's understanding of the Afro-American in this period of his history is incomplete. Detailed statistics on black agricultural workers are available in *Negro Population in the United States, 1790–1915* (U. S. Bureau of the Census, Washington, 1918, reprinted New York, 1968), pt. 6. For succinct summaries of southern agriculture and the place of blacks in it, see Fred A. Shannon, *The Farmer's Last Frontier: Agriculture, 1860–1897* (New York, 1945),* ch. 4; John D. Hicks, *The Populist Revolt* (Minneapolis, 1931),* ch. 2; C. Vann Woodward, *Origins of the New South, 1877–1913* (Baton Rouge, 1951),* chs. 7–8; and Claude H. Nolen, *The Negro's Image in the South: The Anatomy of White Supremacy* (Lexington, Ky., 1967),* chs. 11–12. Three contemporary accounts by whites are Philip A. Bruce, *The Plantation Negro as a Freeman* (New York, 1889, reprinted Wilmington, Del., 1969); Carl Kelsey, *The Negro Farmer* (Chicago, 1903); and Ray Stannard Baker, *Following the Color Line* (New York, 1908),* ch. 4. (The Bruce and Kelsey volumes reflect a biased and insensitive white viewpoint.) Lectures by Booker T. Washington and W. E. B. Du Bois on the economic conditions of blacks in the South are published in *The Negro in the South, His Economic Progress in Relation to His Moral and Religious Development* (Philadelphia, 1907),* chs. 2–3.

For a discussion of the problems involved in the change from slave to free farm labor, see Oscar Zeichner, "The Transition from Slave to Free Agricultural Labor in the Southern States," *Agricultural History*, XIII (Dec. 1939), 22–32. Although a growing number of black farmers obtained their own land and freed themselves from debt, most remained tenants and sharecroppers, constantly in debt to their landlord or to the crossroads merchant. For an article that demonstrates how landownership remained concentrated in white hands after the Civil War, see Roger W. Shugg, "Survival of the Plantation System in Louisiana," *JSH*, III (Aug. 1937), 311–25. The tenant and cropper systems are treated by Thomas J. Edwards, "The Tenant System and Some Changes Since Emancipation," in "The Negro's Progress in Fifty Years," *Annals*, XLIX (Sept. 1913), 38–46. For an account of the crop-lien system which kept so many southern farmers in debt—white as well as black, owner as well as cropper—see Thomas D. Clark, "The Furnishing and Supply System in Southern Agriculture since 1865," *JSH*, XII (Feb. 1946), 24–44. For an account of the actual debt-slavery of many blacks during this period, see Pete Daniel, "Up From Slavery and Down to Peonage: The Alonzo Bailey Peonage Case," *JAH*, LVII (Dec. 1970), 654–70. The following monographs contain chapters on black farmers in three important southern states: Vernon Lane Wharton, *The Negro in Mississippi, 1865–1890* (Chapel Hill, 1947),* chs. 3, 8; George B. Tindall, *South Carolina Negroes, 1877–1900* (Columbia, S.C., 1952),* ch. 6; and Frenise Logan, *The Negro in North Carolina, 1876–1894* (Chapel Hill, 1964), ch. 8.

It is estimated that about 4,000 blacks became cowboys, ranch hands, chuck-wagon cooks, etc., in the range cattle industry, chiefly in Texas. For fascinating studies of this facet of black economic life in the post-Civil War generation, see Kenneth O. Porter, "Negro Labor in the Western Cattle Industry, 1866–1900," *LH*, X (Summer 1969), 346–74;** and Philip Durham and Everett L. Jones, *The Negro Cowboys* (New York, 1965).*

13. Black Workers and the Labor Movement Before World War I

Though most blacks in this period lived and worked on the land, a sizable and increasing percentage, especially in the border states and the North, were engaged in non-agricultural pursuits.

Most of these were in unskilled and service occupations, but a significant proportion worked at skilled and semiskilled trades. For detailed statistics, see Department of Commerce, Bureau of the Census, *Negro Population in the United States, 1790–1915* (Washington, 1918, reprinted New York, 1968), pt. 6. Two basic studies of the black worker in the half century after the Civil War are Charles H. Wesley, *Negro Labor in the United States, 1850–1925* (New York, 1927, reprinted New York, 1967), esp. chs. 5–9, and Lorenzo J. Greene and Carter G. Woodson, *The Negro Wage Earner* (Washington, 1930, reprinted New York, 1970).

Two of the Atlanta University Studies by W. E. B. Du Bois are also of considerable value: *The Negro Artisan* (Atlanta, 1902), and, with Augustus G. Dill, *The Negro American Artisan* (Atlanta, 1912, reprinted New York, 1968). Dean Dutcher, *The Negro in Modern Industrial Society: An Analysis of Changes in the Occupations of Negro Workers, 1910–1920* (Lancaster, Pa., 1930), discusses the impact of World War I on black occupational patterns. A good brief introduction to black labor in the South is Paul B. Worthman and James R. Green, "Black Workers in the New South, 1865–1915," in Nathan I. Huggins, Martin Kilson, and Daniel M. Fox, eds., *Key Issues in the Afro-American Experience*, 2 vols. (New York, 1971),* vol. II, pp. 47–69. The following monographs contain chapters on black labor: Vernon Lane Wharton, *The Negro in Mississippi, 1865–1890* (Chapel Hill, 1947),* ch. 9; George B. Tindall, *South Carolina Negroes, 1877–1900* (Columbia, S.C., 1952),* ch. 7; Frenise Logan, *The Negro in North Carolina, 1876–1894* (Chapel Hill, 1964), ch. 9; W. E. B. Du Bois, *The Philadelphia Negro: A Social Study* (Philadelphia, 1899),* ch. 9; John Daniels, *In Freedom's Birthplace: A Study of the Boston Negroes* (Boston, 1914, reprinted New York, 1968), ch. 9; George E. Haynes, *The Negro at Work in New York City: A Study in Economic Progress* (New York, 1912); Seth M. Scheiner, *Negro Mecca: A History of the Negro in New York City, 1865–1920* (New York, 1965),* chs. 2–3; and Allan H. Spear, *Black Chicago: The Making of a Negro Ghetto, 1890–1920* (Chicago, 1967),* chs. 2, 8.

The interaction between labor unions and black workingmen has been the subject of more scholarly literature than any other facet of black labor. Many blacks in both North and South worked in crafts and industries that brought them into competition with white laborers. All three of the major national unions founded after the Civil War—the National Labor Union, the Knights of Labor, and the American Federation of Labor—officially maintained a non-discriminatory policy, but in practice most local unions barred blacks or segregated them in Jim Crow auxiliaries, and only the Knights of Labor came close to realizing in actuality the ideal of an interracial labor organization. All of the monographs cited in the first two paragraphs above contain references to organized labor and the Negro. In addition, see the following: Sterling D. Spero and Abram L. Harris, *The Black Worker: The Negro and the Labor Movement* (New York, 1931),* pts. 1–4; Frank E. Wolfe, *Admission to American Trade Unions* (Baltimore, 1912), ch. 6; Julius Jacobson, ed., *The Negro and the Labor Movement* (Garden City, N.Y., 1968),* chs. 1–4; Rayford W. Logan, *The Negro in American Life and Thought: The Nadir, 1877–1901* (New York, 1954, rev. paperback ed. 1965, under the title *The Betrayal of the Negro, from Rutherford B. Hayes to Woodrow Wilson*),* ch. 8; Gerald N. Grob, "Organized Labor and the Negro Worker, 1865–1900," *LH*, I (Spring 1960), 164–76; Herman D. Bloch, "Labor and the Negro, 1866–1910," *JNH*, L (July 1965), 163–84; Sumner Eliot Matison, "The Labor Movement and the Negro during Reconstruction," *ibid.*, XXXIII (Oct. 1948), 426–68; Sidney Kessler, "The Organization of Negroes in the Knights of Labor," *ibid.*, XXXVII (July 1952), 248–76;** Bernard Mandel, "Samuel Gompers and the Negro Workers, 1886–1914," *ibid.*, XL (Jan. 1955), 234–60;** Paul B. Worthman, "Black Workers and Labor Unions in Birmingham, Alabama, 1897–1904," *LH*, X (Summer 1969), 375–408,** reprinted in slightly revised form in Milton Cantor, ed., *Black Labor in America* (Westport, Conn., 1970), pp. 53–85; and Philip S. Foner, "The IWW and the Black Worker," *JNH*, LV (Jan. 1970), 45–64.

In areas where discriminatory unions gained substantial control of the labor market, or tried to, black workers were often frozen out of jobs or used as strikebreakers. The result was tension and hostility between working-class whites and blacks which often flared into violence. For studies of strikebreaking, racial friction, and violence, see Sidney Kessler, "The Negro in Labor

Strikes," *Midwest Journal*, XVI (Summer 1954), 16–35; Herbert G. Gutman, "Reconstruction in Ohio: Negroes in the Hocking Valley Coal Mines in 1873 and 1874," *LH*, III (Fall 1962), 243–64;** William M. Tuttle, Jr., "Labor Conflict and Racial Violence: The Worker in Chicago, 1894–1919," *ibid.*, X (Summer 1969), 408–32,** reprinted in slightly revised form in Cantor, ed., *Black Labor in America*, cited above, pp. 86–110; Alma Herbst, *The Negro in the Slaughtering and Meat-Packing Industry in Chicago* (New York, 1932); and Elliott M. Rudwick, *Race Riot at East St. Louis, July 2, 1917* (Carbondale, Ill., 1964).*

Black men and women serving prison sentences were leased by southern states to private contractors, which led to abuses and exploitation that were second only to lynching as a manifestation of cruelty. In some areas of the South, black convict labor provided a considerable part of the labor force and was economically significant. For brief accounts of the convict lease system, consult Fletcher M. Green, "Some Aspects of the Convict Lease System in the Southern States," in Fletcher M. Green, ed., *Essays in Southern History* (Chapel Hill, 1949), pp. 112–23; A. Elizabeth Taylor, "The Origin and Development of the Convict Lease System in Georgia," *Georgia Historical Quarterly*, XXVI (June 1942), 113–28; Mark T. Carleton, "The Politics of the Convict Lease System in Louisiana, 1868–1901," *Louisiana History*, VIII (Winter 1967), 5–26; and Wharton, *The Negro in Mississippi*, ch. 16, Tindall, *South Carolina Negroes*, ch. 13, and Logan, *The Negro in North Carolina*, ch. 18, all cited above. Ch. 6 of Hugh C. Bailey, *Liberalism in the New South: Social Reformers and the Progressive Movement* (Coral Gables, Fla., 1969), recounts efforts by southern liberals to abolish the convict lease system.

14. Black Nationalism and Migration, 1865–1915

The phrase "black nationalism" is often used loosely to describe various forms of ethnocentrism and racial solidarity. For this topic the definition of black nationalism encompasses back-to-

Africa and other emigrationist movements, Pan-Africanism, and cultural nationalism. Other manifestations of racial solidarity are dealt with in topics on the black church, black capitalism, and fraternal societies.

During the Civil War and Reconstruction, antebellum black nationalism almost disappeared as blacks concentrated all their energies on the drive for emancipation, equal rights, and the opportunity to become first-class American citizens. But with the overthrow and abandonment of Reconstruction in the 1870s, the optimistic hopes for assimilation as equals into American society began to fade and the voices of nationalism began to speak out again. Bishop Henry M. Turner of the African Methodist Episcopal Church, the foremost spokesman of nationalism between Reconstruction and the emergence of Marcus Garvey, had a significant impact on the growing racial consciousness of American blacks in the late nineteenth century and helped prepare the way for Garveyism in the 1920s.

Excellent background information and documents on post-Civil War nationalism can be found in John H. Bracey, Jr., August Meier, and Elliott Rudwick, eds., *Black Nationalism in America* (Indianapolis, 1970),* pp. xxxviii–xliii and pt. 3. Other brief accounts are contained in August Meier, *Negro Thought in America, 1880–1915* (Ann Arbor, 1963),* chs. 3–4, and "The Emergence of Negro Nationalism (A Study in Ideologies)," *Midwest Journal,* IV (Summer 1952), 95–111;** Herbert Aptheker, "Consciousness of Negro Nationality to 1900," in Aptheker, *Toward Negro Freedom* (New York, 1956), pp. 104–11; E. U. Essien-Udom, *Black Nationalism: The Search for an Identity in America* (Chicago, 1962),* ch. 2; and Theodore Draper, *The Rediscovery of Black Nationalism* (New York, 1970),* chs. 2–3. The best single study of nationalism in this period, which emphasizes Bishop Turner's role, is Edwin S. Redkey, *Black Exodus: Black Nationalist and Back-to-Africa Movements, 1890–1910* (New Haven, 1969).* See also Redkey's articles, "Bishop Turner's African Dream," *JAH,* LIV (Sept. 1967), 271–90,** and "The Flowering of Black Nationalism: Henry M. Turner and Marcus Garvey," in Nathan I. Huggins, Martin Kilson, and Daniel M. Fox, eds., *Key Issues in the Afro-American Experience,* 2 vols. (New York, 1971),* vol. II, pp. 107–24. Other important nationalists are treated by Hollis R. Lynch, *Edward Wilmot Blyden, Pan-Negro Patriot, 1832–1912* (London, 1967);* William Bittle and Gilbert Geis, "Alfred Charles Sam and an African Return: A Case Study in Negro Despair," *Phylon*, XXIII (2nd Quarter 1962), 178–94,** and *The Longest Way Home: Chief Alfred C. Sam's Back to Africa Movement* (Detroit, 1964); and Kathleen O'Mara Wahle, "Alexander Crummell: Black Evangelist and Pan-Negro Nationalist," *Phylon*, XXIX (Winter 1968), 388–95. For a case study of one of several Liberian emigration projects, see George B. Tindall, "The Liberian Exodus of 1878," *South Carolina Historical Magazine*, LII (July 1952), 133–45;** also see his *South Carolina Negroes, 1877–1900* (Columbia, S.C., 1952),* ch. 8. Africa was not always the goal of emigrationist hopes; for another movement, see J. Fred Rippy, "A Negro Colonization Project in Mexico, 1895," *JNH*, VI (Jan. 1921), 60–73.

The forces of poverty and exploitation that drove many blacks to seek a better life through emigration also produced periodic waves of internal migration from the South to western and northern states, even before the beginnings of massive northward migration during World War I. For a survey of black migration, see Carter G. Woodson, *A Century of Negro Migration* (Washington, 1918, reprinted New York, 1969), esp. chs. 7–8. The Kansas exodus of 1879 was the most famous case of internal migration during this period; see Walter L. Fleming, " 'Pap' Singleton, the Moses of the Colored Exodus," *AJS*, XV (July 1909), 61–82;** John G. Van Dusen, "The Exodus of 1879," *JNH*, XXI (Apr. 1936), 111–29; Roy Garvin, "Benjamin 'Pap' Singleton and His Followers," *ibid.*, XXXIII (Jan. 1949), 7–23; Glen Schwedemann, "St. Louis and the 'Exodusters' of 1879," *ibid.*, XLVI (Jan. 1961), 32–46; Vernon Lane Wharton, *The Negro in Mississippi, 1865–1890* (Chapel Hill, 1947),* ch. 7; Tindall, *South Carolina Negroes, 1877–1900*, cited above, ch. 8; and Frenise Logan, *The Negro in South Carolina, 1876–1894* (Chapel Hill, 1964), ch. 12. Many blacks migrated to Oklahoma, where they settled several all-Negro towns as an expression of racial solidarity and self-sufficiency; there was also talk of trying to make Oklahoma an all-black state: see Mozel C. Hill, "The All-Negro Communities of Oklahoma: The Natural History of a Social Movement," *JNH*, XXXI (July 1946), 254–68,** and William Bittle and Gilbert

Geis, "Racial Self-fulfillment and the Rise of an All-Negro Community in Oklahoma," *Phylon*, XVII (3rd Quarter 1956), 247–60.

While many black Americans during this period were ashamed of or indifferent to their African ancestry, others took pride in it and cultivated a form of Pan-African cultural nationalism. For an appraisal, see George Shepperson, "Pan-Africanism and 'Pan-Africanism': Some Historical Notes," *Phylon*, XXIII (4th Quarter 1962), 346–58.** W. E. B. Du Bois, though he advocated an equalitarian/pluralist solution of the race problem in the United States, was nevertheless the foremost proponent of international cultural and political ties between all peoples of African descent. The principal period of Du Bois' Pan-Africanism came after World War I, but he had begun writing about the subject twenty years earlier and was a leader in the first Pan-African Congress (held in London) in 1900. For analyses of Du Bois' Pan-Africanism and other aspects of his cultural nationalism, see Meier, *Negro Thought in America, 1880–1915*, cited above, ch. 11; Francis L. Broderick, *W. E. B. Du Bois: Negro Leader in a Time of Crisis* (Stanford, 1959),* ch. 5; Elliott M. Rudwick, *W. E. B. Du Bois: A Study of Minority Group Leadership* (Philadelphia, 1960),* ch. 9; and Clarence G. Contee, "The Emergence of Du Bois as an African Nationalist," *JNH*, LIV (Jan. 1969), 48–63. Du Bois' consciousness of the "two-ness" of the black American —his divided loyalties between racial and national identities— is best expressed in his *The Souls of Black Folk* (Chicago, 1903).* See also Du Bois' *The Negro* (New York, 1915),* and his *Dusk of Dawn: An Essay Toward an Autobiography of a Race Concept* (New York, 1940),* esp. chs. 5, 7. Several African students attended American black colleges during the late nineteenth and early twentieth centuries, where they absorbed some of the nationalist ideology then current among elements of the United States black community and took it home with them, where it eventually emerged as African nationalism and anticolonialism. For an account of these developments, see George A. Shepperson, "American Negro Influence on the Emergence of African Nationalism," *Journal of African History*, I (1960), 299–312.**

15. Black Fiction at the Turn of the Century: Charles Waddell Chesnutt and Paul Laurence Dunbar

Between 1890 and 1920 nearly thirty novels by black authors were published in the United States (as opposed to only three known novels before 1890). The authors of these novels were by and large members of the black middle class, and their novels reveal the tension and ambivalence in that class's view of the racial situation in America at the turn of the century. On the one hand these novelists tried to counter myths of racial inferiority by presenting black characters whose values, behavior, and speech are indistinguishable from those of the white middle class. On the other hand, they express from time to time a more self-consciously black sense of pride and outrage, a sense that perhaps the only solution for black Americans is to defy, rather than emulate, the behavior of the whites. It was the task of these novelists to try somehow to resolve the tension between emulation and defiance.

The most important black novelists of this period were Paul Laurence Dunbar and Charles Waddell Chesnutt, both of whom were raised in Ohio. Chesnutt, a successful lawyer, published five volumes of fiction and a biography of Frederick Douglass. His best work is probably contained in his short stories, but his second novel, *The Marrow of Tradition* (Boston, 1901),* deserves particular attention. Dunbar was best known for his poetry, much of it in dialect and much of it appealing to the paternalistic image of white-black relations popularized by the plantation tradition. (See the following topic, "The Portrayal of Blacks by White Writers.") The volumes which made Dunbar's reputation are *Oak and Ivy* (Dayton, Ohio, 1893), *Majors and Minors* (Toledo, Ohio, 1895), which was favorably reviewed by the influential white critic William Dean Howells, and *Lyrics of Lowly Life* (New York, 1896), for which Howells wrote an introduction. Of Dunbar's four novels only the fourth, *The Sport of the Gods* (New York, 1902),* presents important black characters. A comparison of Chesnutt's treatment of black characters and racial conflict in *The Marrow of Tradition* with that of Dunbar in *The Sport of the Gods* illuminates problems Chesnutt and Dunbar faced in dealing with black life.

The best general treatment of Chesnutt and Dunbar and their contemporaries is pt. I, "The Novel of the Rising Middle Class, 1890–1920," of Robert A. Bone, *The Negro Novel in America* (rev. ed., New Haven, 1965).* There is also relevant material in Sterling Brown, *The Negro in American Fiction* (Washington, 1937),* pp. 77–82; Hugh M. Gloster, *Negro Voices in American Fiction* (Chapel Hill, 1948), ch. 2; Vernon Loggins, *The Negro Author: His Development in America* (New York, 1931), pp. 310–31; and Edward Margolies, *Native Sons* (New York, 1968),* pp. 25–26, 29–30. There is a biography of Chesnutt by his daughter, Helen M. Chesnutt, *Charles Waddell Chesnutt: Pioneer of the Color Line* (Chapel Hill, 1952).* Essays on Chesnutt include Russell Ames, "Social Realism in Charles Chesnutt," *Phylon*, XIV (Summer 1953), 199–206, and Samuel Sillen, "Charles W. Chesnutt: A Pioneer Negro Novelist," *Masses and Mainstream*, VI (Feb. 1953), 8–14. There are two biographies of Dunbar: Benjamin Brawley, *Paul Laurence Dunbar: Poet of His People* (Chapel Hill, 1936), and Virginia Cunningham's rather sentimental *Paul Laurence Dunbar and His Song* (New York, 1948). Both emphasize Dunbar's poetry. An effort to analyze and evaluate Dunbar's fiction is ch. 5 of Victor Lawson, *Dunbar Critically Examined* (Washington, 1941). Essays on Dunbar include Edward F. Arnold, "Some Personal Reminiscences of Paul Laurence Dunbar," *JNH*, XVII (Oct. 1932), 400–08; T. W. Daniel, "Paul Laurence Dunbar and the Democratic Ideal," *NHB*, VI (June 1943), 206–08; and Darwin T. Turner, "Paul Laurence Dunbar: The Rejected Symbol," *JNH*, LII (Jan. 1967), 1–13.**

16. The Portrayal of Blacks by White Writers

A. Mark Twain

Writers as different as Stephen Crane (in "The Monster") and Gertrude Stein (in "Melanctha") are among the white authors of major talent who have given increasing attention to the figure of the Afro-American since the Civil War, but Mark Twain was the first to give central importance to black characters in two first-rate works of fiction, *Huckleberry Finn* (New York, 1885)* and *Pudd'nhead Wilson* (Hartford, Conn., 1894).* Both books challenge racism: *Huckleberry Finn* through the hero's growing awareness of the inhumanity of the white world that sanctions slavery and his recognition of the human stature of the slave Jim, *Pudd'nhead Wilson* through a doubly black comedy of mistaken racial identities. Recent criticism, however, has questioned Twain's ability to dissociate himself from the racism he exposes. *Huckleberry Finn* is frequently criticized for its use of racial stereotypes in the figure of Jim. The question of whether the characterization of Jim (or of Roxy, Tom, or Chambers in *Pudd'nhead Wilson*) is stereotyped is complicated by the fact that Twain's parodic comic techniques, particularly in the later book, necessarily exaggerate the contours of his figures. In any case, it is clear that, like other authors (black as well as white), he entertained familiar hypotheses about Afro-American types: the clownish, sensuous, crafty and ingenious, natural, simple, subservient, irresponsible, or villainous black. It is equally clear that he entertained comparable notions about whites.

One view of Twain's handling of black characters can be found in Sterling A. Brown, *The Negro in American Fiction* (Washington, 1937),* pp. 67–69. More recent and provocative views may be found in Richard Chase, *The American Novel and Its Tradition* (Garden City, N.Y., 1956),* pp. 149–56; Henry Nash Smith, *Mark Twain: The Development of a Writer* (Cambridge, Mass., 1962),* pp. 171–83; and especially several works by Leslie A. Fiedler: *Love and Death in the American Novel* (New York, 1960),* pp. 382–92; "As Free as any Cretur . . . !," *New Republic*, CXXXIII (Aug. 15 and 22, 1955), 17–18, 16–18; and "'Come Back to the Raft Ag'n Huck Honey!'," *Partisan Review*, XV (June 1948), 664–71. Seymour L. Gross and John E. Hardy, eds., reprint the section from Fiedler's *Love and Death in the American Novel* in their *Images of the Negro in American Literature* (Chicago, 1966),* pp. 89–99, and also include James M. Cox's excellent "'Pudd'nhead Wilson': The End of Mark Twain's American Dream," pp. 181–93.

Other essays in the voluminous literature on Twain that focus on racial figures and themes are: Lynn Altenbernd, "Huck Finn, Emancipator," *Criticism*, I (1959), 298–307; Francis V. Brownell, "The Role of Jim in *Huckleberry Finn*," *Boston University Studies in English*, I (Spring–Summer 1955), 74–83; Philip Butcher, "Mark Twain Sells Roxy Down the River," *CLAJ*, VIII (Mar. 1965), 225–33, and "Mark Twain's Installment on the National Debt," *Southern Literary Journal*, I (Spring 1969), 48–55;** Abigail Ann Hamblen, "Uncle Tom and 'Nigger Jim': A Study in Contrasts and Similarities," *Mark Twain Journal*, XI (Fall 1961), 13–17; Sakal Morioka, "Pudd'nhead Wilson and the Racial Problem," *Kyusha University Studies in English Literature and Language*, XIII (Jan. 1962), pp. 1–11; Michael Orth, *"Pudd'nhead Wilson* Reconsidered, or The Octoroon in the Villa Viviani," *Mark Twain Journal*, XIV (Summer 1969), 11–15; and two items by Arthur G. Pettit: "Mark Twain, Unreconstructed Southerner, and His View of the Negro, 1835–1860," *Rocky Mountain Social Science Journal*, VII (Apr. 1970), 17–27; and "Mark Twain's Attitude Toward the Negro in the West, 1861–1867," *Western Historical Quarterly*, I (Jan. 1970), 51–62.

Material on Twain's rendering of Afro-American dialect includes J. M. Tidwell, "Mark Twain's Representation of Negro Speech," *American Speech*, XVII (Oct. 1942), 174–76; Lee Pederson, "Negro Speech in *The Adventures of Huckleberry Finn*," *Mark Twain Journal*, XIII (Summer 1966), 1–4; and especially Richard Bridgman, *The Colloquial Style in America* (New York, 1966),* pp. 78–130.

B. The Plantation Myth: Thomas Nelson Page and Joel Chandler Harris

Thomas Nelson Page and Joel Chandler Harris, with less talent than Twain, and less profoundly engaged by the claims of the blacks, won large audiences in post-Civil War America with fiction that perpetuated myths about the South and blacks that still have repercussions in American culture; they were particularly comforting and appealing to whites after the abandonment of Reconstruction. The myth of the southern plantation had great appeal to a South unwilling to accept the consequences of defeat; it was equally popular in the North, tired of sectional strife and determined to reconcile itself to its old foe. Page thought the South's defeat a disaster and the "New South" a travesty of Virginia's former glories; he celebrated an idealized plantation system and portrayed loyal Afro-Americans who testified to the benevolence of their masters and to the dangers of Reconstruction and the new independent blacks. Harris, an adopted son of the plantation system, knew slaves well during his childhood, and in his "Uncle Remus" stories he presented astutely observed but sentimental sketches of life among Georgia blacks.

Important writings by Page include the collection of stories, *In Ole Virginia* (New York, 1887),* the novel *Red Rock* (New York, 1898), and such collections of essays as *The Negro: The Southerner's Problem* (New York, 1904), *The Old South* (New York, 1892), and *The Old Dominion: Her Making and Her Manners* (New York, 1908).

Harris' writings include *Uncle Remus: His Songs and Sayings* (New York, 1881);* *Nights with Uncle Remus* (Boston, 1883); *Told by Uncle Remus: New Stories of the Old Plantation* (New York, 1909).

For comments by black scholars on Page and Harris, see Margaret Just Butcher, *The Negro in American Culture* (New York, 1956), pp. 158–60, and particularly Darwin T. Turner, "Daddy Joel Harris and His Old-Time Darkies," *Southern Literary Journal*, I (Autumn 1968), 20–41.** For the views of a southern white scholar, see Jay B. Hubbell, *The South in American Literature, 1607–1900* (Durham, N.C., 1954), pp. 782–804. An astute essay on Page is Edmund Wilson's in *Patriotic Gore* (New York, 1962),* pp. 604–16. An interesting essay on the beginnings of the plantation myth is the first chapter of Kenneth S. Lynn's *Mark Twain and Southwestern Humor* (Boston, 1959). For the myth of the southern plantation and its celebration after the Civil War, see Francis P. Gaines, *The Southern Plantation: A Study in the Development and Accuracy of a Tradition* (New York, 1924). In chs. 8 and 9 of *The Road to Reunion* (Boston, 1937),* Paul Buck discusses the impact of southern apologists after 1865. For the pervasiveness of nostalgia in northern and southern literature after 1865, see the section "Paradise Lost" in Jay Martin, *Harvests of Change, American Literature, 1865–1914* (Englewood Cliffs,

N.J., 1967),* esp. pp. 81–105. Two recent biographies, which include bibliographies, are Theodore L. Gross, *Thomas Nelson Page* (New York, 1967),* and Paul M. Cousins, *Joel Chandler Harris* (Baton Rouge, 1968).

C. Albion W. Tourgée

A Union officer with literary talent, Albion W. Tourgée moved to North Carolina after the war where he participated in the experiment of Reconstruction. His first novel *Toinette* (New York, 1874, retitled *A Royal Gentleman* in 1881) treats the tragedy of a southern mulatto and her daughter in their relations with northern and southern whites during the war and after. His two best known novels treat the turbulence of Reconstruction and reveal his growing conviction that implacable southern racism could only be countered by an equally determined northern effort to enforce equal rights, an objective he fought for unsuccessfully the rest of his life: *A Fool's Errand* (New York, 1879),* and *Bricks Without Straw* (New York, 1880). Tourgée is discussed by Edmund Wilson in *Patriotic Gore* (New York, 1962),* pp. 529–48. Tourgée is the subject of Otto H. Olsen's *Carpetbagger's Crusade: The Life of Albion Winegar Tourgée* (Baltimore, 1965); chs. 18–23 deal with Tourgée's literary career. See also Robert A. Lively, *Fiction Fights the Civil War* (Chapel Hill, 1957), *passim*; Russell B. Nye, "Judge Tourgée and Reconstruction," *Ohio State Archaeological and Historical Quarterly*, L (1941), 101–14; and George J. Becker, "Albion W. Tourgée: Pioneer in Social Criticism," *American Literature*, XLIX (1947), 59–72. Two other studies that focus on Tourgée's literary career are Roy F. Dibble, *Albion W. Tourgée* (New York, 1921) and Theodore L. Gross, *Albion W. Tourgée* (New York, 1964).*

D. George Washington Cable

Cable was a Louisiana liberal who tried to combine a literary career with a mission as commentator on southern problems after the Civil War and who finally moved to Northampton, Massachusetts, in 1885, still concerned with the South but a virtual expatriate from his native section. His many essays and lectures on the South and the race question provide an opportunity to measure the limits of his understanding of the race problem and to compare his public attitudes and politics to his sympathetic and sensitive portraits of blacks in Creole Louisiana.

His best volumes, besides *Dr. Sevier* (Boston, 1885) and *Madame Delphine* (New York, 1881), are his most famous works: *Old Creole Days* (New York, 1879)* and *The Grandissimes* (New York, 1880).* His writings on the South (*The Silent South*, 1885, and *The Negro Question*, 1890) have been reprinted by Arlin W. Turner in *The Negro Question* (Garden City, N.Y., 1958).* Arlin Turner's biography, *George W. Cable: A Biography* (Durham, N.C., 1956),* may be supplemented by two excellent essays: Edmund Wilson, *Patriotic Gore* (New York, 1962),* pp. 548–604, and Richard Chase, *The American Novel and its Tradition* (Garden City, N.Y., 1957),* pp. 167–76. There is a section on Cable in Jay B. Hubbell, *The South in American Literature*, 1607–1900 (Durham, N.C., 1954), pp. 804–22. The latest biography of Cable is Louis D. Rubin, Jr., *George W. Cable: The Life and Times of a Southern Heretic* (New York, 1969).

17. The Portrayal of Blacks in Paintings by Whites: Winslow Homer and Thomas Eakins

Blacks as an important subject for white painters began to emerge in genre painting before the Civil War, in canvases where Afro-Americans (like everyone else) were threatened by patronizing condescension and by the predilection of painters and viewers alike for charm, quaintness, or the picturesque at the expense of candor, close scrutiny, or uncondescending recognition. But if genre painting abounded with examples of devoted "darkies" at the cabin door or other stereotypes (as in Richard C. Woodville's *Sailor's Wedding*), such works as William Sidney Mount's *The Power of Music* and *Eel Spearing at Setauket* revealed their subjects' distinctive integrity and opened up for the painter a wider variety of Afro-American types.

During and after the Civil War, two painters of major talent were attracted to the figure, color, and circumstances of blacks. One, Winslow Homer, included black subjects in genre paintings of his local scene, traveled to Virginia in 1875 and 1876 to develop subjects, and in the 1890s produced numerous oils and watercolors featuring blacks in ocean and West Indies settings. His paintings have been cited as spanning the full range from genre stereotypes to a mature revelation of the Afro-American's character. The other painter is Thomas Eakins, whose portrait of the black painter Henry O. Tanner is only one of a sizable number of portraits and genre paintings that include Afro-American subjects. Disdaining "respectability" in art and avoiding flattery or idealization of his subjects, Eakins sought to render in art an unvarnished tribute to his subject.

Reproductions of works by the two artists, inadequate though they necessarily are, enable one to examine the postures and coloration of black figures and the circumstances of their surroundings so that one can measure the variety of individuals and types represented and the range of experience or the dignity and beauty revealed in black subjects. Good starting points are the following: the catalogue and notes of the Bowdoin exhibition entitled *The Portrayal of the Negro in American Painting, 1710–1963* (Brunswick, Me., 1964),* a selection of which are included with Sidney Kaplan's essay "The Negro in the Art of Homer and Eakins," in *Massachusetts Review*, III (Winter 1966), 105–20;** Lloyd Goodrich, *Winslow Homer* (New York, 1959),* and *Winslow Homer's America* (New York, 1969); and Fairfield Porter, *Thomas Eakins* (New York, 1959).* Each of these books includes a list of exhibition catalogues that may be consulted for reproductions of the painters' works. The best biographies of both painters are by Lloyd Goodrich: *Winslow Homer* (New York, 1945) and *Thomas Eakins: His Life and Work* (New York, 1933). Both painters are treated by Oliver W. Larkin, *Art and Life in America* (rev. ed., New York, 1960), pp. 272–79, and by Jules Prown, *American Painting, From its Beginnings to the Armory Show* (New York, 1969), pp. 86–96. For earlier genre painters, see Larkin, pp. 214–22; Prown, pp. 79–85; and the following studies: John I. H. Baur, *An American Genre Painter, Eastman Johnson*

(New York, 1940); John F. McDermott, *George Caleb Bingham, River Portraitist* (Norman, Okla., 1959); and Bartlett Cowdrey and Herman Williams, Jr., *William Sidney Mount . . . An American Painter* (New York, 1944).

PART VII

THE NORTHWARD MIGRATION AND THE ROOTS OF CHANGE, 1915–1954

1. The Great Migration

After the Civil War, rural blacks (like southern whites) began to move in substantial numbers to the urban centers of the South, and as early as 1880 black migrants began to show up with increasing frequency in cities outside the South. The northward movement gained momentum in the 1890s, but it was the migration of World War I that shaped the distribution and character of the black population more profoundly than any previous demographic shifts.

The so-called "Great Migration" began in 1915 and peaked during 1916 and 1917; all told, it brought perhaps 300,000 to 400,000 blacks northward in the space of three years. (There is no accurate figure.) The number of blacks in northern cities increased substantially, and by the end of the decade, the migration had confirmed the urban racial ghetto as a permanent feature of the American scene. Much of the impetus for the migration came from long-standing traditions of injustice and lack of opportunity in the South. But the dimensions of the Great Migration were shaped by the special economic circumstances of the war years— on the one hand, depression and crop failures in the South, and on the other, new-found industrial opportunities for blacks in the North as a result of declining immigration from Europe and the demands of war production. Many blacks thought that they were heading for the promised land, but life in new northern ghettos brought profound problems of economic and social adjustment as well as anticipated opportunities.

While the bibliography on the black migration to the North is voluminous, there is still no single comprehensive modern study. William S. Rossiter, *Increase of Population in the United States, 1910–1920*, Census Monographs I (Washington, 1922), and two vols. published by the U. S. Bureau of the Census, *Negro Population: 1790–1915* (Washington, 1918, reprinted New York, 1968)

and *Negroes in the United States, 1920–1932* (Washington, 1935),
provide the raw materials for statistical analysis. Louise V. Kennedy and Frank Ross, *A Bibliography of Negro Migration* (New
York, 1935), is an exhaustive survey of contemporary sources.

R. R. Wright, "The Migration of Negroes to the North," *Annals*, XXVII (May 1906), 559–78; George Edmund Haynes, "The
Movement of Negroes from the Country to the City," *Southern
Workman*, XLII (Apr. 1913), 230–36; Allan H. Spear, *Black Chicago: The Making of a Negro Ghetto, 1890–1920* (Chicago,
1967),* ch. 1; and Gilbert Osofsky, *Harlem: The Making of a
Ghetto; Negro New York, 1890–1930* (New York, 1966),* ch. 2,
are particularly relevant for the prewar migrations.

Contemporary articles which provide a solid introduction to the
Great Migration include Ray Stannard Baker, "The Negro Goes
North," *World's Work*, XXXIV (July 1917), 314–19; George Edmund Haynes, "Negroes Move North," *Survey*, XL (May 4, 1918),
115–22, and XLI (Jan. 4, 1919), 455–61; Henderson H. Donald,
"The Negro Migration of 1916–1918," *JNH*, VI (Oct. 1921),
383–498; William O. Scroggs, "Interstate Migration of Negro Population," *Journal of Political Economy*, XXV (Dec. 1917),
1034–43; and Charles S. Johnson, "How Much is Migration a
Flight from Persecution?" *Opportunity*, I (Sept. 1923), 272–74.

In 1919 the U. S. Department of Labor published a valuable
series of studies under the title *Negro Migrations in 1916–17*
(Washington, 1919). The historical background of black migration culminating in the northward movement during World War I
is traced in Carter G. Woodson, *A Century of Negro Migration*
(Washington, 1918, reprinted New York, 1969), while Thomas
J. Woofter, Jr., *Negro Problems in Cities* (New York, 1928, reprinted College Park, Md., 1969, and Westport, Conn., 1970),
evaluates the migration in the context of the general trend of
movement to urban centers since the beginning of this century.
An earlier Woofter volume, *Negro Migration: Changes in Rural
Organization and Population of the Cotton Belt* (New York,
1920), focuses on Georgia. Emmett J. Scott edited a number of
fascinating letters from the migrants themselves which were published under the title "Letters of Negro Migrants of 1916–1918,"
JNH, IV (July, Oct. 1919), 290–340, 412–75. The following year
Scott also wrote a general study of the movement, *Negro Migra-*

tion During the War (New York, 1920, reprinted New York, 1969). A decade later, Louise V. Kennedy published her scholarly account, *The Negro Peasant Turns Cityward: Effects of Recent Migrations to Northern Cities* (New York, 1930, reprinted College Park, Md., 1969), which deals with the migration itself and problems of urban adjustment. Two less important volumes are Edward E. Lewis, *The Mobility of the Negro: A Study in the American Labor Supply* (New York, 1931), and Clyde Vernon Kiser, *Sea Island to City: A Study of St. Helena Islanders in Harlem and Other Urban Centers* (New York, 1932).* Henderson H. Donald, "The Urbanization of the American Negro," in G. P. Murdock, ed., *Studies in the Science of Society* (New Haven, 1937), is a helpful summary and statistical analysis, while T. Lynn Smith, "The Redistribution of the Negro Population of the United States, 1910–1960," *JNH*, LI (July 1966), 155–73,** and Reynolds Farley, "The Urbanization of Negroes in the United States," *Journal of Social History*, I (Spring 1968), 241–58,** put the movement in demographic perspective. Arna Bontemps and Jack Conroy, *They Seek a City* (Garden City, N.Y., 1945), retitled *Anyplace But Here* (New York, 1966)* for the revised paperback edition, is a popular account. George Edmund Haynes, "Negro Migration: Its Effect on Family and Community Life in the North," *Opportunity*, II (Sept., Oct. 1924), 271–74, 303–06,** is a particularly perceptive analysis of the consequences of migration. Haynes' *Negro New-Comers in Detroit, Michigan* (New York, 1918, reprinted New York, 1969) is a useful case study. The major studies of the development of ghettos—Osofsky's *Harlem*, ch. 9, and Spear's *Black Chicago*, ch. 7, both cited above, and St. Clair Drake and Horace R. Cayton, *Black Metropolis: A Study of Negro Life in a Northern City* (New York, 1945),* ch. 3—treat in some detail the migrations to those black centers and shed light on the entire process.

Articles dealing with the resurgence of substantial migration in the early 1920s include Charles S. Johnson, "The Negro Migration," *Modern Quarterly*, II (1924–25), 314–26;** Joseph A. Hill, "The Effects of the Recent Northward Migration of Negroes," *Publications of the American Sociological Society*, XVIII (1923), 34–46; Guy B. Johnson, "The Negro Migration and Its Consequences," *Journal of Social Forces*, II (Mar. 1924), 404–08;

and William Pickens, "Migrating to Fuller Life," *Forum*, LXXII (Nov. 1924), 600–07. See also Charles S. Johnson, "The American Migrant: The Negro," *Proceedings, National Conference of Social Work* (New York, 1927), pp. 554–58.

The best study of the immigration of blacks to the United States from other countries, chiefly the British West Indies, is Ira De A. Reid, *The Negro Immigrant: His Background, Characteristics and Social Adjustment,* 1899–1937 (New York, 1939).

2. *The Development of the Ghetto*

Conditions which we associate with black life in the contemporary urban ghetto—slum housing, drastic limitation of employment opportunity, large numbers of working mothers, inferior education, lack of police protection and sanitation services, high incidences of crime and delinquency, disease and infant mortality—also prevailed in varying degrees among blacks in northern cities at the beginning of the twentieth century. Although the massive influx of blacks into northern cities dates from World War I, the foundations of black ghettos in major cities were laid as early as the 1890s. Indeed, Gilbert Osofsky argues in "The Enduring Ghetto," *JAH*, LV (Sept. 1968), 243–55, that the basic structure and nature of the black ghetto have remained substantially the same since slavery ended in the North nearly two centuries ago. Allan Spear, "The Origins of the Urban Ghetto, 1870–1915," in Nathan I. Huggins, Martin Kilson, and Daniel M. Fox, eds., *Key Issues in the Afro-American Experience,* 2 vols. (New York, 1971),* vol. II, pp. 153–66, provides a good introduction to this topic.

W. E. B. Du Bois pioneered in the scientific investigation of black city life in his study of *The Philadelphia Negro* (Philadelphia, 1899),* and he continued his efforts when he went to Atlanta University to take charge of its work in sociology and its conferences on black problems. Notable among the Atlanta University publications that deal with aspects of urban life are *Mortality Among Negroes in Cities* (Atlanta, 1896, reprinted

New York, 1968), *Social and Physical Condition of Negroes in Cities* (Atlanta, 1897, reprinted New York, 1968), *The Negro in Business* (Atlanta, 1899, reprinted New York, 1968), *Some Notes on Negro Crime* (Atlanta, 1904, reprinted New York, 1968), *The Health and Physique of the Negro American* (Atlanta, 1906, reprinted New York, 1968), *Economic Cooperation Among Negro Americans* (Atlanta, 1907), *The Negro American Family* (Atlanta, 1908, reprinted New York, 1968), *Efforts for Social Betterment Among Negro Americans* (Atlanta, 1909, reprinted New York, 1968), and *Morals and Manners Among Negro Americans* (Atlanta, 1914, reprinted New York, 1968).

Following Du Bois' lead, a handful of writers after the turn of the century undertook the first serious scholarly study of racial problems since the literature produced by the abolitionists. Contemporary works dealing with conditions among blacks in individual cities and states include "The Negro in the Cities of the North," the entire vol. XV (Oct. 7, 1905) of *Charities*; Mary White Ovington, *Half a Man: The Status of the Negro in New York* (New York, 1911);* R. R. Wright, Jr., *The Negro in Pennsylvania* (Philadelphia, 1912); George Edmund Haynes, *The Negro at Work in New York City: A Study in Economic Progress* (New York, 1912), and his article, "Conditions Among Negroes in the Cities," *Annals*, XLIX (Sept. 1913), 110–17; Louise De Koven Bowen, *The Colored Population of Chicago* (Chicago, 1913); John Daniels, *In Freedom's Birthplace: A History of the Boston Negro* (Boston, 1914, reprinted New York, 1968); William A. Crossland, *Industrial Conditions Among Negroes in St. Louis* (St. Louis, 1914); and Frances Blascoer, *Colored School Children of New York* (New York, 1915). The National Urban League's magazine, *Opportunity*, which was published from 1923–49, regularly included reports on various aspects of urban black life.

It was some decades later, however, that sociologists and historians began the systematic scholarly investigation of the black ghetto. The first major work of this kind is the classic analysis of Chicago by St. Clair Drake and Horace R. Cayton, *Black Metropolis: A Study of Negro Life in a Northern City* (New York, 1945).* Robert Weaver, an eminent black writer and public official, deals especially with the development of residential segregation in *The Negro Ghetto* (New York, 1948). Weaver discusses the founding of black Harlem, as do a number of popular histories of Harlem by black authors, the best of which are James Weldon Johnson, *Black Manhattan* (New York, 1930);* Claude McKay, *Harlem: Negro Metropolis* (New York, 1940); and Roi Ottley, *New World A-Coming* (Boston, 1943, reprinted New York, 1968). Another revealing source is the March 1925, Harlem number (vol. VI) of the *Survey Graphic*. These accounts generally romanticize the Harlem of the 1920s, and they neglect the forces that turned parts of Harlem from the home of the black elite at the turn of the century into the sorry slum of the era of the Harlem renaissance. Such an analysis is ably presented in Gilbert Osofsky's incisive *Harlem: The Making of a Ghetto; Negro New York, 1890–1930* (New York, 1966).* For another useful work see Seth M. Scheiner, *Negro Mecca: A History of the Negro in New York City, 1865–1920* (New York, 1965).* Allan H. Spear, *Black Chicago: The Making of a Negro Ghetto, 1890–1920* (Chicago, 1967),* and Constance McLaughlin Green, *The Secret City: A History of Race Relations in the Nation's Capital* (Princeton, 1967),* are notable studies of other major black communities. Kenneth B. Clark's excellent *Dark Ghetto: Dilemmas of Social Power* (New York, 1965)* focuses on recent problems but also contributes to an understanding of the earlier period. Richard B. Sherman, ed., *The Negro and the City* (Englewood Cliffs, N.J., 1970),* is a reader which illuminates various aspects of urban life since the Great Migration. John H. Bracey, Jr., August Meier, and Elliott Rudwick, eds., *The Rise of the Ghetto* (Belmont, Calif., 1971),* is an excellent collection of articles.

Like the comparative study of slave systems, the comparative history of foreign white and native black groups that immigrated into the cities after 1870 should advance our understanding of the problems which have faced black Americans when they have migrated from southern farms. Whether the "dark ghetto" promises to become a permanent fixture of American urban civilization or whether black Americans—like Polish-Americans, Irish-Americans, and Italian-Americans before them—will become assimilated into the larger urban community, while retaining a good measure of their own distinctive culture, is a question of great moment. Clearly the factor of color makes the black experience unique. Nevertheless, we can learn much from a comparison of the conditions under which these groups of black in-migrants entered the cities in the first place, the attitudes and institutions they brought with them, the receptivity of the larger and dominant city populations toward them, their success in exploiting the urban political process, and other facets of their adjustment to urban life.

While there exists no book devoted exclusively to these problems, good introductions are Nathan Glazer, "Blacks and Ethnic Groups: The Difference, and the Political Difference It Makes," in Huggins, Kilson, and Fox, eds., *Key Issues in the Afro-American Experience*, cited above, vol. II, pp. 193–211, and Oscar Handlin, *The Newcomers: Negroes and Puerto Ricans in a Changing Metropolis* (Cambridge, Mass., 1959),* esp. ch. 4. A short but cogent attempt to compare the histories of black and other urban immigrants is found in the Riot Commission Report, formally *Report of the National Advisory Commission on Civil Disorders* (New York, 1968),* pp. 278–82. There is useful material in Pierre L. van den Berghe, *Race and Ethnicity: Essays in Comparative Sociology* (New York, 1970). Sterling Tucker, *Beyond the Burning: Life and Death of the Ghetto* (New York, 1968),* ch. 3, and Karl E. Taeuber and Alma F. Taeuber, "Is the Negro an Immigrant Group?" *Integrated Education,* I (June 1963), 25–28, argue for the uniqueness of the black ghetto, while Irving Kristol, "The Negro Today Is Like the Immigrant Yesterday," *New York Times Magazine,* Sept. 11, 1966, 50–51 ff., stresses immigrant precedents for the black experience in urban America. Other works that allude to these matters include Gunnar Myrdal, *An American Dilemma: The Negro Problem and Modern Democracy* (New York, 1944),* ch. 3; Nathan Glazer and Daniel P. Moynihan, *Beyond the Melting Pot: The Negroes, Puerto Ricans, Jews, Italians, and Irish of New York* (Cambridge, Mass., 1963),* esp. ch. 1; Herbert J. Gans, *The Urban Villagers: Group and Class in the Life of Italian-Americans* (New York, 1962),* esp. ch. 11; and Charles A. Valentine, *Culture and Poverty: Critique and Counter-Proposals* (Chicago, 1968),* pp. 121–27. Two classic studies of the male subcultures of Italian-Americans and black Americans provide a basis for comparative analysis: William F. White, *Street Corner Society* (2nd ed., Chicago, 1955),* and Elliott Liebow, *Tally's Corner: A Study* *of Negro Streetcorner Men* (Boston, 1967).* John J. Appel, "American Negro and Immigrant Experience: Similarities and Differences," *AQ,* XVIII (Spring 1966), 95–103, reprinted in Leonard Dinnerstein and Frederick Cople Jaher, eds., *The Aliens: A History of Ethnic Minorities in America* (New York, 1970),* pp. 339–47; and Stephan Thernstrom, "Up From Slavery," *Perspectives in American History,* I (1967), 434–39, a review essay of Osofsky's *Harlem* (cited above), raise important questions relevant to all studies of black ghettos and their comparison with other immigrant enclaves. Brewton Berry, *Race and Ethnic Relations* (rev. ed., Boston, 1968) is a sociology textbook that includes comparisons of the immigrant and the black experience. Berry argues that the problems confronting immigrants have not been fundamentally different from those of blacks, but that physical characteristics are the object of greater prejudice than religious or cultural differences.

3. Blacks in World War I

In the words of President Wilson, the United States went to war in 1917 to make the world safe for democracy, and black Americans, hoping that their participation in the war effort might yield a little of that democracy at home, made a significant contribution to the Allied war effort. Some 367,000 blacks were called to military service, and several black regiments fought well in the front lines in France, winning the commendation of American and French officials for their performance. But in the main the American treatment of black fighting men conformed to the country's long-time tradition of prejudice and discrimination. While blacks could be found in most branches of the Army (organized, of course, into separate regiments), none were admitted to the Marines, and the Navy relegated its 5,300 black recruits to the most menial tasks. Altogether, two thirds of the black troops were assigned to labor battalions and service regiments rather than combat units, and most of the black soldiers spent the war unloading ships, setting up camps, digging ditches, and performing other noncombatant functions. The American government was extremely reluctant to establish officers' training camps for blacks and did so only after strong pressure from the NAACP, the black press, and black college students. Fewer than 1,300 black officers were commissioned during the war, and white soldiers sometimes balked at respecting their authority. Discrimination was prevalent in the Army and its civilian service agencies, and frequent clashes between white and black soldiers were reported. Despite all this, the morale of black troops was, with some exceptions, fairly high, and black units usually performed efficiently.

The best general treatment of blacks in the war is that of Emmett J. Scott, the black man who was appointed Special Assistant to the Secretary of War, in *Scott's Official History of the American Negro in the World War* (Chicago, 1919, reprinted New York, 1969). W. E. B. Du Bois' brief contemporary accounts are written from a more critical perspective; see "The Black Man in the Revolution of 1914–1918," *Crisis*, XVII (Mar. 1919), 218–23, "Documents of the War," *ibid.*, XVIII (May 1919), 16–21, and "An Essay Toward a History of the Black Man in the Great War," *ibid.* (June 1919), 63–87.** There is a fine account of both the armed services and manpower mobilization at home in Jane Lang Scheiber and Harry N. Scheiber, "The Wilson Administration and the Wartime Mobilization of Black Americans, 1917–18," *LH*, X (Summer 1969), 433–58, which also appears as ch. 5 of Milton Cantor, ed., *Black Labor in America* (Westport, Conn., 1970). The Division of Negro Economics in the Department of Labor reported on the changing prospects for black labor in *The Negro at Work During the World War and During Reconstruction* (Washington, 1921). Charles Flint Kellogg, *NAACP: A History of the National Association for the Advancement of Colored People*, vol. I: *1909–1920* (Baltimore, 1967), ch. 11, treats the NAACP's efforts to secure officers' training for black men and to combat discrimination in the armed services and in defense industries.

Arthur W. Little, *From Harlem to the Rhine: The Story of New York's Colored Volunteers* (New York, 1936), is an able treatment of both the home front and the battle front, as is Charles H. Williams, *Sidelights on Negro Soldiers* (Boston, 1923). Chester D. Heywood, *Negro Combat Troops in the World War: The*

Story of the 371st Infantry (Worcester, 1928), is an interesting, though at times condescending, study of one of the best black combat regiments. W. Allison Sweeney tends too much toward hero-making in his *History of the American Negro in the Great World War* (Chicago, 1919). Robert R. Moton's autobiography *Finding a Way Out* (London, 1920), ch. 11, tells of Moton's investigations of discrimination in the Army and its service agencies. Addie W. Hunton and Kathryn M. Johnson, *Two Colored Women with the American Expeditionary Forces* (Brooklyn, 1920), gives a firsthand account of YWCA welfare workers assigned to the troops during hostilities in France. Abraham Chew, *A Biography of Colonel Charles Young* (Washington, 1923), describes the career of the highest ranking black officer of that time.

The entire Summer 1943 (vol. XII) issue of the *JNE*, entitled "The American Negro in World Wars I and II," contains articles comparing conditions during the two wars.

4. Race Riots, 1917–1943

By accelerating the urbanization of the black population, the wartime migrations escalated social tensions. Whites found themselves in unaccustomed economic competition with black workers, while urban concentration for the first time created important black voting blocs. Burgeoning ghetto populations, outgrowing available housing, naturally pushed against the tacit boundaries of residential segregation. None of these factors made for good will in interracial relations. Nor did the war experience. Blacks who came home from the fighting front found whites doubly determined to keep them in their place. The rise in lynchings and Ku Klux Klan-style terrorization throughout the South effectively proved the point. And with their hopes raised by the war and their interests actively supported by such organizations as the NAACP, many blacks were unwilling to slip quietly back into second-class citizenship. Within the context of the antiradical reaction and general social dislocation of the war and postwar years there erupted the most serious outbreak of race riots up to that point in American history. Riots hit Houston, Philadelphia, Chester, Pennsylvania, and East St. Louis, Illinois, in 1917, and during the "Red Summer" of 1919 a rash of some two dozen outbreaks plagued cities north and south.

The worst single outbreak of violence, in which at least thirty-nine blacks and nine whites were killed, took place in East St. Louis; it has been excellently chronicled by Elliott M. Rudwick, *Race Riot at East St. Louis, July 2, 1917* (Carbondale, Ill., 1964).* The most comprehensive account of the 1919 riots is Arthur I. Waskow, *From Race Riot to Sit-In, 1919 and the 1960s: A Study in the Connections Between Conflict and Violence* (Garden City, N.Y., 1966).* The most serious riot of 1919 occurred in Chicago, and a full account of the violence is found in the report of the Chicago Commission on Race Relations, *The Negro in Chicago: A Study of Race Relations and a Race Riot* (Chicago, 1922, reprinted New York, 1968), which is well worth comparing to the *Report of the National Advisory Commission on Civil Disorders* (New York, 1968).* For a historian's treatment of the 1919 Chicago riot, see William M. Tuttle, Jr., *Race Riot: Chicago in the Red Summer of 1919* (New York, 1970).* Robert T. Kerlin, *The Voice of the Negro, 1919* (New York, 1920), presents the reaction of the Negro press to the riots.

In their article "Negro Retaliatory Violence in the Twentieth Century," *New Politics*, V (Winter 1966), 41–51, Elliott Rudwick and August Meier have pointed out that the World War I riots typically involved black response to acts of white persecution, followed by retaliation from white mobs, while the riots of the 1960s commonly took the form of black attacks on white-owned property in the ghettos, often touched off by alleged instances of police brutality. This evolution from "communal" to "commodity" riots is also the subject of an incisive essay by Morris Janowitz, "Patterns of Collective Racial Violence," in Hugh Davis Graham and Ted Robert Gurr, eds., *Violence in America: Historical and Comparative Perspectives* (New York, 1969),* ch. 10, the official report to the National Commission on the Causes and Prevention of Violence.

The change in target from white people to white property first became obvious in the Harlem riots of 1935 and 1943, and in the worst riot of the World War II era, in Detroit in 1943. The Detroit riot has been treated in several studies: Harvard Sitkoff, "The Detroit Race Riot of 1943," *Michigan History*, LIII (Fall 1969), 183–94; Robert Shogan and Tom Craig, *The Detroit Race Riot: A Study in Violence* (Philadelphia, 1964); Alfred McClung Lee and Norman Daymond Humphrey, *Race Riot* (New York, 1943); and Earl Brown and George R. Leighton, *Why Race Riots? Lessons from Detroit* (New York, 1944). Various perspectives on the riots of World War II are provided in the essays in chs. 3–4 of Joseph Boskin, ed., *Urban Racial Violence in the Twentieth Century* (Beverly Hills, Calif., 1969). See also Thomas Sancton, "The Race Riots," *New Republic*, CIX (July 5, 1943), 9–12. On Harlem, see Walter F. White, "Behind the Harlem Riot," *ibid.*, CIX (Aug. 16, 1943), 220–22; and Harold Orlansky, *The Harlem Riot: A Study in Mass Frustration* (New York, 1943). Kenneth B. Clark examines sociopsychological aspects of the riots in two articles, "Group Violence: A Preliminary Study of the Attitudinal Pattern of Its Acceptance and Rejection—A Study of the 1943 Harlem Riots," *Journal of Social Psychology*, XIX (Aug. 1944), 319–37, and, in collaboration with James Barker, "The Zoot Effect in Personality: A Race Riot Participant," *Journal of Abnormal and Social Psychology*, XL (Apr. 1945), 143–48.**

For an anthology of primary accounts and retrospective analyses of riots throughout American history, see Allen D. Grimshaw, ed., *Racial Violence in the United States* (Chicago, 1969). A briefer volume, J. Paul Mitchell, ed., *Race Riots in Black and White* (Englewood Cliffs, N.J., 1970),* is a topical collection of source materials drawn from riots over the period 1863–1968. See also Richard Hofstadter and Michael Wallace, eds., *American Violence: A Documentary History* (New York, 1970),* pt. III, "Racial Violence."

Gunnar Myrdal considers riots, lynching, and other forms of racial violence as a sociological phenomenon in ch. 27 of *An American Dilemma: The Negro Problem and Modern Democracy* (New York, 1944).* Various aspects of race riots in American history are discussed in a series of important articles by Allen D. Grimshaw: "Lawlessness and Violence in America and Their Special Manifestations in Changing Negro-White Relationships," *JNH*, XLIV (Jan. 1959), 52–72; "Urban Racial Violence in the United States: Changing Ecological Considerations," *AJS*, LXVI (Sept. 1960), 109–19;** "Relationships Among Prejudice, Discrimination, Social Tension and Social Violence," *Journal of Intergroup Relations*, II (Autumn 1961), 302–10; "Negro-White Relations in the Urban North: Two Areas of High Conflict Potential," *ibid.*, III (Spring 1962), 146–58; "Factors Contributing to Colour Violence in the United States and Britain," *Race*, III (May 1962), 3–19; and "Actions of Police and the Military in American Race Riots," *Phylon*, XXIV (3rd Quarter 1963), 271–89.

On two of the main irritants to race relations after World War I —the resurgence of the Ku Klux Klan and the revival of lynchings —see David M. Chalmers, *Hooded Americanism: The History of the Ku Klux Klan* (Garden City, N.Y., 1965);* Kenneth T. Jackson, *The Ku Klux Klan in the City, 1915–1930* (New York, 1967);* George Brown Tindall, *The Emergence of the New South, 1913–1945* (Baton Rouge, 1967),* ch. 5; and the relevant works on lynching cited in Part VI, topic 3, "Racial Violence: Lynching and Riots."

5. The Origins of Modern Protest and Reform: The NAACP and the National Urban League

The twentieth-century drive for black rights took shape during the Progressive Era with the formation of the two major interracial organizations in the field of racial advancement, the National Association for the Advancement of Colored People and the National Urban League. Although they differed over tactics and short-run emphases, both groups shared a common long-term objective: the integration of blacks into the mainstream of American society on a basis of full equality.

Ch. 4 of C. Vann Woodward, *The Strange Career of Jim Crow* (New York, 1955, rev. ed., 1966)* is an excellent brief survey of the circumstances surrounding the development of organized interracial protest before the civil rights revolution. Pts. 2 and 3 of a book of documents edited by Francis L. Broderick and August Meier, *Negro Protest Thought in the Twentieth Century* (Indianapolis, 1965),* which corresponds to pt. 2 of August Meier, Elliott Rudwick, and Francis L. Broderick, eds., *Black Protest Thought in the Twentieth Century* (rev. ed., Indianapolis, 1971),* provide excellent insights into the drive for equal rights. For general surveys of the various movements in behalf of black advancement, see August Meier and Elliott Rudwick, "Radicals and Conservatives: Black Protest in Twentieth-Century America," in Peter I. Rose, ed., *Americans from Africa*, vol. II: *Old Memories, New Moods* (New York, 1970),* pp. 119–47; Ralph J. Bunche, "A Critical Analysis of the Tactics and Programs of Minority Groups," *JNE*, IV (July 1935), 308–20,** and his "The Programs of Organizations Devoted to the Improvement of the Status of the American Negro," *ibid.*, VIII (July 1939), 539–50; Guy B. Johnson, "Negro Racial Movements and Leadership in the United States," *AJS*, XLIII (July 1937), 57–71; and Roscoe Lewis, "The Role of Pressure Groups in Maintaining Morale Among Negroes," *JNE*, XII (Summer 1943), 464–73. These works deal primarily with blacks in the North, but the roots of protest and agitation were also being established in the South during this period; see, for example, Edwin D. Hoffman, "The Genesis of the Modern Movement for Equal Rights in South Carolina, 1930–1939," *JNH*, XLIV (July 1959), 346–70, and George Brown Tindall, *The Emergence of the New South, 1913–1945* (Baton Rouge, 1967),* ch. 16.

A. The NAACP

Founded in 1909–10 by white liberals and black veterans of the Niagara Movement, the NAACP declared itself in favor of the abolition of all forced segregation, of equal educational opportunities for all, of complete enfranchisement of blacks, and of enforcement of the Fourteenth and Fifteenth Amendments, and it adopted tactics of agitation, as well as court action, to realize those goals. Its major objective during its first half century was to secure legislation and court decisions establishing equal rights for blacks in the areas of voting, civil rights, housing, and education. It carried on vigilant campaigns against lynching and against various forms of private and government discrimination, especially in federal employment, military service, and relief and recovery programs.

Emma Lou Thornbraugh, "The National Afro-American League, 1887–1908," *JSH*, XXVII (Nov., 1961), 494–512,** and Elliott M. Rudwick, "The Niagara Movement," *JNH*, XLII (July 1957), 177–200,** treat important antecedents of the NAACP. The authoritative work on the NAACP's founding and first decade is Charles Flint Kellogg, *NAACP: A History of the National Association for the Advancement of Colored People*, vol. I: 1909–1920 (Baltimore, 1967). Other useful sources are the early portion of Langston Hughes' popular history, *Fight for Freedom: The Story of the NAACP* (New York, 1962); Mary White Ovington, *The Walls Came Tumbling Down* (New York, 1947),* the memoirs of a white woman who played a principal role in the founding of the NAACP; Jack Abramowitz, "Origins of the NAACP," *Social Education*, XV (Jan. 1951), 21–23; and Elliott M. Rudwick, "The National Negro Committee Conference of 1909," *Phylon*, XVIII (4th Quarter 1958), 413–19. Alfreda M. Duster, ed., *Crusade for Justice: The Autobiography of Ida B. Wells* [Ida Wells-Barnett] (Chicago, 1970), is the life story of a black woman who helped to organize the NAACP. Two articles which deal with Booker T. Washington's attitude toward his rival Du Bois' organization are August Meier, "Booker T. Washington and the Rise of the N.A.A.C.P.," *Crisis*, LXX (Feb. 1954), 69–76, and Elliott M. Rudwick, "Booker T. Washington's Relations with the National Association for the Advancement of Colored People," *JNE*, XXIX (Spring 1960), 134–44.

As yet there is no study comparable to Kellogg's for the NAACP's later years, but there is a good brief analysis in Robert L. Zangrando, "The 'Organized Negro': The National Association for the Advancement of Colored People and Civil Rights," in James C. Curtis and Lewis L. Gould, eds., *The Black Experience in America: Selected Essays* (Austin, Tex., 1970),* pp. 145–71. Raymond Wolters, *Negroes and the Great Depression: The Problem of Economic Recovery* (Westport, Conn., 1970),* pt. III, is a thorough account of the changing strategies and tactics of the NAACP during the economic crisis. The organization's work can also be studied in Hughes, *Fight for Freedom*; Warren D. St. James, *The National Association for the Advancement of Colored*

People: A Case Study in Pressure Groups (New York, 1958); Wilson Record, *Race and Radicalism: The NAACP and the Communist Party in Conflict* (Ithaca, N.Y., 1964);* John A. Morsell, "The National Association for the Advancement of Colored People and Its Strategy," *Annals*, CCCLVII (Jan. 1965), 97–101; and in biographies and autobiographies of its major leaders: Francis L. Broderick, *W. E. B. Du Bois: Negro Leader in a Time of Crisis* (Stanford, 1959);* Elliott M. Rudwick, *W. E. B. Du Bois: A Study in Minority Group Leadership* (Philadelphia, 1960);* W. E. B. Du Bois, *Dusk of Dawn: An Essay Toward an Autobiography of a Race Concept* (New York, 1940);* James Weldon Johnson, *Along This Way: The Autobiography of James Weldon Johnson* (New York, 1933);* and Walter F. White, *A Man Called White: The Autobiography of Walter White* (New York, 1948).* Robert L. Jack, *History of the National Association for the Advancement of Colored People* (Boston, 1943), is only of limited value. The NAACP's journal, *The Crisis*, provides a continuing record of the organization's major activities and concerns. For perspectives on the position of the NAACP in the civil rights movement, see Part IX, topic 3, "The Civil Rights Movement," especially section B, "The Question of Tactics: Moderate Legalism vs. Direct Action Radicalism."

Roger L. Rice, "Residential Segregation by Law, 1910–1917," *JSH*, XXXIV (May 1968), 180–99,** is a detailed study of the NAACP's successful battle in this area. Thurgood Marshall, formerly the NAACP's legal counsel, assesses the organization's impact in two articles, "The Rise and Collapse of the 'White Democratic Primary,'" *JNE*, XXVI (Summer 1957), 249–54, and "An Evaluation of Recent Efforts to Achieve Racial Integration in Education through Resort to the Courts," *ibid.*, XXI (Summer 1952), 316–27. For references on the NAACP's victories in the area of educational desegregation, see this Part, topic 9, "Higher Education and Black Scholarship," and Part IX, topic 5, "Since *Brown* v. *Board of Education*: Black Education After 1954." For additional material on the organization's legal efforts, see Part IX, topic 2, "The Supreme Court and Civil Rights." Some of the organization's non-judicial activities are the subject of Gilbert Ware, "Lobbying as a Means of Protest: The NAACP as an Agent of Equality," *JNE*, XXXIII (Spring 1964), 103–10. One of its unsuccessful lobbying attempts—to secure federal legislation against lynching—is treated in Robert L. Zangrando, "The NAACP and a Federal Antilynching Bill, 1934–1940," *JNH*, L (Apr. 1965), 106–17.**

B. The National Urban League

The National Urban League came into existence in response to the plight of blacks in northern cities at the beginning of the twentieth century. From its founding in 1911, the league directed its major efforts toward broadening employment opportunities for blacks and toward providing social services to ease the pain of urbanization. It attacked job discrimination from different angles: by meeting privately with major employers to convince them of the essential fairness and feasibility of hiring black workers; by lobbying the top levels of the American Federation of Labor to persuade organized labor to open its ranks to blacks; and by promoting vocational training and on-the-job counseling for black workers themselves.

While the league's original objective was to stimulate existing welfare agencies to include blacks in on-going programs, it quickly became apparent that the league itself would have to devote extensive attention to direct service activities. To staff its own programs and those of other agencies with competent professionals, the Urban League pioneered in the professional training of black social workers.

The league made scientific social investigation of conditions among blacks in cities an integral part of its program. The results of its surveys, publicized in the league's journal, *Opportunity*, created for the first time an extensive body of reliable information on the life of the urban black population. *Opportunity* also gave black writers and artists a much-needed vehicle for publishing their works.

The best brief account of the founding and purposes of the National Urban League is an article by its long-time executive board chairman, L. Hollingsworth Wood, "The Urban League Movement," *JNH*, IX (Apr. 1924), 117–26. The league's published anniversary booklets—*A Quarter Century of Progress in the Field of Race Relations, 1910–1935* (New York, 1935); *40th Anniversary*

202 THE NORTHWARD MIGRATION

Year Book, 1950 (New York, 1951); and *The Urban League Story, 1910–1960: Golden 50th Anniversary Yearbook* (New York, 1961) —contain a wealth of important material. *Opportunity*, which served as a house organ for the league, is full of information on its development and activities. Two Urban Leaguers who have published autobiographies are Jesse O. Thomas, *My Story in Black and White* (New York, 1967), and John C. Dancy, *Sand Against the Wind: The Memoirs of John C. Dancy* (Detroit, 1966).

Among non-Urban League sources, there are important evaluations in Gunnar Myrdal, *An American Dilemma: The Negro Problem and Modern Democracy* (New York, 1944),* esp. pp. 835, 837–43, 854, 1254–56, and in Ralph J. Bunche, "The Programs of Organizations Devoted to the Improvement of the Status of the American Negro," *JNE*, VIII (July 1939), 539–50. Other articles which deal with the league include Kenneth B. Clark, "The Civil Rights Movement: Momentum and Organization," in Talcott Parsons and Kenneth B. Clark, eds., *The Negro American* (Boston, 1966),* pp. 595–625; Merle Curti, "The Changing Pattern of Certain Humanitarian Organizations," *Annals*, CLXXIX (May 1935), 59–67; Charles S. Johnson, "National Organizations in the Field of Race Relations," *ibid.*, CCXLIV (Mar. 1946), 117–27; "National League on Urban Conditions Among Negroes," *Crisis*, VIII (Sept. 1914), 243–46; "Fifty Years of the Urban League," *NHB*, XXIV (Oct. 1960), 13–14; "The Urban League's First Forty Years," *Survey*, LXXXVII (May 1951), 229–30; and "Urban League's Line: Bias is Bad Business," *Business Week*, Oct. 9, 1954, 180–82, 184.

Robert H. Brisbane, *The Black Vanguard: Origins of the Negro Social Revolution, 1900–1960* (Valley Forge, Pa., 1970),* chs. 2, 11, is a scholarly study that includes important information not published elsewhere, but its usefulness is impaired by a number of factual errors. Arvarh E. Strickland's *History of the Chicago Urban League* (Urbana, Ill., 1966), although limited in certain respects, is valuable in illustrating Urban League activities on a local level.

For evaluations of the position of the Urban League in the civil rights movement, see Part IX, topic 3, "The Civil Rights

Movement," especially section B, "The Question of Tactics: Moderate Legalism vs. Direct Action Radicalism."

6. Black Nationalism: Marcus Garvey

Black separatism, race chauvinism, and black nationalism in one form or another have always existed in this country, especially in times of racial stress and tension (see Part IV, topic 13 and Part VI, topic 14, "Black Nationalism Before the Civil War" and "Black Nationalism and Migration, 1865–1915"). The greatest black nationalist movement of all came in the tension-ridden years after World War I, when Marcus Garvey's Universal Negro Improvement Association won hundreds of thousands of followers, particularly among the black masses of northern cities. Garvey exalted blackness as representing strength and beauty, urged blacks to take pride in their ancestral past, and admonished black men to leave America and build a black nation in Africa. But his "Back-to-Africa" movement never succeeded in resettling any American Negroes, and Garvey himself never set foot in Africa. In the United States, Garvey promoted economic self-sufficiency among blacks through a variety of black-owned and -operated businesses. The best known of these, the Black Star Steamship Line, collapsed from mismanagement, and Garvey was imprisoned for fraudulent use of the mails in raising money for the line.

John H. Bracey, Jr., August Meier, and Elliott Rudwick, eds., *Black Nationalism in America* (Indianapolis, 1970),* is an excellent collection of readings on various aspects of black nationalism throughout American history; pt. 3 deals with the Garvey period. Theodore Draper, *The Rediscovery of Black Nationalism* (New York, 1970),* chs. 3–4; C. Eric Lincoln, *The Black Muslims in America* (Boston, 1961),* ch. 3; and E. U. Essien-Udom, *Black Nationalism: A Search for an Identity in America* (Chicago, 1962),* ch. 2, all deal with Garvey and other twentieth-century nationalist movements prior to the rise of the Black Muslims. For a brief general survey of the separatist phenomenon, see Wilson Record, "Extremist Movements Among American Negroes,"

Phylon, XVII (Spring 1956), 17–23, and Ira De A. Reid, "Negro Movements and Messiahs," *ibid.*, X (4th Quarter 1949), 362–69.

E. David Cronon, *Black Moses: The Story of Marcus Garvey and the Universal Negro Improvement Association* (Madison, 1955),* is excellent. It should be supplemented by two works by Amy Jacques-Garvey, Garvey's second wife—*Garvey and Garveyism* (Kingston, Jamaica, 1963),* and *Philosophy and Opinions of Marcus Garvey*, 2 vols. (New York, 1923, 1925).* Negro sociologist E. Franklin Frazier's "The Garvey Movement," *Opportunity*, IV (Nov. 1926), 346–48, is an important appraisal of Garvey's ability to attract the alienated black masses. Harold Isaacs, *The New World of Negro Americans* (Cambridge, Mass., 1963),* esp. pt. 3, offers a suggestive analysis of Garvey's appeal. Most of the popular studies of blacks in Harlem during the early part of this century contain accounts of Garvey and other black nationalist leaders; see James Weldon Johnson, *Black Manhattan* (New York, 1930),* ch. 18; Claude McKay, *Harlem: Negro Metropolis* (New York, 1940), ch. 10; and Roi Ottley, *New World A-Coming* (Boston, 1943, reprinted New York, 1968), ch. 7. Garvey himself was a Jamaican, and his gospel had considerable appeal to fellow immigrants from the Caribbean; see the relevant portions of Ira De A. Reid, *The Negro Immigrant: His Background, Characteristics and Social Adjustment, 1899–1937* (New York, 1939). Amy Jacques-Garvey gives her views of Marcus Garvey's impact on Jamaica and Africa in a small pamphlet, *Black Power in America* (Kingston, Jamaica, 1968), pp. 14–35. See also George Shepperson, "Notes on Negro American Influences on the Emergence of African Nationalism," *Journal of African History*, I (1960), 299–312.**

Garvey was not the only important black leader in the 1910s and 1920s with a vision of a liberated Africa as the hub of an international black community. W. E. B. Du Bois, at that time editor of the NAACP's magazine *The Crisis*, was instrumental in promoting Pan-Africanism, but he was much less successful than Garvey in winning adherents, and the two men disagreed bitterly in print and in public statements. See Elliott M. Rudwick, "Du Bois Versus Garvey: Race Propagandists at War," *JNE*, XXVIII (Fall 1959), 421–29;** Ben F. Rogers, "William E. B. Du Bois, Marcus Garvey, and Pan-Africa," *JNH*, XL (Apr. 1955),

154–65; on Du Bois' Pan-Africanism, Sterling Stuckey, "Du Bois, Woodson and the Spell of Africa," *Negro Digest*, XVI (Feb. 1967), 20–24, 60–74; and references cited in Part VI, topic 14, "Black Nationalism and Migration, 1865–1915." Richard B. Moore, "Africa Conscious Harlem," in John Henrik Clarke, ed., *Harlem: A Community in Transition* (New York, 1964),* pp. 77–96, deals with nationalism and pro-Africa sentiments from Garvey to the emergence of African nations after World War II.

7. The Black Church in an Era of Urbanization

The rapid acceleration of the northward and cityward movement of the black population after 1915 had important consequences for the black church. A predominantly rural institution whose ministers were often the leading professionals in black society, the church adjusted slowly and often poorly to the shock of urbanization. The impersonality, hectic pace, and secularization of life in northern cities contrasted sharply with the quality of life in the rural South. The history of the black church in this period is in large part a story of efforts to adjust to rapid change and to recapture its role as an agency of social cohesion.

Two brief accounts of the church from World War I to World War II that emphasize the problems of urban adjustment are E. Franklin Frazier, *The Negro Church in America* (New York, 1964),* ch. 4, and Carter G. Woodson, *The History of the Negro Church* (2nd ed., Washington, 1945), ch. 16. An excellent study which analyzes both urban and rural churches in the early 1930s is Benjamin E. Mays and Joseph W. Nicholson, *The Negro's Church* (New York, 1933). Two volumes by Ruby F. Johnston concentrate on the 1940s and early 1950s and deal primarily with urban churches: *The Development of Negro Religion* (New York, 1954) and *The Religion of Negro Protestants: Changing Religious Attitudes and Practices* (New York, 1956). Benjamin E. Mays, *The Negro's God as Reflected in His Literature* (New York, 1938),* chs. 2, 5, 7, deals with religious concepts reflected in sermons, prayers, hymns, and religious writings during the 1920s and 1930s, while William A. Daniel, *The Education of Negro Ministers* (New York, 1925), documents the paucity of formal training for many black preachers. Two studies of the black Methodist denominations during this period are J. Beverly F. Shaw, *The Negro in the History of Methodism* (Nashville, 1954), chs. 10–13, and George A. Singleton, *The Romance of African Methodism* (New York, 1952), chs. 11–16. Charles H. Wesley, "The Religious Attitudes of Negro Youth," *JNH*, XXI (Oct. 1936), 376–93, and E. Franklin Frazier, *Negro Youth at the Crossways, Their Personality Development in the Middle States* (Washington, 1940), ch. 5, demonstrate that the younger generation began to turn away from the church in the 1930s or to demand that it abandon outdated religious practices and adopt a more relevant Christianity.

A. The Urban Church in the North

Black churches reacted in several different ways to the challenges of urbanization. Many of the churches associated with the middle and upper classes responded to the increasing secularization of life by emphasizing material rather than spiritual values and by becoming the focal points of social climbing and status seeking. Others embraced the social gospel and expanded their social welfare services to the black community. Many rural black Baptist churches were transformed into boisterous storefront churches and sects in the city: in 1930 more than one third of the black churches in twelve northern cities were of the storefront variety, often led by "jackleg" preachers with little or no formal training. In the 1930s the holiness cults flourished, especially Father Divine's "Peace Mission Movement" and Daddy Grace's "House of Prayer for All People." Although the emotionalism and exoticism of the storefront churches and the holiness cults were the objects of amused contempt among many whites and of shame among some blacks, they filled an important need for many black peasants uprooted from the soil and set down in the impersonal, confusing, hostile environment of the city. They re-created the warm and close personal relationship of the rural church, gave some meaning and structure to the otherwise chaotic life in the ghetto, and provided a haven from white-controlled institutions. The holiness cults of Father Divine and Daddy Grace functioned in much the same way as the Garvey movement for the masses of rootless urban blacks, by giving them a sense of identity and pride, and many Garveyites joined these cults after the collapse of Garvey's organization.

A good brief introduction to the northern urban church is Seth M. Scheiner, "The Negro Church and the Northern City, 1890–1930," in William G. Shade and Roy C. Herrenkohl, eds., *Seven on Black: Reflections on the Negro Experience in America* (Philadelphia, 1969),* pp. 92–116. Black churches in Chicago are analyzed by St. Clair Drake and Horace R. Cayton, *Black Metropolis: A Study of Negro Life in a Northern City* (New York, 1945),* chs. 15, 19, 21–22, and by Vattel A. Daniel, "Ritual and Stratification in Chicago Negro Churches," *ASR*, VII (June 1942), 352–61. A sharp critique of the storefront churches and cults which describes their ministers as charlatans preying upon the ignorance of the masses is Ira De A. Reid, "Let Us Prey!" *Opportunity*, IV (Sept. 1926), 274–78. James Baldwin's novel, *Go Tell It on the Mountain* (New York, 1953),* paints an unforgettable portrait of the Harlem storefront church. Two useful analyses of the urban cults are Raymond J. Jones, *A Comparative Study of Cult Behavior Among Negroes with Special Reference to Emotional Group Conditioning Factors* (Washington, 1939); and Arthur Huff Fauset, *Black Gods of the Metropolis: Negro Religious Cults of the Urban North* (Philadelphia, 1944).* Father Divine was the subject of several studies, the most useful of which are probably Robert A. Parker, *The Incredible Messiah: The Deification of Father Divine* (Boston, 1937), and Carl Braden, *These Also Believe* (New York, 1949), ch. 1. Two other books on Father Divine that mix analysis with gossip and sensationalism are John Hoshor, *God in a Rolls Royce: The Rise of Father Divine: Madman, Menace, or Messiah* (New York, 1936), and Sara Harris and Harriet Crittenden, *Father Divine: Holy Husband* (New York, 1953).* Hadley Cantril, *The Psychology of Social Movements* (New York, 1941),* ch. 5, also deals with Father Divine's movement. A cult whose theology foreshadowed that of the Black Muslims in some respects is treated by Howard Brotz, *The Black Jews of Harlem: Negro Nationalism and the Dilemmas of Negro Leadership* (New York, 1964).*

B. The Southern Rural Church

Though the northern urban black church during this period has captured the lion's share of historians' attention, the southern rural church remained the backbone of black religion and community life. As late as 1940, three quarters of black Americans still lived in the South and two thirds of the southern black population was still rural. The slowness of some rural churches to adjust to the changing needs of the black population resulted in a decline of their influence, especially among the youth. Several excellent studies of rural and small-town blacks carried out by sociologists during the New Deal contain illuminating chapters on the church: see esp. Charles S. Johnson, *Shadow of the Plantation* (Chicago, 1934),* ch. 5; Arthur F. Raper, *Preface to Peasantry: A Tale of Two Black Belt Counties* (Chapel Hill, 1936),* ch. 18; John Dollard, *Caste and Class in a Southern Town* (New Haven, 1937),* ch. 11; Hortense Powdermaker, *After Freedom: A Cultural Study in the Deep South* (New York, 1939),* pt. 4; and Charles S. Johnson, *Growing Up in the Black Belt: Negro Youth in the Rural South* (New York, 1941),* ch. 5. Three fine studies that describe the rural Negro church in the 1940s are Harry Van Buren Richardson, *Dark Glory: A Picture of the Church Among Negroes in the Rural South* (New York, 1947); William Pipes, *Say Amen Brother! Old-Time Negro Preaching: A Study in American Frustration* (New York, 1951); and Ralph Almon Felton, *Go Down Moses: A Study of 21 Successful Negro Rural Pastors* (Madison, N.J., 1952). See also two articles by Harry W. Roberts: "The Rural Negro Minister: His Personal and Social Characteristics," *SF*, XXVII (Mar. 1949), 291–300,** and "The Rural Negro Minister: His Work and Salary," *Rural Sociology*, XII (Sept. 1947), 284–97.**

C. White Churches and Afro-Americans

Before 1915 the major race relations work of predominantly white denominations had been in black education. After World War I the white churches founded commissions for interracial cooperation and crusaded against lynching, but only within the framework of a segregated society, which the churches did little to challenge before 1950. Indeed, the church remained one of the most segregated institutions in America; a 1946 study concluded that less than one tenth of 1 per cent of black Protestants were in mixed congregations. A balanced treatment of the contributions and shortcomings of white Protestantism during this period is David M. Reimers, *White Protestantism and the Negro* (New York, 1965), chs. 4–6. See also Robert M. Miller, "The Attitudes of American Protestantism Toward the Negro, 1919–1939," *JNH*, XLI (July 1956), 215–40, and Willis D. Weatherford, *American Churches and the Negro* (Boston, 1957), ch. 9. For antilynching activities, consult Robert M. Miller, "The Protestant Churches and Lynching, 1919–1939," *JNH*, XLII (Apr. 1957), 118–31.** Frank S. Loescher, *The Protestant Church and the Negro* (Philadelphia, 1948), is critical of Protestantism's acceptance of segregation. For Methodist and Presbyterian churches, see Dwight Culvert, *Negro Segregation in the Methodist Church* (New Haven, 1953), and Andrew E. Murray, *Presbyterians and the Negro—A History* (Philadelphia, 1966), chs. 7–8. The Roman Catholic Church had a slightly better record on segregation than many of the Protestant denominations, though its black membership was small. See John T. Gillard, *The Catholic Church and the Negro* (Baltimore, 1929, reprinted Chicago, 1968), chs. 4–20, and Albert S. Foley, *God's Men of Color: The Colored Catholic Priests of the United States, 1854–1954* (New York, 1955), chs. 11–25. Another denomination with a small black membership is treated in Erwin E. Krebs, *The Lutheran Church and the American Negro* (Columbus, Ohio, 1950). The spectrum of relationships between Jews and blacks, ranging from alliance to hostility, is examined by Robert G. Weisbord and Arthur Stein, *Bittersweet Encounter: The Afro-American and the American Jew* (Westport, Conn., 1970).

8. *The Black Bourgeoisie*

One of the most influential and controversial studies of black life published since World War II is E. Franklin Frazier's *Black Bourgeoisie* (Glencoe, Ill., 1957).* With rapierlike wit and caustic analysis, Frazier described the "myth" of Negro business, the empty imitativeness of black "society" with its endless parties, debutante balls, gambling, and conspicuous consumption, and the collective inferiority complex of the black upper and middle classes which caused them compensatorily to exaggerate black people's achievements at the same time they privately expressed contempt for lower-class "niggers" and used hair straighteners to escape from Negro-ness. Frazier clearly lacked sympathy or objectivity toward his subjects. Moreover, he frequently lumped the upper and middle classes together in confusing fashion and failed to give due credit to the vital leadership role of black elites in social welfare and protest organizations such as the National Urban League and the NAACP. Nevertheless his book is the most important starting point for an understanding of the black bourgeoisie in the four decades after World War I.

The urban migration created sizable black business and professional classes in such cities as Washington, Atlanta, Durham, New York, and Chicago by the 1920s. The comings and goings of those few hundred wealthy blacks who could afford summer homes, yachts, and European vacations were intensively chronicled by the black press, which also did its best to stimulate black capitalism with "buy black" campaigns and success stories of black entrepreneurs. Yet as Frazier and others pointed out, the elevation of black business to a materialistic religion (see Part VI, topic 10, "Black Capitalism in the Age of Booker T. Washington") and the exaltation of black economic achievements created a myth of business success far out of proportion to the facts. In 1938, for example, black-owned enterprises received only 10 cents of the black consumer's dollar in the Chicago black belt, even though black barbers, beauticians, and morticians had a virtual monopoly of the black trade. Despite the success of black insurance companies (showcases of black capitalism), one national white insurance company had more black business in 1940 than all the black companies combined. In 1950 the total assets of all black banks were less than those of one small-town bank in upstate New York. Black achievements in the professions, despite many outstanding exceptions, were at the same mediocre level, according to Frazier. Yet on this flimsy foundation the black bourgeoisie reared a myth of success and a structure of black "society" that revealed, in Frazier's opinion, a black Babbittry as pretentious as that attributed by Sinclair Lewis to the white middle class.

The basic outlines of Frazier's analysis are presented in more restrained and sympathetic fashion by Gunnar Myrdal, *An American Dilemma: The Negro Problem and Modern Democracy* (New York, 1944),* chs. 14, 32; St. Clair Drake and Horace R. Cayton, *Black Metropolis: A Study of Negro Life in a Northern City* (New York, 1945),* chs. 16–19, 22; Roi Ottley's description of Harlem's "café-au-lait" society in *New World A-Coming* (New York, 1943, reprinted New York, 1968), ch. 13; August Meier and David Lewis, "History of the Negro Upper Class in Atlanta, Georgia, 1890–1958," *JNE*, XXVIII (Spring 1959), 128–39; the accounts of the black upper and middle classes of Indianola and Natchez, Mississippi, and New Orleans, in John Dollard, *Caste and Class in a Southern Town* (New Haven, 1937),* chs. 5, 9, 18, app.; Hortense Powdermaker, *After Freedom: A Cultural Study in the Deep South* (New York, 1939),* chs. 5, 8, 11; Allison Davis and John Dollard, *Children of Bondage: The Personality Development of Negro Youth in the Urban South* (Washington, 1940),* chs. 5–8; and in Frazier's own analysis of middle- and upper-class families in *The Negro Family in the United States* (Chicago, 1939),* chs. 19–20. Wallace Thurman's novel, *The Blacker the Berry* (New York, 1929, reprinted New York, 1969), satirizes class and color consciousness in Harlem. Nathan Hare, *The Black Anglo-Saxons* (New York, 1965),* is an even sharper indictment than Frazier's of the values of the black middle class.

Hylan G. Lewis, "The Negro Business, Professional, and White Collar Worker," *JNE*, VIII (July 1939), 430–45, gives a concise overview of middle-class occupations. Helpful analyses of black professions in the 1930s and 1950s are provided by Carter G. Woodson, *The Negro Professional Man and the Community* (Washington, 1934, reprinted Westport, Conn., 1970), and G. Franklin Edwards, *The Negro Professional Class* (Glencoe, Ill., 1959). The career patterns of black college graduates before 1940, who were recruited almost entirely from the upper and middle classes, are described by Charles S. Johnson, *The Negro College Graduate* (Chapel Hill, 1938). For accounts of black business enterprises ranging from hair straighteners to insurance companies, see the studies by Harris, Trent, Stuart, and Harmon et al. cited in Part VI, topic 10, "Black Capitalism in the Age of Booker T. Washington," which carry the story of black business to the 1930s, and the following four books, which cover the 1940s and include additional material on the earlier period: Joseph A. Pierce, *Negro Business and Business Education* (New York, 1947); Vishnu V. Oak, *The Negro Newspaper* (Yellow Springs, Ohio, 1948), and *The Negro's Adventure in General Business* (Yellow Springs, 1949); and Robert H. Kinzer and Edward Sagarin, *The Negro in American Business: The Conflict Between Separatism and Integration* (New York, 1950). Insurance companies are discussed by E. Franklin Frazier, "Durham: Capital of the Black Middle Class," in Alain L. Locke, ed., *The New Negro* (New York, 1925),* pp. 333–40,** and Robert C. Puth, "Supreme Life: The History of a Negro Life Insurance Company, 1919–1962," *Business History Review*, XLIII (Spring 1969), 1–20.** The condition of black capitalism in Philadelphia in the 1960s is placed in historical perspective by Eugene P. Foley, "The Negro Businessman: In Search of a Tradition," in Talcott Parsons and Kenneth B. Clark, eds., *The Negro American* (Boston, 1966),* pp. 555–92. A case study that takes issue with some of Frazier's indictments of black business is David M. Tucker, "Black Pride and Negro Business in the 1920's: George Washington Lee of Memphis," *Business History Review*, XLIII (Winter 1969), 435–51, which argues that in one case, at least, black business promoted racial pride and militancy.

9. Higher Education and Black Scholarship

The three decades after World War I were a period of rapid growth in black higher education. In 1915 only 2,600 students in black colleges and professional schools were taking college-level subjects. Within fifteen years, however, college enrollment had increased nearly tenfold. During the depression decade of the 1930s it doubled again so that by 1940 there were 44,000 students in southern black colleges, plus several thousand attending integrated northern schools. Before World War I the paucity of high schools and the inadequacy of elementary schools for blacks in the South made it necessary for black colleges to maintain their own elementary and secondary departments. As late as 1921 only 15 per cent of the students in black colleges were enrolled in college-level courses. But in the next decade most colleges dropped their elementary grades and began to phase out their secondary departments as southern states finally built black high schools; in 1932 nearly two thirds of the students in black colleges were enrolled in the college or graduate divisions.

During the same years there was improvement in academic standards, though progress fell short of hopes. A survey of Negro education in 1916 sponsored by the Phelps-Stokes Foundation and the federal government found grave defects in public and private black schools: see Thomas Jesse Jones, ed., *Negro Education: A Study of the Private and Higher Schools for Colored People in the United States*, Bureau of Education, Bulletin #38, 1916, 2 vols. (Washington, 1917, reprinted in 1 vol., New York, 1969). Though the survey's conclusions were challenged by some educators, the report shocked them into a commitment to reform. During the 1920s most southern states increased appropriations for publicly supported black colleges (though such appropriations still lagged far behind those for white schools). The private liberal arts colleges, however, remained at the forefront of black education. They were aided by large grants from foundations and became less dependent on church support. The United Negro College Fund was organized in 1944 to channel contributions to private colleges. Consolidation of the half-dozen black colleges in Atlanta into the Atlanta University Center was begun in 1929, and the next year Dillard University in New Orleans was created out of a merger of formerly competing Congregational and Methodist colleges. The replacement of white faculty members and administrators by blacks, which had begun a decade or more before World War I, continued at an accelerated pace in the 1920s. Black scholars trained at northern graduate schools added real distinction to the faculties of several colleges.

Despite the improvement in quality, most black colleges continued to suffer from defects in library resources, student preparation, and faculty training. Inadequacies of black high schools forced colleges to devote much of their effort to remedial work.

Government surveys of black higher education in 1928 and 1942 documented these problems and found that some colleges, especially the state-supported A. & M. schools, were graduating students who were barely literate. In a controversial and perhaps harsh appraisal of black colleges, Christopher Jencks and David Riesman, *The Academic Revolution* (Garden City, N.Y., 1968),* ch. 10, state that "the Negro college of the 1950s was usually an ill-financed, ill-staffed caricature of white higher education." In the 1970s the future of many of these colleges is in doubt, especially as predominantly white universities increasingly skim off the cream of black college applicants.

Exhaustive statistics and analyses are provided by two government reports: U. S. Bureau of Education, *Survey of Negro Colleges and Universities*, Bulletin #7, 1928 (Washington, 1929, reprinted Westport, Conn., 1970), and U. S. Office of Education, *National Survey of the Higher Education of Negroes*, 4 vols. (Washington, 1942). See also Henry C. Badger, *Statistics of Negro Colleges and Universities: Students, Staff, and Finances, 1900–1950*, Office of Education (Washington, 1951). A good bibliographical guide to the date of its publication is Ambrose Caliver, *Bibliography on the Education of the Negro* (Washington, 1931). The following studies provide general histories of black education during this period: Horace Mann Bond, *The Education of the Negro in the American Social Order* (New York, 1934, rev. ed., 1966), chs. 8 ff.; Dwight O. W. Holmes, *The Evolution of the Negro College* (New York, 1934, reprinted New York, 1969), chs. 12–16; Willard Range, *The Rise and Progress of Negro Colleges in Georgia, 1865–1949* (Athens, Ga., 1951), chs. 9–11; and Henry Allen Bullock, *A History of Negro Education in the South* (Cambridge, Mass., 1967),* chs. 8–9. Virgil A. Clift et al., eds., *Negro Education in America: Its Adequacy, Problems, and Needs* (New York, 1962), includes several essays of value. Frederick L. Brownlee, *New Day Ascending* (Boston, 1946), recounts the development of schools supported by the American Missionary Association. Several contemporary studies of various aspects of black higher education contain useful information: Buell G. Gallagher, *American Caste and the Negro College* (New York, 1938, reprinted New York, 1966); Richard I. McKinney, *Religion in Higher Education Among Negroes* (New Haven, 1945);

Irving A. Derbigny, *General Education in the Negro College* (Stanford, 1947); and Earl J. McGrath, *The Predominantly Negro Colleges and Universities in Transition* (New York, 1965).*

Two scholarly journals devoted to the problems of black education were founded in the 1930s. The more valuable is *The Journal of Negro Education*, affiliated with Howard University, which has been published quarterly since 1932. The July 1933 issue (vol. II) was taken up entirely by a survey of higher education, and the Summer 1960 issue (vol. XXIX) explored all aspects of private and church-related black colleges. *The Quarterly Review of Higher Education Among Negroes*, published since 1933 at Johnson C. Smith University, is another major source of information.

Histories of individual colleges vary in quality, and even the better ones are primarily narrative and laudatory rather than analytical. But they contain material helpful for understanding the period of growth and transition following World War I; see especially Rayford W. Logan, *Howard University, 1867–1967* (New York, 1969); Clarence A. Bacote, *The Story of Atlanta University: A Century of Service, 1865–1965* (Atlanta, 1969); Edward A. Jones, *A Candle in the Dark: A History of Morehouse College* (Valley Forge, Pa., 1967); and Florence Matilda Read, *The Story of Spelman College* (Atlanta, 1961). A readable biography of John Hope, first black president of Morehouse (1906–31) and first president of the affiliated colleges of the Atlanta University Center, is Ridgely Torrence, *The Story of John Hope* (New York, 1948). The autobiography of perhaps the outstanding black educator of the past generation, Benjamin E. Mays, *Born to Rebel: An Autobiography* (New York, 1971), contains a great deal of information on Mays' tenure as president of Morehouse College.

The writings of several black observers and college teachers contain valuable insights. Several of W. E. B. Du Bois' commentaries on black education are reprinted in Meyer Weinberg, ed., *W. E. B. Du Bois: A Reader* (New York, 1970),* pt. 5. Four important essays by Kelly Miller, a dean at Howard University, are "Howard: The National University," in Alain L. Locke, ed., *The New Negro* (New York, 1925),* pp. 312–22;** "The Higher Education of the Negro is at the Crossroads," *Educational Review*, LXXII (Dec. 1926), 272–78; "The Past, Present and Future of the Negro College," *JNE*, II (July 1933), 411–22; and "The Reorganization of the Higher Education of the Negro in Light of Changing Conditions," *ibid.*, V (July 1936), 484–94. The noted sociologist E. Franklin Frazier, who taught at Howard for many years, interpreted the function and significance of black higher education in *The Negro in the United States* (rev. ed., New York, 1957), ch. 18, and *Black Bourgeoisie* (Glencoe, Ill., 1957),* ch. 3. Carter G. Woodson, *The Mis-Education of the Negro* (Washington, 1933)* is an angry critique of the domination of black education by white philanthropy and white values. A black college teacher, Lewis K. McMillan, evaluates higher education for blacks in "Negro Higher Education as I Have Known It," *JNE*, VIII (Jan. 1939), 9–18, and treats the schools, chiefly Claflin College, in one southern state in *Negro Higher Education in the State of South Carolina* (Orangeburg, S.C., 1952). After World War I there was a growing emphasis on race-oriented social science courses in black colleges; John Hope Franklin discusses these in "Courses Concerning the Negro in Negro Colleges," *Quarterly Review of Higher Education Among Negroes*, VIII (July 1940), 138–44. Student unrest and protests against authoritarian restrictions in the 1920s are described by Robert H. Brisbane, *The Black Vanguard: Origins of the Negro Social Revolution, 1900–1960* (Valley Forge, Pa., 1970),* ch. 5, and Herbert Aptheker, "The Negro College Student in the 1920's," *Science and Society*, XXXIII (Spring 1969).

The backgrounds and career patterns of black college students and graduates are analyzed in Ambrose Caliver, *A Personnel Study of Negro College Students* (New York, 1931, reprinted Westport, Conn., 1970) and *A Background Study of Negro College Students* (Washington, 1933, reprinted Westport, Conn., 1970), and Charles S. Johnson, *The Negro College Graduate* (Chapel Hill, 1938, reprinted Westport, Conn., 1970). Most black members of the professions during this period were graduates of black colleges. Their occupations and community roles are described by Carter G. Woodson, *The Negro Professional Man and the Community* (Washington, 1934, reprinted Westport, Conn., 1970), and G. Franklin Edwards, *The Negro Professional Class* (Glencoe, Ill., 1959). Other aspects of higher education and professional training are treated by William A. Daniel,

The Education of Negro Ministers (New York, 1925, reprinted Westport, Conn., 1970); Marion Vera Cuthbert, *Education and Marginality: A Study of the Negro Woman College Graduate* (New York, 1942); and Jeanne L. Noble, *The Negro Woman's College Education* (New York, 1956).

A growing number of black scholars and scientists made major contributions to the community of knowledge in the generation after World War I. Harry Washington Greene enumerates *Holders of Doctorates Among American Negroes* (Boston, 1946), while Richard Bardolph, *The Negro Vanguard* (New York, 1959),* pp. 243–55, 306–24, 419–33, provides capsule biographies of leading scientists, artists, and social scientists. In the historical profession the importance of such black scholars as W. E. B. Du Bois, Carter G. Woodson (who founded the Association for the Study of Negro Life and History in 1915 and launched *The Journal of Negro History* in 1916), Charles H. Wesley, Rayford W. Logan, Benjamin Quarles, John Hope Franklin, and many others who began their careers during this period are attested by the numerous citations of their writings in these bibliographies. Useful analyses of black historians and their work are Earle E. Thorpe, *Negro Historians in the United States* (Baton Rouge, 1958), and *Black Historians: A Critique* (New York, 1971). In sociology, the studies of such men as E. Franklin Frazier, Charles S. Johnson, and Ira De A. Reid have provided much of what we know about the black community from the 1920s to the 1950s. Penetrating treatments of black sociologists are S. P. Fullinwider, *The Mind and Mood of Black America: 20th Century Thought* (Homewood, Ill., 1969),* ch. 5, and John H. Bracey, Jr., August Meier, and Elliott Rudwick, eds., *The Black Sociologists: The First Half Century* (Belmont, Calif., 1971).*

Black scientists are treated in Charles R. Drew, "Negro Scholars in Scientific Research," *JNH*, XXXV (Apr. 1950), 135–49, and Julian H. Taylor, ed., *The Negro in Science* (Baltimore, 1955). Dietrich C. Reitzes, *Negroes in Medicine* (Cambridge, Mass., 1958), and James L. Curtis, *Blacks, Medical Schools, and Society* (Ann Arbor, 1971), document both the shortcomings and strengths of medical education for blacks, while Herbert M. Morais, *The History of the Negro in Medicine* (Washington, 1967), emphasizes the contributions of black medical researchers. A black doctor who pioneered in the development of open-heart surgery, Daniel Hale Williams, is the subject of a biography by Helen Buckler, *Doctor Dan, Pioneer in American Surgery* (Boston, 1954). The achievements of George Washington Carver in agronomy and chemistry became world-famous: two biographies of the "wizard" of Tuskegee are Rackham Holt, *George Washington Carver: An American Biography* (rev. ed., Garden City, N.Y., 1963),* and Elliott Lawrence, *George Washington Carver: The Man Who Overcame* (Englewood Cliffs, N.J., 1966).

The exclusion of blacks from graduate and professional schools in the South was a major hindrance to the training of well-qualified doctors, lawyers, and scholars. In the 1930s the NAACP mounted legal attacks on racial inequality in postgraduate training and, after victory in the Supreme Court case of *Missouri* ex rel. *Gaines* v. *Canada* in 1938, moved in the 1940s to an attack on the principle of segregated state-supported graduate education. Successful challenges of segregated law schools in Oklahoma and Texas (1946 and 1949) laid the groundwork for the assault on segregated public education at all levels, culminating in *Brown* v. *Board of Education of Topeka* in 1954. These developments are treated in Jessie P. Guzman, *Twenty Years of Court Decisions Affecting Higher Education in the South, 1938–1958* (Tuskegee, Ala., 1960), and Samuel Paul Wiggins, *The Desegregation Era in Higher Education* (Berkeley, 1966).* For additional material on the drive for educational desegregation, see this Part, topic 5, "The Origins of Modern Protest and Reform: The NAACP and the National Urban League," Part IX, topic 2, "The Supreme Court and Civil Rights," and Part IX, topic 5, "Since *Brown* v. *Board of Education*: Black Education After 1954."

10. Black Politics

By packing large numbers of blacks into compact geographical areas, migration and urbanization made them a political force to be reckoned with, enabling them to exert pressure more effectively on political parties and government agencies and to elect political representatives of their own race. Historically blacks had felt a special affinity for the Republicans as the party of emancipation, and their national voting patterns regularly reflected that allegiance. But in the presidential election of 1928 the solidly Republican black vote began to break, and by 1936 Franklin D. Roosevelt and his New Deal had moved the black vote firmly within the national Democratic camp (a pattern that has held, with minor exceptions, down to the present day).

Whether dealing with Democratic or Republican authorities, however, at federal and local levels, blacks had to cope with the white power structure, with conservatives in the North and South, farmers and entrenched labor leaders and members of trade unions, and spokesmen for other ethnic groups who played dominant roles in southern, national, or big-city politics. Moreover, organized political action by blacks was complicated by divisions of status, interest, and objectives within the black community itself.

The best starting points for a study of black politics during this period are chs. 20–23 of Gunnar Myrdal's *An American Dilemma: The Negro Problem and Modern Democracy* (New York, 1944);* Ralph J. Bunche, "The Negro in the Political Life of the United States," *JNE*, X (July 1941), 567–84;** Martin Kilson, "Political Change in the Negro Ghetto, 1900–1940's," in Nathan I. Huggins, Martin Kilson, and Daniel M. Fox, eds., *Key Issues in the Afro-American Experience*, 2 vols. (New York, 1971),* vol. II, pp. 167–92; James Q. Wilson, *Negro Politics: The Search for Leadership* (Glencoe, Ill., 1960);* and Harold F. Gosnell, *Negro Politicians: The Rise of Negro Politics in Chicago* (Chicago, 1935).* See also Gosnell's "The Chicago 'Black Belt' as a Political Battleground," *AJS*, XXXIX (Nov. 1933), 329–41;** Allan H. Spear, *Black Chicago: The Making of a Negro Ghetto, 1890–1920* (Chicago, 1967),* chs. 6, 10; and Gilbert Osofsky, *Harlem: The Making of a Ghetto; Negro New York, 1890–1930* (New York, 1966),* ch. 11, a good brief treatment of black politics in New York. Elbert Lee Tatum's *The Changed Political Thought of the Negro, 1915–1940* (New York, 1951) is naïve. So is Henry Lee Moon's *Balance of Power: The Negro Vote* (Garden City, N.Y., 1948), but it contains useful information.

Samuel Lubell's *The Future of American Politics* (New York, 1952),* ch. 5, and *White and Black: Test of a Nation* (New York, 1964),* ch. 4, are much more astute on the subject of the black vote.

Richard B. Sherman has published two articles focusing on the failure of the Republican party to re-establish its image as a champion of black rights—"Republicans and Negroes: The Lessons of Normalcy," *Phylon*, XXVII (Spring 1966), 63–80, and "The Harding Administration and the Negro: An Opportunity Lost," *JNH*, XLIX (July 1964), 151–68. See also John L. Blair, "A Time for Parting: The Negro During the Coolidge Years," *Journal of American Studies*, III (Dec. 1969), 177–99. The Roosevelt administration is treated in the next topic, "Blacks and the New Deal." A special study of the pivotal 1936 election is James A. Harrell, "Negro Leadership in the Election Year 1936," *JSH*, XXXIV (Nov. 1968), 546–65. Harold F. Gosnell's "The Negro Vote in Northern Cities," *National Municipal Review*, XXX (May 1941), 264–67, 278, deals with 1940. For a brief summary of the attitudes of the Presidents and the national parties toward blacks during this period, see Richard Bardolph, ed., *The Civil Rights Record: Black Americans and the Law, 1849–1970* (New York, 1970),* pp. 182–88.

Other interesting case studies of northern black political behavior during this period include John M. Allswang, "The Chicago Negro Voter and the Democratic Consensus: A Case Study, 1918–1936," *Journal of the Illinois State Historical Society*, LX (Summer 1967), 145–75; Ernest M. Collins, "Cincinnati Negroes and Presidential Politics," *JNH*, XLI (Apr. 1956), 131–37; and Edward Litchfield, "A Case Study of Negro Political Behavior in Detroit," *Public Opinion Quarterly*, V (June 1941), 267–74.

In the South blacks suffered from special political disabilities, chief among them systematic disfranchisement through a variety of state and local measures. Paul Lewinson, *Race, Class, and Party: A History of Negro Suffrage and White Politics in the South* (New York, 1932),* pt. 2, is a good brief introduction to the pre-Depression South. George Brown Tindall, *The Emergence of the New South, 1913–1945* (Baton Rouge, 1967),* chs. 16–18, sets the context for the 1930s. Floyd Hunter, *Community Power Structure: A Study of Decision Makers* (Chapel Hill, 1953); V. O. Key, Jr., *Southern Politics in State and Nation* (New

York, 1949);* and Margaret Price, *The Negro Voter in the South* (Atlanta, 1957), include material on both urban and rural black communities in the South. Daniel C. Thompson, *The Negro Leadership Class* (Englewood Cliffs, N.J., 1963),* on New Orleans; M. Elaine Burgess, *Negro Leadership in a Southern City* (Chapel Hill, 1962);* Andrew Buni, *The Negro in Virginia Politics, 1902–1965* (Charlottesville, Va., 1967); Donald S. Strong, "The Rise of Negro Voting in Texas," *APSR*, XLII (June 1948), 510–22;** and Clarence A. Bacote, "The Negro in Atlanta Politics," *Phylon*, XVI (4th Quarter 1955), 333–51, are informative local studies. William M. Brewer discusses efforts to overcome one of the major impediments to black voting in "The Poll Tax and the Poll Taxers," *JNH*, XXIX (July 1944), 260–99.

11. Blacks and the New Deal

The New Deal held out considerable hope for black progress because the national administration for the first time in decades gave particular attention to the problems of blacks, who benefited in sizable numbers from federal relief and recovery programs. But the Roosevelt administration stopped far short of a full-scale commitment to the rights of blacks, and its policies often perpetuated the usual discriminatory injustices toward blacks in America. Moreover, the perilous coalition on which New Deal political power rested made it easier to discriminate against blacks in the administration of federal programs, while making it difficult for blacks to lobby successfully in their own interest. A smaller proportion of unemployed blacks got relief than did unemployed whites, for instance, and black organizations failed in their efforts to secure a federal antilynching law and to amend discriminatory features of the Wagner Act and the Social Security Act. Nevertheless, the Roosevelt administration's policy of using specialists to develop relief and recovery programs led to the formation of a "black cabinet" of advisers in governmental agencies and departments who had some impact on policy development and implementation. Moreover, Mrs. Roosevelt and other prominent New Dealers emerged as public champions of the blacks. These positive factors were reflected in the massive swing of black voters to the Democratic party by 1936.

There is still no single full history of blacks and the New Deal. The most profitable starting point for an overview of the entire subject is Bernard Sternsher's useful anthology, *The Negro in Depression and War: Prelude to Revolution, 1930–1945* (Chicago, 1969).* The lead article in Sternsher's book, Leslie H. Fishel, "The Negro in the New Deal Era," *Wisconsin Magazine of History*, XLVIII (Winter 1964), 111–26, remains the best brief survey. George Brown Tindall, *The Emergence of the New South, 1913–1945* (Baton Rouge, 1967),* ch. 16, is also useful. The major monograph in the field—Raymond Wolters, *Negroes and the Great Depression: The Problem of Economic Recovery* (Westport, Conn., 1970)*—focuses especially on the way in which blacks were affected by the Agricultural Adjustment Act and the National Industrial Recovery Act, and on the response of the NAACP to the economic crisis. Wolters' thesis is that the failure of blacks to receive a fair share in the New Deal recovery program "was not solely the result of the racial insensitivity and/ or prejudice of some prominent officials; it resulted primarily from the fact that Negroes were weak and poorly organized, lacking in political and economic power."

Special studies (many of them quite critical) of the way individual New Deal programs and "alphabet agencies" treated blacks are numerous. The National Recovery Administration: Wolters, *Negroes and the Great Depression*, cited above, pt. II, and contemporary accounts such as John P. Davis, "Blue Eagles and Black Workers," *New Republic*, LXXXI (Nov. 14, 1934), 7–9; Charles L. Franklin, *The Negro Labor Unionist in New York: Problems and Conditions Among Negroes in Manhattan, with Special Reference to the N.R.A. and Post-N.R.A. Situations* (New York, 1936); A. Howard Myers, "The Negro Worker Under the N.R.A.," *JNE*, V (Jan. 1936), 48–53; and Gustav Peck, "The Negro Worker and the NRA," *Crisis*, XLI (Sept. 1934), 262–63, 279. The Tennessee Valley Authority: J. Max Bond, "The Educational Program for Negroes in the TVA," *JNE*, VI (Apr. 1937), 144–51, and "The Training Program of the Tennessee Valley Authority for Negroes," *ibid.*, VII (July 1938), 383–89;

Cranston Clayton, "The TVA and the Race Problem," *Opportunity*, XII (Apr. 1934), 111–13; John P. Davis, "The Plight of the Negro in the Tennessee Valley," *Crisis*, XLII (Oct. 1935), 294–95, 314–15; and Charles H. Houston and John P. Davis, "TVA: Lily-White Reconstruction," *ibid.*, XLI (Oct. 1934), 290–91, 311. The Civilian Conservation Corps: John A. Salmond, "The Civilian Conservation Corps and the Negro," *JAH*, LII (June 1965), 75–88; Marian T. Wright, "Negro Youth and the Federal Emergency Programs: CCC and NYA," *JNE*, IX (July 1940), 397–407; Howard W. Oxley, "The Civilian Conservation Corps and the Education of the Negro," *ibid.*, VII (July 1938), 375–82; and Luther C. Wandall, "A Negro in the CCC," *Crisis*, XLII (Aug. 1935), 244, 253–54. The National Youth Administration: Walter G. Daniel and Carroll L. Miller, "The Participation of the Negro in the National Youth Administration Program," *JNE*, VII (July 1938), 357–65; Catherine Owens Peare, *Mary McLeod Bethune* (New York, 1961); Rackham Holt, *Mary McLeod Bethune: A Biography* (Garden City, N.Y., 1964); and the abovementioned Marian A. Wright article. See also three articles by Robert C. Weaver, a black man who held important advisory positions in various New Deal agencies: "The Public Works Administration School Building Program and Separate Negro Schools," *JNE*, VII (July 1938), 366–74, "The Negro in a Program of Public Housing," *Opportunity*, XVI (July 1938), 198–203, and "Racial Policy in Public Housing," *Phylon*, I (2nd Quarter 1940), 149–56, 161. For the Agricultural Adjustment Administration and aspects of rural blacks and the South during the New Deal, see the next topic, "Shadow of the Plantation: Blacks in the Rural South."

Raymond Wolters deals with unsuccessful efforts to include an antidiscrimination clause in the Wagner Act in "Section 7a and the Black Worker," *LH*, X (Summer 1969), 459–74, reprinted with minor modifications as ch. 6 of Milton Cantor, ed., *Black Labor in America* (Westport, Conn., 1970), and as ch. 7 of Wolters' book, *Negroes and the Great Depression*, cited above. Two articles—Fred Greenbaum, "The Anti-Lynching Bill of 1935: The Irony of 'Equal Justice—Under Law,'" *Journal of Human Relations*, XV (3rd Quarter 1967), 72–85, and Robert L. Zangrando, "The NAACP and a Federal Antilynching Bill, 1934–

1940," *JNH*, L (Apr. 1965), 106–17**—treat another abortive attempt to secure legislation favorable to the Negro.

Various black men wrote contemporary appraisals of the way the New Deal treated their race, and their accounts range in tone from outright hostility to guarded approval. For the spectrum of black opinion, see the following: three articles by John P. Davis, "What Price National Recovery?" *Crisis*, XL (Dec. 1933), 271–72, "A Black Inventory of the New Deal," *ibid.*, XLII (May 1935), 141–42, 154–55, and "A Survey of the Problems of the Negro Under the New Deal," *JNE*, V (Jan. 1936), 3–12; Robert C. Weaver, "The New Deal and the Negro: A Look at the Facts," *Opportunity*, XIII (July 1935), 200–03; Ralph J. Bunche, "A Critique of New Deal Planning as It Affects Negroes," *JNE*, V (Jan. 1936), 59–65; "The Campaign," *Crisis*, XLIII (Nov. 1936), 337; and "The Roosevelt Record," *ibid.*, XLVII (Nov. 1940), 343.

In addition to the biographies of Mrs. Bethune already mentioned, books which deal in part with the "black cabinet" include W. M. Kiplinger, *Washington Is Like That* (New York, 1942); Walter White, *A Man Called White: The Autobiography of Walter White* (New York, 1948);* and Roi Ottley, *New World A-Coming* (Boston, 1943, reprinted New York, 1968). Laurence J. W. Hayes, *The Negro Federal Government Worker: A Study of His Classification Status in the District of Columbia, 1883–1938* (Washington, 1941), treats blacks in the civil service.

The two prominent New Dealers most sympathetic to blacks address themselves to the subject in Harold L. Ickes, "The Negro as Citizen," *Crisis*, XLIII (Aug. 1936), 230–32, and in three articles by Eleanor Roosevelt: "The Negro and Social Change," *Opportunity*, XIV (Jan. 1936), 22–23, "Race, Religion and Prejudice," *New Republic*, CVL (May 11, 1942), 630, and "Some of My Best Friends are Negro," *Ebony*, IX (Feb. 1953), 17–20 ff. Two new biographies treat the First Lady's involvement with black rights: Tamara K. Hareven, *Eleanor Roosevelt: An American Conscience* (Chicago, 1968), ch. 6, and James R. Kearney, *Anna Eleanor Roosevelt: The Evolution of a Reformer* (Boston, 1968), ch. 2. Howard W. Odum describes the reaction to Mrs. Roosevelt's activities from hostile southerners in *Race and Rumors of Race: Challenge to American Crisis* (Chapel Hill, 1943), chs. 9–10. Mary McLeod Bethune, "My Secret Talks with

FDR," *Ebony*, IV (Apr. 1949), 42–51, and Allan Morrison, "The Secret Papers of FDR," *Negro Digest*, IX (Jan. 1951), 3–13, give sympathetic and critical accounts, respectively, of the President's position on race relations, while Frank Freidel, *FDR and the South* (Baton Rouge, 1965),* analyzes the factors which kept the President from taking an active stand in behalf of black rights. See also ch. 18, "Southern Politics and the New Deal," of Tindall's *The Emergence of the New South, 1913–1945*, cited early in this topic.

Sociologists, economists, and novelists have all made important contributions to our understanding of the impact of the Depression on black life. Among the social science studies, one should consult three works by Fisk University sociologist Charles S. Johnson—*The Economic Status of the Negro* (Nashville, 1933), "The Negro," *AJS*, XLVII (May 1942), 854–64,** and "Incidence upon the Negroes," *ibid.*, XL (May 1935), 737–45—as well as Newell D. Eason, "Attitudes of Negro Families on Relief," *Opportunity*, XIII (Dec. 1935), 367–69, 379; Thyra J. Edwards, "Attitudes of Negro Families on Relief—Another View," *ibid.*, XIV (July 1936), 213–15; anonymous letters from destitute blacks in *Crisis*, XLI (Nov. 1934), 330–31; T. Arnold Hill, *The Negro and Economic Reconstruction* (Washington, 1937); and the January 1936 issue (vol. V) of the *JNE*, devoted to blacks and the economic crisis. But no one can gain a real sense of what it meant to be black during the Depression without reading two powerful novels, Ralph Ellison's *Invisible Man* (New York, 1947),* and Richard Wright's *Native Son* (New York, 1940),* as well as Wright's autobiography, *Black Boy: A Record of Childhood and Youth* (New York, 1945).*

Gunnar Myrdal's massive study, *An American Dilemma: The Negro Problem and Modern Democracy* (New York, 1944),* is an over-all assessment of the status of blacks at the close of the Depression and the Roosevelt administration.

12. Shadow of the Plantation: Blacks in the Rural South

In 1938 President Franklin D. Roosevelt described the South as "the Nation's no. 1 economic problem," and without question the foremost socioeconomic problem within the South was the plight of black and white tenant farmers. Living under semifeudal conditions, existing on per-family annual incomes of $300 or less, suffering from widespread malnutrition, pellagra, and hookworm, and residing in squalid cabins where they "could study astronomy through the openings in the roof and geology through holes in the floor," they were "the most impoverished and backward" element in the American economy. The problem of tenancy was nothing new to the South in the 1930s, but while in 1880 only 36 per cent of southern farms had been operated by tenants, a half century later this figure had grown to 55 per cent. In 1930 more than two thirds of the black farmers were tenants or sharecroppers. In the 1920s the ravages of the boll weevil and increasing competition from synthetic fibers had plunged cotton farming into recession, and the Great Depression drove cotton prices to their lowest level in nearly forty years.

Agricultural recovery was one of the New Deal's top priorities, but the enforcement of the Agricultural Adjustment Act (AAA) in the South, controlled as it was by the planters, exacerbated rather than alleviated the plight of sharecroppers, especially those with black skins. In 1934 tenants organized the interracial Southern Tenant Farmers' Union (STFU)—the most significant interracial movement in the rural South since the Populists—whose success helped bring about the creation of the Farm Security Administration. But neither the union nor federal agricultural programs substantially improved the lot of southern black farmers. The problem of the sharecropper was "solved" in the generation after 1940 by the mechanization of cotton farming and the consequent displacement of tenants, who exchanged rural misery for the dubious advantages of the urban ghetto.

A good introduction to the condition of rural blacks is provided by Gunnar Myrdal, *An American Dilemma: The Negro Problem and Modern Democracy* (New York, 1944),* chs. 11–12. Three recent studies portray the plight of southern farmers and the inadequate efforts of the New Deal to help them: George Brown Tindall, *The Emergence of the New South, 1913–1945* (Baton Rouge, 1967),* chs. 4, 12; David Eugene Conrad, *The Forgotten Farmers: The Story of the Sharecroppers in the New Deal* (Urbana, Ill., 1965); and Raymond Wolters, *Negroes and the Great Depression: The Problem of Economic Recovery* (Westport, Conn., 1970),* pt. 1. A survey of the condition of black farmers on the eve of the Depression can be found in Carter G. Woodson, *The Rural Negro* (Washington, 1930, reprinted New York, 1969).

During the New Deal a number of remarkable studies, carried out by black and white sociologists, brought the problem of southern rural poverty to national attention as never before. The best of these studies were Charles S. Johnson, *Shadow of the Plantation* (Chicago, 1934),* which deals with Macon County, Alabama, where Tuskegee is located; Charles S. Johnson, Edwin R. Embree, and Will W. Alexander, *The Collapse of Cotton Tenancy* (Chapel Hill, 1935); Arthur F. Raper, *Preface to Peasantry: A Tale of Two Black Belt Counties* (Chapel Hill, 1936),* a survey of Greene and Macon counties, Georgia; Thomas J. Woofter, *Landlord and Tenant on the Cotton Plantation* (Washington, 1936),* sponsored by the Works Projects Administration (WPA); and Charles S. Johnson, *Growing Up in the Black Belt: Negro Youth in the Rural South* (New York, 1941),* based on a study of eight counties in five deep South states. Two classic accounts of race relations and the black subculture in the small town of Indianola, Mississippi, also contain penetrating insights into rural Negro life during the 1930s: John Dollard, *Caste and Class in a Southern Town* (New Haven, 1937),* and Hortense Powdermaker, *After Freedom: A Cultural Study in the Deep South* (New York, 1939).* Also valuable are pts. 1 and 2 of Arthur F. Raper and Ira De A. Reid, *Sharecroppers All* (Chapel Hill, 1941). For an unforgettable essay, with photographs, on white tenant farmers, see James Agee and Walker Evans, *Let Us Now Praise Famous Men* (Boston, 1941). The January 1936 issue (vol. V) of the *JNE* was devoted to an analysis of the economic status of blacks; two useful articles on the black rural population are Olive M. Stone, "The Present Position of the Negro Farm Population" and J. Phil Campbell, "The Government's Farm Policies and the Negro Farmer," *ibid.*, 20–39.

A moving account of the Southern Tenant Farmers' Union by one of its leaders is Howard Kester, *Revolt Among the Share-croppers* (New York, 1936, reprinted New York, 1969). An important monograph is Donald H. Grubbs, *Cry From the Cotton: The Southern Tenant Farmers' Union and the New Deal* (Baton Rouge, 1971). Articles that cover various aspects of the STFU and New Deal agricultural policies are John Beecher, "The Share Croppers' Union in Alabama," *SF*, XIII (Oct. 1934), 124–32;** Jerold S. Auerbach, "Southern Tenant Farmers: Socialist Critics of the New Deal," *LH*, VII (Winter 1966), 3–18;** Donald H. Grubbs, "Gardner Jackson, That 'Socialist' Tenant Farmers' Union, and the New Deal," *Agricultural History*, XLIII (Apr. 1968), 125–37; M. S. Venkataramani, "Norman Thomas, Arkansas Sharecroppers, and the Roosevelt Agricultural Policies, 1933–37," *MVHR*, XLVII (Sept. 1960), 225–46; and Louis Cantor, "A Prologue to the Protest Movement: The Missouri Sharecropper Roadside Demonstration of 1939," *JAH*, LV (Mar. 1969), 804–22, which was expanded into a book of the same title (Durham, N.C., 1969).

13. Organized Labor and Blacks

Until the Depression of the 1930s and the founding of the Congress of Industrial Organizations (CIO) in 1935, the record of organized labor with respect to blacks was largely negative. Only a few unions, notably the Knights of Labor in the 1880s and the United Mine Workers after 1890, made any serious efforts to recruit black members. While the American Federation of Labor (AFL) consistently espoused non-discrimination in principle, its constitution after 1902 sanctioned the issuance of Jim Crow charters to all-black unions, and the AFL never enforced its non-discriminatory policy on member unions. Thousands of black workers were effectively denied the advantages of union organization, and their employment as strikebreakers sharpened the animosities between black and white workers. By 1940, however, the CIO's vigorous campaign to recruit blacks had brought some 200,000 blacks into its constituent unions, and black men had become an important part of the American labor movement.

For brief accounts of organized labor and blacks, see ch. 50 of Philip Taft, *Organized Labor in American History* (New York, 1964), and the relevant portions of Charles H. Wesley, *Negro Labor in the United States* (New York, 1927), and Sterling D. Spero and Abram L. Harris, *The Black Worker: The Negro and the Labor Movement* (New York, 1931).* Alexander Saxton, "Race and the House of Labor," in Gary B. Nash and Richard Weiss, eds., *The Great Fear: Race in the Mind of America* (New York, 1970),* pp. 98–120, is an able treatment of the rise of racial exclusion policies (against Orientals as well as blacks) in the American labor movement. National Urban League research director Ira De A. Reid made a comprehensive study of union discrimination in *Negro Membership in American Labor Unions* (New York, 1930, reprinted Westport, Conn., 1969, and Wilmington, Del., 1971). Ray Marshall, *The Negro and Organized Labor* (New York, 1965), and Julius Jacobson, ed., *The Negro and the American Labor Movement* (Garden City, N.Y., 1968),* chs. 3–5, carry the study of blacks and organized labor through the Depression and war and include some specialized industrial studies. Raymond Wolters recounts the AFL's treatment of blacks in the 1930s in "Section 7a and the Black Worker," *LH*, X (Summer 1969), 459–74, reprinted with minor modifications as ch. 6 of Milton Cantor, ed., *Black Labor in America* (Westport, Conn., 1970), and as ch. 7 of Wolters' book, *Negroes and the Great Depression: The Problem of Economic Recovery* (Westport, Conn., 1970).* Two black leaders express their views of unions in Lester B. Granger, "The Negro—Friend or Foe of Organized Labor?" *Opportunity*, XIII (May 1935), 142–45, and A. Philip Randolph, "The Trade Union Movement and the Negro," *JNE*, V (Jan. 1936), 54–58. Brailsford R. Brazeal, *The Brotherhood of Sleeping Car Porters: Its Origin and Development* (New York, 1946), treats the most important all-black union.

When the CIO was established in 1935 it vigorously and successfully recruited black members in its constituent industrial unions. There are several good studies of blacks and the unions since 1935, among them: Horace R. Cayton and George S. Mitchell, *Black Workers and the New Unions* (Chapel Hill, 1939, reprinted College Park, Md., 1969); Herbert R. Northrup, *Organized Labor and the Negro* (New York, 1944); and Charles L. Franklin, *The Negro Labor Unionist of New York* (New York, 1936, reprinted New York, 1969). A short pamphlet issued by the CIO, *The CIO and the Negro Worker Together for Victory* (Washington, 1941), sets forth its racial policies. The increasingly favorable attitudes of blacks toward unions is the subject of James S. Olson, "Organized Black Leadership and Industrial Unionism: The Racial Response, 1936–1945," *LH*, X (Summer 1969), 475–86 (reprinted with minor modifications as ch. 7 of Cantor, ed., *Black Labor in America*, cited above). A contemporary book on the status of black labor at the conclusion of the war is Robert C. Weaver, *Negro Labor: A National Problem* (New York, 1946).

Useful case studies of individual unions include Herbert R. Northrup, "The Negro and the United Mine Workers of America," *Southern Economic Journal*, IX (Apr. 1943), 313–27; Lloyd H. Bailer, "The Negro Automobile Worker," *Journal of Political Economy*, LI (Oct. 1943), 415–29; and Irving Howe and B. J. Widick, "The U.A.W. Fights Race Prejudice: Case History on the Industrial Front," *Commentary*, VIII (Sept. 1949), 261–68. Other articles worth consulting include Preston Valien, "The Mentalities of Negro and White Workers: An Experimental School Interpretation of Negro Trade Unionism," *SF*, XXVII (May 1949), 433–38;** William Kornhauser, "The Negro Union Official: A Study of Sponsorship and Control," *AJS*, LVII (Mar. 1952), 443–52;** Abram L. Harris, "The Negro and Economic Radicalism," *Modern Quarterly*, II (1924–25), 198–208; and William M. Tuttle, Jr., "Labor Conflict and Racial Violence: The Black Worker in Chicago, 1894–1919," *LH*, X (Summer 1969), 408–32** (reprinted with minor modifications as ch. 4 of Cantor, ed., *Black Labor in America*, cited above).

14. Blacks and Communism

As the most obviously oppressed and exploited minority in the United States, black Americans, according to Communist theory, should have been ripe for revolution. Beginning shortly after its formation at the close of World War I, the American Communist party has tried through various approaches to recruit black members and to promote black interests. By and large, however, black Americans have shown little interest in Communist ideology and overtures, and the party has failed to make any important headway in its designs. Part of this failure is probably attributable to its particular reading of the major objectives of blacks in the United States; while blacks were seeking legal equality and integration, Communist policy, based on a view of blacks as an oppressed colonial nation, called for their self-determination as a separate nation in the American South. The slogan of self-determination was officially adopted in 1928, and it prevailed with some exceptions through the 1950s. Communist tactics in trying to win black support have varied in relation to changes in international Communist strategy; the party has tried at different times to infiltrate, destroy, duplicate, or co-operate with existing black organizations. Yet despite successful infiltration of some groups and despite the affinity some blacks have felt for Communism, especially during the 1930s and 1940s, the party's gains have remained minimal.

William A. Nolan, *Communism Versus the Negro* (Chicago, 1951), and Wilson Record, *The Negro and the Communist Party* (Chapel Hill, 1951), both amply document the failure of the party properly to understand and exploit the plight of blacks in the United States—findings which, as Vaughn D. Bornet has pointed out, were enforced by the anti-Communist suspicion and hysteria of the era in which they were published. Bornet points up some scholarly deficiencies in the two works in his review essay, "Historical Scholarship, Communism, and the Negro," *JNH*, XXXVII (July 1952), 304–24. They should be supplemented by several articles and by the relevant portions of the standard histories of Communism in America: Wilson Record, "The Development of the Communist Position on the Negro Question in the United States," *Phylon*, XIX (3rd Quarter 1958), 306–26; John W. Van Zanten, "Communist Theory and the Negro Question," *Review of Politics*, XXIX (Oct. 1967), 435–56; T. H. Kennedy and T. F. Leary, "Communist Thought and the Negro," *Phylon*, VIII (2nd Quarter 1947), 116–23; Joseph C. Mouledos, "From Browderism to Peaceful Co-Existence: An Analysis of Developments in the Communist Position on the American Negro," *ibid.*, XXV (4th Quarter 1964), 79–90; Theodore Draper, *American Communism and Soviet Russia: The Formative Period* (New York, 1960),* ch. 15; David A. Shannon, *The Decline of American Communism: A History of the Communist Party of the United States since 1945* (New York, 1959), pp. 58–67; and Nathan Glazer, *The Social Basis of American Communism* (New York, 1961), ch. 5. William Z. Foster, *History of the Communist Party of the United States* (New York, 1952), esp. pp. 225–35, 266–69, 308–09, 444–46, 476–79, gives the party line. Wilson Record's second major book, *Race and Radicalism: The NAACP and the Communist Party in Conflict* (Ithaca, N.Y., 1964),* is an important case study which tells the story of the party's shifting strategies. Raymond Wolters, *Negroes and the Great Depression: The Problem of Economic Recovery* (Westport, Conn., 1970),* ch. 13, deals with the relationship between the Communists and the National Negro Congress.

Major black leaders discuss the subject in Walter White, "The Negro and the Communists," *Harper's*, CLXIV (Dec. 1931), 62–72; W. E. B. Du Bois, "Postscript," *Crisis*, XL (Sept. 1931), 313–15 ff.; A. Philip Randolph, "A. Philip Randolph Tells . . . 'Why I Would Not Stand for Reelection as President of the National Negro Congress,'" *American Federationist*, XLVIII (July 1940), 24–25; and a round-table debate, "Have Communists Quit Fighting for Negro Rights?" *Negro Digest*, III (Dec. 1944), 56–70. During the 1930s, the party's *Communist* often included relevant articles. Benjamin J. Davis, a leading black Communist, explains his allegiance in "Why I Am A Communist," *Phylon*, VIII (2nd Quarter 1947), 105–16. Angelo Herndon, *Let Me Live* (New York, 1937, reprinted New York, 1969),* is a moving autobiography of a young black Communist jailed for his activities in behalf of the party. Harold Cruse gives a fine account of the flirtation of black artists and writers with Communism in *The Crisis of the Negro Intellectual* (New York, 1967),* pt. 2, while Richard Wright, one of those who later became disaffected from the party, tells his story in Richard Crossman, ed., *The God That Failed* (New York, 1949).* On Wright and Communism, see also Constance Webb, *Richard Wright: A Biography* (New York, 1968), esp. chs. 9–11, 22, 28, and Wright's well-known novel, *Native Son* (New York, 1940).* Ralph Ellison, *Invisible Man* (New York, 1947),* is another important fictional treatment of blacks and Communism.

The Scottsboro Case was a microcosm of Communist efforts to make headway among blacks. The charge that nine black youths had raped two white prostitutes on a freight train in Alabama in 1931 quickly became an international *cause célèbre*. It resulted in 1935 in the important Supreme Court ruling that blacks may not be systematically excluded from jury service. During the 1930s it created a crisis for black leadership in which liberal groups, including the American Civil Liberties Union (ACLU) and the NAACP, initially fought Communist efforts to conduct the boys' legal defense, but later co-operated with the party in a joint Scottsboro Defense Committee. The campaign to free the defendants from jail continued for two decades. Dan T. Carter's excellent *Scottsboro: A Tragedy of the American South* (Baton Rouge, 1969)* is the definitive study. Two works by participants in the case, Haywood Patterson (the last Scottsboro defendant to be freed) and Earl Conrad's dramatic *Scottsboro Boy* (Garden City, N.Y., 1950),* and Allan K. Chalmers (the chairman of the Scottsboro Defense Committee), *They Shall Be Free* (Garden City, N.Y., 1951), should also be consulted.

During the 1950s and 1960s the Communist party found itself increasingly at odds with rising black nationalist sentiment. The party line has been officially critical of the Black Muslims, and, in an about-face from its earlier doctrine of self-determination, it has condemned the idea of black separatism. For an indication of the hostility between black nationalists and Communists, see Benjamin J. Davis, *The Negro People on the March* (New York, 1956); Harold W. Cruse, "Revolutionary Nationalism and the Afro-American," *Studies on the Left*, II (1962), 12–25;** "Exchange: Revolutionary Nationalism and the Afro-American," *ibid.*, III (1962), 57–71;** chs. 10, 13 of Cruse's *Rebellion or Revolution?* (New York, 1968);* A. James Gregor, "Black Nationalism: A Preliminary Analysis of Negro Radicalism," *Science and Society*, XXVII (Fall 1963), 415–32;** and two works by Claude M. Lightfoot, *Ghetto Rebellion to Black Liberation* (New York, 1968),* and "Negro Nationalism and the Black Muslims," *Political Affairs*, XLI (July 1962), 3–20.

15. Blacks in World War II

At the outbreak of World War II, American blacks found themselves faced with the job of reconciling the international "Four Freedoms" enunciated in President Franklin D. Roosevelt's 1941 State of the Union address with the deprivations of freedom they experienced as second-class citizens in the United States. Sharing the national revulsion against Nazism, and hoping that the war against Hitler's brand of racism might point up the continuing indignities of racism at home, blacks participated extensively in the war effort. Military service and defense industries opened up new opportunities for training in technological skills, and service abroad exposed blacks to foreign cultures with more tolerant attitudes toward blacks than those prevailing in the United States. In some small measure, black hopes that the war might act as a catalyst to improve American race relations were eventually justified. During the war, however, blacks encountered and worked to redress discrimination in two special areas: the armed services and defense-related employment.

The war itself saw a considerable improvement in the status of black troops over that of World War I. Integrated officers' candidates schools were established, for instance, and the Army Air Corps and the Marines for the first time opened their ranks to blacks, while the Navy, which had previously restricted blacks to service as messmen, allowed them to enlist throughout its branches. Black women served in the WACS and WAVES. Individual black soldiers and entire black combat units were decorated for bravery and meritorious performance on the fighting front.

But these improvements were not representative of the entire picture. The War Department persisted in organizing black soldiers into separate units, although it experimented briefly (and successfully) with mixed fighting units in Germany just before the war ended in 1945. Black pilots were trained at a segregated base at Tuskegee Institute. About one million black men and women served in the armed forces, nearly half of them in foreign theaters, but they were still heavily overrepresented in the service forces (for example, engineering, supply, transportation, and port companies) and underrepresented in the air corps and ground combat companies. Blacks were subjected to segregation in recreational and transportation facilities on army posts, and clashes between black and white soldiers were commonplace. Serious race riots broke out at several army camps during the war. Although black troops generally performed capably, segregation practices inevitably had some detrimental effect on their morale and their operational efficiency.

Whereas labor shortages during World War I had opened extensive employment opportunities for blacks in northern industries, unemployment among both whites and blacks at the outbreak of World War II put the black worker in a much less advantageous position on the home front; employers in industries converting for war production were predictably loath to hire blacks. Only after A. Philip Randolph, head of the all-black Brotherhood of Sleeping Car Porters, made public plans for a massive "March on Washington" to persuade the federal government to insure employment of blacks in defense industries did President Roosevelt agree to issue Executive Order 8802 forbidding discrimination in defense industries. A clause barring discrimination was thenceforth included in all defense contracts, and a Committee on Fair Employment Practices was set up to hear complaints of violations. In effect, FEPC had few "teeth" in it, but it contributed to a considerable improvement in the status of black employment by the end of the war.

Ulysses Lee, *The Employment of Negro Troops* (Washington, 1966), an exceptionally detailed volume in the multivolume official history, *United States Army in World War II*, is the definitive work on blacks in the Army, while Richard M. Dalfiume, *Fighting on Two Fronts: Desegregation of the U.S. Armed Forces, 1939–1953* (Columbia, Mo., 1969), is the authoritative account of the slow process of breaking down discrimination against black troops. Contemporary studies of the position of blacks in the armed services include two informed articles by L. D. Reddick in the *JNH*: "The Negro in the United States Navy During World War II," XXXII (Apr. 1947), 201–19, and "The Negro Policy of the United States Army, 1775–1945," XXXIV (Jan. 1949), 9–29. See also Dennis D. Nelson, *The Integration of the Negro into the U.S. Navy* (New York, 1951). Charles E. Francis describes the war experiences of blacks in the Army Air Corps in *The Tuskegee Airmen: The Story of the Negro in the U.S. Air Force* (Boston, 1955). The situation of black Americans early in World War II is taken up by John Temple Graves, "The Southern Negro and the War Crisis," *Virginia Quarterly Review*, XVIII (Autumn 1942), 500–17; Earl Brown, "American Negroes and the War," *Harper's*, CLXXXIV (Apr. 1942), 545–52; "The Negro's War," *Fortune*, XXV (June 1942), 77–80 ff.; and Earl Brown and George R. Leighton, *The Negro and the War* (New York, 1942). Walter White, the executive secretary of the NAACP, provides a fine account of activities among blacks on the fighting front in *A Rising Wind* (Garden City, N.Y., 1945) and *A Man Called White: The Autobiography of Walter White* (New York, 1948),* chs. 28–36. John D. Silvera, *The Negro in World War II* (Baton Rouge, 1946, reprinted New York, 1969), is a good source for pictures.

Black writers particularly concerned with problems of black morale include Charles S. Johnson and others, *To Stem This Tide: A Survey of Racial Tension Areas in the United States* (Boston, 1943), chs. 7–8; James A. Bayton, "The Psychology of Racial Morale," *JNE*, XI (Apr. 1942), 150–53; Horace M. Bond, "Should the Negro Care Who Wins the War?" *Annals*, CCXXIII (Sept. 1942), 81–85; Guion G. Johnson, "The Impact of the War upon the Negro," *JNE*, X (July 1941), 596–611; and J. Saunders Redding, "A Negro Looks at This War," *American Mercury*, LV (Nov. 1942), 585–92. Sociological and psychological studies of racial tensions during wartime, the performance of black soldiers, and the impact of increasing integration in the armed forces include Eli Ginzberg, *The Negro Potential* (New York, 1956), ch. 4; David G. Mandelbaum, *Soldier Groups and Negro Soldiers* (Berkeley, 1952); and the chapter on blacks in Samuel Andrew Stauffer, *The American Soldier*, 2 vols. (Princeton, 1949).

During the war, several journals devoted entire issues to the impact of the war on black Americans. These include "Color, Unfinished Business of Democracy," *Survey Graphic*, XXX (Nov. 1942); "World War II and Negro Higher Education," *JNE*, XI (July 1942); "Minority Peoples in a Nation at War," *Annals*, CCXXIII (Sept. 1942); "The American Negro in World Wars I and II," *JNE*, XII (Summer 1943); and two issues of the *Journal of Educational Sociology*, ed. by L. D. Reddick, "The Negro in the North During Wartime," XVIII (Jan. 1944), and "Race Relations on the Pacific Coast," XIX (Nov. 1945).

The impact of the war on the determination of blacks to fight for democracy at home is the subject of a perceptive analysis by Richard M. Dalfiume, "The 'Forgotten Years' of the Negro Revolution," *JAH*, LV (June 1968), 90–106.** Gunnar Myrdal offers a suggestive introduction to the influence of the war on the status of blacks in the United States in ch. 45 of *An American Dilemma: The Negro Problem and Modern Democracy* (New York, 1944).* For a sampling of black thought on the racial situation in this period, see Rayford W. Logan, ed., *What the Negro Wants* (Chapel Hill, 1944). A key point of contention on the home front —the employment of blacks in defense industries—is treated in Robert C. Weaver, *Negro Labor: A National Problem* (New York, 1946), and in his two-part "Racial Employment Trends in National Defense," *Phylon*, II (4th Quarter 1941), 337–59, and *ibid.* (1st Quarter 1942), 21–31; Council for Democracy, *The Negro and Defense* (New York, 1941); Lester B. Granger, "Barriers to Negro War Employment," *Annals*, CCXXIII (Sept. 1942), 72–81; Herbert R. Northrup, *Organized Labor and the Negro* (New York, 1944); Race Relations Program of the American Missionary Association and the Julius Rosenwald Fund, *The Negro War Worker in San Francisco* (San Francisco, 1944); and W. Y. Bell, Jr., "The Negro Warrior's Home Front," *Phylon*, V (3rd Quarter 1944), 271–79.

A. Philip Randolph explains the program of the March on Washington movement in "Why Should We March?" *Survey*

Graphic, XXXI (Nov. 1942), 488–89. There are three major studies of this movement and the creation of the FEPC: Louis C. Kesselman, *The Social Politics of FEPC: A Study in Reform Pressure Movements* (Chapel Hill, 1948); Louis Ruchames, *Race, Jobs, and Politics: The Story of FEPC* (New York, 1953); and Herbert R. Garfinkel, *When Negroes March: The March on Washington Movement in the Organizational Politics for FEPC* (Glencoe, Ill., 1959).*

PART VIII

*BLACKS IN AMERICAN
CULTURE, 1900–1970*

1. The Harlem Renaissance

The ferment generated by the migration of blacks into the urban North stirred the ambitions of black intellectuals, buoyed their self-confidence, and enabled them in the 1920s to launch a movement that has been named the "Harlem renaissance." Black sociologists and historians, as well as poets, novelists, and artists, were involved. The movement produced a large number of impressive anthologies, memoirs, and promotional works whose impact continued strong through the 1930s. They were designed to display the cultural and intellectual achievements of Afro-Americans in order to gain new respect from the community at large and to strengthen the cultural aspirations and traditions of the black community itself. Confident that Harlem was becoming a "race capital," some black spokesmen ran the risk of racial chauvinism. Yet they also ran the risks of appealing, consciously or unconsciously, to conventional conceptions of cultural excellence as defined by the white middle class or of appealing to stereotyped notions about black life.

The literature produced by the movement was vast, but a good starting point is the collection of writings that brought the movement into focus, *The New Negro: An Interpretation* (New York, 1925),* ed. by Alain L. Locke, a Harvard-trained Rhodes Scholar and professor at Howard University. The following items by leaders of the movement are also important primary material: Claude McKay's autobiography, *A Long Way from Home* (New York, 1937);* James Weldon Johnson's autobiography, *Along This Way* (New York, 1933);* the last sixteen chapters of James Weldon Johnson's *Black Manhattan* (New York, 1930);* and Langston Hughes' autobiography, *The Big Sea* (New York, 1940).* The entire issue of *Survey Graphic*, VI (Mar. 1925), "Harlem, Mecca of the New Negro," contains material, notably James Weldon Johnson's "The Making of Harlem," pp. 635–39. Johnson's anthology, *The Book of American Negro Poetry* (New York, 1922),* with its introduction entitled "The Negro's Creative Genius," was an important early product of the movement. Other essays by blacks connected with the renaissance include James Weldon Johnson's "The Dilemma of the Negro Author," *American Mercury*, XV (Dec. 1928), 477–81, and "Race Prejudice and the Negro Artist," *Harper's*, CLVII (Nov. 1928), 769–76; Alain L. Locke's "The Negro Intellectual," *New York Herald Tribune Books*, May 20, 1920, p. 12; W. E. B. Du Bois' "Criteria for Negro Art," *Crisis*, XXXII (Oct. 1926), 290–97; Countee Cullen's introduction to his *Caroling Dusk* (New York, 1927); Benjamin Brawley's "The Negro Literary Renaissance," *Southern Workman*, LVI (Apr. 1927), 177–84; and Langston Hughes' important "The Negro Artist and the Racial Mountain," *Nation*, CXXII (June 23, 1926), 692–94.** Benjamin Brawley's *The Negro Genius* (first published as *The Negro in Literature and Art* in 1910) was enlarged in 1918 and again in 1927 and 1937;* its introduction is reprinted in Darwin W. Turner and Jean M. Bright, eds., *Images of the Negro in America* (Boston, 1965),* pp. 51–56. Contemporary analyses by white critics include V. F. Calverton, "The Negro's New Belligerent Attitude," *Current History*, XXX (Sept. 1929), 1081–88, and John Chamberlain, "The Negro as a Writer," *Bookman*, LXX (Feb. 1930), 603–11.

Some of the participants in the renaissance later evaluated the movement's impact. See especially Alain L. Locke, "Self-Criticism: The Third Dimension in Culture," *Phylon*, XI (4th Quarter 1950), 391–94, and George S. Schuyler, "The Van Vechten Revolution," *ibid.*, 362–68, a discussion of the influence of white patrons on black writers of the renaissance. Analyses and criticisms of the renaissance by the subsequent generation of black writers and intellectuals include Arna Bontemps, "The Harlem Renaissance," *Saturday Review*, XXX (Mar. 22, 1947), 12–13 ff.; William S. Braithwaite, "Alain Locke's Relationship to the Negro in American Literature," *Phylon*, XVIII (2nd Quarter 1957), 166–73; Eugene C. Holmes, "Alain Leroy Locke: A Sketch," *ibid.*, XX (1st Quarter 1959), 82–89; and Harold Cruse, *Crisis of the Negro Intellectual* (New York, 1967),* pt. 1.

The fullest scholarly treatment of the renaissance is Nathan I. Huggins, *Harlem Renaissance* (New York, 1971). For excellent brief surveys of the renaissance, see S. P. Fullinwider, *The Mind and Mood of Black America* (Homewood, Ill., 1969),* ch. 6, and Gilbert Osofsky, *Harlem: The Making of a Ghetto; Negro New York, 1890–1930* (New York, 1966),* epilogue. Both Robert A. Bone, *The Negro Novel in America* (rev. ed., New Haven, 1965),* pt. 2, and Hugh M. Gloster, *Negro Voices in American Fiction* (Chapel Hill, 1948), chs. 3–4, have relevant material on various writers connected with the renaissance, and Stephen H. Bronz, *The Roots of Negro Racial Consciousness: The 1920's: Three Harlem Renaissance Authors* (New York, 1964),* discusses James Weldon Johnson, Countee Cullen, and Claude McKay. Two important biographies are Blanche E. Ferguson, *Countee Cullen and the Negro Renaissance* (New York, 1966),* and James A. Emanuel, *Langston Hughes* (New York, 1967).

For other works connected with the movement and material on their authors, see this Part, topic 2, "Black Poetry," topic 4, "Fiction of the Renaissance: Jean Toomer and Claude McKay," and topic 8, "Black Painters and Sculptors."

2. Black Poetry

Among the best writers who played important roles in the Harlem renaissance were three poets: Langston Hughes, Countee Cullen, and James Weldon Johnson. Since 1930, and with increasing frequency since 1950, black poets with impressive talents have gained prominence on the literary scene. (For the earlier case of Paul Laurence Dunbar, see Part VI, topic 15, "Black Fiction at the Turn of the Century: Charles Waddell Chesnutt and Paul Laurence Dunbar.") The first Pulitzer prize awarded to a black poet was won in 1950 by Gwendolyn Brooks for *Annie Allen*.

But successful or not, black poets have encountered particular problems not faced by white poets. One was presented by the dialect tradition: To use dialect might encourage a surrender to stereotypes and sentimentality, and (as with all dialect literature) might render the poetry difficult to read; to ignore dialect, on the other hand, might mean failure to render the rich idiom and cadences of Afro-American speech. Another problem was how to register the black's racial consciousness, his sense of alienation from the dominant white culture, his protest against the injustices of his position in American society. Did black life and protest demand simplicity of subject matter and directness of appeal to the audience? Or did the black's responsibilities to his art demand that he master the modes of poetry becoming dominant in white culture? As members of the black community and citizens of the larger community as well, black poets have responded to world-wide currents of taste in modern literature as well as to black traditions in music, religious literature, and folklore in pursuit of their professional careers.

Anthologies have been one important means for gaining recognition, and they display the range of talent among black poets. Two anthologies whose combined comprehensiveness is impressive are Langston Hughes and Arna Bontemps, eds., *The Poetry of the Negro, 1746–1970* (rev. ed., Garden City, N.Y., 1970), and Alan Lomax and Raoul Abdul, eds., *3000 Years of Black Poetry* (New York, 1970).* For the 1920s and the Harlem renaissance poets, see the following important collections: James Weldon Johnson's *The Book of American Negro Poetry* (New York, 1922; rev. ed., New York, 1931);* Countee Cullen, ed., *Caroling Dusk: An Anthology of Verse by Negro Poets* (New York, 1927); Robert T. Kerlin, ed., *Contemporary Poetry of the Negro* (Hampton, Va., 1923) and *Negro Poets and Their Poems* (Washington, 1923); Alain L. Locke's selection of poems by Claude McKay, Countee Cullen, Jean Toomer, and Langston Hughes, entitled *Four Negro Poets* (New York, 1927); Newman White and W. C. Jackson, eds., *An Anthology of Verse by American Negroes* (Durham, N.C., 1924, reprinted Durham, 1968).

For general collections and anthologies of recent poetry, see particularly the following: Arna Bontemps, ed., *American Negro Poetry* (New York, 1963);* Herbert Hill, ed., *Soon, One Morning: New Writing by American Negroes, 1940–1962* (New York, 1963); Darwin T. Turner, ed., *Black American Literature: Poetry* (Columbus, Ohio, 1969);* Clarence Major, ed., *The New Black Poetry* (New York, 1969);* June M. Jordan, ed., *Soulscript: Afro-American Poetry* (Garden City, N.Y., 1970);* Ted Wilentz and

Tom Weatherly, eds., *Natural Process: An Anthology of New Black Poetry* (New York, 1970);* Walter Lowenfels, ed., *In a Time of Revolution: Poems from Our Third World* (New York, 1970);* LeRoi Jones and Larry Neal, eds., *Black Fire: An Anthology of Afro-American Writing* (New York, 1968);* and R. Baird Shuman, ed., *Nine Black Poets* (Durham, N.C., 1968). Other fine collections include Rosey E. Pool, ed., *Beyond the Blues: New Poems by American Negroes* (Kent, England, 1962);* Langston Hughes, ed., *New Negro Poets U.S.A.* (Bloomington, Ind., 1964);* Robert Hayden, ed., *Kaleidoscope, Poems by Negro Poets* (New York, 1967);* and *Ten: An Anthology of Detroit Poets* (Fort Smith, Ark., 1968). Recent volumes of verse include the following: Gil Scott-Hern, *Small Talk at 125th and Tenth* (New York, 1970);* Julius Lester, *Search for the New Land* (New York, 1969);* June M. Jordan, *Who Look at Me* (New York, 1969); and Lucille Clifton, *Good Times* (New York, 1969).*

Commentary that emphasizes the particular problems of black poets and distinctive features of their traditions and productions includes several early pieces in addition to the introductions to the anthologies by Johnson and Cullen listed above: Newman White, "American Negro Poetry," *SAQ,* XX (Oct. 1921), 304–22, and "Racial Feeling in Negro Poetry," *ibid.,* XXI (Jan. 1922), 14–29; and Charlotte E. Taussig, "The New Negro as Revealed in his Poetry," *Opportunity,* V (Apr. 1927), 108–11. See also two important pieces by J. Saunders Redding, *To Make a Poet Black* (Chapel Hill, 1939) and "The Problems of the Negro Writer," *Massachusetts Review,* VI (Autumn–Winter 1964), 57–70. Dialect problems are discussed by Eugenia W. Collier, "James Weldon Johnson: Mirror of Change," *Phylon,* XXI (Winter 1960), 351–59. The following articles are also important: Edward Bland, "Racial Bias and Negro Poetry," *ibid.,* LXIII (4th Quarter 1944), 328–33; Walter I. Daykin, "Race Consciousness in Negro Poetry," *Sociology and Social Research,* XX (Nov.–Dec. 1935), 98–105; Charles I. Glicksberg, "Negro Poets and the American Tradition," *Antioch Review,* VI (Summer 1946), 243–53; and Carolyn M. Rodgers, "Black Poetry—Where It's At," *Negro Digest,* XVIII (Sept. 1969), 7–16. Ch. 6 in Margaret Just Butcher, *The Negro in American Culture* (New York, 1956) is a brief summary of black poetry.

In the 1960s influential black poets and critics attempted to define the "black aesthetic" in terms of the black writer's relation to his audience and by what June M. Jordan called the "particular human voice" derived from the "black experience." For relevant material, see June Jordan's introduction to *Soulscript*, cited above, pp. xvi–xix; Addison Gayle, ed., *The Black Aesthetic* (Garden City, N.Y., 1971); and two items in LeRoi Jones and Larry Neal, eds., *Black Fire: An Anthology of Afro-American Writing*, cited above: James T. Stewart's "The Development of the Black Revolutionary Artist," pp. 3–10, and Larry Neal's "And Shine Swam On," pp. 637–56. See also Ishmael Reed's introduction to *Nineteen Necromancers from Now* (Garden City, N.Y., 1970);* the symposium by Romare Bearden et al., "The Black Artist in America," cited in this Part, topic 8, "Black Painters and Sculptors"; and items cited in this Part, topic 6, "After Protest: Black Writers in the 1950s and 1960s." Two illuminating reviews that discuss the "black aesthetic," the first by a white reviewer and the second by a black novelist, are Thomas Lask, "Why Don't You Just Get Lost?" New York *Times*, Jan. 23, 1971, p. 27, and Toni Morrison, "*Amistad 2, New African Literature and the Arts, The Black Aesthetic*," in the *New York Times Book Review*, Feb. 28, 1971, pp. 5, 34. For a white critic's defense of the "black aesthetic," see "White Standards and Black Writing" and "Black Writing and White Criticism" in Richard Gilman, *The Confession of Realms* (New York, 1970),* pp. 3–12, 13–21.

A. Countee Cullen

Cullen's poetry includes *Color* (New York, 1925); *Copper Sun* (New York, 1927); *The Black Christ and Other Poems* (New York, 1929); *The Medea and Other Poems* (New York, 1935); and selected poems, *On These I Stand* (New York, 1947).

Helen J. Dinger, *A Study of Countee Cullen* (New York, 1953); Stephen H. Bronz, *Roots of Negro Racial Consciousness: The 1920's: Three Harlem Renaissance Authors* (New York, 1964),* pp. 47–64; Margaret Perry, *A Bio-Bibliography of Countee P. Cullen* (Westport, Conn., 1969); and Blanche E. Ferguson's uncritical *Countee Cullen and the Negro Renaissance* (New York, 1966),* are the most complete studies. Two touching tributes to Cullen are Arna Bontemps, "Countee Cullen, American Poet," *The People's Voice*, V (Jan. 1946), 52–53, and Owen Dodson, "Countee Cullen (1903–1946)," *Phylon*, VII (1st Quarter 1946), 19–21. See also Arthur Davis, "The Alien-Exile Theme in Countee Cullen's Poems," *ibid.*, XIV (4th Quarter 1953), 390–400; Beulah Reimherr, "Race Consciousness in Countee Cullen's Poetry," *Susquehanna University Studies*, VII (1963), 65–82; Harvey Webster, "A Difficult Career," *Poetry*, LXX (July 1947), 222–25; and Bertram Woodruff, "The Poetic Philosophy of Countee Cullen," *Phylon*, I (3rd Quarter 1940), 213–23.

B. Langston Hughes

The Selected Poems of Langston Hughes (New York, 1959) draws on his earlier volumes, the most important of which were *The Weary Blues* (New York, 1926); *Fine Clothes to the Jew* (New York, 1927); *The Dream Keeper and Other Poems* (New York, 1932); *Scottsboro Limited: Four Poems and a Play in Verse* (New York, 1932); and *Montage of a Dream Deferred* (New York, 1951). More recent is *The Panther and the Lash: Poems of Our Times* (New York, 1967). Hughes' autobiographical writings include *The Big Sea* (New York, 1940);* *I Wonder as I Wander* (New York, 1956);* "My Adventures as a Social Poet," *Phylon*, VIII (3rd Quarter 1947), 205–13; and "Simple and Me," *ibid.*, VI (4th Quarter 1945), 349–54. For Hughes' folk hero Simple and his fiction and drama, see Darwin T. Turner's bibliography, *Afro-American Writers* (New York, 1970),* pp. 58–61.

James A. Emanuel, *Langston Hughes* (New York, 1967) is an excellent introduction. Milton Meltzer has written *Langston Hughes: A Biography* (New York, 1968). Material emphasizing Hughes's poetry includes Countee Cullen, "Our Book Shelf: Poet on Poet," *Opportunity*, IV (Feb. 1926), 73; Arthur P. Davis, "The Harlem of Langston Hughes' Poetry," *Phylon*, XIII (3rd Quarter 1952), 276–83, and "Langston Hughes: Cool Poet," *CLAJ*, XI (June 1968), 280–96;** Darwin Turner, "Langston Hughes," *ibid.*, 297–309; James Presley, "The American Dream of Langston Hughes," *Southwest Review*, XLVIII (Autumn 1963), 380–86; and Aaron Kramer, "Robert Burns and Langston Hughes," *Freedomways*, VIII (Spring 1968), 159–66.

C. James Weldon Johnson

When James Weldon Johnson published his autobiographical *Along This Way* (New York, 1933),* his *Fifty Years and Other Poems* (Boston, 1917) and his most famous work, *God's Trombones: Seven Negro Sermons in Verse* (New York, 1927), had already appeared. His *Saint Peter Relates an Incident: Selected Poems* (New York, 1935) is a collection of some of his best works.

Stephen H. Bronz, *The Roots of Negro Racial Consciousness: The 1920's: Three Harlem Renaissance Authors* (New York, 1964),* pp. 18–46, is the best introduction to Johnson. Earlier comment appeared in Benjamin Brawley, *The Negro Genius* (New York, 1937),* pp. 206–14, and *The Negro in Literature and Art* (New York, 1929), pp. 79–82; Sterling A. Brown, *Negro Poetry and Drama* (Washington, D.C., 1937),* pp. 68–69; and J. Saunders Redding, *To Make a Poet Black* (Chapel Hill, 1939, reprinted College Park, Md., 1968), pp. 120–25. An important article on Johnson's position as a black intellectual is Herbert Aptheker, "Du Bois on James Weldon Johnson," *JNH*, LII (Apr. 1967), 128–45. Articles on Johnson's poetry include Eugenia W. Collier, "James Weldon Johnson, Mirror of Change," *Phylon*, XXI (4th Quarter 1960), 351–59, and Joseph Auslander, "Sermon Sagas," *Opportunity*, V (Sept. 1927), 274–75.

D. Melvin B. Tolson

Tolson's most notable work is *Libretto for the Republic of Liberia* (New York, 1953). More recent is *Harlem Gallery, Book I: The Curator* (New York, 1965).* He has also published *Rendezvous with America* (New York, 1944) and "A Poet's Odyssey," an interview in Herbert Hill, ed., *Anger and Beyond: The Negro Writer in the United States* (New York, 1966),* pp. 181–203.

The commentary on Tolson's work includes the poet Allen Tate's preface to the *Libretto for the Republic of Liberia*, cited above; Dan McCall, "The Quicksilver Sparrow of M. B. Tolson," *AQ*, XVIII (Fall 1966), 538–42; and the poet Karl Shapiro's "A Foot in the Door," *New York Herald Tribune Book Week*, Jan. 10, 1965, p. 1, reprinted in *Negro Digest*, XIV (May 1965),

75–77. See also Sarah W. Fabio, "Who Speaks Negro?" *Negro Digest*, XVI (Dec. 1966), 54–58, and D. G. Thompson, "Tolson's Gallery Brings Poetry Home," *NHB*, XXIX (Dec. 1965), 69–70.

E. Gwendolyn Brooks

Gwendolyn Brooks' *Selected Poems* (New York, 1963)* draws on earlier volumes that include the following: *A Street in Bronzeville* (New York, 1945); *Annie Allen* (New York, 1949); *Bronzeville Boys and Girls* (New York, 1956), a volume for children; *The Bean Eaters* (New York, 1960); and *In the Mecca* (New York, 1968). A brief statement of her intentions as a black poet, "Poets Who Are Negro," appeared in *Phylon*, XI (4th Quarter 1950), 312. She contributed a brief foreword to Langston Hughes' *New Negro Poets U.S.A.* (Bloomington, Ind., 1964).* A recent interview conducted by George Stavros, under the title "An Interview with Gwendolyn Brooks," appeared in *Contemporary Literature*, XI (Winter 1970), 1–20. See also Frank L. Brown, "Chicago's Great Lady of Poetry," *Negro Digest*, XI (Dec. 1961), 53–57; "Gwendolyn Brooks: Poet Laureate," in Phillip T. Drotning and Wesley W. South, *Up From the Ghetto* (New York, 1970), pp. 170–76; J. Crockett, "An Essay on Gwendolyn Brooks," *NHB*, XIX (Nov. 1955), 37–39; B. Cutler, "Long Reach, Strong Speech," *Poetry*, CIII (Mar. 1964), 388–89; Stanley Kunitz, "Bronze by Gold," *ibid.*, LXXI (Apr. 1950), 52–56; and particularly two articles by Arthur P. Davis, "The Black-and-Tan Motif in the Poetry of Gwendolyn Brooks," *CLAJ*, VI (Dec. 1962), 90–97, and "Gwendolyn Brooks: A Poet of the Unheroic," *ibid.*, VII (Dec. 1963), 114–25.

F. LeRoi Jones

LeRoi Jones' volumes of poems include *Preface to a Twenty-Volume Suicide Note* (New York, 1961);* *The Dead Lecturer* (New York, 1964);* and *Black Magic* (New York, 1969). Two important essays by Jones are "The Myth of a 'Negro Literature,'" in his *Home: Social Essays* (New York, 1966),* pp. 105–15; and "Philistinism and the Negro Writer," in Herbert Hill, ed., *Anger and Beyond: The Negro Writer in the United States* (New York,

1966).* Commentary on Jones' poetry includes Denise Levertov, "Poets of the Given Ground," *Nation*, CXCII (Oct. 14, 1961), 251–52; Clarence Major, "The Poetry of LeRoi Jones," *Negro Digest*, XIV (Mar. 1965), 54–56; Donald B. Costello, "LeRoi Jones: Black Man as Victim," *Commonweal*, LXXXVIII (June 28, 1968), 436–40; and Kathryn Jackson, "LeRoi Jones and the New Black Writers of the Sixties," *Freedomways*, IX (Summer 1969), 232–48. For Jones' career as a black militant and as a playwright, see this Part, topic 6, "After Protest: Black Writers in the 1950s and 1960s," and this Part, topic 9, "Blacks and the American Theater."

3. Exotic Primitivism in the White Novel

The attempt of Harlem renaissance writers to define the black's identity and the culture of the black community was complicated by a durable myth about Afro-Americans that was given new currency during the 1920s, the myth of the exotic black primitive. The myth has roots in the ancient past (see Part II, topic 2, "The Figure of the Black in English Renaissance Drama") and colors such American works as Mark Twain's *Pudd'nhead Wilson* and Gertrude Stein's "Melanctha." In the 1920s a number of important white novelists published works that celebrated the black as the enviable paradigm of physical and psychic freedom. The popularity of Freud, jazz, and African sculpture, as well as attacks on middle-class values in the writings of social critics, reinforced the cult of primitivism. The movement had a pronounced effect on Afro-American fiction as well as on white conceptions of the black character and the black community.

The vogue of primitivism centered in Carl Van Vechten and his novel, *Nigger Heaven* (New York, 1926).* Other important examples are Sherwood Anderson's *Dark Laughter* (New York, 1924),* Waldo Frank's *Holiday* (New York, 1923), and E. E. Cummings' *The Enormous Room* (New York, 1922).*

There is useful material scattered through Robert A. Bone's *The Negro Novel in America* (rev. ed., New Haven, Conn.,

1965),* and Hugh M. Gloster's *Negro Voices in American Fiction* (Chapel Hill, 1948), esp. pp. 157–73, and in Frederick J. Hoffman, *Freudianism and the Literary Mind* (Baton Rouge, 1945),* pp. 230–55 (Anderson), 256–76 (Frank). On Van Vechten see Bruce Kellner, *Carl Van Vechten and the Irreverent Decades* (Norman, Okla., 1968); Edward Lueders, *Carl Van Vechten and the Twenties* (Albuquerque, N.M., 1955);* Oscar Cargill, *Intellectual America* (New York, 1941), pp. 507–11; G. S. Schuyler, "Carl Van Vechten," *Phylon*, XI (4th Quarter 1950), 363–68; and Edmund Wilson, *The Shores of Light* (New York, 1952),* pp. 68–72. For Anderson and Cummings, consult Irving Howe, *Sherwood Anderson* (New York, 1951),* and Charles Norman, *The Magic-Maker: E.E. Cummings* (New York, 1958). An important article is Sterling A. Brown, "Negro Stereotypes as Seen by White Authors," *JNE*, II (Jan. 1933), 179–203.

4. Fiction of the Renaissance: Jean Toomer and Claude McKay

The ferment of the Harlem renaissance was an important influence on black novelists. They turned for material from the black professional middle class to the black "masses," the "folk"— whether in urban North or rural South. Blackness became, in their fiction, a positive value, not simply a quality to be minimized or excused. They turned from the civilized to the primitive, from the respectable to the exotic—encouraged not only by the new cultural awakening but also by the example of such white novelists as Sherwood Anderson, in *Dark Laughter* (New York, 1925),* and Carl Van Vechten, in *Nigger Heaven* (New York, 1926)* (see the preceding topic, "Exotic Primitivism in the White Novel"). Whereas dialect had been a mark of sometimes comic inferiority in the fiction of earlier black writers, it became for these new novelists a serious and vibrant form of communication. At its best, this movement allowed the novelist to come closer to the richness and reality of black life than had such "genteel" writers as Charles W. Chesnutt and Paul Laurence Dunbar. At its worst, however, the movement simply moved the black novelist from one stereotype—the genteel, middle-class Negro—to another —the exotic primitive.

The most important writers of fiction in this movement were Jean Toomer and Claude McKay. Toomer's reputation rests on his collection of short prose pieces and poems, *Cane* (New York, 1932),* which may be the most important work of black fiction before 1940. Claude McKay wrote three novels. *Home to Harlem* (New York, 1928)* chronicles the adventures of a World War I deserter in Harlem. *Banjo* (New York, 1929)* concerns the life of a similar black vagabond. And in *Banana Bottom* (New York, 1933), set in the West Indies, a black woman forsakes the ways of white Protestant gentility to embrace her sexual and racial identity. McKay also published several volumes of poetry (see this Part, topic 2, "Black Poetry"), and an autobiography, *A Long Way from Home* (New York, 1937).* McKay and Toomer may be compared with respect to the nature and authenticity (insofar as this quality can be judged) of the black identity evoked in their fiction.

For general discussions of the fiction of the Harlem renaissance, which also include material on Toomer and McKay, see Robert A. Bone, *The Negro Novel in America* (rev. ed., New Haven, 1965),* chs. 3, 4; Edward Margolies, *Native Sons* (Philadelphia, 1968),* pp. 30–35, 38–42; and Hugh M. Gloster, *Negro Voices in American Fiction* (Chapel Hill, 1948), chs. 3, 4. For discussions specifically of Toomer and *Cane*, see Gorham Munson, "The Significance of Jean Toomer," *Opportunity*, III (Sept. 1925), 262–63; Paul Rosenfeld, "Jean Toomer," in *Men Seen* (New York, 1925); S. P. Fullinwider, "Jean Toomer, Lost Generation, or Negro Renaissance?" *Phylon*, XXVII (Winter 1966), 396–403;** Darwin T. Turner, "Jean Toomer's *Cane*: A Critical Analysis," *Negro Digest*, XVIII (1969), 54–61;** two somewhat overlapping essays by Arna Bontemps—"Jean Toomer and the Harlem Writers of the 1920's," in Herbert Hill, ed., *Anger and Beyond: the Negro Writer in the United States* (New York, 1966),* and the introduction to the Harper Perennial paperback edition of *Cane* (New York, 1969);* and Todd Lieber, "Design and Movement in *Cane*," *CLAJ*, XIII (Sept. 1969), 35–50. Discussions of McKay and his fiction can be found in Stephen H. Bronz, *Roots of Negro Racial Consciousness: The 1920's: Three Harlem Renaissance Authors*

(New York, 1964);* Wayne Cooper, "Claude McKay and the New Negro of the 1920's," *Phylon*, XXV (Fall 1964), 297–306; Blyden Jackson, "The Essential McKay," *ibid.*, XIV (2nd Quarter 1953), 216–17; and Robert A. Smith, "Claude McKay: An Essay in Criticism," *ibid.*, IX (3rd Quarter 1948), 270–73. Rebecca C. Barton's "*A Long Way from Home*: Claude McKay," in *Witnesses for Freedom* (New York, 1948), concerns McKay's autobiography, but it is still relevant to this topic. Also of interest is McKay's article, really a manifesto for the concerns of the Harlem renaissance in fiction, "A Negro to His Critics," *New York Herald Tribune Books*, Mar. 6, 1932, pp. 1, 6.

5. Black Social Fiction: The "Protest School"

In the early 1930s the economic and cultural hopes represented by the Harlem renaissance gave way to the realities of the Depression. This disappointment profoundly affected the ways in which black novelists dealt with black life. Like the writers of the Harlem renaissance, the new writers chose the black masses as their subject, but with the aim of protesting against, rather than celebrating, the unique conditions of black life in America. More and more, in the 1930s and 1940s, black novelists turned their attention to white oppression. Like many white radical writers in the Depression decades these new black writers sought to make literature an instrument of social protest.

An early example of the so-called "protest school" in black fiction is Arna Bontemps' *Black Thunder* (New York, 1936),* a historical novel dealing with the Prosser slave conspiracy of 1800. But social protest was established as the dominant mode for black fiction by Richard Wright, whose *Native Son* (New York, 1940)* was extraordinarily popular and influential. Besides Wright, the most important writers of black protest fiction in the 1930s and 1940s would seem in retrospect to have been Ann Petry and Chester Himes.

For an excellent general discussion of black protest fiction, see Robert A. Bone, *The Negro Novel in America* (rev. ed., New

Haven, 1965),* chs. 7, 8. For a discussion of the debate between advocates of protest fiction and those in reaction against protest see the following topic, "After Protest: Black Writers in the 1950s and 1960s." A suggestive general essay is Tilman C. Cothran's "White Stereotypes in Fiction by Negroes," *Phylon*, XI (Autumn 1950), 252–56.

A. Richard Wright

Besides *Native Son*, Wright's most important works are his autobiography, *Black Boy* (New York, 1945),* and his two collections of short fiction, *Uncle Tom's Children* (New York, 1938)* and *Eight Men* (New York, 1961).* His other novels are: *Lawd, Today!* (written 1936, published New York, 1963),* *The Outsider* (New York, 1953),* *Savage Holiday* (New York, 1954),* and *The Long Dream* (New York, 1958).* Wright also wrote two books of travel and journalism: *Black Power* (New York, 1954), describing a trip to Ghana, and *The Color Curtain* (New York, 1956). In *White Man, Listen!* (New York, 1957)* he collected a number of speeches. He discussed his radicalism in an essay in Richard Crossman's *The God That Failed* (New York, 1949). See also his 1937 essay, "Blueprint for Negro Literature," printed in full for the first time in John A. Williams and Charles F. Harris, eds., *Amistad 2: Writings on Black History and Culture* (New York, 1971),* pp. 3–20.

Much of the critical discussion of Wright has concentrated on assessing the effects of protest in Wright's fiction. Some critics have complained that Wright falsifies or oversimplifies black life for the sake of protest, that he is not able to get beyond stereotypes in his portrayal of black (and white) characters. For an answer to such an argument, focusing on *Native Son*, see Wright's essay, "How Bigger Was Born," which appeared in the *Saturday Review of Literature*, XXII (June 1, 1940), 3–4, 17–20, and which is reprinted as the introduction to the Harper Perennial Paperback edition of *Native Son* (New York, 1966).*

Of the countless articles on Wright, those by James Baldwin and Irving Howe are among the best (see the following topic, "After Protest: Black Writers in the 1950s and 1960s"). An early and favorable appraisal by Ralph Ellison, "Richard Wright's Blues," appears in Ellison's *Shadow and Act* (New York, 1964).* See also Nathan A. Scott, Jr., "The Dark and Haunted Tower of Richard Wright," in Addison Gayle, Jr., ed., *Black Expression: Essays by and about Black Americans in the Creative Arts* (New York, 1969),* pp. 296–311.** For biographical information, see Constance Webb, *Richard Wright: A Biography* (New York, 1968). Of the two book-length critical studies of Wright, Edward Margolies' *The Art of Richard Wright* (Carbondale, Ill., 1969) is useful, and Dan McCall's *The Example of Richard Wright* (New York, 1969) is excellent.

B. Chester Himes

Chester Himes is probably the most prolific of black social novelists. He is also the author of a number of Harlem detective novels. His first novel, *If He Hollers Let Him Go* (New York, 1945), deals with racial discrimination at a California shipyard during World War II. *Lonely Crusade* (New York, 1947) presents the trials of a black union organizer and also is Himes' first exploration of the theme of interracial sex. *Cast the First Stone* (New York, 1952), a novel of prison life, has mainly white characters. *The Third Generation* (New York, 1954), which is at least partly autobiographical, portrays the education of a young middle-class black. In *The Primitive* (New York, 1956) Himes again explores the brutality of an interracial sexual relationship. His more recent novels include *Pinktoes* (New York, 1965)* and, perhaps the best-known of Himes' detective novels, *Cotton Comes to Harlem* (New York, 1966).*

With Himes as with Wright, critical discussion has concentrated on the novelist's ability to integrate the functions of art and protest. There is useful critical material on Himes in Bone's *Negro Novel in America*, cited above, chs. 8, 9, and Edward Margolies, *Native Sons* (Philadelphia, 1968),* ch. 5. For a long interview with Himes conducted by John A. Williams, see "My Man Himes: An Interview with Chester Himes," in John A. Williams and Charles F. Harris, eds., *Amistad 1: Writings on Black History and Culture* (New York, 1970),* pp. 25–93.

C. Ann Petry

The classification of Ann Petry as a "protest novelist" stems largely from the subject matter of her first novel, *The Street* (Boston, 1946),* which deals with the efforts of a black woman to maintain her middle-class values in Harlem. Mrs. Petry's other two novels take place in small New England towns. While *The Narrows* (Boston, 1953) deals with racial tensions in such a town, *Country Place* (Boston, 1947) deals primarily with white characters. By comparing *Country Place* to either *The Street* or *The Narrows*, one may examine the effects of racial pressures on Mrs. Petry's art. One may also try to determine whether freedom from the demands of racial protest seems to enrich or to impoverish *Country Place*, and whether Mrs. Petry is freer from stereotypes in treating white characters or black characters.

On *The Street*, see James W. Ivy, "Ann Petry Talks About Her First Novel" and "Mrs. Petry's Harlem," in *Crisis*, LIII (Feb. 1946), 43–46, 48–49. *Country Place* is discussed at some length in Bone's *Negro Novel in America*, cited above, pp. 180–85. An enthusiastic but rather vague "special case" for Ann Petry's fiction is made in David Littlejohn, *Black on White: A Critical Survey of Writings by American Negroes* (New York, 1966),* pp. 154–56.

6. After Protest: Black Writers in the 1950s and 1960s

After 1940 many black writers, following the example of Richard Wright's *Native Son*, chose social protest as the proper form for the portrayal of black life. But as time has passed, younger writers have become restive under Wright's influence. Their dissatisfaction with the demands of protest literature gave rise to a critical debate that deserves close attention. It involved the two most important black novelists to follow Wright, Ralph Ellison and James

Baldwin, who used the debate to define their own conceptions of the nature of black literature and of literature in general. And this debate brought into the open the central dilemma of the black writer in an age of racial upheaval: How shall he reconcile his role as *writer* with his identity as a *black* man? Must his fiction always be protest fiction? And if not, how shall he counter the accusation that he is abandoning his people?

The debate over Richard Wright and protest literature began with two essays James Baldwin published in *The Partisan Review*: "Everybody's Protest Novel," XVI (June 1949), 578–85,** and "Many Thousands Gone," XVIII (Nov.–Dec. 1951), 665–80. Both are reprinted in Baldwin's *Notes of a Native Son* (Boston, 1955).* Baldwin also wrote three more essays on Wright, which were collected under the title "Alas, Poor Richard," in his *Nobody Knows My Name* (New York, 1961).* In 1963 the white critic Irving Howe rose to defend Wright's reputation and position in an essay entitled "Black Boys and Native Sons," *Dissent*, X (Fall 1963), 353–68. In this essay Howe grouped Ralph Ellison with Baldwin as a younger black writer desecrating the example of Wright, and Ellison replied with his own essay, "The World and the Jug," *New Leader*, XLVI (Dec. 9, 1963), 22–26. Howe and Ellison went one more round in "The Writer and Critic: An Exchange," *ibid.*, XLVII (Feb. 3, 1964), 12–22. Ellison's part in this exchange appears, along with his original reply to Howe, as "The World and the Jug," in his *Shadow and Act* (New York, 1964).* Howe's original essay is reprinted in his *A World More Attractive* (New York, 1963) and also in his *Decline of the New* (New York, 1970), where it is accompanied by his 1969 reflections on the debate. But Howe's contribution to "The Writer and Critic: An Exchange" has not been reprinted. The argument over the relative merits of Wright, Baldwin, and Ellison is still smoldering, a recent contribution being Eldridge Cleaver's attack on Baldwin (and praise of Wright) in "Notes on a Native Son," *Soul on Ice* (New York, 1968),* pp. 97–111.

Several viewpoints on the role of black authors are expressed in Conference of Negro Writers, *The American Negro Writer and His Roots: Selected Papers* (New York, 1960). For a recent collection of interpretive essays, see Donald B. Gibson, ed., *Five*

Black Writers: Essays on Wright, Ellison, Baldwin, Hughes and LeRoi Jones (New York, 1970).*

Four important black writers whose careers illuminate the issues of this debate are James Baldwin, Ralph Ellison, LeRoi Jones, and John A. Williams. Each has attempted to resolve or simply confront the conflict between his political or racial conscience and his artistic conscience, and the attempts of the four writers taken together raise important questions about the assumptions of the Wright-Baldwin, Howe-Ellison debate. For one thing, are a writer's racial and artistic consciences always necessarily in conflict? Do the motives and conventions of protest necessarily impose constrictions and stereotypes on the black writer? In the case of Baldwin and Ellison, two more specific questions arise. To what extent do their novels actually embody the values they recommend for black fiction and which they find lacking, apparently, in the fiction of Wright's followers? And do they manage, in fact, to write about contemporary black life without involving themselves in "protest"?

A. James Baldwin

Baldwin's literary output includes four novels—*Go Tell It on the Mountain* (New York, 1953),* *Giovanni's Room* (New York, 1956),* *Another Country* (New York, 1962),* and *Tell Me How Long the Train's Been Gone* (New York, 1968);* a collection of short stories—*Going to Meet the Man* (New York, 1965);* two plays—*Blues for Mister Charlie* (New York, 1964)* and *The Amen Corner* (New York, 1968); and three volumes of essays— *Notes of a Native Son* (Boston, 1955),* *Nobody Knows My Name* (New York, 1961),* and *The Fire Next Time* (New York, 1963).* The shape of Baldwin's career to date is suggested by comparing *Go Tell It on the Mountain*, Baldwin's most concerted effort to treat black life while avoiding the formulas of protest fiction, to *Tell Me How Long the Train's Been Gone*, which seems much closer to the conventions of protest. In Baldwin's writings of the 1960s, social and political ideas seem to have a larger place than the earlier essays on Wright saw to be desirable. For further amplification of Baldwin's social and political views see also Kenneth B. Clark, ed., *The Negro Protest: James Bald-*

win, Malcolm X, Martin Luther King Talk with Kenneth B. Clark (Boston, 1963).

The following are useful assessments of Baldwin's work: Robert Coles, "Baldwin's Burden," *Partisan Review*, XXXI (Summer 1964), 409–16; Dan Jacobson, "James Baldwin as Spokesman," *Commentary*, XXXII (Dec. 1961), 497–502; Robert A. Bone, *The Negro Novel in America* (rev. ed., New Haven, 1965),* ch. 10; Edward Margolies, *Native Sons* (Philadelphia, 1968),* ch. 6; and Calvin C. Hernton, "Blood of the Lamb: the Ordeal of James Baldwin," in John A. Williams and Charles F. Harris, eds., *Amistad 1: Writings on Black History and Culture* (New York, 1970),* pp. 183–225. Fern Marja Eckman's *The Furious Passage of James Baldwin* (New York, 1966)* is an essay on Baldwin's career based largely on personal interviews. Also of interest is Margaret Mead and James Baldwin, *A Rap on Race* (Philadelphia, 1971).

B. Ralph Ellison

Ralph Ellison's very considerable reputation as a novelist rests entirely on one work, *Invisible Man* (New York, 1952),* although a new novel is now in progress. Portions of this work in progress have been published as "The Roof, the Steeple and the People," *Quarterly Review of Literature*, X, no. 3 (1960), 115–28; "Juneteenth," *ibid.*, XIII, nos. 3–4 (1965), 262–76; and "Night-Talk," *ibid.*, XVI, nos. 3–4 (1969), 317–29. Ellison has collected a number of his essays—many of them dealing with American literature and the place of the black writer in that literature—in *Shadow and Act* (New York, 1964).*

Ellison has frequently expressed himself in interviews, of which the following are the most important: Robert Penn Warren and Ralph Ellison, "A Dialogue," *Reporter*, XXII (Mar. 25, 1965), 42–48—which also appears, along with an essay by Warren on *Shadow and Act*, in Warren's *Who Speaks for the Negro?* (New York, 1965),* pp. 325–54; John Corry, "An American Novelist Who Sometimes Teaches," *New York Times Magazine*, Nov. 20, 1966, 54 ff.; James Thompson, Lennox Raphael, and Steve Cannon, "'A Very Stern Discipline,' An Interview with Ralph Ellison," *Harper's*, CCXXXIV (Mar. 1967), 76–95; and Ralph Ellison and James Alan McPherson, "Indivisible Man," *Atlantic*, CCXXVI (Dec. 1970), 45–60. There is useful biographical and critical material in Robert A. Bone, *The Negro Novel in America* (rev. ed., New Haven, 1965),* pp. 196–212, and in Edward Margolies, *Native Sons* (New York, 1968),* ch. 7. Essays on Ellison and *Invisible Man* include: Jonathan Baumbach, "Nightmare of a Native Son: Ellison's Invisible Man," in *The Landscape of Nightmare; Studies in the Contemporary American Novel* (New York, 1965);* Robert Bone, "Ralph Ellison and the Uses of Imagination," in Herbert Hill, ed., *Anger and Beyond: The Negro Writer in the United States* (New York, 1966),* pp. 86–111; Charles I. Glicksberg, "The Symbolism of Vision," *Southwest Review*, XXXIX (Summer 1954), 259–65; Marcus Klein, "Ralph Ellison," in *After Alienation* (Cleveland, 1964); Richard Kostelanetz, "The Politics of Ellison's Booker: *Invisible Man* as Symbolic History," *Chicago Review*, XIX, no. 2 (1967), 5–26; Earl Rovit, "Ralph Ellison and the American Comic Tradition," *Wisconsin Studies in Contemporary Literature*, I (Winter 1960), 34–42; and Raymond Olderman, "Ralph Ellison's Blues and *Invisible Man*," *ibid.*, VII (Spring 1966), 142–59. Several of the foregoing plus additional critical essays are reprinted in John M. Reilly, ed., *Twentieth Century Interpretations of Invisible Man* (Englewood Cliffs, N.J., 1970).*

C. LeRoi Jones

While Ralph Ellison has been stressing the primacy of art over direct political action, at least for the artist, and has been stressing the place of the black writer in the American literary tradition, LeRoi Jones—poet, novelist, playwright, essayist—would appear to be doing just the opposite. Since his first successes in the early 1960s, he has moved closer to an art of direct, even propagandistic political statement—designed exclusively for a black audience. While some critics have accused Ellison of "selling out" his race, a rather different group accuses Jones of "selling out" his art. One must pierce through the heated controversy surrounding Jones to evaluate his particular solution to the conflict between artistic and political obligations and to understand how that solution changed (if it did change) during the 1960s.

For Jones's earlier poetry, see *Preface to a Twenty-Volume Suicide Note* (New York, 1961),* and *The Dead Lecturer* (New York, 1964).* Four plays are collected in *Dutchman and The Slave* (New York, 1964),* and *The Baptism & The Toilet* (New York, 1966).* Jones has published one novel, *The System of Dante's Hell* (New York, 1963).* The essays in *Home: Social Essays* (New York, 1966),* especially "The Myth of a 'Negro Literature,'" and Jones's volume of music history, *Blues People: Negro Music in White America* (New York, 1963),* are also important.

For Jones's recent poetry, see *Black Magic* (Indianapolis, 1969).* His recent plays include: *Arm Yourself, or Harm Yourself! A One Act Play* (Newark, 1967); *Slave Ship: A One Act Play* (Newark, 1969); and *The Death of Malcolm X*, in Ed Bullins, ed., *New Plays from the Black Theatre* (New York, 1969),* pp. 1–20. See also the anthology of essays, fiction, poetry, and drama by younger black writers, which Jones edited with Larry Neal, *Black Fire: An Anthology of Afro-American Writing* (New York, 1968);* it includes another recent Jones play, *Madheat: A Morality Play*.

Ch. 10 of Edward Margolies's *Native Sons* (Philadelphia, 1968)* deals with Jones. For various reactions to Jones and his plays, see George Dennison, "The Demagogy of LeRoi Jones," *Commentary*, XXXIX (Feb. 1965), 67–70 (reviewing *The Toilet* and *The Slave*); Philip Roth, "Channel X: Two Plays on the Race Conflict," *New York Review of Books*, II (May 28, 1964), 10–13 (reviewing *Dutchman* and James Baldwin's *Blues for Mister Charlie*); Stephen Schneck, "LeRoi Jones, or Poetics & Policemen," *Ramparts*, VII (July 13, 1968), 14–19 (a discussion of Jones's career); and Gerald Weales, "The Day LeRoi Jones Spoke on Penn Campus What Were the Blacks Doing in the Balcony?" *New York Times Magazine*, May 4, 1969, 38 ff. There is an essay on *Blues People* in Ralph Ellison's *Shadow and Act* (New York, 1964),* pp. 241–50. Two interviews with Jones are Askai Muhammed Touré, Marvin X, and Faruk, "An Interview with Ameer Baraka (LeRoi Jones)," *Journal of Black Poetry*, I (Fall 1968), 2–14, and Ida Lewis and LeRoi Jones, "Conversation," *Essence*, I (Sept. 1970), 20–25.

D. John A. Williams

At a time when many black writers seem torn between political commitment and literary calling, John A. Williams seems able to follow both. His growing commitment to social and political issues has not, apparently, affected his productivity as a novelist. In his most recent novels, Williams deals quite directly with contemporary social and racial controversies. It is no coincidence that Williams greatly admires such a writer as Chester Himes; for by treating social issues directly in his fiction, Williams is in effect continuing the tradition of the "protest school" in black fiction. The question remains as to whether he has managed to avoid what many critics take to be the shortcomings of that school. Does he manage to transcend, to convert to the purposes of art, the issues with which he deals? This is partly to ask whether social issues, in his fiction, become significant literary themes as well. But it is also to ask whether Williams is able to transmit, along with his issues, a sense of the life that makes the issues important.

Williams's most recent novel, *Sons of Darkness, Sons of Light* (Boston, 1969),* deals with a black professor who, as he becomes increasingly active in the cause of civil rights, also becomes increasingly militant. Even more provocative is *The Man Who Cried I Am* (Boston, 1967),* whose hero, Max Reddick, is a writer in many ways similar to Williams and whose subject is the pressure which acts on a black writer in modern Europe and America. Many of the characters in this novel are clearly based to some extent on real people, most notably Harry Ames, who corresponds in many respects to Richard Wright. Two earlier works are *Night Song* (New York, 1961), a novel of the jazz world, and *Sissie* (New York, 1963),* the story of a black woman in the North.

For Williams's more direct contributions to literary and/or political controversy see: "Literary Ghetto," *Saturday Review*, XLVI (Apr. 20, 1963), 21 ff.; the two introductions and "Postscript Concerning the Times" in Williams's anthology, *Beyond the Angry Black* (New York, 1966, expansion of *The Angry Black*, 1962); "William Styron's Faked Confessions," in John Henrik Clarke, ed., *William Styron's Nat Turner: Ten Black Writers Respond*

(Boston, 1968),* pp. 45–49; the introduction and "My Man Himes" in John A. Williams and Charles F. Harris, eds., *Amistad 1: Writings on Black History and Culture* (New York, 1970);* and *The King God Didn't Save: Reflections on the Life and Death of Martin Luther King, Jr.* (New York, 1970). Also of interest is *This Is My Country Too* (New York, 1965),* a collection of observations on the American scene derived from a trip through the country Williams took for *Holiday* magazine. See also "This Is My Country Too: a Pessimistic Postscript," *Holiday*, XLI (June 1967), 8 ff.

E. Toward a "Black Aesthetic"

At the beginning of the 1970s young black writers, and a number of slightly older black writers who have been publishing steadily through the 1960s, are once again attempting to break free of the apparent conflict between social commitment and aesthetics. Like the writers of the Harlem renaissance, whom they admire and from whom some of them often borrow, these young writers believe in the positive assertion of black folk characteristics as a source of vitality in black art. Like Ralph Ellison they object strongly to the subordination of black life to sociological ideas; they insist that black literature, like white, must be judged on *aesthetic* grounds. But in direct opposition to Ellison, these young writers hold that the aesthetic by which black literature is to be judged (and written) is quite distinct from the aesthetic established to explain and justify white art. Whereas Ellison describes himself as being primarily and essentially an American writer, Ishmael Reed writes (in his introduction to the anthology *19 Necromancers from Now* [Garden City, N.Y., 1970]*): "What distinguishes the present crop of Afro-American and black writers from their predecessors is a marked independence from Western form."

This notion that the "form" of black art must separate it from white art is the keystone of the attempt to define a "black aesthetic." Although these writers reject social and political classifications of art they are nonetheless separatists, because in their view social and political separation have produced in the United States two radically opposed aesthetic traditions. Thus the task of these younger writers is double. They must tap the black aesthetic tradition, in Africa or in America, in music, language, voodoo, dance, and so on. And to prove the separateness of this tradition, they must show that white aesthetic terminology, for all its avowed lack of social involvement, is rooted in the racism of white society and therefore inappropriate for judging black expression. One of the most important essays in connection with this second goal is Addison Gayle, Jr., "Cultural Hegemony: The Southern White Writer and American Letters," in John A. Williams and Charles F. Harris, eds., *Amistad 1: Writings on Black History and Culture* (New York, 1970),* pp. 3–24. In more general terms, the literary call for a "black aesthetic" is only part of a larger assertion of black cultural separatism, discussed in Part IX, topic 14, "Black Life-Styles in the Ghetto."

Generalizations about literary movements are inevitably made at the cost of oversimplification, especially when the movement is only in the process of emerging. A sense of the range and diversity of the "black aesthetic" can be gained from several recent anthologies. Examples of the different forms of the new literature, and of the historical and critical ideas that accompany it, may be found in LeRoi Jones and Larry Neal, eds., *Black Fire: An Anthology of Afro-American Writing* (New York, 1968);* Williams and Harris, eds., *Amistad 1*, cited above, and *Amistad 2: Writings on Black History and Culture* (New York, 1971);* and Reed, ed., *19 Necromancers from Now*, cited above. An anthology specifically devoted to poetry is Clarence Major, ed., *The New Black Poetry* (New York, 1969).* For drama, see Ed Bullins, ed., *New Plays from the Black Theatre* (New York, 1969).* For collections of critical essays see Addison Gayle, Jr., *Black Expression: Essays by and about Black Americans in the Creative Arts* (New York, 1969),* and Addison Gayle, Jr., ed., *The Black Aesthetic* (Garden City, N.Y., 1971).

It is difficult at this stage to isolate "major" figures of the movement. A list of novelists would include Ishmael Reed, author of *The Free-Lance Pallbearers* (Garden City, N.Y., 1967),* and *Yellow Back Radio Broke-Down* (Garden City, N.Y., 1969);* William Melvin Kelley, author of *A Different Drummer* (New York, 1962),* *A Drop of Patience* (Garden City, N.Y., 1965), *dem* (Garden City, N.Y., 1967),* *Dunfords Travels Everywheres*

(Garden City, N.Y., 1970), and a collection of stories, *Dancers on the Shore* (Garden City, N.Y., 1964); Charles S. Wright, author of *The Messenger* (New York, 1963) and *The Wig* (New York, 1966); Cecil Brown, author of *The Life and Loves of Mr. Jiveass Nigger* (New York, 1969);* Clarence Major, author of *All-Night Visitors* (New York, 1970); Ronald Fair, author of *World of Nothing* (New York, 1970); and John A. Williams, although the particular nature of his fiction has led to separate discussion of his works in section D of the present topic. John Oliver Killens, although somewhat older than most of the writers listed here, should be included—especially for his latest novel, *The Cotillion: or One Good Bull is Half the Herd* (New York, 1971). Killens' earlier works include three novels—*Youngblood* (New York, 1954), *And Then We Heard the Thunder* (New York, 1963) and *'Sippi* (New York, 1967)—and a work of non-fiction, *Black Man's Burden* (New York, 1965).* For particular poets, see the anthologies listed above, especially Major's *The New Black Poetry*, and see also this Part, topic 2, "Black Poetry."

Like many literary movements, this one has produced a good deal of critical work—manifestoes, revaluations of earlier work, and analyses of the works of the writers themselves. Among the most impressive of these younger critics is Addison Gayle, Jr. Essays by him may be found in the anthologies listed above, two of which he edited. See also Gayle's *The Black Situation* (New York, 1970). Another relevant long essay is Stephen E. Henderson, "'Survival Motion,' A Study of the Black Writer and the Black Revolution in America," in Mercer Cook and Stephen E. Henderson, *The Militant Black Writer in Africa and the United States* (Madison, 1969),* pp. 63–129.

7. Black Figures in the Writings of White Southerners: Lillian Smith and William Faulkner

Few white southern novelists writing in the twentieth century have ignored blacks as a subject for fiction. (For William Styron's fictional treatment of Nat Turner's rebellion, see Part III, topic 4,

"Slave Revolts.") But the writings of Lillian Smith and William Faulkner have a particular interest, beyond their intrinsic merits, because of the authors' public positions on the civil rights revolution. Each gave close attention to the racial attitudes of southern whites and examined candidly his or her own feelings about the black community and racial conflict, as well as treating black life and such themes as miscegenation in their writings. Miss Smith became an outspoken champion of the civil rights revolution, while Faulkner emerged after 1954 as an ambivalent southern moderate with deeply divided and obsessively guilt-ridden attitudes toward blacks and their aspirations.

Lillian Smith's novel about interracial love and violence, *Strange Fruit* (New York, 1944),* launched a career that soon revealed her as the most outspoken white critic of the racial status quo in the deep South. Attempts to suppress the instantly popular book were made in Detroit, New York City, and, successfully, in Massachusetts, where an obscenity charge was fought through to the State Supreme Court. Miss Smith was an editor of *South Today* for ten years, until 1946, and later published (with Paula Schnelling) *The North Georgia Review.* She was an active member of the advisory committee of the Congress of Racial Equality (CORE) until, shortly before her death in 1966, she resigned in protest against the militant advocates of black power.

By contrast, William Faulkner was decidedly less sympathetic to the "cause" of the blacks, and, while he spoke less often directly on civil rights questions, certain statements he made after 1954 were widely condemned by blacks and white liberals. The complicated attitudes toward Afro-Americans expressed in his fiction had been a matter of controversy for decades. His fiction presents the most probing exploration of black life ever undertaken by a white American and presents also the most revealing expressions of the fears, rage, guilt, and admiration provoked among whites by blacks in the American South.

A. Lillian Smith

Besides her novel, see the dramatic version, written with Esther Smith, of *Strange Fruit* (New York, 1945);* *Killers of the Dream* (New York, 1949),* and *Now Is the Time* (New York, 1955), both non-fiction; and *The Journey* (Cleveland, 1954),* a volume of reminiscences. Among her articles on the civil rights movement are the detailed letter entitled "How to Work for Racial Equality," *New Republic*, CXIII (July 4, 1945), 23–24; "The South's Moment of Truth," *Progressive*, XXIV (Sept. 1960), 32–35; and "Words That Chain Us and Words That Set Us Free," *New South*, XVII (Mar. 1962), 3–12.

For information and comment on the court case involving *Strange Fruit*, see "De Voto Issues Statement Against Strange Fruit Decision," *Publishers Weekly*, CXLVIII (Oct. 6, 1945), 1664; H. Williams, "The Decision in the 'Strange Fruit' Case," *ibid.*, (Oct. 20, 1945), 1831–32; *Commonwealth* v. *Isenstadt*, Supreme Judicial Court of Massachusetts, reprinted in Edward De Grazia, ed., *Censorship Landmarks* (New York, 1969), pp. 125–30; Bernard De Voto, "The Easy Chair," *Harper's*, CXC (Feb. 1945), 225–28; and Max Lerner, "On Lynching a Book," *Public Journal: Marginal Notes on Wartime America* (New York, 1945), reprinted in Robert B. Downs, ed., *The First Freedom* (Chicago, 1960), pp. 131–34.

There is material on Lillian Smith in Margaret Just Butcher, *The Negro in American Culture* (New York, 1956), pp. 172–73, esp. pp. 266–70. For material on the stage version of *Strange Fruit*, see *Opportunity*, XXIV (Jan. 1946), 24–35; and *Theatre Arts*, XXIX (Dec. 1945), 674, and *ibid.*, XXX (Feb. 1946), 73–75. See also S. Grafton, "We're Mighty Fond of Our Miss Lil," *Collier's*, CXXV (Jan. 28, 1950), 8–9; and particularly Nancy M. Tischler, *Black Masks: Negro Characters in Modern Southern Fiction* (University Park, Pa., 1969), passim.

B. William Faulkner

Few of Faulkner's major works ignore black people. *The Sound and the Fury* (New York, 1929)* treats the connections between a black family and a declining white family. *Light in August* (New York, 1932)* presents the gothic tragedy of a white-skinned Negro who is eventually lynched. *Absalom, Absalom!* (New York, 1936)* sets a drama of miscegenation against the background of the Civil War and United States history from 1833 to 1910. The novel that posed most explicitly the question of Faulkner's attitudes toward civil rights was *Intruder in the Dust* (New York, 1948),* the story of an ambitious black, tied by blood to whites, who is successfully defended from an unjust charge of murder. The work that probes most deeply into the emotional lives, family tragedies, and social aspirations of the black is the collection of related short stories focusing on the black branch of the McCaslin family, *Go Down Moses and Other Stories* (New York, 1942).

For colorful recollections of Faulkner's relations with blacks in his home town, see John Cullen, with Floyd C. Watkins, *Old Times in the Faulkner Country* (Chapel Hill, 1961), chs. 6, 8, 13, and Earl Wortham, "So I Could Ride Along with Him," the reminiscences of a black blacksmith in Oxford, in James B. Webb and A. Wigfall Green, eds., *William Faulkner of Oxford* (Baton Rouge, 1965),* pp. 165–70. A letter of 1960 in which Faulkner refused the request of his former servant for a donation to the NAACP was published in the New York *Times*, Aug. 3, 1967, p. 16. Faulkner's statements that disturbed blacks and white liberals appeared in Russell W. Howe, "A Talk with William Faulkner," *Reporter*, XIV (Mar. 22, 1956), 18–20; letters provoked by the interview, including Faulkner's own protest that the article attributed to him "statements which no sober man would make," appeared in *ibid.*, XIV (Apr. 19, 1956), 5–7. Faulkner's most considered statement on the civil rights crisis was his 1955 speech, "American Segregation and the World Crisis," to the Southern Historical Association which was published by the Southern Regional Council, *Three Views of the Segregation Decisions* (Atlanta, 1956), pp. 9–12. Faulkner's own comments on black characters in his fiction are scattered through Frederick L. Gwynn and Joseph L. Blotner, eds., *Faulkner in the University* (Charlottesville, Va., 1959).*

The body of criticism on Faulkner that gives some attention to his fictional treatment of blacks is too voluminous to itemize. Brief comments are in Margaret Just Butcher, *The Negro in American Culture* (New York, 1956), pp. 262–66, and Chester E. Eisinger, *Fiction of the Forties* (Chicago, 1963),* pp. 178–86, which places Faulkner as a southern conservative. The most thorough examination of Faulkner's public statements on civil rights and of his fictional treatment of blacks is Charles H. Nilon, *Faulkner and the Negro* (New York, 1965); see also Nancy M.

Tischler, *Black Masks: Negro Characters in Modern Southern Fiction* (University Park, Pa., 1969), *passim*. The most probing essays on the subject include the following: Melvin Backman, "The Wilderness and the Negro in Faulkner's *The Bear*," PMLA, LXXVI (Dec. 1961), 595–600; Daniel Bradford, "Faulkner on Race," *Ramparts*, II (Dec. 1963), 43–49; Melvin Seiden, "Faulkner's Ambiguous Negro," *Massachusetts Review*, IV (Summer 1963), 675–90; Robert M. Slabey, "Joe Christmas, Faulkner's Marginal Man," *Phylon*, XXI (Fall 1960), 266–77; Victor Strandberg, "Faulkner's Poor Parson and the Technique of Inversion . . . ," *Sewanee Review*, LXXIII (Spring 1965), 181–90; Edmund Wilson, "William Faulkner's Reply to the Civil-Rights Program," in *Classics and Commercials, A Literary Chronicle of the Forties* (New York, 1950),* pp. 460–70; and particularly essays by three fellow novelists: James Baldwin, "Faulkner and Desegregation," in *Nobody Knows My Name* (New York, 1962),* ch. 7; Ralph Ellison, "Twentieth Century Fiction and the Black Mask of Humanity," *Shadow and Act* (New York, 1964),* pp. 24–44; and Robert Penn Warren, "Faulkner: The South, the Negro, and Time," in Warren, ed., *Faulkner: Twentieth Century Views* (Englewood Cliffs, N.J., 1966),* pp. 251–71.

8. Black Painters and Sculptors

While America had produced black artists before 1920 (notably two expatriates, the sculptor Edmonia Lewis and the painter Henry O. Tanner), the 1920s and the Harlem renaissance brought a larger number of artists with more impressive and varied talents to the fore. (In Alain L. Locke, ed., *The New Negro* [New York, 1925], however, the paintings intending to present black subjects without evasion or sentimentality were the work of German-born Winold Reiss, a white artist.) Yet, even with their new prominence in American cultural life and the somewhat expanding opportunities for their talents, black artists faced all the problems familiar to most American artists, plus those attendant on being a black professional. A good number (like

Tanner before them and Beauford De Laney later) became expatriates in their search for a stimulating and stable environment for their work.

One problem was how to find a tradition or how to establish a relation with conflicting traditions and current movements in American and European art. New modes of "realism" assigned heightened importance to the unvarnished treatment of subjects and scenes, including the Afro-American community that was intimately known to most black artists and was "invisible" to most whites. Yet new modes of "abstraction" or non-figurative art diminished the importance of representational subjects, black or white.

Another problem was how to define the artist's role in connection with the social goals of the black community and with the art world that was dominated by whites and seldom bought or even displayed the works of black artists. Some black artists and spokesmen felt that art should be enlisted in the service of black protest and social action, risking propaganda or sensationalism and the disdain of the white community. Others felt that the artists should reveal and celebrate, for black and white alike, the essentially middle-class values dominant in American society. Still others felt that the Afro-American could best prove his talent by pursuing his craft without overt racial aims or content. The issue was complicated by the vogue of African artifacts in European and American art circles and the demand that the Afro-American should base his art on an African tradition.

There is material on painting in Margaret Just Butcher, *The Negro in American Culture* (New York, 1956), ch. 10; James A. Porter's illustrated *Modern Negro Art* (New York, 1943); and in Alain L. Locke, *Negro Art: Past and Present* (Washington, 1936). But the most thorough and best illustrated work is Cedric Dover, *American Negro Art* (New York, 1960; 3rd ed., New York, 1965).* Martha M. Mathews, *Henry Ossawa Tanner: American Artist* (Chicago, 1969), is a full-length study. A provocative brief work that discusses the significance of modernist and primitive traditions for the black painter is Benjamin Brawley's introduction to his *The Negro Genius* (New York, 1937);* first published in 1910 and extensively revised, it has been reprinted by Darwin T. Turner and Jean M. Bright, eds., *Images* *of the Negro in America* (Boston, 1965),* pp. 51–56. Equally illuminating is the symposium "The Negro in Art: How Shall He Be Portrayed?" *Crisis,* XXXI (Mar. 1926), 219–20, 278–80, and *ibid.,* XXXII (May 1926), 35–36, 71–73. A most important symposium of black artists, particularly an exchange between the sculptors Richard Hunt and Tom Lloyd, discusses the relation of the black artist to both white and black communities and argues the question of whether there is such a thing as "black art." See Romare Bearden et al., "The Black Artist in America," *Metropolitan Museum of Art Bulletin,* XXVII (Jan. 1969), 245–60. J. Edward Atkinson, ed., *Black Dimensions in Contemporary American Art* (New York, 1971),* is a book of reproductions with brief commentaries on the artists whose works are included.

Much of the commentary generated by the Harlem renaissance relates directly or indirectly to the role of the black artist, notably the following: Alain L. Locke's introduction and "The Legacy of the Ancestral Arts," and Albert C. Barnes's "Negro Art and America" in Locke's *The New Negro* (New York, 1925),* pp. 19–28, 254–70; George Schuyler's "Negro Art Hokum" and Langston Hughes's "The Negro Artist and the Racial Mountain" in *Nation,* CXXII (June 16 and June 23, 1926), 662–63** and 692–94.** Comment on particular artists includes: Lucy E. Smith, "Some American Artists in Paris," *American Magazine of Art,* XVIII (Mar. 1927), 134–36; Francis C. Holbrook, "A Group of Negro Artists," *Opportunity,* I (July 1923), 211–13; and Worth Tuttle, "Negro Artists Are Developing True Racial Art," an account of an exhibition at the New York Public Library, West 135th St. Branch, New York *Times,* May 14, 1933, sect. 9, p. 8. See also, particularly for illustrations, Alain L. Locke, *The Negro in Art: a Pictorial Record of the Negro Artist and of the Negro Theme in Art* (Washington, 1940).

Important essays on the position of black artists during the Depression are Meyer Shapiro, "Race, Nationality, and Art," *Art Front,* II (Mar. 1936), 10; the black painter Aaron Douglas, "The Negro in American Culture," *The First American Writers' Congress* (New York, 1936); and Vernon Winslow, "Negro Art and the Depression," *Opportunity,* XIX (Feb. 1941), 40–42. More recent material on individual artists includes: "And the Migrants Kept Coming: A Negro Artist [Jacob Lawrence] Paints the Story of the Great American Minority," *Fortune*, XXIV (Nov. 1941), 102–09; James V. Herring, "The Negro Sculptor," *Crisis*, XLIX (Aug. 1942), 261–63; Elizabeth McCausland, "Jacob Lawrence," *Magazine of Art*, XXXVIII (Nov. 1945), 251–54; Henry Miller, *The Amazing and Invariable Beauford De Laney* (Yonkers, N.Y., 1945); "Negro Artists," *Life*, XXI (July 22, 1946), 62–65; American Federation of Artists, *Jacob Lawrence* (New York, 1960); Charles White, *Images of Dignity: The Drawings of Charles White* (Los Angeles, 1967); and the State University of New York, The Art Gallery, *Romare Bearden* (Albany, 1968). See also James A. Porter, *The Progress of the Negro in Art During the Last Fifty Years* (Pittsburgh, 1950); Lindsay Patterson, ed., *The Negro in Music and Art* (New York, 1967); and particularly Addison Gayle, Jr., ed., *Black Expression: Essays by and about Black Americans in the Creative Arts* (New York, 1969).*

For catalogues and descriptive accounts of exhibitions including black artists, see Chicago American Negro Exposition, *Exhibition of the Art of the American Negro* (Chicago, 1911); Negro Library Association, *Exhibition Catalogue: First Annual Exhibition of . . . Paintings, Engravings, Sculpture, etc. . . .* (New York, 1916); New York Public Library, 135th St. Branch, *Annual Exhibition of Negro Artists* (New York, 1924); Ruby M. Kendrick, "Art at Howard University," *Crisis*, XXXIX (Nov. 1932), 348–49; Harmon Foundation Inc., *Exhibit of Fine Arts by American Negro Artists* (New York, 1928, 1929, 1930, 1931, 1933) and *Negro Artists* (New York, 1935); Baltimore Museum of Art, *Contemporary Negro Art* (Baltimore, 1939); Associated American Artists, *Catalogue of Exhibit of Karamu Artists* (New York, 1942); Albany Institute of History and Art, *The Negro Artist Comes of Age* (Albany, 1945); Cultural Exchange Center, *Prints by American Negro Artists* (Los Angeles, 1965); National Conference of Artists, *A Print Portfolio by Negro Artists* (Chicago, 1963); Jeanne Siegel, "Why Spiral?" an account of an exhibit by a group of black painters called "Spiral," *Art News*, LXV (Sept. 1966), 48–51; The City University of New York, *Evolution of the Afro-American Artist* (New York, 1967); and the Minneapolis Institute of Arts, *30 Contemporary Black Artists* (Minneapolis, 1968). There is useful material scattered through Edward Bruce

and Forbes Watson, eds., *Art in Federal Buildings* . . . , vol. I,
Mural Designs, 1934–1936 (Washington, 1936); Museum of Mod-
ern Art, *New Horizons in American Art* (New York, 1936); and
De Young Museum, *Frontiers of American Art: WPA Federal
Art Project* (San Francisco, 1939).

9. Blacks and the American Theater

The theater has always been an important institution for bind-
ing communities together, for altering or shaping the relations
among their components or classes, and for providing employment and outlets for creative talent. Racial repression in the
United States, however, has severely hampered the performance
of these functions by the American stage. Blacks have been un-
welcome when not actually excluded from the audience in white-
dominated theaters; the American, British, and European plays
most often produced provided few black roles for Afro-American
actors to play, and white producers often assigned white actors
to such roles (in *Othello*, for instance) while never casting a black
actor in a white role; black dramatists have had trouble getting
their plays produced and holding a serious audience in a white
theater. As a result, neither the black nor the white community
has found Afro-American life dramatized in its particularity in
the American theater; plays dealing directly with the black community or with such explosive themes as racial violence and miscegenation have been a rarity. For decades the American theater
left black performers to shift for themselves in ghetto theaters or
virtually confined them to a corner of the theatrical world that
was devoted to light popular entertainment and restricted black
performers to demeaning, stereotyped roles; the buffoonlike antics
of shuffling blacks in the minstrel shows and vaudeville entered
into the musical comedy tradition in the 1920s and gained further
popularity with white audiences in radio and the film.

Since about 1917, however, with the short-lived but influential
production of Ridgely Torrence's *Three Plays for a Negro
Theatre*, blacks have made gains in two significant directions:

(1) notable success for some black performers and playwrights in the Broadway and white-dominated theater; and (2) the establishment of black companies and theaters, such as the Gilpin or Karamu Players in Cleveland and currently the Negro Ensemble Company in New York City.

Besides Margaret Just Butcher's brief ch. 9 in *The Negro in American Culture* (New York, 1956), a number of important works deal with all aspects of the subject. For "Books and Articles Related to Black Theater Published from 1/1960 to 2/1968," see *Drama Review*, XII (Summer 1968), 176–80. Useful for reference are Frederick W. Bond, *The Negro and the Drama* (Washington, 1940, reprinted College Park, Md., 1969) and Lindsay Patterson, ed., *Anthology of the American Negro in the Theater* (New York, 1967). Good starting points are the entire issue devoted to "The Negro in the Theater," *Drama Critique*, VII (Spring 1964); Edith J. R. Isaacs's illustrated *The Negro in the American Theater* (New York, 1947, reprinted College Park, Md., 1969); and particularly the more recent and impassioned survey by the black playwright Loften Mitchell, *Black Drama: The Story of the American Negro in the Theatre* (New York, 1967).* Langston Hughes and Milton Meltzer, *Black Magic: A Pictorial History of the Negro in American Entertainment* (Englewood Cliffs, N.J., 1967), is a survey in words and pictures of minstrelsy, vaudeville, music, the theater, and films.

A. Minstrels, Vaudeville, and Popular Entertainment

Minstrel shows, usually featuring white actors in blackface but later including a larger proportion of black performers, were popular before and after the Civil War, and contributed to the vaudeville tradition that sustained a sizable number of talented black comedians after 1900, notably the team of Bert Williams and George Walker. Playing before largely white audiences (and billed as "Two Real Coons") they kept to the stereotype of the shuffling, shiftless, happy "darky." Black composers for the vaudeville stage wrote "coon songs" and the "ragtime" melodies that comprise one of the sources of jazz, and James Weldon Johnson, the poet and future executive secretary of the NAACP, earned his living for several years by writing lyrics for such songs. In the 1920s Broadway musical comedy hits included such all-black productions as *Shuffle Along, Chocolate Dandies,* and the annual *Blackbirds* revues, and featured the stars Josephine Baker, Bill Robinson, and Ethel Waters. The "shuffle along" image was soon established in radio by "Amos 'n' Andy" (played by white actors) and in films where talented black actors like Lincoln Perry ("Stepin Fetchit") and Hattie McDaniel played watermelon-stealing "darkies" and "mammies." Many of these actors were the antithesis in real life of the characters they portrayed on the stage, but until the 1920s there were few opportunities for them to portray "respectable," militant, or other serious black roles, and it is only in very recent years that attempts have been made to excise the image of the buffoon from the entertainment media.

The best starting points for material on this topic are Isaacs, *The Negro in the American Theater,* cited above, pp. 21–27; Mitchell, *Black Drama,* cited above, chs. 2, 3; Joseph Boskin, "Sambo: The National Jester in Popular Culture," in Gary B. Nash and Richard Weiss, eds., *The Great Fear: Race in the Mind of America* (New York, 1970),* pp. 165–85; and Joseph Boskin, *The Life and Death of Sambo* (New York, 1971). Brief summaries are in Butcher, *The Negro in American Culture,* cited above, pp. 188–92, and Richard Bardolph, *The Negro Vanguard* (New York, 1959),* pp. 175–81, 303–09. There is background material in Hans Nathan, *Dan Emmett and the Rise of Early Negro Minstrelsy* (Norman, Okla., 1962); Tom Fletcher, *One Hundred Years of the Negro in Show Business* (New York, 1954); and Langston Hughes and Milton Meltzer, *Black Magic: A Pictorial History of the Negro in American Entertainment,* cited above. There is additional information scattered in James Weldon Johnson, *Along This Way* (New York, 1933),* and *Black Manhattan* (New York, 1930),* and in Rudi Blesh and Harriet Janis, *They All Played Ragtime: The True Story of An American Music* (rev. ed., New York, 1959).* Biographical and autobiographical material that illuminates the performing styles and the struggles of talented black entertainers includes Mabel Rowland, ed., *Bert Williams, Son of Laughter* (New York, 1923); Ethel Waters (with Charles Samuels), *His Eye Is on the Sparrow* (Garden City, N.Y., 1951); Eartha Kitt, *Thursday's Child* (New York, 1956); Lena Horne and Richard Schickel, *Lena* (New York, 1965);

Sammy Davis, Jr., with Jane and Burt Boyar, *Yes I Can: The Story of Sammy Davis, Jr.* (New York, 1965);* Hy Steirman, ed., *Harry Belafonte: His Complete Life Story* (New York, 1957); Arnold Shaw, *Belafonte: An Unauthorized Biography* (Philadephia, 1960); and Dorothy Dandridge and Earl Connor, *Everything and Nothing: The Dorothy Dandridge Story* (New York, 1970).

B. Ridgely Torrence's and Eugene O'Neill's "Negro Plays"

Stereotyped characterizations of white ethnic minorities and of blacks dominated the American stage in the first decades of the twentieth century, but the virulence with which blacks were presented in such plays as Thomas Dixon's *The Clansman* (New York, 1905) was extreme. The first attempts by white dramatists to do full justice to the richness of black life were those of Ridgely Torrence in *Three Plays for a Negro Theater* (1917) and of Eugene O'Neill in *The Emperor Jones* (New York, 1921)* and *All God's Chillun Got Wings* (New York, 1924), though these plays still reflected some white stereotypes about blacks. *The Emperor Jones* brought the black actor Charles Gilpin into prominence (though he later returned to jobs as an elevator operator and farmer) and both O'Neill plays later brought Paul Robeson to stardom. Torrence's plays were published in *Granny Maumee and Other Plays* (New York, 1917).

What these productions meant to the black community is conveyed by James Weldon Johnson, *Black Manhattan* (New York, 1930),* ch. 15; by Jessie Fauset's "The Gift of Laughter," in Alain L. Locke, ed., *The New Negro* (New York, 1925),* pp. 161–67; and by Montgomery Gregory's "The Drama of Negro Life" in the same collection, pp. 153–60. Information on the importance of the plays for Paul Robeson's career may be gathered from biographies: Eslanda R. Robeson, *Paul Robeson, Negro* (New York, 1930); Shirley Graham, *Paul Robeson: Citizen of the World* (New York, 1946), and Edwin P. Hoyt, *Paul Robeson: The American Othello* (New York, 1967). The plays and their impact are discussed by both Isaacs, *The Negro in the American Theater*, chs. 3–4, and Mitchell, *Black Drama*, chs. 6–7, both cited above. Works that emphasize the impact of the plays on the black actors and on the scandalized white community include John H. Raleigh, *The Plays of Eugene O'Neill* (Carbondale, Ill., 1965), pp. 107–18; and Arthur and Barbara Gelb, *O'Neill* (New York, 1962), pp. 399–400 (on *The Dreamy Kid*), pp. 438–50 (on *The Emperor Jones*), and pp. 547–57 (on *All God's Chillun*). Marie Seton, *Paul Robeson* (London, 1958), gives attention to the O'Neill productions, notably those abroad, pp. 29–41, 60–71. On Torrence, see John M. Clum, "Ridgely Torrence's Negro Plays: A Noble Beginning," *SAQ*, LXVIII (Winter 1969), 96–108.

For material on the treatment of black characters by white dramatists and other white authors before 1917, see Durant Da Ponte, "The Greatest Play of the South," a study of *The Clansman*, in *Tennessee Studies in Literature*, II (1957), 15–24; and two surveys by Sterling A. Brown: "A Century of Negro Portraiture in American Literature," *Massachusetts Review*, VII (Winter 1966), 73–96, and "Negro Character as Seen by White Authors," *JNE*, II (Apr. 1933), 179–203. On O'Neill, consult Van Wyck Brooks, "Eugene O'Neill: Harlem," in *The Confident Years: 1885–1915* (New York, 1952), pp. 539–53; J. Lowell, "Eugene O'Neill's Darker Brother," *Theater Arts*, XXXII (Jan. 1948), 45–58; Edwin W. Engel, *The Haunted Heroes of Eugene O'Neill* (Cambridge, Mass., 1953), pp. 48–53, 117–26; Doris V. Falk, *Eugene O'Neill and the Tragic Vision* (New Brunswick, N.J., 1958), pp. 66–71, 87–90; and Timo Tiusanen, *O'Neill's Scenic Images* (Princeton, 1968), pp. 97–112, 174–82. For an attack on the treatment of the blacks in a recent play by a white writer, see Carl M. Moss, "'The Great White Hope,'" *Freedomways*, IX (Spring 1969), 127–38.

C. Black Performers and Black Theater

There are abundant materials on (1) the problems of black performers in the American theater and (2) the black theaters that have been founded with increasing frequency in recent decades. Items are listed under these two categories below though they overlap considerably with each other and with Section D, "Black Dramatists," that follows.

1. In the 1940s and 1950s, wide-ranging reviews under the title "The Negro on Broadway" were published annually by Miles M.

Jefferson in *Phylon*, which may be consulted (along with the books by Bond, Isaacs, and Mitchell listed above) for all aspects of the theater's relations to the blacks. See vol. VI (1st Quarter 1945), 42–52; VII (2nd Quarter 1946), 185–96; VIII (2nd Quarter 1947), 146–59; IX (2nd Quarter 1948), 99–107; X (2nd Quarter 1949), 103–11; XI (2nd Quarter 1950), 105–13; XII (2nd Quarter 1951), 128–36; XIII (2nd Quarter 1952), 199–208; XIV (3rd Quarter 1953), 268–79; XV (3rd Quarter 1954), 253–60; XVII (3rd Quarter 1956), 227–37; and XVIII (3rd Quarter 1957), 286–95. For the 1960s, a spirited introduction is ch. 4, "The Negro Revolution," in Gerald C. Weales' *The Jumping-Off Place: American Drama in the 1960's* (New York, 1969). For a highly critical view of Afro-American achievements in the theater, see Harold Cruse, *The Crisis of the Negro Intellectual* (New York, 1967),* pp. 520–43.

The acting career of an early black expatriate is covered by C. L. Lewis, "Black Knight of the Theater: Ira Aldridge," *Negro Digest*, XVII (Apr. 1968), 44–47, and Herbert Marshall and Mildred Stock, *Ira Aldridge, The Negro Tragedian* (New York, 1958). For the career of Paul Robeson, see the items listed above in Section B, "Ridgely Torrence's and Eugene O'Neill's 'Negro Plays.'" For the problems of black performers in the contemporary legitimate theater, see Ossie Davis, "The Flight from Broadway," *Negro Digest*, XV (Apr. 1956), 14–19; Ruby Dee, "The Tattered Queens," *ibid.*, 32–36; and Woodie King, Jr., "The Problems Facing Negro Actors," *ibid.*, 53–59. Ossie Davis' success as performer, playwright, and now movie director is reflected in his account of an assignment to direct a film in Nigeria, "When is a Camera a Weapon?" New York *Times*, Sept. 20, 1970, sect. 2, pp. 17, 24. A piercing analysis of the problems which light-skinned black actors face during the vogue for "black theater" appeared in a letter by Ellen Holly, entitled "How Black Do You Have to Be?" *ibid.*, Sept. 15, 1968, sect. 2, pp. 1, 5. See also L. J. Cotton, "The Negro in the American Theater," *NHB*, XXIII (May 1960), 172–78.

2. Theaters where black artists are in control of production have been established sporadically since 1821 in the United States, and the emergence of Harlem and black colleges as cultural centers, the black federal theater units during the Great Depression, and the recent assertions of black identity have given renewed im-

petus to the movement. Some black companies have produced plays from the current and classical repertories by white authors as well as plays by black playwrights, some have employed white as well as black actors, some have played to mixed audiences, and some have catered particularly to the black community or devoted their productions to plays written by blacks.

There is material on black theaters scattered through the items by Bond and Isaacs cited above, but see particularly Hoyt W. Fuller, "Black Theater in America," *Negro Digest*, XVII (Apr. 1968), 83–93, and chs. 6, 8 (on the Crescent and Lafayette Theaters and the Harlem WPA Negro unit) in Mitchell, *Black Drama*, cited above. References to black companies and productions sponsored by the WPA are scattered through the following: Wilson Whitman, *Bread and Circuses: A Study of the Federal Theater* (New York, 1937); Pierre de Rohan, ed., *Federal Theater Plays*, 2 vols. (New York, 1938); Jane De H. Mathews, *The Federal Theatre, 1935–1939* (Princeton, 1967);* and particularly Hallie F. Flanagan, *Arena* (New York, 1940). See also Morgan Y. Himelstein, *Drama Was a Weapon: The Left-Wing Theatre in New York, 1929–1941* (New Brunswick, N.J., 1963). Two articles on particular theaters are Terrence Tobin, "Karamu Theatre: 1915–1964," *Drama Critique*, VII (Spring 1964), 86–91, and "Krigwa Players' Little Negro Theatre," *Crisis*, XXXIII (Dec. 1926), 70–71.

The motives and strategies guiding the black theater movement are illuminated by the following: Dick Campbell, "Is There a Conspiracy Against Black Playwrights?" *Negro Digest*, XVII (Apr. 1968), 11–15; John O. Killens, "Broadway in Black and White," *A Forum*, I, no. 3 (1965), 66–70; Jim Williams, "The Need for a Harlem Theater," *Freedomways*, III (Summer 1963), 307–11, and "Pieces on Black Theatre and the Black Theatre Worker," *ibid.*, IX (Spring 1969), 146–55; Melvin Dixon, "Black Theater: The Aesthetics," *Negro Digest*, XVIII (July 1969), 41–44; Woodie King, Jr., "Black Theater: Present Condition," *The Drama Review*, XII (Summer 1968), 117–24; Adam D. Miller, "It's a Long Way to St. Louis: Notes on the Audience for Black Drama," *ibid.*, 147–50; Larry Neal, "The Black Arts Movement," *ibid.*, 29–39; Frank Silvera, "Towards a Theater of Understanding," *Negro Digest*, XVIII (Apr. 1969), 33–35; Ed Bullins,

"Theater of Reality," *ibid.*, XV (Apr. 1966), 60–66; and two important pieces by the actor and playwright Douglas Turner Ward, co-founder of the Negro Ensemble Company in New York City: "American Theater: For Whites Only?" New York *Times*, Aug. 14, 1966, sect. 2, pp. 1 ff.; "Needed: A Theater for Black Themes," *Negro Digest*, XVII (Dec. 1967), 34–39. An early plea for black drama was an anonymous piece, "Why Not a Negro Drama for Negroes by Negroes?" *Current Opinion*, LXXII (May 1922), 639–40. For the strategic use of theatrical troupes and activities in the civil rights struggle, see Thomas C. Dent and Richard Schecker, *The Free Southern Theatre* (Indianapolis, 1969).*

D. Black Dramatists

Doris E. Abramson gives a general account in *Negro Playwrights in the American Theatre, 1925–1959* (New York, 1969); and check lists of plays by black playwrights include Charles Fineberg, *Negro Plays* (New York, n.d.) and *Fifteen One-Act Plays* (New York, 1936), and Frank Silvera, *A List of Negro Plays* (New York, 1938). The bibliographies and texts in the works by Frederick Bond, Edith Isaacs, and Loften Mitchell, cited above, are important for reference. Collections of plays by blacks include the following: Alain L. Locke and Montgomery Gregory, eds., *Plays of Negro Life: A Source-Book of Native American Drama* (New York, 1927); Willis Richardson, ed., *Plays and Pageants from the Life of the Negro* (Washington, 1930); Willis Richardson and May Miller, eds., *Negro History in Thirteen Plays* (Washington, 1935); LeRoi Jones and Larry Neal, eds., *Black Fire: An Anthology of Afro-American Writing* (New York, 1968);* and William Couch, Jr., ed., *New Black Playwrights* (Baton Rouge, 1968).* (Couch's collection includes Ed Bullins' *Goin' a Buffalo*; Lonne Elder's *Ceremonies in Dark Old Men*; Adrienne Kennedy's *A Rat's Mass*; William W. Mackey's *Family Meeting*; and Douglas Turner Ward's *Happy Ending* and *Day of Absence*.) Another recent collection is Clayton Riley, ed., *A Black Quartet: Four New Black Plays* (New York, 1970).* (Riley's collection includes Ben Caldwell's *Prayer Meeting*; Ronald Milner's *The Warning*; Ed Bullins' *The Gentleman Caller*; and LeRoi Jones' *Great Good-*

ness of Life.) A recent collection, edited by Alice Childress, is *Black Scenes* (Garden City, N.Y., 1971).

Critical studies of black playwrights and their materials include Sterling A. Brown, *Negro Poetry and Drama* (Washington, 1937);* Montgomery Gregory, "The Drama of Negro Life," in Alain L. Locke, ed., *The New Negro* (New York, 1925),* pp. 153–60; William Couch, Jr., "The Problem of Negro Character and Dramatic Incident," *Phylon*, XI (2nd Quarter 1950), 127–33; Gerald Bradley, "Goodbye, Mr. Bones: The Emergence of Negro Themes and Characters in American Drama," *Drama Critique*, VII (Spring 1964), 79–85; Owen Dodson, "Playwrights in Dark Glasses," *Negro Digest*, XVII (Apr. 1968), 30–36; Waters E. Turpin, "The Contemporary American Negro Playwright," *CLAJ*, IX (Sept. 1965), 12–24; three important articles by Darwin T. Turner: "The Negro Dramatist's Image of the Universe," *ibid.*, V (Dec. 1961), 106–20;** "Negro Playwrights and the Urban Negro," *ibid.*, XII (Sept. 1968), 19–25; and "Past and Present in Negro Drama," *Negro American Literature Forum*, II (Summer 1968), 26–27; and Christopher W. E. Bigsby, *Confrontation and Commitment: A Study of Contemporary American Drama, 1959– 1966* (Columbia, Mo., 1969), pp. 115–73. Alice Childress, a black playwright, has written "A Woman Playwright Speaks Her Mind," *Freedomways*, VI (Winter 1966), 75–80.

The following section lists the published plays of seven leading black playwrights plus critical commentary and analysis.

1. James Baldwin

Baldwin's plays are *Blues for Mister Charlie* (New York, 1964),* and *The Amen Corner* (New York, 1968). Commentary includes Christopher W. E. Bigsby, "The Committed Writer: James Baldwin as Dramatist," *Twentieth Century Literature*, XIII (Apr. 1967), 39–48; Joseph Featherstone, "Blues for Mr. Baldwin," *New Republic*, CLIII (Nov. 27, 1965), 34–36; Philip Roth, "Channel X: Two Plays on the Race Conflict," *New York Review of Books*, II (May 28, 1964), 10–13; and Louis Phillips, "The Novelist as Playwright: Baldwin, McCullers, and Bellow," in William E. Taylor, ed., *Modern American Drama: Essays in Criti-*

cism (Deland, Fla., 1968), pp. 145–62. A full-length study is Fern M. Eckman, *The Furious Passage of James Baldwin* (New York, 1967).*

2. Ed Bullins

Bullins' plays include *How Do You Do?* (Mill Valley, Calif., 1967) and *Five Plays* (Indianapolis, 1969),* which includes *Goin' a Buffalo, In the Wine Time, A Son, Come Home, The Electronic Nigger,* and *Clara's Ole Man.* (*Goin' a Buffalo* is published also in Couch's *New Black Playwrights,* cited above.) Bullins' *The Gentleman Caller* is printed in Riley's collection cited above. An important article by Bullins is "Theater of Reality," *Negro Digest,* XV (Apr. 1966), 60–66.

3. Ossie Davis

Davis wrote *Purlie Victorious: A Comedy in Three Acts* (New York, 1961). Gerald C. Weales, *The Jumping-Off Place,* cited in section C, ch. 4, contains an analysis of Davis's work as a writer, actor, and director. For additional material by and about Davis, see the titles cited above in section C, "Black Performers and Black Theater."

4. Lorraine Hansberry

Lorraine Hansberry's published plays are *A Raisin in the Sun* (New York, 1959)* and *The Sign in Sidney Brustein's Window* (New York, 1965). See also her *The Movement: Documentary of a Struggle for Equality* (New York, 1964)* and "Me Tink Me Hear Sounds in De Night," *Theater Arts,* XLV (Oct. 1961), 9–11. Commentary includes Harold Isaacs, "Five Writers and Their African Ancestry: Part III," *Phylon,* XXI (4th Quarter 1960), 317–36; John O. Killens, "Broadway in Black and White," *A Forum,* I, no. 3 (1965), 66–70; Theophilus Lewis, "Social Protest in *A Raisin in the Sun,*" *Catholic World,* CXC (Oct. 1959), 31–35; Anon., "Playwright," *New Yorker,* XXXV (May 9, 1959), 33–35; Christopher W. E. Bigsby, *Confrontation and Commitment,* cited above, pp. 156–73; Gerald C. Weales, *The Jumping-*

Off Place, cited above, ch. 4; and Harold Cruse, "Lorraine Hansberry," in *The Crisis of the Negro Intellectual* (New York, 1967),* pp. 267–84.

5. Langston Hughes

Hughes' plays are published in Smalley Webster, ed., *Five Plays by Langston Hughes*, including *Little Ham, Mulatto, Simply Heavenly, Soul Gone Home*, and *Tambourines to Glory* (Bloomington, Ind., 1963). Commentary includes Arthur P. Davis, "The Tragic Mulatto Theme in Six Works of Langston Hughes," *Phylon*, XVI (2nd Quarter 1955), 195–204, and Darwin T. Turner, "Langston Hughes as Playwright," *CLAJ*, XI (June 1967), 297–309.

6. LeRoi Jones

Jones' plays include *The Baptism & The Toilet* (New York, 1966);* *Dutchman and The Slave* (New York, 1964);* "Black Mass," in *The Liberator* (June 1966); and *Great Goodness of Life* published in Riley's collection cited above. Of particular note in Jones, *Home: Social Essays* (New York, 1966),* are "The Myth of a 'Negro Literature,'" pp. 105–15; "Black Writing," pp. 161–65; "Expressive Language," pp. 166–72; and "The Revolutionary Theatre," pp. 210–15. Commentary includes Maria K. Mootry, "Themes and Symbols in Two of LeRoi Jones' Plays," *Negro Digest*, XVIII (Apr. 1969), 42–47; Hugh Nelson, "LeRoi Jones' *Dutchman*: A Brief Ride on a Doomed Ship," *Educational Theatre Journal*, XX (Feb. 1968), 53–59; Philip Roth, "Channel X: Two Plays on the Race Conflict," *New York Review of Books*, II (May 28, 1964), 10–13; Christopher W. E. Bigsby, *Confrontation and Commitment*, cited above, pp. 138–55; Gerald C. Weales, *The Jumping-Off Place*, cited above, ch. 4; and George Dennison, "The Demagogy of LeRoi Jones," *Commentary*, XXXIX (Feb. 1965), 67–76. See also the sections on Jones in this Part, topic 2, "Black Poetry," and topic 6, "After Protest: Black Writers in the 1950s and 1960s."

7. Douglas Turner Ward

Ward's plays are *Happy Ending* and *Day of Absence* (New York, 1968), available also in William Couch, Jr., ed., *New Black Playwrights*, cited above, pp. 3–59; and *The Reckoning* (New York, 1970). See also the items by Ward listed above in section C, "Black Performers and Black Theater." For commentary see Gerald C. Weales, *The Jumping-Off Place*, cited above, ch. 4.

10. Afro-Americans in Films

The Afro-American's relation to the motion picture—as audience, performer or artist, and subject—has paralleled his experience in the theater, though the irony of his mistreatment is sharpened by an art that speaks of its medium as "black-and-white" or "color." Movie audiences were segregated by race in much of the country until recently. Black performers had fewer opportunities than whites for employment and the exercise of their talent. (The first "talking" movie featured a white singer in blackface.) It was virtually impossible for blacks to become directors of films, and there were (and still are) even fewer opportunities for black writers and producers in films than in the theater; directors like Lloyd Richardson and script writers like Carl Lee remain a rarity. The content of Hollywood films until recently has tempted black audiences with enticing images of a white world that either ignored Afro-Americans or presented debased stereotypes of black life, perpetuating for white audiences the dangerous myths of racial superiority. The insinuating power of the film in modern culture makes all the more important the efforts, notably since 1963, to expand the opportunities for blacks in the movie industry and to treat more maturely and candidly the subjects that customarily are distorted by racist attitudes and stereotypes such as life in the black ghetto, the domestic lives and erotic experience of blacks, miscegenation, and racial conflict.

Peter Noble, *The Negro in Films* (London, 1948, reprinted Port

Washington, N.Y., 1969), is a good introduction to the subject to the date of its publication and contains a listing of films from 1902 to 1948 featuring blacks or dealing with racial themes. V. J. Jerome, *The Negro in Hollywood Films* (New York, 1950), is a Marxist interpretation. Most of the black movie stars up to 1966 are portrayed in Langston Hughes and Milton Meltzer, *Black Magic: A Pictorial History of the Negro in American Entertainment* (Englewood Cliffs, N.J., 1967). A useful monograph on D. W. Griffith's epoch-making but extremely biased film is Seymour Stern, *The Birth of a Nation* (New York, 1946).

The entire issues of *Close Up*, V (Aug. 1929), and *New Theatre*, II (July 1935), are devoted to the Afro-American in the theater and the films. An article critical of Hollywood's depiction of black characters is Arthur Draper, "Uncle Tom Will You Never Die?" *New Theatre*, III (Jan. 1936), 30–31. William Harrison, "The Negro and the Cinema," *Sight and Sound*, VIII (Spring 1939), 16–17, deals with *The Emperor Jones* as well as with the problems of independent black producers. Articles emphasizing more recent films include two by Thomas R. Cripps, "The Death of Rastus: Negroes in American Films Since 1945," *Phylon*, XXVIII (Fall 1967), 267–75,** and "Movies in the Ghetto, B.P. [Before Poitier]," *Negro Digest*, XVIII (Feb. 1969), 21–27, 45–48; Martin S. Dworkin, "The New Negro on the Screen," *Progressive*, XXIV (Oct., Nov., Dec. 1960), 39–41, 33–36, 34–36; and Calvin Hernton, "And You, Too, Sidney Poitier," in Hernton, *White Papers for White Americans* (Garden City, N.Y., 1966), pp. 53–70. Stanley Kauffmann's collection of reviews, *A World on Film* (New York, 1966),* pp. 151–54, 164–66, 167–68, includes evaluations of several important recent films dealing with Afro-American life: *A Raisin in the Sun, Take a Giant Step, The Cool World,* and *Nothing But a Man.* For Renata Adler's perceptive analysis, see "The Negro That Movies Overlook," New York *Times,* Mar. 3, 1968, sect. 2, p. 1. Three articles examining the content and production problems of specific films dealing with blacks are Vinicius De Moraes, "The Making of *The Quiet One,*" *Hollywood Quarterly*, IV (Summer 1950), 375–84; Dorothy B. Jones, "William Faulkner: Novel into Film," on *Intruder in the Dust, The Quarterly of Film, Radio, and Television*, VIII (Fall 1953), 51–57; and James Baldwin, "*Carmen Jones:* The

Dark Is Light Enough," in *Notes of a Native Son* (New York, 1955),* pp. 46–54. Ralph Ellison's astute comments on five films (*Birth of a Nation, Home of the Brave, Lost Boundaries, Pinky,* and *Intruder in the Dust*) are in *Shadow and Act* (New York, 1964),* pp. 273–81. Two indispensable studies of films in the 1950s and 1960s are by Albert Johnson: "Beige, Brown, or Black," *Film Quarterly,* XIII (Fall 1959), 38–43, and "The Negro in American Films: Some Recent Works," *ibid.,* XVIII (Summer 1965), 14–30. See also Carl M. Moss, "The Negro in American Films," *Freedomways,* III (Spring 1963), 134–42. For a highly critical appraisal of past and present Hollywood treatments of black life, see Stephen Fay, "The Era of Dummies and Darkies," *Commonweal,* XCIII (Oct. 30, 1970), 125–28.

11. Soul Music: Blues, Jazz, and Variations

Music is an expression of a people's deepest cultural values, and this is especially true of Afro-Americans. The constricted status of blacks has limited their opportunities for social and political expression and forced them to rely upon songs and folklore, often containing hidden or double meanings, to express sorrow, resignation, humor, satire, anger, and protest. Black music reflects the changing conditions of Afro-Americans over time: the spirituals help us understand slavery; work songs and country blues tell us much about blacks in the postemancipation South; urban blues and jazz are keys to the urban black experience. "Laughin' on the outside, cryin' on the inside," a blues theme, is a microcosm of much black history in America. Black music can also tell us a great deal about the dominant white culture, for it held that culture up to a sharp and often unflattering mirror image; at the same time, black music has penetrated all aspects of popular American culture in the twentieth century and has become one of the most important influences on American popular music. For the function of music as an expression of an urban black subculture, see Part IX, topic 14, "Black Life-Styles in the Ghetto."

One of the earliest forms of American black music was the

spiritual. For the abundant literature on the spirituals, see the references cited in Part II, topic 4, "African Cultural Survivals Among Black Americans," Part III, topic 1, "Plantation Slavery in the Antebellum South," and Part IV, topic 4, "The Antebellum Black Church." The blues were an amalgam of the spirituals and secular work songs; in their pure "country" form they date from the late nineteenth century. The "classic" blues, to use LeRoi Jones's terminology, belonged to the world of vaudeville and cabaret entertainment in the period around and after World War I and made famous such names as Ma Rainey and Bessie Smith. The "urban" blues, reflecting the adjustment to the conflicts and strangeness of the city, were harder, crueler, more stoical than country or classic blues. Two excellent books trace the origins of the blues and the life-styles they express: LeRoi Jones, *Blues People: Negro Music in White America* (New York, 1963),* and Charles Keil, *Urban Blues* (Chicago, 1966).* Other accounts are Samuel Charters, *The Country Blues* (New York, 1959), and *The Poetry of the Blues* (New York, 1963);* Paul Oliver, *Blues Fell This Morning: The Meaning of the Blues* (London, 1960),* *Conversation with the Blues* (New York, 1965), and *Screening the Blues* (London, 1968); Frederic Ramsey, *Been Here and Gone* (New Brunswick, N.J., 1960);* and George Mitchell, *Blow My Blues Away* (Baton Rouge, 1971). All of these studies devote attention to personalities in the blues tradition; in addition, see the autobiographies of two outstanding early bluesmen: Perry Bradford, *Born With the Blues: Perry Bradford's Own Story* (New York, 1965);* and W. C. Handy, *Father of the Blues*, ed. by Arna Bontemps (New York, 1941).*

Jazz was not a successor to the blues, but a parallel development that was at first the purely instrumental form of the blues and soon moved off into its own paths of change and refinement. Its origins were associated with the vice districts in black neighborhoods of southern cities. By the 1920s, however, jazz had become an American and not an exclusively black idiom. Blues and jazz were the basic forms of black-originated popular music, but they spawned many offshoots: "ragtime" in the early 1900s, "boogiewoogie" in the 1930s, "bebop" in the 1940s, "rock 'n' roll" in the 1950s, and "soul music" in the 1960s. During all this time the blues and jazz themselves underwent permutations of such bewildering complexity that even experts have difficulty sorting them out.

The literature on jazz and its offshoots is enormous and falls roughly into three overlapping classifications: (1) sociocultural history; (2) biographies, reminiscences, and feature articles concentrating on personalities; (3) musicological analysis. A good bibliography to the date of its publication is Robert G. Reisner, *The Literature of Jazz: A Selective Bibliography* (2nd ed., rev., New York, 1959).

1. Perhaps the best sociocultural history of jazz is Marshall Stearns, *The Story of Jazz* (New York, 1956).* A good general treatment of blues and jazz is found in pts. III and IV of Eileen Southern, *The Music of Black Americans: A History* (New York, 1971).* Other studies include Barry Ulanov, *A History of Jazz in America* (New York, 1952); Rudi Blesh, *Shining Trumpets: A History of Jazz* (New York, 1958); Samuel B. Charters, *Jazz: New Orleans, 1885–1963* (New York, 1963);* Samuel B. Charters and Leon Kunstadt, *Jazz: A History of the New York Scene* (Garden City, N.Y., 1962); and Nat Hentoff and Albert J. McCarthy, eds., *Jazz: New Perspectives in the History of Jazz by Twelve of the World's Foremost Jazz Critics and Scholars* (New York, 1959). Two early analyses that probably overemphasize the primacy of New Orleans are Wilder Hobson, *American Jazz Music* (New York, 1939); and Hugues Panassié, *The Real Jazz* (New York, 1942). A history of Afro-American dance forms is Marshall and Jean Stearns, *Jazz Dance* (New York, 1968). The best history of ragtime is Rudi Blesh and Harriet Janis, *They All Played Ragtime: The True Story of an American Music* (rev. ed., New York, 1959).* For an account of the New York scene in the early years of the century by a man who wrote lyrics for many ragtime tunes, see James Weldon Johnson, *Black Manhattan* (New York, 1930),* esp. chs. 9–11, and *Along This Way: The Autobiography of James Weldon Johnson* (New York, 1933),* esp. chs. 17–20.

2. Books that emphasize personalities and their life-styles include Frederic Ramsey and Charles Smith, eds., *Jazzmen* (New York, 1939); two volumes edited by Nat Hentoff and Nat Shapiro, *Hear Me Talkin' to Ya—The Story of Jazz by the Men Who Made It* (New York, 1955),* and *The Jazzmakers* (New York, 1957); Nat Hentoff, *The Jazz Life* (New York, 1961); LeRoi Jones,

Black Music (New York, 1967);* Louis Armstrong, *Satchmo: My Life in New Orleans* (New York, 1954);* Jeannette Eaton, *Trumpeter's Tale: The Story of Young Louis Armstrong* (New York, 1955); Robert Goffin, *Horn of Plenty: The Story of Louis Armstrong* (New York, 1947); Alan Lomax, *Mister Jelly Roll: The Fortunes of Jelly Roll Morton* (New York, 1950); Peter Gammond, ed., *Duke Ellington: His Life and Music* (New York, 1958); Barry Ulanov, *Duke Ellington* (New York, 1946); Stanley Dance, *The World of Duke Ellington* (New York, 1970), and Max Harrison, *Charlie Parker* (New York, 1961).*

3. One of the first efforts toward a serious musicological analysis of jazz was Winthrop Sargeant, *Jazz: Hot and Hybrid* (rev. ed., New York, 1946). A recent study, the first of two projected volumes, is the most complete analysis of early jazz and related musical forms: Gunther Schuller, *Early Jazz: Its Roots and Musical Development* (New York, 1968).

Useful reference works on jazz include Leonard Feather, *The Encyclopedia of Jazz* (New York, 1955), and *The Encyclopedia of Jazz in the Sixties* (New York, 1966); Barry Ulanov, *A Handbook of Jazz* (New York, 1957);* and Ralph J. Gleason, ed., *Jam Session: An Anthology of Jazz* (New York, 1958). Two periodicals that contain articles and news in the field, plus discography, are *Jazz Review* and *Jazz*.

A fine study that contains analyses and examples of all kinds of black folk music, including blues and jazz, is Harold Courlander, *Negro Folk Music U.S.A.* (New York, 1963).* An anthology that covers classical as well as popular and folk music is Lindsay Patterson, ed., *The Negro in Music and Art* (New York, 1967). Three fine essays dealing with the impact of black music, especially jazz, on white Americans and Europeans are Morroe Berger, "Jazz: Resistance to the Diffusion of a Culture Pattern," *JNH*, XXXII (Oct. 1947), 461–94; Arnold Shaw, "Popular Music from Minstrel Songs to Rock 'n' Roll," in Paul Henry Land, ed., *One Hundred Years of Music in America* (New York, 1961), pp. 140–68; and Martin Cooper, "Revolution in Musical Taste," in Bertrand Russell, ed., *The Impact of America on European Culture* (Boston, 1951), pp. 67–78.

The civil rights movement was expressed and sustained by song;

for a collection of more than seventy songs, see Guy and Candie Carawan, eds., *We Shall Overcome! Songs of the Southern Freedom Movement* (New York, 1963).* A recent study that charts the impact of the new militancy on black music is Frank Kofsky, *Black Nationalism and the Revolution in Music* (New York, 1970).*

12. Blacks in Opera and Symphonic Music

It has been particularly difficult for talented black musicians to pursue careers in serious music because of the high cost of training, the difficulties of gaining access to orchestras, concert stages, or opera companies, and the elitist rituals that surround the performance of serious music in the institutions dominated by white Americans. Concert singers have had the most conspicuous success since the 1930s, but even those most widely recognized for their talents have been excluded from certain opportunities and subjected to indignities when off the concert stage. (Paul Robeson starred in Eugene O'Neill's play *The Emperor Jones*, but the role in the opera based on the play was assigned at the Metropolitan Opera to a white singer, Lawrence Tibbett, who sang it in "black-voice.") Many first-rate singers have established their reputations in European opera companies which welcomed them when America's few companies remained segregated, and some have preferred to remain expatriates in recent years, though opera companies and concert stages have opened their stage doors to such stars as Shirley Verrett, Robert McFerrin, William Warfield and Leontyne Price.

The career of the great contralto Marian Anderson best represents the black concert artists' struggles in recent decades. The refusal of the Daughters of the American Revolution to let her hold a concert in Constitution Hall in Washington in 1939 became a *cause célèbre* and provoked the First Lady, Mrs. Eleanor Roosevelt, to resign from the organization in protest; the Easter concert at the Lincoln Memorial organized by Mrs. Roosevelt and others to counter the racism of the DAR was a triumph attended by an audience of 75,000. Miss Anderson's debut at the

Metropolitan Opera in 1955 (in a subordinate role, and after her voice had passed its prime), was a landmark in the Afro-American quest for recognition and equality, though not until late in her career did she insist that blacks be admitted on an equal basis to her audiences in the South.

Black composers of serious music have had notable, if less conspicuous, success, marked by the performances in the 1930s of William Levi Dawson's *Negro Folk Symphony* and William Grant Still's *Afro-American Symphony*. Dawson was director of music at Tuskegee until 1955; Still produced operas and symphonic compositions on Afro-American themes while composing also for radio and motion pictures. The best representative of the serious black composer's position in American culture is Howard Swanson, who has worked as a locomotive greaser, mail clerk, and Internal Revenue employee both before and during his career as a symphonic composer. Among his many compositions are the *Second ("Short") Symphony*, which was awarded the New York Music Critics' Circle Prize for 1950-1951, and seven songs set to poems by Carl Sandburg, Vachel Lindsay, and Langston Hughes.

The following collections and bibliographies cover symphonic and operatic music by black composers: Dominique-René de Lerma, ed., *Black Music in Our Culture: Curricular Ideas on the Subjects, Materials, and Problems* (Kent, Ohio, 1970), *The Legacy of Black Music* (Kent, Ohio, 1971), *Black Music: A Preliminary Register of the Composers and Their Works* (Bloomington, Ind., 1971); and Eileen Southern, ed., *Source Readings in Black American Music* (New York, 1971).

There is material on black concert artists and composers in the following: Benjamin G. Brawley, *The Negro Genius* (New York, 1937),* ch. 11; Margaret Just Butcher, *The Negro in American Culture* (New York, 1956), ch. 4; Maude Cuney Hare, *Negro Musicians and Their Music* (Washington, 1936), chs. 14, 15; and particularly Lindsay Patterson, ed., *The Negro in Music and Art* (New York, 1967), chs. 10, 11. Richard Bardolph traces the Negro musicians' climb up the ladder of success in *The Negro Vanguard* (New York, 1959),* pp. 156-66, 284-95. There is detailed information on the appearances of Negro soloists at both the New York City Center Opera and the Metropolitan Opera in Irving Kolodin, *The Metropolitan Opera, 1883-1966: A Candid His-*

tory (New York, 1966), esp. pp. 547–48, 745 (on Marian Anderson), and 653–59 (on Leontyne Price's performance at a glittering Metropolitan opening night). Brief but detailed comments on William Grant Still and Howard Swanson are in Gilbert Chase, *America's Music From Pilgrims to the Present* (2nd ed., New York, 1966), pp. 512–13, 541–42, and in John Tasker Howard and George K. Bellows, *A Short History of Music in America* (New York, 1957),* pp. 292–93, 385–86. There is up-to-date information on black performers and composers in Eileen Southern, *The Music of Black Americans: A History* (New York, 1971),* chs. 14–16. The situation of black composers in 1971 is discussed by Howard Klein, "Overdoing 'Benign Neglect'?" in New York *Times*, Mar. 7, 1971, sect. 2, pp. 1, 9.

Biographies, memoirs, and autobiographical material include: William G. Still, "An Afro-American Composer's Point of View," in Henry Cowell, ed., *American Composers on American Music* (Stanford, Calif., 1933),* ch. 27; Verna Arvey, *William Grant Still* (New York, 1939); Charles J. Harris, *Reminiscences of My Days with Roland Hayes* (Orangeburg, S.C., 1944); Helen Mackinley, *Angel Mo' and Her Son, Roland Hayes* (Boston, 1932); Marian Anderson, *My Lord, What a Morning!* (New York, 1956);* and Vehamen Kosti, *Marian Anderson* (New York, 1941). For biographies of Paul Robeson, see this Part, topic 9, "Blacks and the American Theater." In Ernest Dunbar, ed., *The Black Expatriates: A Study of American Negroes in Exile* (New York, 1968),* are interviews with the black conductor Dean Dixon (pp. 188–201) and the Negro opera stars Reri Grist (pp. 114–26), Gloria Davy (pp. 176–87), and Mattiwilda Dodds (pp. 207–23). Edward R. Clarke has published *Negro Art Songs* (New York, 1946).

Among the works by Afro-American composers that have been recorded on discs and listed in recent catalogues are the following: William Levi Dawson, *Negro Folk Symphony* (Decca #710077); Howard Swanson, *Short Symphony* (American Recording Society #7 and Composers' Recordings, Inc., #S-254), *Night Music* (Decca #3215, 8511), and *Seven Songs* (Desto #6422 and American Recording Society #10). Selections from black composers are on two recent releases: *The Black Composers in Amer-*

ica (Desto #DC7107) and *Natalie Hinderas Plays Music by Black Composers* (Desto #7102/3).

13. The Black Press Since Booker T. Washington

The earliest black newspapers emerged in the service of abolitionist protest, and the promotion of racial advancement has continued to be a primary function of the black press. But the black newspaper has traditionally served another important function insofar as it provides additional news about blacks not available in the regular white daily press. In particular, black society, sports, business, crime, and sensationalism have been the major sources of news in the black press (as in much of the white press). The news and editorial columns of the leading twentieth-century black newspapers provide a detailed chronicle of events in the black community and of trends in black protest, and they also afford important insights into the views of their readers and of their middle-class black establishment owners. Chief among these papers are: two dailies, the Chicago *Defender* (founded in 1905) and the Atlanta *World* (1928); and the Pittsburgh *Courier* (1910), the *Afro-American* (a chain publication, best known for its Baltimore [1892] and Washington [1933] papers, which publishes several editions for various parts of the country), the New York *Amsterdam News* (1909), and the Norfolk *Journal and Guide* (1899), published weekly or semiweekly.

These papers offer rich opportunities for fruitful analysis, but the literature about the black press has thus far been weak. N. W. Ayer & Son's *Directory of Newspapers and Periodicals*, published annually in Philadelphia, is the best source for up-to-date listings of black papers. Warren Brown, *Check List of Negro Newspapers in the United States* (1827–1946) (Jefferson City, Mo., 1946), lists dates of founding and expiration, the location of all known copies, and editors' names for 467 papers during that period. The best brief introduction to the history and role of the black press is still ch. 42 of Gunnar Myrdal, *An American Dilemma: The Negro Problem and Modern Democracy* (New York, 1944).*

E. Franklin Frazier interprets the press as the creator of "a world of make-believe" for the black middle class in ch. 8 of *Black Bourgeoisie* (Glencoe, Ill., 1957).* Monographs in the field are dated and seriously limited in value; see Vishnu V. Oak, *The Negro Newspaper* (Yellow Springs, Ohio, 1948); Frederick G. Detweiler, *The Negro Press in the United States* (Chicago, 1922, reprinted College Park, Md., 1968); and George William Gore, Jr., *Negro Journalism: An Essay on the History and Present Conditions of the Negro Press* (Greencastle, Ind., 1922). Several articles that survey the press and its changing role include Eugene Gordon, "The Negro Press," *Annals*, CXL (Nov. 1928), 248–56; P. B. Young (publisher of the Norfolk *Journal and Guide*), "The Negro Press—Today and Tomorrow," *Opportunity*, XVII (July 1939), 204–05; P. L. Prattis, "The Role of the Negro Press in Race Relations," *Phylon*, VII (3rd Quarter 1946), 273–83, and his "Race Relations and the Negro Press," *ibid.*, XIV (4th Quarter 1953), 373–83; Doxey A. Wilkerson, "The Negro Press," *JNH*, XVI (Fall 1947), 511–21; John H. Burma, "An Analysis of the Present Negro Press," *SF*, XXVI (Dec. 1947), 172–80; James A. Bayton and Ernestine Bell, "An Exploratory Study of the Role of the Negro Press," *JNH*, XX (Winter 1951), 8–15; Lewis H. Fenderson, "The Negro Press As a Social Instrument," *ibid.* (Spring 1951), 181–88; Bernard C. Rosen, "Attitude Changes Within the Negro Press Toward Segregation and Discrimination," *Journal of Social Psychology*, LXII (Feb. 1964), 77–84; and Thelma T. Gorham, "The Negro Press, Past, Present and Future," in *Directory of U.S. Negro Newspapers, Magazines and Periodicals, 1966* (New York, 1966). Maxwell Brooks, *The Negro Press Re-Examined: Political Content of Leading Negro Newspapers* (Boston, 1959), studies five papers during 1948. Richard L. Beard and Cyril E. Zoerner II, "Associated Negro Press: Its Founding, Ascendency and Demise," *Journalism Quarterly*, XLVI (Spring 1969), 47–52, treats the news service that provided news concerning blacks to Afro-American newspapers in the United States and Africa during the period 1919–66.

There are still only two important biographies of black editors—Roi Ottley, *The Lonely Warrior: The Life and Times of Robert S. Abbott* (Chicago, 1955), editor of the Chicago *Defender*, and Stephen R. Fox, *The Guardian of Boston: William Monroe*

Trotter (New York, 1970).* Trotter, the militant editor of the Boston *Guardian*, is also treated in Charles W. Puttkammer and Ruth Worthy, "William Monroe Trotter, 1872–1934," *JNH*, XLIII (Oct. 1958), 298–316. A long-time columnist for the Pittsburgh *Courier*, George S. Schuyler, who began his career as an editor of the socialist *Messenger*, has written two books—*Fifty Years of Progress in Negro Journalism* (Pittsburgh, 1950), and an autobiography, *Black and Conservative* (New Rochelle, N.Y., 1966). Richard Bardolph, *The Negro Vanguard* (New York, 1959),* pp. 142–46, 249–54, presents a group portrait of black journalists in the twentieth century. Roy L. Hill, *Who's Who in the American Negro Press* (Dallas, 1960), includes biographical sketches. For an account of "Negroes on White Newspapers," see *Ebony*, XI (Nov. 1955), 77–82.

In the aftermath of the riots of the 1960s, special attention has been paid to the relative importance of blacks—as news and as reporters—in white newspapers and broadcast media. The white media have been indicted on several counts: for reporting racial strife while ignoring constructive developments in the black community; for helping to spread racial violence by the intensive coverage they give to riots; and for failing to employ blacks in any significant numbers as reporters, editors, researchers, broadcasters, technicians, and actors in commercials and regular programming. Ch. 15 of the *Report of the National Advisory Commission on Civil Disorders* (New York, 1968)* is a succinct introduction to these problems. In recent years, several conferences have been held on the subject, some journalism training programs for minority groups have been instituted, and newspapers and broadcasting networks have begun to hire increasing numbers of blacks. For discussion of the media's coverage of racial news, see Paul L. Fisher and Ralph L. Lowenstein, eds., *Race and the News Media* (New York, 1967), and Armistead S. Pride et al., *The Black American and the Press* (Los Angeles, 1968), ed. by Jack Lyle. Three recent articles in the *Journalism Quarterly*—Royal D. Colle, "Negro Image in the Mass Media: A Case Study in Social Change," XLV (Spring 1968), 55–60; Edward J. Trayes, "The Negro in Journalism: Surveys Show Low Ratios," XLVI (Spring 1969), 5–8; and Melvin Mencher, "Journalism: The Way It Is, as

Seen by Black Reporters and Students," XLVI (Autumn 1969), 499–504, 554—are especially relevant here.

During this century, special-interest periodicals have emerged to supplement black newspapers. Some of these, the organs of important protest and welfare organizations—for example, the NAACP's *Crisis*, the Urban League's *Opportunity*, *The Black Panther*—shed important light not only on the activities of the sponsoring group but also on major trends in black protest and culture. On *Opportunity*, see "*Opportunity*—How It Began," *Opportunity*, XXV (Oct.–Dec. 1947), 184, and the magazine's entire final issue, vol. XXVII (Winter 1949). For an account of the origins and early development of *Crisis*, see Charles Flint Kellogg, *NAACP: A History of the National Association for the Advancement of Colored People*, vol. I: 1909–1920 (Baltimore, 1967), esp. pp. 50–53, 149–54. Michael A. Malec, "Some Observations on the Content of *Crisis*, 1932–1962," *Phylon*, XXVIII (2nd Quarter 1967), 161–67, looks at the changing emphasis of its civil rights articles. Radical black magazines and newspapers, chief among them *The Messenger*, *The Liberator*, *Freedom*, and *Freedomways*, are the subject of extended analysis in Harold Cruse, *The Crisis of the Negro Intellectual* (New York, 1967).* The Johnson Publishing Company of Chicago has established an immensely successful publishing empire by creating black counterparts for the mass circulation white popular magazines. *Ebony*, founded in 1945, is the major Johnson publication; others include *Jet*, *Tan*, and *Negro Digest*. There is a brief biographical sketch of the head of the publishing company, John H. Johnson, in Phillip T. Drotning and Wesley W. South, *Up from the Ghetto* (New York, 1970),* ch. 13. On the history and contents of *Ebony*, see "The Story of *Ebony*," *Ebony*, XI (Nov. 1955), 122–28, and Paul M. Hirsch, "An Analysis of *Ebony*: The Magazine and Its Readers," *Journalism Quarterly*, XLV (Summer 1968), 261–70, 292. For an early general study, see Sidney V. Reedy, "The Negro Magazine: A Critical Study of Its Educational Significance," *JNH*, XIX (Oct. 1934), 598–604.

The advertisements in black magazines and newspapers can be as informative as their news and feature articles. For example, hair straighteners and skin whiteners were for many years widely advertised in the black press. An analysis of more recent advertising, studying the impact of "black is beautiful," would reveal important sociological as well as commercial developments.

14. Blacks in Sports

For the tough, talented, and "hungry" youth of many minority groups, sports has been an avenue of escape from the ghetto to fame and fortune. For blacks this avenue, as usual, remained closed long after it was opened to other minorities. Until after World War II the only integrated professional sport was boxing, and except for occasional black athletes at northern high schools and colleges or track stars in the Olympics, amateur sports also drew the color line. But since 1945 a major breakthrough has made sports one of the most integrated institutions in America, at least on the playing field. Jackie Robinson's debut with the Brooklyn Dodgers in 1947 was an event in American social history almost comparable in importance with President Harry Truman's integration directive to the armed forces the following year. By 1970 the proportion of blacks in major league baseball and football was three times their percentage of the population; more than half the players in the National Basketball Association were blacks. The exploits of black athletes have made them heroes in the ghetto and focal points for race pride and identity.

But there is another side to this success story. Black athletes suffer many kinds of discrimination, overt and subtle. Prejudiced white coaches, teammates, and fans can make a black player's life a hell. Black athletes often feel exploited as "animals." In 1970 there were no black managers in major league baseball and no black head coaches in the National Football League. Professional sports is big business, but only recently have black personnel been employed even on a token basis in the teams' front offices. The growing discontent of black athletes has led to numerous protests and boycotts, climaxed by the clenched-fist salute of American blacks at the 1968 Olympics in Mexico City. A black sociologist, Harry Edwards, has been a leader of these protests; see his *The Revolt of the Black Athlete* (New York, 1969). For an incisive discussion of racial discrimination and black discontent in sports, see Jack Olsen, *The Black Athlete: A Shameful Story, The Myth of Integration in American Sport* (New York, 1968). Olsen's study first appeared as a five-part series in *Sports Illustrated* and, with Edwards' book, has led to considerable soul-searching and some changes in the athletic establishment. For an assessment of these changes and of what remains to be done, see Bernard E. Garnett and Frye Gaillard, *The Black Athlete—1970* (Nashville, 1970).

The best introduction to the history of blacks in sports is Edwin B. Henderson and the Editors of *Sport Magazine, The Black Athlete: Emergence and Arrival* (New York, 1968), which includes a comprehensive bibliography. Other general histories and appraisals are Edwin Bancroft Henderson, *The Negro in Sports* (Washington, 1939, rev. ed., 1949); Robert L. Nelson, *The Negro in Athletics* (New York, 1940); Harold U. Ribalou, *The Negro in American Sports* (New York, 1954); Arthur S. T. Young, *Negro Firsts in Sports* (Chicago, 1963); and Arna Bontemps, *Famous Negro Athletes* (New York, 1964).*

In the days of slavery, white planters would sometimes put two or more of the strongest neighborhood slaves into a ring and make them fight it out, for the amusement of white men, until all but one were pulverized into unconsciousness. After the Civil War several black boxers made names for themselves, but the white champions of the day usually refused to fight blacks. Finally in 1908 the white heavyweight champion, Tommy Burns, agreed to fight Jack Johnson, a black stevedore from Galveston. Johnson won and reigned for several years as champion. A controversial and unconventional hero, Johnson was in constant trouble with the white establishment. In 1937 a more modest black boxer won the heavyweight crown, and for many years Joe Louis was a model for black decorum and restraint in the world of sports. Since World War II boxing has become overwhelmingly a black sport, with Cassius Clay (who has taken the name of Muhammad Ali) setting an example for the new-style black athlete. The fullest history of black boxers up to 1938 is Nathaniel S. Fleischer, ed., *Black Dynamite: The Story of the Negro in the Prize Ring from 1782 to 1938*, 5 vols. (New York, 1938–47). For Jack Johnson, the best studies are Denzil Batchelor, *Jack Johnson and His Times*

(London, 1956) and Finis Farr, *Black Champion: The Life and Times of Jack Johnson* (New York, 1964).* Johnson is also the subject of Howard Sackler's fine play, *The Great White Hope* (New York, 1968).* For Joe Louis, see *The Joe Louis Story*, an autobiography written with the editorial aid of Chester L. Washington and Haskell Cohen (New York, 1953); and Margery Miller, *Joe Louis, American* (rev. ed., New York, 1966). Other fighters are treated in Gene Schoor, *Sugar Ray Robinson* (New York, 1951); Henry Armstrong, *Gloves, Glory, and God: An Autobiography* (Westwood, N.J., 1956); Floyd Patterson with Milton Gross, *Victory over Myself* (New York, 1962); and Jack Olsen, *Black is Best: The Riddle of Cassius Clay* (New York, 1967).

For the story of Jackie Robinson and the "grace under pressure" that enabled him to break the color line in professional baseball, see Arthur W. Mann, *The Jackie Robinson Story* (New York, 1951), and John R. Robinson, with Carl Rowan, *Wait Till Next Year: Life Story of Jackie Robinson* (New York, 1956). For the career of the next best-known black baseball player, see Willie Mays, with Charles Einstein, *My Life in and out of Baseball* (New York, 1966), and Arnold Hano, *Willie Mays* (New York, 1966). The story of the Negro leagues before the integration of professional baseball is told by Robert W. Peterson, *Only the Ball Was White* (Englewood Cliffs, N.J., 1970). The progress of blacks in basketball from the clowning of the Harlem Globetrotters to the dignity of perhaps the best player the game has produced, Bill Russell, who became the first black coach in any major league sport, can be traced by a reading of Dave Zinkoff and Edgar Williams, *Around the World with the Harlem Globetrotters* (Philadelphia, 1953), and William Russell with William McSweeney, *Go up for Glory* (New York, 1966).*

Long an upper-class sport, tennis was slow to lower its racial barriers, but in the 1950s the talented Althea Gibson could no longer be kept out of major tournaments; in 1957 she won at Wimbledon, the National Clay Courts Championship, and at Forest Hills. See her autobiography, *I Always Wanted to Be Somebody* (New York, 1958).* For the impressive story of the 1968 Forest Hills men's champion, see Arthur Ashe, with Clifford G. Gewecke, *Advantage Ashe* (New York, 1967), and esp. John McPhee, *Levels of the Game* (New York, 1969).*

Much information about black athletes appears in periodicals, especially *The Negro History Bulletin, Ebony, Sport,* and *Sports Illustrated.* For a guide to articles in these and other periodicals through 1967, consult the bibliography in *The Black Athlete: Emergence and Arrival,* cited above.

PART IX

THE CIVIL RIGHTS
REVOLUTION, 1954–1970

1. Congress, the Executive, and Civil Rights

The decade of the 1940s marked the first time in this century that a national political party, and in fact the President himself, publicly affirmed the idea that the federal government has a responsibility actively to seek improvement in the status of black people. President Franklin D. Roosevelt's Executive Order 8802 in 1941, establishing the Fair Employment Practices Committee (FEPC), was a first step in this direction, but it was President Harry S Truman and the Democratic party in the latter part of the 1940s who established civil rights as a major political issue.

The national and international climate of the 1940s made the time propitious for the promotion of black rights. World War II and its aftermath provided an extremely powerful catalyst in this respect. After a war to defend democracy against fascism and Nazi racism, and later during a "Cold War" against Communist totalitarianism, segregation became increasingly untenable in the context of the democratic faith. The substantial participation of black soldiers in the war effort underscored the irony of continued segregation on the home front. The emergence of new African nations made racial discrimination a diplomatic embarrassment, and the United Nations Charter firmly endorsed the rights of racial, ethnic, and religious minorities as a guiding principle of international society. On the home front, Afro-Americans were enjoying new economic opportunities, and wartime migrations to urban centers created a clear base for the exercise of some black political leverage. Blacks had not only important new power, but also heightened racial pride, growing out of their war service and reflecting the movements for African independence. All of these factors provided an important impetus for action in behalf of equal rights. The three branches of the federal government played important roles from the administration of Harry S Truman through that of Lyndon B. Johnson. But most of the initiative came from blacks and their white allies who formed the ranks of the modern civil rights movement.

A. The Truman Administration

In 1946 President Truman appointed a committee to investigate and report on the status of civil rights in America. Following its report, *To Secure These Rights* (Washington, 1947), the President urged the enactment of a fair employment practices law, the outlawing of poll taxes and lynching, and the elimination of segregation in interstate transportation. Later these recommendations were incorporated into the 1948 Democratic platform. Although no civil rights legislation was passed during Truman's administration, the President himself made a significant move on his own executive authority in 1948 when he ordered the desegregation of the armed forces and of the federal civil service.

The basic civil rights documents of the Truman administration (including excerpts from the report of the President's Committee on Civil Rights) can be found in Henry Steele Commager, ed., *The Struggle for Racial Equality: A Documentary Record* (New York, 1967),* pp. 35–48, and in Barton J. Bernstein and Allen J. Matusow, eds., *The Truman Administration: A Documentary History* (New York, 1966),* pp. 95–114. Truman himself makes brief reference to problems of civil rights in the second volume of his *Memoirs: Years of Trial and Hope, 1946–1952* (New York, 1956),* ch. 13, and in several speeches in David S. Horton, ed., *Freedom and Equality: Addresses by Harry S. Truman* (Columbia, Mo., 1960), chs. 1–3. For a critical assessment of Truman's civil rights record, see Barton J. Bernstein, "The Ambiguous Legacy: The Truman Administration and Civil Rights," in Barton J. Bernstein, ed., *Politics and Policies of the Truman Administration* (Chicago, 1970),* pp. 269–314. The fullest historical treatment is William C. Berman, *The Politics of Civil Rights in the Truman Administration* (Columbus, Ohio, 1970).

The President's Committee on Equality of Treatment and Opportunity in the Armed Forces published its report in *Freedom to Serve: Equality of Treatment and Opportunity in the Armed Forces* (Washington, 1950). The authoritative study by Richard M. Dalfiume, *Desegregation of the U.S. Armed Forces: Fighting*

on Two Fronts, 1939–1953 (Columbia, Mo., 1969), now super-
sedes Lee Nichols' *Breakthrough on the Color Front* (New York,
1954). Richard J. Stillman, *Integration of the Negro in the U.S.
Armed Forces* (New York, 1968), is less well done but is useful
particularly for the post-Korean era. L. D. Reddick, "The Negro
Policy of the American Army Since World War II," *JNH*,
XXXVIII (Apr. 1953), 194–215, is a perceptive contemporary
analysis. See also Dennis D. Nelson, *The Integration of the Ne-
gro into the United States Navy* (New York, 1951), and Isham
G. Newton, "The Negro and the National Guard," *Phylon*,
XXIII (Spring 1962), 18–28. Sociological and psychological
studies of Negro soldiers and the process of desegregation include
David G. Mandelbaum, *Soldier Groups and Negro Soldiers*
(Berkeley, 1952); Eli Ginzberg, *The Negro Potential* (New York,
1956),* ch. 4; Robert J. Dwyer, "The Negro in the U.S. Army,"
Sociology and Social Research, XXXVIII (1953), 103–12;
Charles C. Moskos, Jr., "Racial Integration in the Armed Forces,"
AJS, LXXII (Sept. 1966), 132–48;** and Leo Bogart, ed., *Social
Research and the Desegregation of the U.S. Army* (Chicago,
1969), which presents the two major troop opinion surveys under-
taken in 1951.

B. The Eisenhower Administration

Republican Dwight D. Eisenhower took a considerably less
activist view of the role of the federal executive with respect to
civil rights. Feeling that it was inappropriate to comment directly
on the work of the Supreme Court, Eisenhower during his presidency refrained from urging compliance with the 1954 *Brown*
decision. The President often voiced the conviction that "you
cannot change people's hearts merely by laws," and he clearly
preferred state rather than federal action against racial discrimination. Nevertheless, he sent federal troops to Little Rock, Arkansas, in 1957 to enforce court-ordered public school desegregation, and beginning in 1956 he sent some cautious civil rights
proposals to the Congress. Thanks largely to the influence of Senate Majority Leader Lyndon B. Johnson, the Congress in 1957
passed its first piece of civil rights legislation since 1875.

There are telling commentaries on Eisenhower's reluctance to move on civil rights in his own memoirs, *The White House Years*, vol. I: *Mandate for Change, 1953–1956* (Garden City, N.Y., 1963),* pp. 286–87, 292–94, and vol. II: *Waging Peace, 1956–1961* (Garden City, N.Y., 1965),* ch. 6, and in an account by his one-time speechwriter, Emmet John Hughes, *The Ordeal of Power: A Political Memoir of the Eisenhower Years* (New York, 1963), pp. 200–01, 241–45, 261. Wilson Record and Jane Cassels Record, eds., *Little Rock U.S.A.: Materials for Analysis* (San Francisco, 1960),* and Virgil T. Blossom, *It Has Happened Here* (New York, 1959), chs. 7–9 and p. 184, deal with the role of the Eisenhower administration in the Little Rock crisis. The story of the 1957 Civil Rights Act is best told in John W. Anderson, *Eisenhower, Brownell, and the Congress: The Tangled Origins of the Civil Rights Bill of 1956–57* (University, Ala., 1964); C. Vann Woodward, "The Great Civil Rights Debate," *Commentary*, XXIV (Oct. 1957), 283–91; and Foster Rhea Dulles, *The Civil Rights Commission, 1957–1965* (East Lansing, Mich., 1968).

The second Civil Rights Act of the Eisenhower administration, which dealt with voting rights and was intended to plug loopholes in the 1957 statute, was passed in 1960 against the backdrop of black sit-ins, and it provides the first clear-cut example of the impact of non-violent direct action on the legislative progress of civil rights. In addition to Dulles, see especially Daniel M. Berman, *A Bill Becomes a Law: The Civil Rights Act of 1960* (New York, 1962),* and Charles W. Havens, "Federal Legislation to Safeguard Voting Rights: The Civil Rights Act of 1960," *Virginia Law Review*, XLVI (June 1960), 945–75. Vern Countryman, ed., *Discrimination and the Law* (Chicago, 1965), is a collection of papers exploring the power of the law to curb racial and religious discrimination in employment, housing, education, and public accommodations. E. Frederic Morrow describes Eisenhower's public commitment to civil rights as frustratingly inconclusive in *Black Man in the White House: A Diary of the Eisenhower Years by the Administrative Officer for Special Projects, the White House, 1955–1961* (New York, 1963).* The biannual *Report* of the Civil Rights Commission (first published in 1959), and the appropriate sections of the general histories and documentary anthologies of the civil rights movement cited in this Part, topic 3, "The Civil Rights Movement," help fill out the

Eisenhower record on civil rights. These sources should also be consulted for the Kennedy and Johnson administrations.

C. The Kennedy Administration

The events of the early 1960s—the "freedom rides," James Meredith's attempt to enter the University of Mississippi, the crises at Birmingham and Montgomery—changed President John F. Kennedy's position on black rights from one of mild sympathy to one of vigorous, unqualified support during the course of his presidency. The Justice Department gave positive aid to the freedom riders in 1961, and in November 1962 President Kennedy issued an executive order prohibiting discrimination in federally supported housing. In 1963, after the violence in Birmingham, he asked Congress for civil rights legislation which, among other provisions, would guarantee equal access to places of public accommodation. The bill was mired in a legislative impasse at the time of President Kennedy's assassination in November 1963, but he succeeded during his presidency in wholeheartedly committing the federal government to action in behalf of civil rights, and blacks generally identified strongly with his leadership.

The best material on civil rights during the Kennedy years includes the two major biographies: Arthur M. Schlesinger, Jr., *A Thousand Days: John F. Kennedy in the White House* (Boston, 1965),* chs. 35–36, and Theodore Sorenson, *Kennedy* (New York, 1965),* ch. 28; see also chs. 2–3 of Alexander M. Bickel, *Politics and the Warren Court* (New York, 1965). The President's addresses on race relations and civil rights during 1962 and 1963 are included in ch. 6 of John F. Kennedy, *The Burden and the Glory*, ed. by Allan Nevins (New York, 1964).* Harry L. Golden gives a sympathetic, popular account in *Mr. Kennedy and the Negroes* (Cleveland, 1964). Doris E. Saunders, ed., *The Kennedy Years and the Negro* (Chicago, 1964),* includes information on black appointees and excerpts from presidential messages and speeches on civil rights as well as excellent pictures. Burke Marshall, an assistant attorney general during the Kennedy administration, assesses the potential for federal action in *Federalism and Civil Rights* (New York, 1964).

D. The Johnson Administration

President Lyndon B. Johnson's Congress finally moved to assert decisive leadership in behalf of black rights. The Twenty-fourth Amendment to the Constitution prohibiting poll taxes in federal elections went into effect in January 1964, and with full moral support and indeed urging from the White House, Congress passed the civil rights legislation President Kennedy had requested. The murders of civil rights workers Andrew Goodman, James Chaney, and Michael Schwerner in 1964, and the brutal police excesses in Selma and Montgomery in 1965, provoked congressional passage of the Voting Rights Act of 1965. In 1968, directly after the assassination of Martin Luther King, Jr., the Congress approved another Civil Rights Act whose best-known title established open housing as the law of the land.

There have been several studies of the Civil Rights Act of 1964, chief among them Benjamin Muse, *The American Negro Revolution: From Nonviolence to Black Power, 1963–1967* (Bloomington, Ind., 1968),* chs. 6, 12; Alexander M. Bickel, "The Civil Rights Act of 1964," *Commentary*, XXXVIII (Aug. 1964), 33–39; Clifford M. Lytle, "The History of the Civil Rights Bill of 1964," *JNH*, LI (Oct. 1966), 275–96; "The Controversy over the 'Equal Opportunity' Provisions of the Civil Rights Bill," *Congressional Digest*, XLIII (Mar. 1964), 67–96; Leslie A. Carothers, *The Public Accommodations Law of 1964: Arguments, Issues and Attitudes in a Legal Debate* (Northampton, Mass., 1968); Gary Orfield, *The Reconstruction of Southern Education: The Schools and the 1964 Civil Rights Act* (New York, 1969); and Bureau of National Affairs, *The Civil Rights Act of 1964: Text, Analysis, Legislative History, What It Means to Employers, Businessmen, Unions, Employees, Minority Groups* (Washington, 1964). Donald S. Strong, *Negroes, Ballots, and Judges: National Voting Rights Legislation in the Federal Courts* (University, Ala., 1968), finds the impact of the Civil Rights Acts of 1957, 1960, and 1964 on black voting to be relatively modest. On the Voting Rights Act of 1965, consult *Congressional Quarterly Weekly Report*, Aug. 6, 1965, 1539–40, and Muse, *The American Negro Revolution*, cited above, pp. 177–81, for a brief summary of the legislative history and contents; Henry Steele Commager, ed., *The Struggle for Equality: A Documentary Record* (New York, 1967),* pp. 208–30, for the President's message to Congress, the text of the bill, and the major court cases testing its legality (see also the other documentary anthologies cited in the following topic, "The Supreme Court and Civil Rights," and topic 3, "The Civil Rights Movement"); and for accounts of its initial implementation, two reports by the U.S. Commission on Civil Rights, *The Voting Rights Act: The First Months* (Washington, 1965), and *Political Participation: A Study of the Participation by Negroes in the Electoral and Political Processes in 10 Southern States Since Passage of the Voting Rights Act of 1965* (Washington, 1968). On the failure to secure civil rights legislation in 1966, see Muse, *The American Negro Revolution*, cited above, ch. 17. Topic 7, below, "Housing for Black Americans," includes references for the Civil Rights Act of 1968.

Bickel's *Politics and the Warren Court*, cited above, provides a good summary of the federal government's activities respecting civil rights during the Johnson administration. In addition, see Tom Wicker, *JFK and LBJ: The Influence of Personality Upon Politics* (New York, 1968),* ch. 11, and the relevant portions of Eric F. Goldman, *The Tragedy of Lyndon Johnson* (New York, 1969).* Harold C. Fleming, "The Federal Executive and Civil Rights: 1961–1965," *Daedalus*, XCIV (Fall 1965), 921–48, which also appears as pp. 371–400 of Talcott Parsons and Kenneth B. Clark, eds., *The Negro American* (Boston, 1966),* is an important essay that surveys the precedents for executive action in civil rights since World War II and evaluates the Kennedy-Johnson record in three respects: "administrative action and executive orders, law enforcement, and presidential leadership and legislative proposals." Ruth P. Morgan, *The President and Civil Rights: Policy-Making by Executive Order* (New York, 1970),* analyzes developments from the Roosevelt through the Johnson administrations. For a documentary account of federal executive and legislative action in behalf of blacks from Truman through Johnson, see Richard Bardolph, ed., *The Civil Rights Record: Black Americans and the Law, 1849–1970* (New York, 1970),* pp. 242–43, 246–50, 302–08, 352–66, 394–425. Joseph Parker Witherspoon, *Admin-*

310 THE CIVIL RIGHTS REVOLUTION

istrative Implementation of Civil Rights (Austin, Tex., 1968) is
a detailed study on the federal, state, and local level.

E. State and Local Legislation

Duane Lockard treats non-federal FEPC, fair housing, and
public accommodations legislation during this period in *Toward
Equal Opportunity: A Study of State and Local Antidiscrimination
Laws* (New York, 1968).* Theodore Leskes looks at "State Law
Against Discrimination" in these same areas and in education in
chs. 6–9 of Milton R. Konvitz, *A Century of Civil Rights* (New
York, 1961).* In addition, see the Bureau of National Affairs, *State
Fair Employment Laws and Their Administration: Texts, Federal-
State Cooperation, Prohibited Acts* (Washington, 1964), and
Witherspoon, *Administrative Implementation of Civil Rights*,
cited above. Bardolph, *The Civil Rights Record*, also cited above,
includes a representative sampling of state laws protecting civil
rights and discriminating against blacks. See pp. 188–98, 250–64 for
1910–54, and pp. 366–93 on the period since 1954. Leon H. May-
hew, *Law and Equal Opportunity: A Study of the Massachusetts
Commission Against Discrimination* (Cambridge, Mass., 1968),
is a sociological case study of the role of antidiscrimination laws
and the legal agency responsible for their implementation in regu-
lating race relations in Boston. Morroe Berger examines New
York State laws against employment discrimination as a case study
in ch. 4 of *Equality by Statute: The Revolution in Civil Rights*
(Garden City, N.Y., 1952, rev. ed., 1967).* For further information on New York, see Jay Anders Higbee, *Development and Administration of the New York Law Against Discrimination* (University, Ala., 1966).

2. The Supreme Court and Civil Rights

Beginning during World War I, but especially after *Brown* v.
Board of Education in 1954, the Supreme Court has established
itself as a major protector of black rights. Before *Brown*, the

Court's attack against segregation centered on two major areas, the right to vote and equal access to education. A series of cases wiped out the "grandfather clauses" and the white primary systems which southern states had devised to exclude blacks from voting; others established the right of blacks to attend previously all-white institutions of higher education. *Brown*, which struck down legal segregation in public education (see topic 5, below, "Since *Brown* v. *Board of Education*: Black Education After 1954"), is generally regarded as a major factor in the emergence of the modern civil rights movement. In the decade after *Brown*, the Warren Court concerned itself with cases testing the constitutionality of federal civil rights legislation, which it uniformly upheld, and with cases testing the legality of sit-ins and similar demonstrations, which it confirmed with few exceptions.

There are several excellent collections of documents on the Court and civil rights. Among the best are Joseph Tussman, ed., *The Supreme Court on Racial Discrimination* (New York, 1963);* Norman Dorsen, *Discrimination and Civil Rights: Cases, Text, and Materials* (Boston, 1969);* and Richard Bardolph, ed., *The Civil Rights Record: Black Americans and the Law, 1849–1970* (New York, 1970),* pp. 199–214, 265–93, 426–536. Of the secondary studies, the best include Loren Miller, *The Petitioners: The Story of the Supreme Court of the United States and the Negro* (New York, 1966),* chs. 14–29; Jack Greenberg, *Race Relations and American Law* (New York, 1959); Alexander M. Bickel, *Politics and the Warren Court* (New York, 1965), chs. 1–3; Archibald Cox, *The Warren Court: Constitutional Decision as an Instrument of Reform* (Cambridge, Mass., 1968), chs. 2–3; and Robert J. Harris, *The Quest for Equality: The Constitution, Congress and the Supreme Court* (Baton Rouge, 1960), chs. 3–6. Other useful works include Benjamin Munn Ziegler, ed., *Desegregation and the Supreme Court* (Boston, 1958);* Milton R. Konvitz, *The Constitution and Civil Rights* (New York, 1947), and, with Theodore Leskes, *A Century of Civil Rights* (New York, 1961),* ch. 5; Morroe Berger, *Equality by Statute: The Revolution in Civil Rights* (Garden City, N.Y., 1952, rev. ed., 1967),* chs. 1–3; Paul A. Freund, "Civil Rights and the Frontiers of Law," in Talcott Parsons and Kenneth B. Clark, eds., *The Negro American* (Boston, 1966),* pp. 363–70, and "Separate-But-Equal: A

Study of the Career of a Constitutional Concept," *Race Relations Law Reporter*, I (Feb. 1956), 283–92; Edward F. Waite, "The Negro in the Supreme Court," *Minnesota Law Review*, XXX (Mar. 1946), 219–304; Ernest Kaiser, "The Federal Government and the Negro, 1865–1955," *Science and Society*, XX (Winter 1956), 27–58; and A. E. Dick Howard, "Mr. Justice Black: The Negro Protest Movement and the Rule of Law," *Virginia Law Review*, LIII (June 1967), 1030–90. Vols. 3 and 4 of Leon Friedman and Fred L. Israel, comps., *The Justices of the United States Supreme Court, 1789–1961: Their Lives and Major Opinions*, 4 vols. (New York, 1969), cover the period since 1915; several decisions concerning black rights are treated in detail. Major cases are classified according to type, with appropriate legal references, in "A Chronology of Principal Cases on Segregation, 1878–1959," *New South*, XIV (Oct. 1959), 8–13. The U. S. Commission on Civil Rights, *Freedom to the Free: Century of Emancipation, 1863–1963* (Washington, 1963), is a brief review which also includes a bibliography of court cases and legislation. Charles S. Mangum, Jr., gives a comprehensive accounting of *The Legal Status of the Negro* (Chapel Hill, 1940) on the basis of state and federal court cases and statutes.

On school desegregation, see Albert P. Blaustein and Clarence C. Ferguson, Jr., *Desegregation and the Law: The Meaning and Effect of the School Segregation Cases* (New Brunswick, N.J., 1957, rev. ed., New York, 1962);* Daniel M. Berman, *It Is So Ordered: The Supreme Court Rules on School Segregation* (New York, 1966);* Leon Friedman, ed., *Argument: The Complete Oral Argument Before The Supreme Court in Brown v. Board of Education of Topeka, 1952–55* (New York, 1969), and additional references in Part VII, topic 9, "Higher Education and Black Scholarship," and topic 5, below, "Since *Brown v. Board of Education*: Black Education After 1954." Harry Kalven, Jr., *The Negro and the First Amendment* (Columbus, Ohio, 1965),* and Archibald Cox, "Direct Action, Civil Disobedience, and the Constitution," in Cox, Mark De Wolfe Howe, and J. R. Wiggins, *Civil Rights, the Constitution, and the Courts* (Cambridge, Mass., 1967), pp. 2–29, consider the legality of sit-ins and other forms of protest, but the wide range of law review articles on the sit-in cases (which can best be located through notes in Dorsen, cited above, and similar sources) should also be consulted. Voting rights cases are treated in Charles Aikin, ed., *The Negro Votes* (San Francisco, 1962),* chs. 3–5; R. W. Hainsworth, "The Negro and the Texas Primaries," *JNH*, XVIII (Oct. 1933), 426–50; Bernard Taper, *Gomillion versus Lightfoot: The Tuskegee Gerrymander Case* (New York, 1963); and a sequel by Taper, "A Reporter at Large: A Break with Tradition," *New Yorker*, XLI (July 24, 1965), 58 ff. Other useful studies of particular aspects of the drive for equal rights in the courts include Bernard Nelson, *The Fourteenth Amendment and the Negro Since 1920* (Washington, 1946); Clement E. Vose, *Caucasians Only: The Supreme Court, the NAACP and the Restrictive Covenant Cases* (Berkeley, 1959);* and Sarah M. Lemmon, "Transportation Segregation in the Federal Courts since 1865," *JNH*, XXXVIII (Apr. 1953), 174–93. S. Sidney Ulmer, "Supreme Court Behavior in Racial Exclusion Cases: 1935–1960," *APSR*, LVI (June 1962), 325–30, is a quantitative analysis of the Court's handling of cases involving the exclusion of blacks from jury service in state courts.

The Warren Court has usually been regarded as a major champion of black rights. In "A Critic's View of the Warren Court— Nine Men in Black Who Think White," *New York Times Magazine*, Oct. 13, 1968, 56–57 ff., Lewis Steel registers a surprising and controversial dissent, charging instead that the Court "has not departed from the American tradition of treating Negroes as second-class citizens." The upshot of the publication of this article was Steel's dismissal as associate counsel of the NAACP and the subsequent resignation of most of its legal staff to protest Steel's ouster.

In 1967 U. S. Solicitor General Thurgood Marshall, formerly the director–counsel of the NAACP's Legal Defense and Education Fund, became the first black man ever to sit on the Supreme Court. See John P. MacKenzie, "Thurgood Marshall," in Friedman and Israel, *The Justices of the United States Supreme Court*, cited above, vol. 4, pp. 3063–92, and Ronald R. Davenport, "The Second Justice Marshall," *Duquesne University Law Review*, VII (1968), 44–60.

On civil rights and the state courts during the twentieth century, see Bardolph, *The Civil Rights Record*, cited above, pp. 215–32, 294–300.

3. The Civil Rights Movement

At the close of World War II, blacks in the United States were still treated as second-class citizens. Throughout the South, and in many northern states and communities as well, blacks were denied equal access with whites to places of public accommodation such as restaurants, parks, and movie theaters, and they were relegated to the back of the bus or to separate railroad cars. Black children were segregated in separate and inferior public schools, while adults were often denied their rightful franchise and almost always severely restricted in their employment opportunities.

The NAACP had for decades worked laboriously through the courts to secure the legal establishment of black rights, while the National Urban League had concerned itself primarily with the attainment of economic opportunities and the provision of social services. These activities would continue through the 1950s and 1960s, but legal petitioning, interracial teamwork, and private entreaties were to be joined then by a new style of black protest: large-scale, non-violent direct action to achieve the desired goal of full integration into every aspect of American life. To be sure, the philosophy and techniques of non-violent direct action had been developed by the Congress of Racial Equality (CORE) during World War II, and the concept of mass black action to redress discrimination had been central to A. Philip Randolph's "March on Washington" movement in the early 1940s. But it was not until the 1950s and especially the 1960s that their effectiveness as weapons in the civil rights struggle was actually tested and confirmed.

As yet we have no scholarly history of the momentous efforts of blacks and whites during the 1950s and 1960s to secure black rights, but Anthony Lewis and the New York *Times, Portrait of a Decade: The Second American Revolution* (New York, 1964),* and two vols. by Benjamin Muse, *Ten Years of Prelude: The Story of Integration Since the Supreme Court's 1954 Decision* (New York, 1964), and *The American Negro Revolution: From Nonviolence to Black Power, 1963–1967* (Bloomington, Ind., 1968),* provide an informed narrative of the major events beginning with the *Brown* decision. Chs. 4 and 5 of C. Vann Woodward's interpretive essay, *The Strange Career of Jim Crow* (New York, 1955, rev. ed., 1966),* with a suggestive analysis of the civil rights movement as a "Second Reconstruction," ought not to be missed. Simeon Booker, *Black Man's America* (Englewood Cliffs, N.J., 1964), is a popular history of the struggle for civil rights. Debbie Louis, *And We Are Not Saved: A History of the Movement as People* (Garden City, N.Y., 1970),* is an account with special emphasis on the involvement of young people, written from the perspective of a young white CORE worker. An exceptionally rich documentary record makes it easy to study various aspects of the movement. The most thorough of the many collections already published is Leon Friedman, ed., *The Civil Rights Reader: Basic Documents of the Civil Rights Movement* (New York, 1967).* Other volumes of primary source materials are August Meier and Elliott Rudwick, eds., *Black Protest in the Sixties* (Chicago, 1970);* Henry Steele Commager, ed., *The Struggle for Racial Equality: A Documentary Record* (New York, 1967);* Albert P. Blaustein and Robert L. Zangrando, eds., *Civil Rights and the American Negro: A Documentary History* (New York, 1968),* chs. 7, 8; Richard A. Bardolph, ed., *The Civil Rights Record: Black Americans and the Law, 1849–1970* (New York, 1970),* pt. 6; Joanne Grant, ed., *Black Protest: History, Documents, and Analyses, 1619 to the Present* (New York, 1968),* pts. 6, 7; and Staughton Lynd, ed., *Nonviolence in America: A Documentary History* (Indianapolis, 1966),* pt. 9. The *Civil Rights Digest, A Quarterly of the U.S. Commission on Civil Rights* includes articles and bibliography on various aspects of civil rights. Lester A. Sobel, ed., *Civil Rights, 1960–66* (New York, 1967),* is a detailed journalistic narrative drawn largely from *Facts on File*. The Congressional Quarterly Service provides a summary of Supreme Court decisions, congressional action, proposals, reports, as well as charts, statistics, and brief accounts of major events in *Revolution in Civil Rights, 1945–1968* (4th ed., Washington, June 1968).* Alan F. Westin, ed., *Freedom Now! The Civil Rights Struggle in America* (New York, 1964), pt. 3, gives a detailed accounting of the kinds of discriminatory practices the civil rights movement strove to reverse. Frank W. Hale, Jr.,

The Cry for Freedom: An Anthology of the Best That Has Been Said and Written on Civil Rights Since 1954 (South Brunswick, N.J., and New York, 1969), is an anthology of the most important civil rights speeches. A Boston minister, Jack Mendelsohn, presents sympathetic biographical accounts of the movement's best-known casualties from the decade 1955-65 in *The Martyrs: Sixteen Who Gave Their Lives for Racial Justice* (New York, 1966). Lerone Bennett, Jr., *Confrontation: Black and White* (Chicago, 1965),* esp. pts. 4-5 and the epilogue, provides a thoughtful overview of the black revolt. James A. Geschwender, "Social Structure and the Negro Revolt: An Examination of Some Hypotheses," *SF*, XLIII (Dec. 1964), 248-56,** is a critical evaluation of common sociological explanations of the emergence of black protest. For analyses of the forces that came to dissipate the energy and achievements of the movement, see C. Vann Woodward, "What Happened to the Civil Rights Movement?" *Harper's*, CCXXXIV (Jan. 1967), 29-37, and John Herbers, *The Lost Priority: What Happened to the Civil Rights Movement in America?* (New York, 1970).

A. Montgomery: Non-violent Direct Action and the Emergence of Martin Luther King

The modern civil rights movement is generally dated from the Supreme Court's landmark decision in *Brown* v. *Board of Education* in 1954. Nineteen fifty-five marked the emergence of non-violent direct action as the blacks of Montgomery, Alabama, staged an eleven-month boycott of the city's buses to protest discriminatory treatment. Although it took a 1956 Supreme Court decision to end segregation on Montgomery's buses, the boycott demonstrated the possibilities of non-violent direct action as a technique in the civil rights struggle. It became a model for subsequent civil rights activity, and it set the dominant style of the civil rights movement for the next decade. It showed conclusively that blacks could unite on their own initiative to seek their rights, and it introduced a new group of young, southern, black leaders, notably the Reverend Dr. Martin Luther King, Jr.

The best sources for an understanding of the events and significance of the Montgomery bus boycott are King's own account, *Stride Toward Freedom: The Montgomery Story* (New York,

1958),* and several contemporary articles, chief among them Norman W. Walton's five-part series, "The Walking City, A History of the Montgomery Boycott," *NHB*, XX (Oct., Nov. 1956, Feb., Apr. 1957), 17–21, 27–33, 102–04, 147–52, 166; XXI (Jan. 1958), 75–76, 81; "Attack on Conscience," *Time*, LXIX (Feb. 18, 1957), 17–20; Abel Plenn, "Report on Montgomery a Year After," *New York Times Magazine*, Dec. 29, 1957, 11, 36, 38; and two conflicting views in Martin Luther King, Jr., and Grover C. Hall, Jr. (editor of the Montgomery *Advertiser*), "Alabama's Bus Boycott: What It's All About," *U.S. News & World Report*, XLI (Aug. 3, 1956), 82–89. Preston Valien, "The Montgomery Bus Protest as a Social Movement," in Jitsuichi Masuoka and Preston Valien, eds., *Race Relations: Problems and Theory* (Chapel Hill, 1961),* pp. 112–27, and Donald H. Smith, "Martin Luther King, Jr.: In the Beginning at Montgomery," *Southern Speech Journal*, XXXIV (Fall 1968), 8–17, are also useful. Jacquelyne Clark compares the work of the Montgomery Improvement Association to the (Birmingham) Alabama Christian Movement for Human Rights and the Tuskegee Civic Association over the period 1954–59 in *These Rights They Seek: A Comparison of the Goals and Techniques of Local Civil Rights Organizations* (Washington, 1962).

One of the significant consequences of Montgomery was the emergence of Dr. King as a major figure in the civil rights movement. King's own writings provide a capsule history of important events in civil rights as well as an insight into the evolution of his personal objectives and the tactics he was willing to espouse in order to realize them. In addition to *Stride Toward Freedom*, his most important works are *Why We Can't Wait* (New York, 1964),* an account of the movement against segregation in Birmingham in 1963 which includes the famous "Letter from a Birmingham Jail"; *Where Do We Go From Here: Chaos or Community?* (New York, 1967),* in which he reaffirms non-violent direct action and rejects black power as a form of separatism; and *The Trumpet of Conscience* (New York, 1968), a collection of addresses delivered months before he died, in which he advocates mass civil disobedience to combat poverty and racism.

David L. Lewis' *King: A Critical Biography* (New York, 1970)* is an excellent study of its subject. Among the laudatory biographies, the best are Lawrence D. Reddick, Jr., *Crusader Without*

318 THE CIVIL RIGHTS REVOLUTION

Violence: A Biography of Martin Luther King, Jr. (New York, 1959); Lerone Bennett, Jr., *What Manner of Man: A Biography of Martin Luther King, Jr.* (Chicago, 1964, rev. ed., 1968),* and William Robert Miller, *Martin Luther King, Jr.: His Life, Martyrdom and Meaning for the World* (New York, 1968).* C. Eric Lincoln, ed., *Martin Luther King, Jr.: A Profile* (New York, 1970),* is a handy combination of selections from King's own writings and the assessments of other writers. Hanes Walton, Jr., *The Political Philosophy of Martin Luther King, Jr.* (Westport, Conn., 1971), is a critical analysis of King's political thought. John A. Williams presents an elaborate conspiracy theory of King's assassination in *The King God Didn't Save: Reflections on the Life and Death of Martin Luther King, Jr.* (New York, 1970). Coretta Scott King tells of her husband's career in *My Life With Martin Luther King, Jr.* (New York, 1969).* Among the numerous articles on King, the most important assessment is by August Meier, "On the Role of Martin Luther King," *New Politics*, IV (Winter 1965), 52–59,** which describes King as a "conservative militant" whose "enormous success" is attributable to a "combination of militancy with conservatism and caution, of righteousness with respectability." David Halberstam, "The Second Coming of Martin Luther King," *Harper's*, CCXXXV (Aug. 1967), 39–51, treats King's emergence as an important spokesman against the war in Vietnam. King himself discusses the war in *The Trumpet of Conscience*, cited above.

For the Southern Christian Leadership Conference (SCLC), the organization of southern black ministers that King founded, see Edward T. Clayton, ed., *The SCLC Story* (Atlanta, 1964), and Nat Hentoff, "A Peaceful Army," *Commonweal*, LXXII (June 10, 1960), 275–78. Three studies that focus on the technique of non-violence are William Robert Miller, *Nonviolence: A Christian Interpretation* (New York, 1966);* Howard Thurman, *Disciplines of the Spirit* (New York, 1963); and Frederic Solomon and Jacob R. Fishman, "The Psychosocial Meaning of Nonviolence in Student Civil Rights Activities," *Psychiatry*, XXVII (May 1964), 91–99.

B. The Question of Tactics: Moderate Legalism vs. Direct Action Radicalism

In the wake of Montgomery, sit-ins, freedom rides, boycotts, and mass marches became better known than court fights as the hallmark of civil rights activity, and direct action challenged the old moderate legalism as the governing strategy of the civil rights movement. Once supreme in civil rights leadership, the NAACP in the early 1960s found itself largely eclipsed by the newly-emerged SCLC and SNCC (Student Nonviolent Coordinating Committee) and the resurgent CORE (Congress of Racial Equality), all more successful than the NAACP in appealing to the black masses. For an introduction to the viewpoints of the major organizations and leading individuals, the best place to start is in documentary anthologies, particularly Alan F. Westin, ed., *Freedom Now! The Civil Rights Struggle in America* (New York, 1964), pts. 1, 4, 5, and Francis L. Broderick and August Meier, eds., *Negro Protest Thought in the Twentieth Century* (Indianapolis, 1965),* pt. 4, which corresponds to pt. 3 of August Meier, Elliott Rudwick, and Francis L. Broderick, eds., *Black Protest Thought in the Twentieth Century* (rev. ed., Indianapolis, 1971).* Richard Bardolph, ed., *The Civil Rights Record: Black Americans and the Law, 1849–1970* (New York, 1970),* pp. 311–51, is also useful. Kenneth B. Clark provides a succinct analysis of the methods of the major organizations working for black advancement in "The Civil Rights Movement: Momentum and Organization," in the book he edited with Talcott Parsons, *The Negro American* (Boston, 1966),* pp. 595–625. Another important interpretive essay on this subject is August Meier and Elliott Rudwick, "Radicals and Conservatives: Black Protest in Twentieth-Century America," in Peter I. Rose, ed., *Americans from Africa*, vol. II: *Old Memories, New Moods* (New York, 1970),* pp. 119–47. Arnold M. Rose, ed., *The Negro Protest* (Philadelphia, 1965) (the entire vol. CCCLVII, Jan. 1965, issue of the *Annals*), esp. the last section entitled "Different Means to the Goal," is an excellent series of articles. Kenneth B. Clark, ed., *The Negro Protest: James Baldwin, Malcolm X, Martin Luther King Talk with Kenneth B. Clark* (Boston, 1963), affords an interesting comparison of the views of these major figures. W. Haywood Burns analyzes the relationship among legal-judicial, non-violent, and radical-separatist forms of protest in *The Voices of Negro Protest in America* (New York, 1963), while Robert Penn Warren considers the alternatives in *Who Speaks for the Negro?* (New York, 1965).* See also James Q. Wilson, "The Strategy of Protest: Problems of Negro Civic Action," *Journal of Conflict Resolution*, V (Sept. 1961), 291–303,** and Richard P. Young, ed., *Roots of Rebellion: The Evolution of Black Politics and Protest Since World War II* (New York, 1970),* pts. 4–5.

Louis E. Lomax, *The Negro Revolt* (New York, 1962),* is an extremely provocative although at times superficial review of civil rights activities and leadership through the early 1960s. August Meier's "The Revolution Against the NAACP: A Critical Appraisal of Louis E. Lomax's *The Negro Revolt*," *JNE*, XXXII (Spring 1963), 146–52, points up Lomax's shortcomings and, together with Meier's "Negro Protest Movements and Organizations," *ibid.* (Fall 1963), 437–50, sets forth the thesis that rivalries among the various organizations are "not due so much to differences in philosophy, tactics or degree of militancy as much as to a power struggle for hegemony in the civil rights movement." A third Meier article, "New Currents in the Civil Rights Movement," *New Politics*, II (Summer 1963), 27–29, deals with the role of radical revolutionary groups in black protest movements. Charles Silberman, *Crisis in Black and White* (New York, 1964),* ch. 5, comments on the development of civil rights activities beyond NAACP-style tactics, while Robert L. Zangrando discusses the rejection of the NAACP by militants in the 1960s in "The 'Organized Negro': The National Association for the Advancement of Colored People and Civil Rights," in James C. Curtis and Lewis L. Gould, eds., *The Black Experience in America: Selected Essays* (Austin, Tex., 1970),* pp. 145–71. Three interpretive treatments of the changing thrust of the movement are Vincent Harding, "Black Radicalism: The Road from Montgomery," in Alfred F. Young, ed., *Dissent: Explorations in the History of American Radicalism* (De Kalb, Ill., 1968),* pp. 319–54; Robert L. Zangrando, "From Civil Rights to Black Liberation: The Unsettled 1960's," *Current History*, LVII (Nov. 1969), 281–86, 299; and Elliott Rudwick and August Meier, "Organizational

Structure and Goal Succession: A Comparative Analysis of the NAACP and CORE, 1964–1968," *SSQ*, LI (June 1970), 9–41.

A consistent voice of moderation supporting the old legalistic approach to civil rights and arguing for the importance of coalition with white allies is Bayard Rustin, who sets forth his views in several important articles: "From Protest to Politics: The Future of the Civil Rights Movement," *Commentary*, XXXIX (Feb. 1965), 25–31; "'Black Power' and Coalition Politics," *ibid.*, XLII (Sept. 1966), 35–40; "The Failure of Black Separatism," *Harper's*, CCXL (Jan. 1970), 25–34; "The Meaning of Birmingham," *Liberation*, VIII (June 1963), 7–9, 31; and "The Meaning of the March on Washington," *ibid.*, VIII (Oct. 1963), 11–13. Oscar Handlin suggests that insistence on integration (which he labels "a false issue") as such is a mistake insofar as it obscures the real issue of achieving equality within our urban industrial society; see his essay "The Goals of Integration," in Parsons and Clark, eds., *The Negro American*, cited above, pp. 659–77, and his book *Fire-Bell in the Night: The Crisis in Civil Rights* (Boston, 1964).*

Two books by James Boggs, *The American Revolution: Pages from a Negro Worker's Notebook* (New York, 1963),* and *Racism and the Class Struggle: Further Pages from a Black Worker's Notebook* (New York, 1970),* and Robert Williams, *Negroes with Guns* (New York, 1962), are radical black critiques of the approach of moderate civil rights organizations. The position of the Black Muslims is treated below in topic 10, "Black Nationalism Since World War II." On the other end of the spectrum, the views of the most conservative of the organizations working for black advancement, the National Urban League, are set forth in three works by its late executive director, Whitney M. Young, Jr. —*To Be Equal* (New York, 1964);* "Civil Rights Action and the Urban League," in Arnold M. Rose, ed., *Assuring Freedom to the Free: A Century of Emancipation in the USA* (Detroit, 1964), pp. 210–19; and "Civil Rights and a Militant Profession," National Conference on Social Welfare, *The Social Welfare Forum, 1965* (New York, 1965), pp. 42–54—and in Allan Morrison, "'New Look' for the Urban League," *Ebony*, XXI (Nov. 1965), 164–75. For an introduction to CORE, see its former national director James Farmer's book *Freedom—When?* (New York,

1966), and Inge Powell Bell, *CORE and the Strategy of Non-violence* (New York, 1968).* Its origins in the 1940s are best treated in August Meier and Elliott Rudwick, "How CORE Began," *SSQ*, XLIX (Mar. 1969), 789–99.**

Howard Zinn's *SNCC: The New Abolitionists* (Boston, 1964)* is a solid history which carries SNCC from its birth at the outset of the sit-in movement to 1964. For an insight into the major changes in SNCC since the publication of Zinn's book, the best sources are Allen J. Matusow, "From Civil Rights to Black Power: The Case of SNCC, 1960–1966," in Barton J. Bernstein and Allen J. Matusow, eds., *Twentieth-Century America: Recent Interpretations* (New York, 1969),* pp. 531–57; Jack Newfield, "The Question of SNCC," *Nation*, CCI (July 19, 1965), 38–40; Gene Roberts, "The Story of Snick: From 'Freedom High' to 'Black Power,'" *New York Times Magazine*, Sept. 25, 1966, 27–29 ff.; Anne Braden, "The SNCC Trends: Challenge to White America," *Southern Patriot*, XXIV (May 1966), 1–3; Lerone Bennett, Jr., "SNCC: Rebels with a Cause," *Ebony*, XX (July 1965), 146–53; E. J. Shoben, Jr., and P. R. Werdell, "SDS and SNCC: Profiles of Two Student Organizations," *School and Society*, XCVI (Oct. 26, 1968), 365–73; Paul Good, "Odyssey of a Man—And a Movement," *New York Times Magazine*, June 25, 1967, 5, 44–48 (on John Lewis); two articles by Andrew Kopkind in the *New Republic*, "New Radicals in Dixie: Those 'Subversive' Civil Rights Workers," CLII (Apr. 10, 1965), 13–16, and "The Future of 'Black Power': A Movement in Search of a Program," CLVI (Jan. 7, 1967), 16–18; and H. Rap Brown, *Die Nigger Die!* (New York, 1969),* chs. 9–11.

Three public opinion surveys sponsored by *Newsweek*—William Brink and Louis Harris, *The Negro Revolution in America* (New York, 1964),* esp. ch. 7; their *Black and White: A Study of U.S. Racial Attitudes Today* (New York, 1967),* esp. ch. 3; and Peter Goldman, *Report from Black America* (New York, 1970), ch. 2, app. C—reveal black attitudes toward the spectrum of civil rights leadership.

C. The Early 1960s: Special Studies

The major events of the civil rights movement in the early 1960s are treated in the material cited above. In addition, there is a growing literature on particular aspects of the movement. Studies of the sit-ins include Glenford E. Mitchell and William H. Peace III, eds., *The Angry Black South* (New York, 1962),* a collection of essays by participants in the original sit-in; Miles Wolff, *Lunch at the Five and Ten: The Greensboro Sit-ins—A Contemporary History* (New York, 1970); *Diary of a Sit-In* (Chapel Hill, 1962),* Merrill Proudfoot's day-by-day account of events in Knoxville, Tennessee, in June and July 1960; Jack L. Walker, *Sit-Ins in Atlanta: A Study in the Negro Revolt* (New York, 1964); Ruth Searles and J. Allen Williams, Jr., "Negro College Students' Participation in Sit-ins," *SF*, XL (Mar. 1962), 215–20; and Charles U. Smith, "The Sit-Ins and the New Negro Student," *Journal of Intergroup Relations*, II (Summer 1961), 223–29. "Negro Students and the Protest Movement," ch. 14 of Donald R. Matthews and James W. Prothro, *Negroes and the New Southern Politics* (New York, 1966),* deals with participants in the sit-ins and freedom rides. Two former CORE officials, James Farmer and James Peck, have written of the freedom rides in *Freedom—When?* (New York, 1966) and *Freedom Ride* (New York, 1962), respectively.

James Forman, *Sammy Younge, Jr.* (New York, 1968),* a biography of the first southern black college student to be killed in the course of the civil rights movement, contains revealing insights into SNCC and the black community in the South. Michael Dorman gives his view of events in the South from "Ole Miss" in the fall of 1962 through Tuscaloosa the following summer in *We Shall Overcome: A Reporter's Eyewitness Account of the Year of Racial Strife and Triumph* (New York, 1965).* Walter Lord, *The Past That Would Not Die* (New York, 1965), is a popular narrative of the struggle to enroll James Meredith at the University of Mississippi. John Ehle, *The Free Men* (New York, 1964), the best case study thus far of a local civil rights movement, describes efforts to desegregate Chapel Hill, North Carolina, during 1963–64. Pt. 3 of Howard Zinn, *The Southern Mystique* (New York, 1964), deals with the battle over civil rights in Albany, Georgia, during the early 1960s. David Stahl, Frederick B. Sussman, and Neil J. Bloomfield, *The Community and Racial Crises* (New York, 1966), presents case studies of the efforts of several communities to handle racial demonstrations and discusses the appropriate legal tools. William M. Kunstler, a northern lawyer prominent in defending civil rights workers, tells of his activities in the South from 1961 to 1964 in *Deep in My Heart* (New York, 1966). Anne Moody, *Coming of Age in Mississippi* (New York, 1968),* is a moving autobiography of a young black girl actively involved in the movement. Martin Oppenheimer and George La Rey give step-by-step practical pointers on how it's done in *A Manual for Direct Action: Strategy and Tactics for Civil Rights and All Other Nonviolent Protest Movements* (Chicago, 1965).* Lorraine Hansberry, *The Movement: Documentary of a Struggle for Equality* (New York, 1964),* provides excellent pictures of the civil rights movement of the early 1960s; Guy and Candie Carawan, eds., capture much of its mood in *We Shall Overcome! Songs of the Southern Freedom Movement* (New York, 1963).*

On the 1963 March on Washington, see "For Jobs and Freedom: Three Views of the Washington March," *Midwest Quarterly*, V (Winter 1964), 99–116; Bayard Rustin, "The Meaning of the March on Washington," *Liberation*, VIII (Oct. 1963), 11–13; Margaret Long, "March on Washington," *New South*, XVIII (Sept. 1963), 3–17; Martin Luther King, Jr., *Why We Can't Wait* (New York, 1964),* pp. 122–25; and the photographic record in Doris E. Saunders, *The Day They Marched* (Chicago, 1963).* Anna Arnold Hedgeman, the sole woman member of the executive committee for the march, discusses the planning for it in her autobiography, *The Trumpet Sounds: A Memoir of Negro Leadership* (New York, 1964), ch. 9.

D. Mississippi Summer

Participants and journalists have given us a graphic account of the "Freedom Summer" of 1964, sponsored by COFO (Council of Federated Organizations), which had three major foci: "Freedom Schools," community service projects, and a massive voter education and registration drive in the interests of the Mississippi Freedom Democratic Party (MFDP). The best of the histories by participants is SNCC worker Sally Belfrage's evocative *Freedom Summer* (New York, 1965).* For other perspectives, see William McCord, *Mississippi: The Long Hot Summer* (New York, 1965); Tracy Sugarman, *Stranger at the Gates: A Summer in Mississippi* (New York, 1966); and Elizabeth Sutherland, ed., *Let-*

ters from Mississippi (New York, 1965),* a moving collection of writings by northern white youths who participated in the project. Florence Howe has studied "Mississippi's Freedom Schools: The Politics of Education," *Harvard Educational Review*, XXXV (Spring 1965), 141–60. Students who attended the schools speak in Langston Hughes, ed., *Freedom School Poetry* (Atlanta, 1966).

Len Holt tells the story of Mississippi 1964 from the perspective of a key black civil rights lawyer in *The Summer That Didn't End* (New York, 1965), while newspaper reporter Nicholas Von Hoffman provides a disturbing portrait in his *Mississippi Notebook* (New York, 1964). William Bradford Huie recounts the murders of civil rights workers Andrew Goodman, James Chaney, and Michael Schwerner in *Three Lives for Mississippi* (New York, 1965).* For a different perspective, see Don Whitehead, *Attack on Terror: The FBI Against the Ku Klux Klan in Mississippi* (New York, 1970). James W. Silver, *Mississippi: The Closed Society* (New York, 1964, rev. ed., 1966),* provides excellent background by a former professor at "Ole Miss" who is highly critical of his native state. Bruce Hilton, *The Delta Ministry* (New York, 1969),* tells of civil rights activities in Mississippi after the Freedom Summer.

The related story of a voter registration effort in Fayette County, Tennessee, is told in Fayette County Project Volunteers, *Step by Step: Evolution and Operation of the Cornell Students' Civil-Rights Project in Tennessee, Summer, 1964* (New York, 1965).

On the Mississippi Freedom Democratic Party, see below, topic 9, "Black Political Power."

4. The Church and the Civil Rights Movement

Except for a brief period during the Civil War and Reconstruction, established leaders of white churches have generally supported the status quo in race relations. A radical minority of churchmen always challenged the status quo and furnished leadership for such protest movements as abolitionism and the NAACP, but the institutional church confined its efforts largely to such safe activities as education and mission work. In the quarter century since World War II and especially during the 1960s, however, white clergymen of all faiths have become increasingly radical on the race issue. A revived commitment to the social gospel has focused with growing intensity on the civil rights struggle. Ministers, nuns, rabbis, and priests have been conspicuous in the freedom rides, marches, and demonstrations of the past decade; several clergymen of both races have become martyrs to the cause. The churches have also tried to set their own house in order: synods, conferences, and dioceses have been integrated, parochial schools in some parts of the South have taken the lead in educational desegregation, and many churches have tried to forge a creative response to the challenges of black power. Yet individual congregations remain largely uniracial; churches are still more segregated than most other institutions in the United States; and the liberal pronouncements of bodies such as the National Council of Churches are translated into action at the local level slowly and with great difficulty, if at all. It is debatable whether the church has been a leader or follower in the civil rights revolution.

The civil rights struggle has also confronted the black church with formidable challenges. The internal contradictions of a partly self-segregated institution which has served as a social center and refuge from the white man's world but at the same time has furnished much civil rights leadership have intensified in the 1960s. The growing secularization of the black community and especially of the civil rights movement has forced fundamentalist-oriented churches to modernize or become obsolete. The evolution from a crusade for desegregation led by churches of the black bourgeoisie to a quasi-separatist effort to mobilize the ghetto masses has left black religious institutions in a state of confusion and divided purpose. And the increasing openness of white churches to assimilation has posed a threat, albeit a distant one, to the independence of the black church. The Afro-American church appears to stand at a crossroads in its history, but there are no clear signs of which road it will take. Very likely it will move in several directions at once.

A brief general survey of the church and race in the mid-1960s is Liston Pope, "The Negro and Religion in America," *Review of Religious Research*, V (Spring 1964), 142–52. Joseph H. Fichter, "American Religion and the Negro," in Talcott Parsons and Kenneth B. Clark, eds., *The Negro American* (Boston, 1966),* pp. 401–22, describes the growing activism of black and white churches in the civil rights movement. Daisuke Kitagawa, *Race Relations and Christian Mission* (New York, 1964),* analyzes black and white churches in Africa and the United States. Two books by Joseph R. Washington—*Black Religion: The Negro and Christianity in the United States* (Boston, 1964)* and *The Politics of God: The Future of the Black Churches* (Boston, 1967)* —describe the shortcomings of both black and white churches and suggest programs for change.

The best introduction to the role of the white church in race relations since World War II is chs. 5–7 of David M. Reimers, *White Protestantism and the Negro* (New York, 1965). A black theologian challenges the church to reject racism in George D. Kelsey, *Racism and the Christian Understanding of Man* (New York, 1965).* The freedom movement since the Montgomery bus boycott of 1955–56 has inspired an extraordinary number of soul-searching books by white Protestants urging Christianity to practice the brotherhood it has always supposedly preached. Many of these works reflect a deep sense of collective guilt for the church's indifferent record on the rights of blacks: Liston Pope, *The Kingdom Beyond Caste* (New York, 1957); Kyle Haselden, *The Racial Problem in Christian Perspective* (New York, 1959);* Matthew Ahmann, ed., *Race: Challenge to Religion* (Chicago, 1963);* Robert Warren Spike, *The Freedom Revolution and the Churches* (New York, 1965); Ralph L. Moellering, *Christian Conscience and Negro Emancipation* (Philadelphia, 1965), chs. 7–10; Kyle Haselden, *Mandate for White Christians* (Richmond, Va., 1966); Russell B. Barbour, *Black and White Together: Plain Talk for White Christians* (Philadelphia, 1967);* Jean Russell, *God's Lost Cause: A Study of the Church and the Racial Problem* (London, 1968);* Andrew Schulze, *Fire From the Throne: Race Relations in the Church* (St. Louis, 1968); John R. Fry, *Fire and Blackstone* (Philadelphia, 1969);* John Howard Griffin, *The Church and the Black Man* (New York, 1969);* and Donald G.

Holtrop, *Notes on Racism for White Christians* (Grand Rapids, Mich., 1970).*

Daisuke Kitagawa, *The Pastor and the Race Issue* (New York, 1965), is a primer for ministerial action. Paul Ramsey, *Christian Ethics and the Sit-In* (New York, 1961), is a religious justification of non-violent civil disobedience. The prominence of clergymen in the Selma, Alabama, demonstrations of 1965 is described in John Cogley, "The Clergy Heeds a New Call," *New York Times Magazine*, May 2, 1965, 42–43 ff. Henry Clark, *The Church and Residential Desegregation: A Case Study of an Open Housing Covenant Campaign* (New Haven, 1965), Robert L. Wilson and James H. Davis, Jr., *The Church and the Racially Changing Community* (Nashville, 1966), and John Fish, Gordon Nelson, Walter Stuhr, and Lawrence Witmer, *The Edge of the Ghetto: A Study of Church Involvement in Community Organization* (New York, 1966)* study the response of urban churches to changing racial neighborhoods. Joseph C. Hough urges white Protestants to support the creative pluralism and positive community programs of black power in *Black Power and White Protestants: A Christian Response to the New Negro Pluralism* (New York, 1968).* Another attempt to reconcile black power with Christian ethics is Charles Freeman Sleeper, *Black Power and Christian Responsibility: Some Biblical Foundations for Social Ethics* (Nashville, 1969). A variety of responses to James Forman's call for reparations from white churches for their long support of racial repression are presented in Robert S. Lecky and H. Elliott Wright, eds., *Black Manifesto: Religion, Racism, and Reparations* (New York, 1969).* On most racial issues, from integration to black power, the white clergy are considerably in advance of their congregations; for an analysis of this gap, see Jeffrey K. Hadden, "Ideological Conflict between Protestant Clergy and Laity on Civil Rights," in Norval D. Glenn and Charles M. Bonjean, eds., *Blacks in the United States* (San Francisco, 1969), pp. 310–21.

In the recurring crises over desegregation of schools and public accommodations in the South since 1954, white clergymen have been caught in a cross fire between the racism of many parishioners and the dictates of their consciences or the edicts of national church organizations. Some southern white ministers responded with outspoken courage which cost them their pulpits; others hewed the segregationist line; still others maintained a cowardly silence. Earnest Q. Campbell and Thomas F. Pettigrew, *Christians in Racial Crisis: A Study of Little Rock's Ministry* (Washington, 1959), is critical of the white clergy for failing to exercise its potential moral leadership. Several viewpoints are expressed in Lewis S. C. Smythe, ed., *Southern Churches and Race Relations* (Lexington, Ky., 1961). For an interesting dialogue see George McMillan, "Silent White Ministers of the South," *New York Times Magazine*, April 5, 1964, 22 ff., and Robert Collie, "A Silent Minister Speaks Up," *ibid.*, May 24, 1964, 12 ff. The moving stories of two pastors who lost their pulpits because of support for civil rights are presented by Robert McNeill, *God Wills Us Free: The Ordeal of a Southern Minister* (New York, 1965), and Thomas J. Holmes, Jr., and Garner E. Bryan, Jr., *Ashes for Breakfast* (Valley Forge, Pa., 1969). Sermons of liberal southern Presbyterians are published in Donald W. Shriver, Jr., ed., *The Unsilent South: Prophetic Preaching in Racial Crisis* (Richmond, Va., 1965).* P. Allen Krause, "Rabbis and Negro Rights in the South, 1954–1967," *American Jewish Archives*, XXI (Apr. 1969), 20–47, is critical of southern Jewish religious leadership for reluctance to act vigorously in support of civil rights.

The Roman Catholic Church has become increasingly concerned with race relations in the 1960s, and Catholic writers have produced a number of books urging the church to play a more aggressive role in the drive for equal rights. See especially Joseph T. Leonard, *Theology and Race Relations* (Milwaukee, 1963); Philip Berrigan, *No More Strangers* (New York, 1965);* Joseph Eugene O'Neill, *A Catholic Case Against Segregation* (New York, 1966); Matthew Ahmann and Margaret Roach, eds., *The Church and the Urban Racial Crisis* (Techny, Ill., 1967);* and Lawrence E. Lucas, *Black Priest/White Church: Catholics and Racism* (New York, 1970). The impact of black power in the convents is discussed by Pat Kiely, "Cry for Black Nun Power," *Commonweal*, LXXXVIII (Sept. 27, 1968), 650, and "Black Nuns Relate to Black Power," *Christian Century*, LXXXV (Oct. 16, 1968), 1320–22. The campaigns of the militant priest Father James E. Groppi for open housing and black power in Milwaukee are chronicled in Frank A. Aukofer, *City with a Chance* (Milwaukee, 1968).

The literature on the black church as an institution during the last two decades of rapid racial change is less voluminous and less critical than that on the white church, but in recent years a number of penetrating essays have appeared. Still the best brief treatment is ch. 5 of E. Franklin Frazier, *The Negro Church in America* (New York, 1964),* which should be supplemented by C. A. Green, "The Negro Church: A Power Institution," *NHB*, XXVI (Oct. 1962), 20–22; Norval D. Glenn, "Negro Religion and Negro Status in the United States," in Louis Schneider, ed., *Religion, Culture, and Society* (New York, 1964), pp. 623–39; E. Wilbur Bock, "The Decline of the Negro Clergy: Changes in the Formal Religious Leadership in the United States in the Twentieth Century," *Phylon*, XXIX (Spring 1968), 48–64; and seven essays on "The Negro Church in the U.S.A.," in *Risk: A Publication of the World Council of Churches*, IV (1968). Elizabeth Yates, *Howard Thurman: Portrait of a Practical Dreamer* (New York, 1964), is a biography of the prominent black theologian.

For the role of black ministers in the civil rights movement, particularly Martin Luther King and the Southern Christian Leadership Conference, see section A of topic 3, above, "The Civil Rights Movement." Bruce Hilton, *The Delta Ministry* (New York, 1969),* is a fascinating account of an interracial but predominantly black group of ministers and laymen, supported by the National Council of Churches, who are carrying forward the work of voter registration and community action in the Mississippi Delta counties. A widely reprinted article by Gary T. Marx, "Religion: Opiate or Inspiration of Civil Rights Militancy Among Negroes?" *ASR*, XXXII (Feb. 1967), 64–72,** measures the militancy of black denominations and finds the middle- and upperclass churches to be considerably more activist than the lower-class churches and holiness cults, where otherworldly concerns often prevail; Marx's conclusions are confirmed by surveys of church members in Watts, Oakland, and Houston reported by William McCord, John Howard, Bernard Friedberg, and Edwin Harwood, *Life Styles in the Black Ghetto* (New York, 1969),* pp. 107–17. Hylan Lewis, *Blackways of Kent* (Chapel Hill, 1955),* ch. 6, describes the black churches in a southern community, while

Gerhard Lenski, *The Religious Factor* (Garden City, N.Y., 1961),* is a comparative analysis of Catholics, Jews, and white and black Protestants in Detroit.

Despite their increasing social concern, middle-class black churches have largely failed to reach the black urban proletariat, especially in the North, a factor which is commented upon in many of the foregoing studies but has not received adequate systematic treatment. James H. Cone, *Black Theology and Black Power* (New York, 1969),* and *A Black Theology of Liberation* (Philadelphia, 1970),* and Albert B. Cleage, Jr., *The Black Messiah* (New York, 1968),* attempt to mobilize Christianity in the service of the black power movement; the latter book argues that "Jesus was the non-white leader of a non-white people struggling for national liberation against the rule of a white nation, Rome," and urges the church to "reinterpret its message in terms of the needs of a Black Revolution." Hiley H. Ward, *Prophet of the Black Nation* (Philadelphia, 1969), is a study of Albert Cleage, the militant black nationalist preacher of Detroit.

Howard O. Jones, *Shall We Overcome: A Challenge to Negro and White Christians* (Westwood, N.J., 1966, retitled in paperback ed. *For This Time*),* is a plea by a black minister who is critical of the church's involvement in civil rights movements and urges a return to a solely spiritual and evangelistic mission.

5. *Since* Brown *v.* Board of Education: *Black Education After 1954*

Few events have altered the history of black Americans as profoundly as the 1954 decision of the United States Supreme Court in *Brown* v. *Board of Education of Topeka*. In a remarkably brief opinion written by Chief Justice Earl Warren, a unanimous Court struck down the separate-but-equal holding of *Plessy* v. *Ferguson* (1896). "In the field of public education," the Court announced, "the doctrine of 'separate but equal' has no place. Separate educational facilities are inherently unequal." Although the decision embraced only education and failed directly to affect voting rights and segregated public accommodations, it nevertheless sent through the nation massive social and political reverberations which have yet to come to an end.

Specifically, of course, the *Brown* decision affected public education, at first in the segregated school systems of the South, by enjoining the *de jure* separation of the races. By the mid-1960s, however, its influence had permeated every major issue in public education, both North and South, and had aroused heated controversies everywhere regarding integration and educational enrichment, the busing of school children, administrative and political control of the schools (the chief issue of which is centralization versus decentralization or community control), and other such issues related to *de facto* segregation—the separation of the races in schools by social conditions (such as housing patterns) rather than by statute. Moreover, by the late 1960s, these issues had in turn spawned a new version of an old controversy about the intellectual capacity of the black American. It is not too much to say that the *Brown* decision, coming on top of other major social changes such as the transformation of American cities and suburbs, intensified, as nothing else had before, the general postwar crisis in American education.

The *Brown* Case and *de jure* Segregation

The initial *Brown* decision of 1954 and its often overlooked companion case, *Bolling* v. *Sharpe*, are to be found in the official *Reports of the United States Supreme Court* (known as the *U.S. Reports*) at 347 U.S. 483 (that is, at p. 483 of vol. 347 of the *U.S. Reports*) and 347 U.S. 497. The equally important second *Brown* decision is to be found in the *U.S. Reports* at 349 U.S. 294; it helped appreciably to confuse the law on desegregation by setting forth the legal guidelines, including the expedient but imprecise criterion of "all deliberate speed," under which desegregation was to take place in accordance with *Brown I*. These decisions, plus the momentous arguments by attorneys for both sides before the Supreme Court, have been brought together in the compendious work of Leon Friedman, ed., *Argument: The Complete Oral Argument Before the Supreme Court in Brown v. Board of Education of Topeka, 1952–55* (New York, 1969).

A definitive history of the *Brown* cases is yet to be written, but useful introductions include the essays by Alfred Kelly, a participant in the preparation of plaintiffs' briefs, "The School Desegregation Case," in John A. Garraty, ed., *Quarrels That Have Shaped the Constitution* (New York, 1962),* pp. 243–68; Jack Greenberg, director and counsel of the NAACP Legal Defense and Educational Fund, who provides an overview of the *Brown* and other desegregation cases from the NAACP perspective, in ch. 7 and apps. B and C of *Race Relations and American Law* (New York, 1959); Anthony Lewis and the New York *Times, Portrait of a Decade: The Second American Revolution* (New York, 1964),* ch. 2; and Loren Miller, *The Petitioners: The Story of the Supreme Court of the United States and the Negro* (New York, 1966),* chs. 23–24. Albert P. Blaustein and Clarence C. Ferguson, *Desegregation and the Law: The Meaning and Effect of the School Segregation Cases* (New Brunswick, N.J., 1957, rev. ed., New York, 1962),* is another intelligent discussion of the *Brown* case and its immediate repercussions.

Most of the subsequent cases regarding the desegregation of the schools, as well as cases in other fields of civil rights, decided in lower as well as high court jurisdictions, are to be found in the issues of *The Race Relations Law Reporter*, which ceased publication in 1967 after an eleven-year existence. Many of the most important of these cases have been brought together in Joseph Tussman, ed., *The Supreme Court on Racial Discrimination* (New York, 1963).* Don Shoemaker, ed., *With All Deliberate Speed: Segregation-Desegregation in Southern Schools* (New York, 1957), and Hubert Horatio Humphrey, ed., *School Desegregation: Documents and Commentaries* (New York, 1964),* also published as *Integration vs. Segregation*, provide additional commentaries. Detailed coverage of desegregation activities in the South after 1954 may be followed in the files of the *Southern School News*, published until 1965 by the Southern Educational Reporting Service. Moreover, the issues of the *Journal of Negro Education*, especially vols. XXIV (Summer 1955), XXV (Summer 1956), XXVII (Summer 1958), and XXXIV (Summer 1965), provide important continuing assessments of the progress of educational desegregation.

Not surprisingly, *Brown* and its companion cases failed to bring about immediate or large-scale integration of the school systems in the South. As late as 1970 some districts in the South had not yet abandoned *de jure* segregation, dual school systems, and other obstructionist tactics. Reviews of the confused history of school desegregation in the South since 1954 are to be found in Benjamin Muse, *Ten Years of Prelude: The Story of Integration Since the Supreme Court's 1954 Decision* (New York, 1964), and Gary Orfield's incisive *Reconstruction of Southern Education: The Schools and the 1964 Civil Rights Act* (New York, 1969). See also John H. McCord, *With All Deliberate Speed: Civil Rights Theory and Reality* (Urbana, Ill., 1969).

As these three studies make clear, many tactics were used by southern opponents of desegregation, including pupil-placement laws (which gave to state or local boards the authority to place students in designated schools, thus perpetuating segregation), the gerrymandering of school districts to circumvent legal orders, the establishment of private schools, and the actual shutting of the schools, for both whites and blacks. These actions, which came to be known as "massive resistance," plus the recalcitrance of courts staffed by southern judges to carry out the mandates of *Brown I* and *II*, actually pushed the Supreme Court into its tougher stance. Besides the Orfield, Muse, and McCord studies, the history of these obstructionist tactics is detailed in Numan V. Bartley, *The Rise of Massive Resistance: Race and Politics in the South in the 1950s* (Baton Rouge, 1969); Robbin L. Gates, *The Making of Massive Resistance* (Chapel Hill, 1964); Jack Peltason, *58 Lonely Men: Southern Federal Judges and School Desegregation* (New York, 1961);* Neil R. McMillen, *The Citizen's Council: A History of Organized Resistance to the Second Reconstruction* (Urbana, Ill., 1971); Robert C. Smith, *They Closed Their Schools* (Chapel Hill, 1965), a study of "massive resistance" in Prince Edward County, Virginia, one of the respondent school districts in the *Brown* cases; and Benjamin Muse, *Virginia's Massive Resistance* (Bloomington, Ind., 1961).

For a useful review of southern attitudes toward integration and of the pre-1954 status of education for blacks in the southern schools, consult Harry S. Ashmore, *The Negro and the Schools* (Chapel Hill, 1954).* And for more direct criticism of the role of the Supreme Court in advancing integration, see, for example,

Peter A. Carmichael, *The South and Segregation* (Washington, 1965), esp. chs. 1–5, and James Jackson Kilpatrick, *The Southern Case for School Segregation* (New York, 1962).

The effects of integration upon those involved has naturally become a matter of importance. The best and most evocative study of some of these effects on southern students and teachers, white and black, is by the psychiatrist Robert Coles, *Children of Crisis* (Boston, 1967).* Polly Greenberg has written a full account of the tribulations of the embattled Child Development Group of Mississippi, an organization that provided compensatory schooling for black children in that state, in *The Devil Has Slippery Shoes: A Biased Biography of the Child Development Group of Mississippi* (New York, 1969).

The origins of desegregation in southern colleges, universities, and professional schools are touched upon in many of the works already noted. The integration of previously all-white institutions of higher learning, mandated by a series of earlier Supreme Court decisions such as *Missouri* ex rel. *Gaines* v. *Canada* (1938), *Sipuel* v. *Board of Regents* (1948), *Sweatt* v. *Painter* (1950), and *Mc-Laurin* v. *Oklahoma Regents* (1950), was bound to threaten the isolated black colleges, most of them in the South. A straightforward discussion of the effects of desegregation on these institutions is Earl J. McGrath, *The Predominantly Negro Colleges and Universities in Transition* (New York, 1965).* See also Frank Bowles and Frank DeCosta, *Between Two Worlds: A Profile of Negro Higher Education* (New York, 1971). A pessimistic evaluation of the future of these institutions is ch. 10 of Christopher Jencks and David Riesman, *The Academic Revolution* (Garden City, N.Y., 1968).* For further references to black higher education see Part VII, topic 9, "Higher Education and Black Scholarship."

Efforts to desegregate the southern school systems became by 1960 just one thrust of the national movement for civil rights. The part played by integration efforts in this larger crusade and the crosscurrents affecting education because of other campaigns of the movement are suggested in the general works cited above under topic 3, "The Civil Rights Movement."

De facto Segregation

It was only a matter of time, of course, before demands for legal (de jure) desegregation would be translated into demands for real (de facto) integration of the races in the schools. But by the early 1960s it also became clear that it was far easier to terminate legally mandated segregation, most of it in the South, than to bring about true integration throughout the country, and especially in the great metropolitan areas and their suburbs where the question of integration became ensnared with the newer issues of community control, compensatory education, and black culture which to this day continue to defy simple solution.

There exists no general study of de facto segregation. Nevertheless, much of the controversy originates over the condition of education for Afro-Americans in the northern cities. On this question, ch. 9 of Charles E. Silberman, Crisis in Black and White (New York, 1964),* and ch. 6 of Kenneth B. Clark, Dark Ghetto: Dilemmas of Social Power (New York, 1965),* are extremely useful. Joan I. Roberts, ed., School Children in the Urban Slum (New York, 1967), brings together a fine collection of readings from the social sciences on the subject. Also useful is the report of the U. S. Civil Rights Commission, Racial Isolation in the Public Schools (Washington, 1967). Many of the publications of the Office of Education of the Department of Health, Education, and Welfare are also pertinent and illuminating, especially its magazine American Education.

Much of the debate over de facto segregation, like that over de jure segregation, revolves about questions of law. For legal definitions, reviews of the history of school law, and reasonably up-to-date compendia of school laws, three studies are particularly important: Lee O. Garber and E. Edmund Reutter, Jr., The Yearbook of School Law 1969 (Danville, Ill., 1969), an annual publication; Meyer Weinberg, Race and Place: A Legal History of the Neighborhood School (Washington, 1968), which forcibly brings home the fact that the "neighborhood" schools which historically have aroused such impassioned defense have generally been all-white schools; and E. Edmund Reutter, Jr., "The Law, Race, and School Districting," in Carroll Johnson and Michael

Usdan, eds., *Decentralization and Racial Integration* (New York, 1968), pp. 45–59.

It remains a moot question whether the integration of the races in the public schools does or does not work—that is, whether or not it improves the performance of the formerly segregated black pupils, whether or not it works better than the strategy of sharply enriching their school environment and their schooling while leaving them in separate all-black schools, and whether or not it injures the quality of education available for the whites. The major document in this debate is what has come to be known as the "Coleman Report," formally, James S. Coleman et al., *Equality of Educational Opportunity* (Washington, 1966), of whose lengthy findings pp. 3–34 are a summary. Its data argue strongly that black children throughout the nation are educationally deprived and that they benefit appreciably by their integration with white students. The report has been questioned in Samuel Bowles and Henry M. Levin, "The Determinants of Scholastic Achievement—An Appraisal of Some Recent Evidence," *Journal of Human Resources*, III (Winter 1968), 3–24, to which Coleman has replied, *ibid.*, 237–46. A wide ranging discussion of the report is *Equal Educational Opportunity* (Cambridge, Mass., 1969).

A second document, which brilliantly illuminates the complex problems of integration and quality schooling, is the extraordinary legal opinion of Judge J. Skelly Wright of the U. S. District Court for the District of Columbia in *Hobson v. Hansen*, 269 Fed. Supp. 401 (1957), which struck down the Washington, D.C., tracking system developed by the city's then superintendent of schools, Carl F. Hansen. See also John H. Fischer, "Race and Reconciliation: The Role of the School," in Talcott Parsons and Kenneth B. Clark, eds., *The Negro American* (Boston, 1966),* pp. 491–511. Meyer Weinberg reviews much of this debate in *Desegregation Research: An Appraisal* (Bloomington, Ind., 1968).* A superb bibliography is Weinberg, *The Education of the Minority Child: A Comprehensive Bibliography* (Chicago, 1970).*

By the 1960s, the fight for school integration had moved out of the courts and become a vital political issue to be determined through elections, lobbying, and civic struggles. Studies of the political issues involved in urban education and race include Robert L. Crain, *The Politics of School Desegregation: Comparative Case Studies of Community Structure and Policy-Making* (Chicago, 1968),* of which pts. 2, 4, and 5 concern *de facto* segregation; Marilyn Gittell and Alan S. Hevese, eds., *The Politics of Urban Education* (New York, 1969),* a collection of articles; David Rogers, *110 Livingston Street: Politics and Bureaucracy in the New York City Schools* (New York, 1968), a study of New York City's educational bureaucracy, of which chs. 1–6 are especially pertinent; T. Bentley Edwards and Frederick M. Wort, *School Desegregation in the North: The Challenge and the Experience* (San Francisco, 1967);* Raymond W. Mack, *Our Children's Burden: School Desegregation in Ten American Communities* (New York, 1968),* some case studies; Donald Bouma and James Hoffman, *The Dynamics of School Integration: Problems and Approaches in a Northern City* (Grand Rapids, Mich., 1970);* and the Nov. 1967 issue of *Law and Society,* for other studies on the politics of integration. The experiences of the communities of Teaneck, New Jersey, and Berkeley, California, both of which integrated their school systems, are treated in Reginald G. Damerell, *Triumph in a White Suburb* (New York, 1968);* and Neil V. Sullivan, with Evelyn S. Stewart, *Now Is the Time: Integration in the Berkeley Schools* (Bloomington, Ind., 1970).

The fight for integration in the urban school systems began to break down in the mid-1960s, first around 1964 in New York City and elsewhere later on. Not all citizens lost hope in integration, nor did all lose hope in the ability of the political system to bring it about. Nevertheless, after 1965 more and more people began to search for new means to improve the schools and especially to better the education available to black children. Generally speaking, professional educators turned from the battle for integration to the battle for compensatory education for blacks, while black residents of the cities, and especially the parents of black pupils, turned toward community control.

On compensatory education, three studies are particularly germane: Martin Mayer, *The Teachers Strike: New York, 1968* (New York, 1969),* and Maurice R. Berube, *Confrontation at Ocean Hill-Brownsville: The New York School Strikes of 1968* (New York, 1969),* examinations of New York City's 1968 public school teachers' walk-out, a crisis precipitated in part by efforts to alter the racial composition of the city's schools and to improve educational quality in the ghetto; and Peter Schrag, *Village School Downtown: Politics and Education* (Boston, 1967).* On community control likewise, two studies bear special examination: Henry M. Levin, ed., *Community Control of Schools* (Washington, 1970),* the best study to date, and Miriam Wasserman, *The School Fix, NYC, USA* (New York, 1970), a study of the struggle over the control of New York Public School 201. Three additional and more partisan studies on the same subject are Annette T. Rubinstein, ed., *Schools Against Children: The Case for Community Control* (New York, 1970);* Mario Fantini et al., *Community Control and the Urban School* (New York, 1970);* and Alan A. Altschuler, *Community Control: The Black Demand for Participation in Large American Cities* (New York, 1970).* On urban education generally, the contents of *The Urban Review*, a journal published between 1966 and 1970, are useful.

Not surprisingly, an important product of the controversies regarding *de facto* segregation of urban schools has been a concern for the conditions of learning in these schools and a renewed interest in the kinds of teaching needed to surmount them. Among the many treatments of these themes, four are especially sensitive and intelligent: Jonathan Kozol, *Death at an Early Age: The Destruction of the Hearts and Minds of Negro Children in the Boston Schools* (New York, 1967);* Herbert Kohl, *36 Children* (New York, 1967);* George Dennison, *The Lives of Children: The Story of the First Street School* (New York, 1968);* and Nat Hentoff, *Our Children Are Dying* (New York, 1966).* See also Gerald Levy, *Ghetto School: Class Warfare in an Elementary School* (New York, 1970),* and Jim Haskins, *Diary of a Harlem Schoolteacher* (New York, 1970). For a general survey of the problems of urban education, see Harry L. Miller and Roger R. Woock, *Social Foundations of Urban Education* (Hinsdale, Ill., 1970).

One venerable issue revived by all of these controversies concerns the intellectual capacity of blacks compared with whites. Probably no issue relating to race relations is more sensitive than this. If evidence to this fact is needed, the furor aroused by the publication of Arthur R. Jensen, "How Much Can We Boost IQ and Scholastic Achievement?" *Harvard Educational Review*,

XXXIX (Winter 1969), 1–123, supplies it; *ibid.*, XXXIX (Spring 1969), 273–356, is devoted to replies to Jensen, to which Jensen himself responds, *ibid.*, XXXIX (Summer 1969), 449–83. On the revival of racial inferiority arguments in the 1950s and 1960s, see also I. A. Newby, *Challenge to the Court: Social Scientists and the Defense of Segregation, 1954–1966* (Baton Rouge, 1967).

6. *The Economic Status of Black Americans*

Since World War II there has been considerable absolute improvement in the economic status of blacks in the United States. While blacks are still heavily overrepresented in the lowest paying, lowest status jobs, many have benefited from new skilled labor and white-collar employment opportunities opened through the positive efforts of business and industry in accord with the developing "fair employment" machinery of federal, state, and local governments. Urbanization and education have also helped to decrease the disproportionate concentration of blacks in agricultural and service occupations. The absolute median family income of black Americans has risen substantially, and the percentage of blacks living below the poverty level has declined significantly. Despite the persistence of notorious racial discrimination in the building trades and other unions, blacks have made considerable progress toward overcoming racial barriers within the ranks of organized labor.

Yet there has been little if any real improvement in the relative or comparative economic status of black Americans. Factors advancing black economic fortunes have benefited whites as well, and the economic gap between blacks and whites failed to narrow during the 1950s and 1960s. Since the 1940s the unemployment differential between blacks and whites has widened to the point that blacks are out of work at more than twice the rate of whites, and there is little prospect for change, since blacks are clustered in those jobs most susceptible to obsolescence through the advances of technology and automation. While blacks represent some 10 per cent of the nation's population, they account for roughly a third of America's poor, and some writers predict that without massive private and governmental efforts to correct the situation, this country may have a permanent black proletariat.

For an overview of the different elements that bear on the economic status of blacks in the United States, the best place to start is in anthologies, particularly Arthur M. Ross and Herbert Hill, eds., *Employment, Race, and Poverty* (New York, 1967);* Louis A. Ferman, Joyce L. Kornbluh, and J. A. Miller, eds., *Negroes and Jobs: A Book of Readings* (Ann Arbor, 1968);* and Herbert R. Northrup and Richard L. Rowan, eds., *The Negro and Employment Opportunity: Problems and Practices* (Ann Arbor, 1965).*

There have been many studies of the changing occupational status and income level of black Americans since World War II. Raw data are available in two publications of the U. S. Bureau of Labor Statistics, *Negroes in the United States: Their Economic and Social Situation* (Washington, 1966), and *Social and Economic Conditions of Negroes in the United States* (Washington, 1967). Among the general surveys, the following are useful: two works by Charles C. Killingsworth, *Jobs and Income for Negroes* (Ann Arbor, 1968),* and a summary, "Jobs and Income for Negroes," in Irwin Katz and Patricia Gurin, eds., *Race and the Social Sciences* (New York, 1969), ch. 5; Dawn Day Wachtel, *The Negro and Discrimination in Employment* (Ann Arbor, 1965),* which has an especially useful bibliography; Peter M. Blau and Otis Dudley Duncan, *The American Occupational Structure* (New York, 1967), esp. pp. 207–27, 404–08, which deals with the impact of a "vicious circle of cumulative disadvantages" on inequality of occupational opportunities for blacks; four articles in Talcott Parsons and Kenneth B. Clark, eds., *The Negro American* (Boston, 1966)*—St. Clair Drake, "The Social and Economic Status of the Negro in the United States," pp. 3–46; Philip M. Hauser, "Demographic Factors in the Integration of the Negro," pp. 71–101; Rashi Fein, "An Economic and Social Profile of the Negro American," pp. 102–33; and Daniel Patrick Moynihan, "Employment, Income, and the Ordeal of the Negro Family," pp. 134–59—which originally appeared in *Daedalus*, XCIV (Fall 1965), 771–814, 847–77, 815–46, and 745–70, respectively; Leonard Broom and Norval D. Glenn, *Transformation of* *the Negro American* (New York, 1965),* ch. 6; Herbert Hill, "Racial Inequality in Employment: The Patterns of Discrimination," *Annals,* CCCLVII (Jan. 1965), 30–47; Ray Marshall, *The Negro Worker* (New York, 1967),* esp. ch. 6; Nathan Hare, "Recent Trends in the Occupational Mobility of Negroes, 1930–1960: An Intracohort Analysis," *SF,* XLIV (Dec. 1965), 166–73; and Richard P. Young, ed., *Roots of Rebellion: The Evolution of Black Politics and Protest Since World War II* (New York, 1970),* pt. 2. Eli Ginzberg, *The Negro Potential* (New York, 1956),* deals with the changed economic position of blacks over the period 1940–55; see also Norval D. Glenn, "Some Changes in the Relative Status of American Nonwhites, 1940 to 1960," *Phylon,* XXIV (Summer 1963), 109–22. Walter G. Daniel, "The Relative Employment and Income of American Negroes," *JNE,* XXXII (Fall 1963), 349–57, is a thorough analysis of relative progress during the 1950s. For the 1960s, see Jack P. Gibbs, "Occupational Differentiation of Negroes and Whites in the United States," *SF,* XLIV (Dec. 1965), 159–65, an analysis for each state as of 1960; Norval D. Glenn, "Changes in the Social and Economic Conditions of Black Americans during the 1960's," and Daniel O. Price, "Occupational Changes among Whites and Nonwhites, with Projections for 1970," in Norval D. Glenn and Charles M. Bonjean, eds., *Blacks in the United States* (San Francisco, 1969), chs. 3, 4. Jack Rosenthal, "Census Data Show Blacks Still Poor," New York *Times,* Feb. 12, 1971, pp. 1, 22, summarizes the Census Bureau's analysis of black and white income levels during the 1960s.

Gary S. Becker develops a model for analyzing the economic effects of discrimination in *The Economics of Discrimination* (Chicago, 1957); he finds that the occupational position of blacks relative to whites remained essentially stable over the period 1910–50. Elton Rayack, "Discrimination and the Occupational Progress of Negroes," *Review of Economics and Statistics,* XLIII (May 1961), 209–14, argues instead that blacks enjoyed a better relative occupational position after World War II than before it. For another explanation, see Anne O. Krueger, "The Economics of Discrimination," *Journal of Political Economy,* LXXI (Oct. 1963), 481–86. Harry J. Gilman, "Economic Discrimination and Unemployment," *American Economic Review,* LV (Dec. 1965), 1077–96, studies the impact of color on the white–non-white unemployment differential. Stanley Lieberson and Glenn V. Fuguitt make projections concerning "Negro-White Occupational Differences in the Absence of Discrimination" in *AJS*, LXXIII (Sept. 1967), 188–200.

Other works of interest include two articles by Alan B. Batchelder, "Decline in the Relative Income of Negro Men," *Quarterly Journal of Economics*, LXXVIII (Nov. 1964), 525–48, and "Economic Forces Serving the Ends of the Negro Protest," *Annals*, CCCLVII (Jan. 1965), 80–88; Mollie Orshansky, "The Aged Negro and His Income," *Social Security Bulletin*, XXVII (Feb. 1964), 3–12; W. Ellison Chalmers and Nathaniel W. Dorsey, "Research on Negro Job Status," *Journal of Intergroup Relations*, III (Fall 1962), 344–59; two sections of Eli Ginzberg, ed., *The Negro Challenge to the Business Community* (New York, 1964)*—Charles E. Silberman, "The Economics of the Negro Problem," pp. 15–24, and Whitney M. Young, Jr., "Jobs and Income," pp. 25–37; Vivian W. Henderson, *The Economic Status of Negroes: In the Nation and in the South* (Atlanta, 1963); Otis Dudley Duncan, "Patterns of Occupational Mobility Among Negro Men," *Demography*, V, no. 1 (1968), 11–22;** a pamphlet by Harold L. Sheppard and Herbert E. Striner, *Civil Rights and the Social Status of American Negroes* (Kalamazoo, Mich., 1966);* Aaron Antonovsky and Lewis L. Lorwin, eds., *Discrimination and Low Incomes: Social and Economic Discrimination Against Minority Groups in Relation to Low Incomes in New York State* (New York, 1959);* and Irving Kovarsky and William Albrecht, *Black Employment: The Impact of Religion, Economic Theory, Politics, and Law* (Ames, Iowa, 1970).

National concern with poverty during the 1960s focused attention also on the special circumstances of the black poor. The problem of poverty in the United States was thrust into the public consciousness by Michael Harrington's provocative book, *The Other America: Poverty in the United States* (New York, 1962);* Harrington argues in ch. 4 that "Negro poverty is unique in every way." Among the many subsequent studies of poverty, the following (only a partial selection) deal especially with blacks: Daniel M. Fox, "Black Americans and the Politics of Poverty," in Nathan I. Huggins, Martin Kilson, and Daniel M. Fox, eds., *Key Issues in the Afro-American Experience*, 2 vols. (New York,

1971),* vol. II, pp. 212–26; Ben B. Seligman, *Permanent Poverty: An American Syndrome* (Chicago, 1968), ch. 3; Harold L. Sheppard, "Poverty and the Negro," in Ben B. Seligman, ed., *Poverty as a Public Issue* (New York, 1965),* pp. 118–38; Otis Dudley Duncan, "Inheritance of Poverty or Inheritance of Race?" (which argues that black "poverty stems largely not from the legacy of poverty but from the legacy of race") in *Perspectives on Poverty*, vol. I: *On Understanding Poverty: Perspectives from the Social Sciences*, ed. by Daniel P. Moynihan (New York, 1968), ch. 4; Louis A. Ferman, Joyce L. Kornbluh, and Alan Haber, eds., *Poverty in America* (Ann Arbor, 1965),* *passim*; Herman P. Miller, *Rich Man, Poor Man* (New York, 1964),* ch. 6; Ben H. Bagdikian, *In the Midst of Plenty: The Poor in America* (Boston, 1964);* Alan Batchelder, "Poverty: The Special Case of the Negro," *American Economic Review*, LV (May 1965), 530–40; Lester C. Thurow, *Poverty and Discrimination* (Washington, 1969); John F. Kain, ed., *Race and Poverty: The Economics of Discrimination* (Englewood Cliffs, N.J., 1969);* Jeremy Larner and Irving Howe, eds., *Poverty: Views from the Left* (New York, 1969),* *passim*; Alphonso Pinkney and Roger R. Woock, *Poverty and Politics in Harlem* (New Haven, 1971);* Paul Good, *The American Serfs* (New York, 1968),* on rural black poverty in the South; and the moving photographic essay by Robert Coles and Al Clayton, *Still Hungry in America* (New York, 1969). Kenneth B. Clark finds poverty at the root of the pathology of the ghetto in *Dark Ghetto: Dilemmas of Social Power* (New York, 1965),* ch. 3. David Street and John C. Leggett, "Economic Deprivation and Extremism: A Study of Unemployed Negroes," *AJS*, LXVII (July 1961), 53–57,** posits a causal link between economic deprivation and political radicalism and violence. See also John C. Leggett, "Economic Insecurity and Working-Class Consciousness," *ASR*, XXIX (Apr. 1964), 226–34.** Michael Harrington, "The New Lost Generation: Jobless Youth," *New York Times Magazine*, May 24, 1964, 13 ff., treats problems of unemployment among young blacks. Claude Brown's powerful autobiography, *Manchild in the Promised Land* (New York, 1965),* affords a compelling insight into the psychology of poverty. For a discussion of the relationship of poverty to the culture of the black ghetto, see below, topic 14, "Black Life-Styles in the Ghetto."

After the legislative victories of the early 1960s, jobs and income for poor blacks became the major thrusts of what remained of the civil rights movement. Charles Fager, *Uncertain Resurrection: The Poor People's Washington Campaign* (Grand Rapids, Mich., 1969),* tells the story of the unsuccessful effort of the Southern Christian Leadership Conference during the summer of 1968 to force federal action in behalf of the poor through non-violent disruption of government operations. See also Jill Freedman, *Old News: Resurrection City* (New York, 1971).*

In recent years, with special impetus from civil rights legislation and from riots, business and industry have substantially accelerated their efforts in training, hiring, and promoting blacks. Louis A. Ferman, *The Negro and Equal Employment Opportunities: A Review of Management Experiences* (New York, 1968); Richard D. Alexander, et al., *The Management of Racial Integration in Business: Special Report to Management* (New York, 1964); Paul H. Norgren, Albert N. Webster, Roger D. Borgeson, and Maud B. Patten, *Employing the Negro in American Industry: A Study of Management Practices* (New York, 1959); and Jack G. Gourlay, *The Negro Salaried Worker* (New York, 1965),* all analyze the experiences of businesses in employing blacks. John S. Morgan and Richard L. Van Dyke, *White-Collar Blacks: A Breakthrough?* (New York, 1970), is based on interviews with blacks in managerial or professional capacities in the predominantly white business establishment. See also Eli Ginzberg, ed., *Business Leadership and the Negro Crisis* (New York, 1968), on the opportunities and responsibilities of business in ameliorating the status of blacks in the United States.

Articles that deal especially with the efforts of private business in the aftermath of the riots to train and hire the hard-core unemployed and to relocate plants in the ghetto include Linda Liston, "Industry Answers Urban Crisis with Action," *Industrial Development and Manufacturers Record*, CXXXVII (May–June 1968), 19–24; Norbert R. Berg, "Control Data Builds Plant, Brings Hope to Ghetto," *ibid.*, 25–26; "Core Cities: The Logical Location for Industry," *ibid.*, 27–32; Ben S. Gilmer, "Business Involvement in Urban Problems: A Look at One Company's

Search for Solution," *Business Horizons*, XI (June 1968), 15–22; Stanley Marcus, "Who Is Responsible? A Businessman Looks at Civil Rights," *ibid.*, 23–28; "Pushing Harder for Ghetto Jobs," *Business Week*, Jan. 20, 1968, 123–26; "Business Joins War on Urban Ills," *ibid.*, Apr. 27, 1968, 84–90; "Dealing the Negro In," *ibid.*, May 4, 1968, 64–84; Barbara Flower, "Riots—An Ounce of Prevention," *Conference Board Record*, V (July 1968), 23–25; "Employing the Unemployable," *Fortune*, LXXVIII (July 1968), 29–30, 34; Robert C. Albrook, "Business Wrestles with Its Social Conscience," *ibid.* (Aug. 1968), 88–90, 178; Robert Haakenson, "The Urban Crisis: What One Company Is Doing," *Management Review*, LVII (July 1968), 8–16; John T. Garrity, "Red Ink for Ghetto Industries?" *Harvard Business Review*, XLVI (May–June 1968), 4–6; and Theodore V. Purcell, "Break Down Your Employment Barriers," *ibid.* (July–Aug. 1968), 65–76. See also John S. Morgan, *Business Faces the Urban Crisis* (Houston, Tex., 1969), and National Citizens' Committee for Community Relations, *Putting the Hard-Core Unemployed Into Jobs* (Washington, 1968). Two books that deal especially with the ghetto economy are Carolyn Shaw Bell, *The Economics of the Ghetto* (Indianapolis, 1971),* and William K. Tabb, *The Political Economy of the Black Ghetto* (New York, 1971).*

Industry-by-industry studies conducted by the Industrial Research Unit of the Wharton School of Finance and Commerce provide the most complete picture of blacks in specific sectors of the economy. Those published thus far include Herbert R. Northrup, *The Negro in the Chemical Industry*, Report No. 1 (Philadelphia, 1968); Herbert R. Northrup, *The Negro in the Aerospace Industry*, Report No. 2 (Philadelphia, 1968);* Richard L. Rowan, *The Negro in the Steel Industry*, Report No. 3 (Philadelphia, 1968); Edward C. Koziara and Karen C. Koziara, *The Negro in the Hotel Industry*, Report No. 4 (Philadelphia, 1968); Carl B. King and Howard W. Risher, Jr., *The Negro in the Petroleum Industry*, Report No. 5 (Philadelphia, 1969); Herbert R. Northrup and Alan B. Batchelder, *The Negro in the Rubber Tire Industry*, Report No. 6 (Philadelphia, 1969); William Howard Quay, Jr., *The Negro in the Chemical Industry*, Report No. 7 (Philadelphia, 1969); and Herbert R. Northrup, *The Negro in the Paper Industry*, Report No. 8 (Philadelphia, 1969).

Jerome H. Holland, *Black Opportunity* (New York, 1969), gives an encouraging assessment of the industrial employment prospects of black youth.

Paul Bullock, *Merit Employment: Nondiscrimination in Industry* (Los Angeles, 1960),* surveys methods of combating racial and religious discrimination in employment. Machinery and Allied Products Institute and Council for Technological Advancement, *Equal Employment Opportunity . . . a MAPI Symposium* (Washington, 1969), is a collection of papers on government and industry programs dealing with employment discrimination, while Peter B. Doeringer, ed., *Programs to Employ the Disadvantaged* (Englewood Cliffs, N.J., 1969), includes case studies of the experiences of management, labor, government, and civil rights groups with programs to provide job opportunities. Richard P. Nathan, *Jobs and Civil Rights: The Role of the Federal Government in Promoting Equal Opportunity in Employment and Training* (Washington, 1969), is a thorough study of the various federal weapons in this area. Michael I. Sovern, *Legal Restraints on Racial Discrimination in Employment* (New York, 1966), surveys state and federal legislation and executive orders. Title VII of the 1964 Civil Rights Act prohibited discrimination in employment. This act and other federal action against employment discrimination can also be studied in the appropriate works in topic 1, above, "Congress, the Executive, and Civil Rights." See also Paul H. Norgren and Samuel E. Hill, *Toward Fair Employment* (New York, 1964); "Toward Equal Opportunity in Employment," the entire Fall 1964 (vol. XIV) issue of the *Buffalo Law Review*; and Alfred W. Blumrosen, "The Newport News Agreement—One Brief Shining Moment in the Enforcement of Equal Employment Opportunity," in John H. McCord, ed., *With All Deliberate Speed: Civil Rights Theory and Reality* (Urbana, Ill., 1969), pp. 97–158. On progress in black employment in the federal government since World War II, see Samuel Krislov, *The Negro in Federal Employment: The Quest for Equal Opportunity* (Minneapolis, 1967); Norgren and Hill, *Toward Fair Employment*, cited above, ch. 8; and John Hope II and Edward E. Shelton, "The Negro in the Federal Government," *JNE*, XXXII (Fall 1963), 367–74.

Whether blacks advance in industrial employment is integrally related to their success within the ranks of organized labor. Two books by Ray Marshall provide the best accounts of recent changes in the relationship between blacks and labor unions—*The Negro and Organized Labor* (New York, 1965) and *The Negro Worker* (New York, 1967).* For a brief summary of developments over the decade 1950–60, see Marshall's article, "The Negro and Organized Labor," *JNE*, XXXII (Fall 1963), 375–89.** *The Negro and Apprenticeship* (Baltimore, 1967), which Marshall co-authored with Vernon M. Briggs, Jr., explores problems of apprenticeship opportunities for blacks in the skilled trades. See also Julius Jacobson, ed., *The Negro and the American Labor Movement* (Garden City, N.Y., 1968),* intro., chs. 3, 6–9. Scott Greer, *Last Man In: Racial Access to Union Power* (Glencoe, Ill., 1959), is a study of the status of Mexicans and blacks in Los Angeles labor unions. For a case study of the efforts of one union to implement a policy of non-discrimination, see John Hope II, *Equality of Opportunity: A Union Approach to Fair Employment* (Washington, 1956).

A number of writers have argued that ending discrimination by employers and unions is only a partial answer to the economic disabilities of black Americans. In addition, they urge compensatory programs and special efforts on the part of government and industry to close the economic gap between blacks and whites. See two works by Whitney M. Young, Jr., *To Be Equal* (New York, 1964),* in which he argues for a domestic Marshall Plan, and *Beyond Racism: Building an Open Society* (New York, 1969), which portrays black America as "an economic disaster area"; also see Charles E. Silberman, *Crisis in Black and White* (New York, 1964),* esp. ch. 8; Nat Hentoff, *The New Equality* (New York, 1964),* chs. 7, 13; and Donald Canty, *A Single Society: Alternatives to Urban Apartheid* (New York, 1969). Tom Kahn, *The Economics of Equality* (New York, 1964),* links improvement in the economic status of blacks to thoroughgoing reform of the nation's economic institutions. Dale L. Hiestand, *Economic Growth and Employment Opportunities for Minorities* (New York, 1964), studies the connections between general economic growth and the expansion of job opportunities for blacks. See also James Tobin, "On Improving the Economic Status of the Negro," in Parsons and Clark, eds., *The Negro*

American, cited early in this topic, pp. 451–71 as well as Sidney Wilhelm, *Who Needs the Negro?* (Cambridge, Mass., 1970),* an outstanding economic analysis saying that blacks are no longer needed in the postindustrial society.

The black power movement, with its emphasis on racial pride and indigenous control of institutions in the black community, brought with it an interest in the development of black capitalism. Black capitalism involves the growth of black entrepreneurship and of employment opportunities for black workers in businesses owned and operated by Afro-Americans. William F. Haddad and G. Douglas Pugh, eds., *Black Economic Development* (Englewood Cliffs, N.J., 1969),* is a good general introduction to the subject. Theodore L. Cross, *Black Capitalism: Strategy for Business in the Ghetto* (New York, 1969), suggests roles white business might take in helping to develop black capitalism. For a review essay of Cross as well as articles treating different aspects of black capitalism, see "Black Capitalism: Prospects and Problems," the entire vol. LII (Aug. 23, 1969) of *Saturday Review.* Articles that deal with recent efforts of government and the banking industry to promote black business enterprise include "Aiding Negro Businessmen," *Business Week,* Apr. 18, 1964, 141; "Where Negro Business Gets Credit," *ibid.,* June 8, 1968, 98–100; "Aiding Black Capitalism," *ibid.,* Aug. 17, 1968, 33; Carter Henderson, "Helping Negro Business Prosper," *Nation's Business,* LVI (Aug. 1968), 50–54; "Drive to Set Negroes up in Business," *U.S. News & World Report,* LVII (Aug. 31, 1964), 82; and "Banks: Black Capitalism," *Newsweek,* LXXII (Aug. 26, 1968), 71. For critiques of "separate but equal" economic development, see Frederick D. Sturdivant, "The Limits of Black Capitalism," *Harvard Business Review,* XLVII (Jan.–Feb. 1969), 122–28; and Paul Feldman, "The Pathos of 'Black Power,'" *Dissent,* XIV (Jan.–Feb. 1967), 69–79. For black attacks on the capitalist premises of black capitalism, see Robert L. Allen, *Black Awakening in Capitalist America: An Analytic History* (Garden City, N.Y., 1969),* and Earl Ofari, *The Myth of Black Capitalism* (New York, 1970).* For special studies of different approaches to economic development in black communities, see Henry Etzkowitz and Gerald M. Schaflander, *Ghetto Crisis: Riots or Reconciliation?* (Boston, 1969), on the Bedford-Stuyvesant

Community Co-op Center in Brooklyn; and Leon H. Sullivan, *Build, Brother, Build* (Philadelphia, 1969), pp. 85–160, 180–86, on the Philadelphia Opportunities Industrialization Center, and pp. 161–79 on the Zion Non-profit Charitable Trust, a vehicle for black ownership of apartments, manufacturing concerns, a shopping center, and other businesses in the Philadelphia area. James Heilbrun and Stanislaw H. Wellisz, "An Economic Program for the Ghetto," in Robert H. Connery, ed., *Urban Riots: Violence and Social Change* (New York, 1968),* pp. 76–89, assesses ways of developing black enterprise in Harlem. Studies of black businessmen include two works by Eugene P. Foley, *The Achieving Ghetto* (Washington, 1968),* and "The Negro Businessman: In Search of a Tradition," in Parsons and Clark, eds., *The Negro American*, cited above, pp. 555–92; Broom and Glenn, *Transformation of the Negro American*, cited earlier in this topic, ch. 7; Harding B. Young, "Negro Participation in American Business," *JNE*, XXXII (Fall 1963), 390–401; "The Negro Businessman in America," *Congressional Record*, 88th Cong., 1st Sess., vol. CIX, pt. 18 (Dec. 6, 1963), 23674–79; "The Ordeal of the Black Businessman," *Newsweek*, LXXI (Mar. 4, 1968), 72–74; Phillip T. Drotning and Wesley W. South, *Up from the Ghetto* (New York, 1970),* chs. 8, 10; H. Naylor Fitzhugh, ed., *Problems and Opportunities Confronting Negroes in the Field of Business* (Washington, 1962); Wilmoth A. Carter, *The Urban Negro in the South* (New York, 1961), on black business in Raleigh, North Carolina; and especially John Seder and Berkeley G. Burrell, *Getting It Together: Black Businessmen in America* (New York, 1971).

7. Housing for Black Americans

Because it involves living arrangements that bear directly on the most intimate personal and social relationships, housing has remained one of the most impregnable bastions of racial segregation. Clinging to the traditional belief that a man's home is his castle, most white Americans have been loath to sell, rent, or live in close proximity to blacks. Housing discrimination has been fostered by government policies, the practices of the housing industry, and private prejudices alike, and it has been facilitated by the economic disabilities borne by black Americans. Historically the constraint of residential segregation has combined with the push of black migration to confine blacks to overpriced, low-quality housing within racial ghettos. Traditionally, blacks have gotten less for their housing dollar than whites, and until recent years even those able to afford decent homes have been blocked from entering white residential neighborhoods by barriers of law and private agreement. The impact of housing discrimination goes well beyond the location and quality of the homes of black Americans, for residential segregation lays the basis for a wide-ranging pattern of segregation in schools, public accommodations, commercial establishments, public services, and social contacts.

The changing distribution of black population in the United States has directly influenced the circumstances in which black Americans live. Steadily increasing migration to urban centers for two decades after World War II resulted in a rising index of residential segregation. The major study of the relationship between migration patterns and degree of residential segregation is Karl E. Taeuber and Alma F. Taeuber, *Negroes in Cities: Residential Segregation and Neighborhood Change* (Chicago, 1965),* which finds that "Negroes are by far the most residentially segregated urban minority group in recent American history." For a brief summary, see Karl E. Taeuber, "Residential Segregation," *Scientific American*, CCXIII (Aug. 1965), 12–19. Similar findings are revealed in Wendell Bell and Ernest M. Willis, "The Segregation of Negroes in American Cities," *Social and Economic Studies*, VI (Mar. 1957), 59–75. For comparative insights into the immigrant experience, see Stanley Lieberson, *Ethnic Patterns in American Cities* (New York, 1963). Karl E. Taeuber, "Patterns of Negro-White Residential Segregation," *Milbank Memorial Fund Quarterly*, XLVIII (Apr. 1970), 69–93, is a summary assessment of the quantitative studies of racial residential segregation. Morton Grodzins, "Metropolitan Segregation," *Scientific American*, CXCVII (Oct. 1957), 33–41, and his pamphlet, *The Metropolitan Area as a Racial Problem* (Pittsburgh, 1958), are predictions of overwhelming ghettoization in the central cities of the urban North. Leo F. Schnore and Philip C. Evenson, "Segregation in Southern Cities," *AJS*, LXXII (July 1966), 58–67, finds that older cities are less segregated residentially. Richard L. Morrill, "The Negro Ghetto: Problems and Alternatives," *Geographical Review*, LV (July 1965), 339–61,** develops a model for explaining the process of ghetto expansion. Statistics presented in U. S. Housing and Home Finance Agency, *Our Nonwhite Population and Its Housing: The Changes Between 1950 and 1960* (Washington, 1963),* point up the increasing urban ghettoization during that decade. Otis Dudley Duncan and Beverly Duncan, *The Negro Population of Chicago: A Study of Residential Succession* (Chicago, 1957), is a fine case study of demographic changes in that city during the first half of this century; chs. 5–8 deal especially with residential patterns, with particular emphasis on the decade 1940–50.

Studies that deal with postwar changes in black population distribution include Donald J. Bogue, *The Population of the United States* (Glencoe, Ill., 1959), ch. 7; Daniel O. Price, "Urbanization of the Blacks," *Milbank Memorial Fund Quarterly*, XLVIII (Apr. 1970), 47–67; two works by Harry Sharp and Leo F. Schnore, "The Changing Color Composition of Metropolitan Areas," *Land Economics*, XXXVIII (May 1962), 169–85, and "Racial Change in Metropolitan Areas, 1950–1960," *SF*, XLI (Mar. 1963), 247–53; two articles by Karl E. Taeuber and Alma F. Taeuber, "The Changing Character of Negro Migration," *AJS*, LXX (Jan. 1965), 429–41, and "The Negro as an Immigrant Group: Recent Trends in Racial and Ethnic Segregation in Chicago," *ibid.*, LXIX (Jan. 1964), 374–82; Donald O. Cowgill, "Trends in Residential Segregation of Nonwhites in American Cities, 1940–1950," *ASR*, XXI (Feb. 1956), 43–47; Reynolds Farley and Karl E. Taeuber, "Population Trends and Residential Segregation Since 1960," *Science*, CLIX (Mar. 1, 1968), 953–56; Karl E. Taeuber, "The Effect of Income Redistribution on Racial Residential Segregation," *Urban Affairs Quarterly*, IV (Sept. 1968), 5–14; Theodore G. Clemence, "Residential Segregation in the Mid-Sixties," *Demography*, IV, no. 2 (1967), 562–68; Robert C. Weaver, *The Urban Complex: Human Values in Urban Life* (Garden City, N.Y., 1964),* ch. 6, "The Urbanization of the Negro"; Bruce C. Straits, "Residential Movement Among Negroes and Whites in Chicago," *SSQ*, XLIX

(Dec. 1968), 573–92, which also appears as ch. 10 of Norval D. Glenn and Charles M. Bonjean, eds., *Blacks in the United States* (San Francisco, 1969); T. Lynn Smith, "The Redistribution of the Negro Population of the United States, 1910–1960," *JNH*, LI (July 1966), 155–73;** and Reynolds Farley, "The Urbanization of Negroes in the United States," *Journal of Social History*, I (Spring 1968), 241–58.** Recent studies that show increasing black migration to the suburbs and a slowing down in the rapid growth of black population in the central cities are David L. Birch, *The Economic Future of City and Suburb*, Supplementary Paper No. 30, Committee for Economic Development (New York, 1970),* and Reynolds Farley, "The Changing Distribution of Negroes Within Metropolitan Areas: The Emergence of Black Suburbs," *AJS*, LXXV (Jan. 1970, pt. 1), 512–29. According to the 1970 Census, the black population of the central cities increased by 3.4 million, or from 18 to 23 per cent, over the decade of the 1960s, while the black suburban population grew by 762,000, a gain of 42 per cent. See Jack Rosenthal, "More Blacks in Suburbs, but Ratio Stays Stable," New York *Times*, Feb. 11, 1971, pp. 1, 24. At the same time, black migration from the South to the North during the 1960s remained at a rate comparable to the high level of the 1940s and 1950s. For a summary of the Census Bureau's findings on the regional distribution of the black population, see Jack Rosenthal, "Negro Migration to North Found Steady Since '40's," *ibid.*, Mar. 4, 1971, pp. 1, 20, and "One-Third of Blacks Found in 15 Cities," *ibid.*, May 19, 1971, p. 39.

General demographic studies of blacks in America also include information relevant to residential distribution; see, for example, two articles by Preston Valien, "General Demographic Characteristics of the Negro Population in the United States," *JNE*, XXXII (Fall 1963), 329–36, and "Overview of Demographic Trends and Characteristics by Color," *Milbank Memorial Fund Quarterly*, XLVIII (Apr. 1970), 21–45, as well as Irene B. Taeuber, "Change and Transition in the Black Population of the United States," *Population Index*, XXXIV (Apr.–June 1968), 121–51; and Philip M. Hauser, "Demographic Factors in the Integration of the Negro," *Daedalus*, XCIV (Fall 1965), 847–77, which also appears as pp. 71–101 of Talcott Parsons and Kenneth B. Clark, eds., *The Negro American* (Boston, 1966).*

The most thorough treatment of the history and ramifications of housing discrimination in the United States is Davis McEntire, *Residence and Race* (Berkeley and Los Angeles, 1960), the final report of the Commission on Race and Housing, a private organization founded in 1955 to undertake a broad investigation of inequality of housing opportunity for this country's racial and ethnic minorities. See also a briefer volume summarizing the commission's findings, *Where Shall We Live?* (Berkeley and Los Angeles, 1958),* for a good general introduction to problems of residential segregation. Charles Abrams, *Forbidden Neighbors: A Study of Prejudice in Housing* (New York, 1955), is another useful general work which deals with the development of housing discrimination, its institutionalization in the private housing market, and its intensification by public policy. See also Linton C. Freeman and Morris H. Sunshine, *Patterns of Residential Segregation* (Cambridge, Mass., 1970).

Many studies sketch the contours of residential segregation over the past several decades. Briefer treatments of the problem can be found in *Report of the United States Commission on Civil Rights, 1959* (Washington, 1959),* pp. 336–97; Charles Abrams, "The Housing Problem and the Negro," *Daedalus,* XCV (Winter 1966), 64–76, which also appears as pp. 512–24 of Parsons and Clark, eds., *The Negro American,* cited above; Karl E. Taeuber, "The Problem of Residential Segregation," in Robert H. Connery, ed., *Urban Riots: Violence and Social Change* (New York, 1968),* pp. 105–14; two works by Eunice and George Grier, "Equality and Beyond: Housing Segregation in the Great Society," which also appears as pp. 525–54 of Parsons and Clark, eds., *The Negro American,* and the Griers' book *Equality and Beyond: Housing Segregation and the Goals of the Great Society* (Chicago, 1966);* Marion P. Yankauer and Milo B. Sunderhauf, "Housing: Equal Opportunity to Choose Where One Shall Live," *JNE,* XXXII (Fall 1963), 402–14; Whitney M. Young, Jr., *To Be Equal* (New York, 1964),* ch. 5; Michael Harrington, *The Other America: Poverty in the United States* (New York, 1962),* ch. 8; and Robert C. Weaver, *Dilemmas of Urban America* (Cambridge, Mass., 1965),* ch. 4.

Case studies of housing opportunities for blacks in individual cities and states include National Committee Against Discrimination in Housing, *Jobs and Housing: A Study of Employment and Housing Opportunities for Racial Minorities in Suburban Areas of the New York Metropolitan Region* (New York, 1970);* Nathan Glazer and Davis McEntire, eds., *Studies in Housing and Minority Groups* (Berkeley and Los Angeles, 1960), chs. 1–4, 7; Beverly Duncan and Philip M. Hauser, *Housing A Metropolis— Chicago* (Glencoe, Ill., 1960); U. S. Commission on Civil Rights, *Civil Rights U.S.A.: Housing in Washington, D.C.* (Washington, 1962);* Charles Tilly, Wagner D. Jackson, and Barry Kay, *Race and Residence in Wilmington, Delaware* (New York, 1965); a pamphlet by Eunice and George Grier, *In Search of Housing: A Study of Experiences of Negro Professional and Technical Personnel in New York State* (New York, 1958); and James B. McKee, "Changing Patterns of Race and Housing: A Toledo Study," *SF*, XLI (Mar. 1963), 253–60.

For many years federal policies sanctioned and indeed actively sustained housing discrimination. The Federal Housing Administration supported restrictive covenants and expressly favored racially segregated housing projects. Blacks found it difficult if not impossible to participate in federally sponsored mortgage financing programs. The first breakthrough came with a 1948 Supreme Court ruling in *Shelley* v. *Kraemer*, which held restrictive covenants in private housing to be legally unenforceable. Thereafter federal housing policies began very slowly to change. By 1962, when President John F. Kennedy issued his executive order prohibiting discrimination in the sale or rental of housing owned, operated, or financed by the federal government, a number of states and localities had already passed fair housing statutes and ordinances. Title VIII of the 1968 Civil Rights Act established the principle of open occupancy in nearly every form of private and public housing, and in the same year the Supreme Court ruled in *Jones* v. *Alfred H. Mayer Co.* that all racial discrimination with respect to real or personal property was a violation of federal law.

The best review of federal housing policies previous to President Kennedy's executive order is U. S. Commission on Civil Rights, *Report 1961*, vol. IV: *Housing* (Washington, 1961).* See also *Report of the United States Commission on Civil Rights, 1959*, cited above, pp. 451–505. The authoritative study of *Shelley* v. *Kraemer* and its companion cases is Clement E. Vose, *Cauca-*

sians Only: The Supreme Court, the NAACP, and the Restrictive Covenant Cases (Berkeley, 1959).* A contemporary appraisal by an NAACP lawyer who argued the cases before the Court is Loren Miller, "Supreme Court Covenant Decision—An Analysis," *Crisis*, LV (Sept. 1948), 265–66, 285. Beginning in 1952 the U. S. Housing and Home Finance Agency published annual reports, variously titled *Open Occupancy in Housing Programs of the Public Housing Administration* (Washington, 1952–55), *Trends Toward Open Occupancy in Housing Programs of the Public Housing Administration* (Washington, 1956), and *Trends Toward Open Occupancy in Low-Rent Housing Programs of the Public Housing Administration* (Washington, 1957–63), which reflect the status of segregation in federally assisted public housing before the Kennedy order took effect. Margaret Fisher and Frances Levenson, *Federal, State and Local Action Affecting Race and Housing*, published by the National Association of Intergroup Relations Officials, Sept. 1962, provides a full accounting of action at all governmental levels prior to the issuance of the order. The context of the President's decision to issue the order is treated in Arthur M. Schlesinger, Jr., *A Thousand Days: John F. Kennedy in the White House* (Boston, 1965),* ch. 35, and in Theodore M. Sorenson, *Kennedy* (New York, 1965),* pp. 480–82. The order's scope and impact are assessed in *Civil Rights '63: 1963 Report of the United States Commission on Civil Rights* (Washington, 1963),* pp. 93–103; Charles Abrams, "The Housing Order and Its Limits," *Commentary*, XXXV (Jan. 1963), 10–14; and Arthur J. Levin, *The Federal Role in Equal Housing Opportunity: An Affirmative Program to Implement Executive Order 11063* (Washington, 1964). The President's comments on the order can be found in John F. Kennedy, *The Burden and the Glory*, ed. by Allan Nevins (New York, 1964),* pp. 172–73. For a southern senator's critique, see John Sparkman, "Civil Rights and Property Rights," *Federal Bar Journal*, XXIV (Winter 1964), 31–46.

On the 1968 Civil Rights Act, see "Opening the Doors," *Time*, XCI (Apr. 19, 1968), 20–21; "Open Housing . . . Riot Control— How the New Law Will Work," *U.S. News & World Report*, LXIV (Apr. 22, 1968), 10, 12; Alexander M. Bickel, "The Belated Civil Rights Legislation of 1968," *New Republic*, CLVIII

(Mar. 30, 1968), 11–12; "Open Housing Law Credited to Mitchell's Lobbying," *Congressional Quarterly Weekly Report*, XXVI (Apr. 26, 1968), 931–34; "Discrimination in Employment and in Housing: Private Enforcement Provisions of the Civil Rights Acts of 1964 and 1968," *Harvard Law Review*, LXXXII (Feb. 1969), 834–63; Alexander A. Kolben, *Enforcing Open Housing: An Evaluation of Recent Legislation and Decisions* (New York, 1969), pt. 2; Edward W. Brooke, T. A. Smedley, Arthur Kinoy, and Sam J. Ervin, "Non-discrimination in the Sale or Rental of Real Property: Comments on *Jones* v. *Alfred H. Mayer Co.* and Title VIII of the Civil Rights Act of 1968," *Vanderbilt Law Review*, XXII (Apr. 1969), 455–502; and Frank I. Michelman, "The Advent of a Right to Housing: A Current Appraisal," *Harvard Civil Rights-Civil Liberties Law Review*, V (Apr. 1970), 207–26. The text of the housing title is reprinted in Norman Dorsen, *Discrimination and Civil Rights: Cases, Text, and Materials* (Boston, 1969),* pp. 391–94.

The text of the Supreme Court's opinion in *Jones* v. *Mayer* appears in *ibid.*, pp. 395–401. For analyses, see Gerhard Casper, "*Jones* v. *Mayer*: Clio, Bemused and Confused Muse," in Philip B. Kurland, ed., *Supreme Court Review* (Chicago, 1968), pp. 89–132; the *Vanderbilt Law Review* symposium cited in the preceding paragraph; "*Jones* v. *Mayer*: The Thirteenth Amendment and the Federal Anti-discrimination Laws," *Columbia Law Review*, LXIX (June 1969), 1019–56; "Housing Gets a New Message," *Business Week*, June 22, 1968, 30–31; Kolben, *Enforcing Open Housing*, cited above, pt. 3; and William B. Ball, "Housing and the Negro: New Life for the Thirteenth Amendment," *America*, CXIX (July 6, 1968), 11–13.

Other treatments of federal housing policies and programs include Davis McEntire, "Government and Racial Discrimination in Housing," *Journal of Social Issues*, XIII, no. 4 (1957), 60–67; Loren Miller, "Government's Role in Housing Equality," *Journal of Intergroup Relations*, I (Winter 1959–60), 56–61; B. T. McGraw, "The Housing Act of 1954 and Implications for Minorities," *Phylon*, XVI (2nd Quarter 1955), 171–82; Congressional Quarterly Service, *Housing A Nation* (Washington, 1966);* John H. Denton, ed., *Race and Property* (Berkeley, 1964); Lawrence M. Friedman, *Government and Slum Housing: A Century of Frustra-*

tion (Chicago, 1968);* and Loren Miller, "The Protest Against Housing Segregation," *Annals*, CCCLVII (Jan. 1965), 73–79. References on state and local fair housing legislation include: Fisher and Levenson, *Federal, State and Local Action Affecting Race and Housing*, cited above; two publications of the U. S. Housing and Home Finance Agency, *State Statutes and Local Ordinances and Resolutions Prohibiting Discrimination in Housing and Urban Renewal Operations* (Washington, 1961),* and *Fair Housing Laws . . . Summaries and Text of State and Municipal Laws* (Washington, 1964);* New York State Commission Against Discrimination, *Legislation on Discrimination in Housing: Federal, State and City* (Albany, 1956); *Report of the United States Commission on Civil Rights, 1959*, cited above, pp. 399–450; Lee H. Kozol, "Fair Housing Practices Law," *Massachusetts Law Quarterly*, XLVII (Sept. 1962), 295–305; Marshall Kaplan, "Discrimination in California Housing: The Need for Additional Legislation," *California Law Review*, L (Oct. 1962), 635–49; Alfred W. Blumrosen, "Antidiscrimination Laws in Action in New Jersey: A Law-Sociology Study," *Rutgers Law Review*, XIX (Winter 1965), 187–287; Alfred W. Blumrosen, Frank Askin, and Richard H. Chused, *Enforcing Fair Housing Laws: Apartments in White Suburbia* (Newark, 1970),* which deals with the New Jersey State Law Against Discrimination in Housing; Richard J. Roberts, "Fair Housing Laws: A Tool for Racial Equality," *Social Order*, XII (Jan. 1962), 20–34; and Kolben, *Enforcing Open Housing*, cited above. *Trends in Housing*, a bimonthly publication of the National Committee Against Discrimination in Housing, provides up-to-date information on the status of antidiscrimination laws and ordinances throughout the country.

Alfred Avins, ed., *Open Occupancy vs. Forced Housing under the Fourteenth Amendment: A Symposium on Anti-Discrimination Legislation, Freedom of Choice, and Property Rights in Housing* (New York, 1963), incorporates a broad range of criticisms of fair housing legislation. Before the 1968 legislation and Supreme Court decision, real estate associations seeking to overturn fair housing legislation successfully promoted anti-fair housing referenda and constitutional amendments in several states and cities. A well-publicized example of this tactic involved the adoption of Proposition 14 in California in the 1964 election; see

John H. Denton, *Apartheid American Style* (Berkeley, 1967).* The United States Supreme Court struck down Proposition 14 in 1967 in *Reitman* v. *Mulkley.*

Federal urban renewal programs have generated widespread controversy. Critics charge, in part, that "urban renewal" is tantamount to "Negro removal." For an introduction to the urban renewal debate, see James Q. Wilson, ed., *Urban Renewal: The Record and the Controversy* (Cambridge, Mass., 1966);* Charles Abrams, *The City Is the Frontier* (New York, 1965);* Scott Greer, *Urban Renewal and American Cities: The Dilemma of Democratic Intervention* (Indianapolis, 1965);* Thomas F. Johnson, James R. Morris, and Joseph G. Butts, *Renewing America's Cities* (Washington, 1962); and an exchange in *Commentary*, Herbert J. Gans, "The Failure of Urban Renewal: A Critique and Some Proposals," XXXIX (Apr. 1965), 29–37, and George M. Raymond, Malcolm D. Rivkin, and Herbert J. Gans, "Urban Renewal," XL (July 1965), 72–80. A strongly negative assessment is Martin Anderson, *The Federal Bulldozer: A Critical Analysis of Urban Renewal, 1949–1962* (Cambridge, Mass., 1964).* Donald Canty, *A Single Society: Alternatives to Urban Apartheid* (New York, 1969),* offers another critique. A more positive appraisal can be found in Weaver, *Dilemmas of Urban America*, cited above, chs. 3–4. Studies that focus especially on the relationship between race and urban renewal include Wolf Von Eckardt, *Bulldozers and Bureaucrats: Cities and Urban Renewal* (Washington, 1963),* ch. 5, which also appears as "Black Neck in the White Noose," *New Republic*, CXLIX (Oct. 19, 1963), 14–17; L. K. Northwood, "The Threat and Potential of Urban Renewal: A Workable Program for Better Race Relations," *Journal of Intergroup Relations*, II (Spring 1961), 101–14; Robert C. Weaver, "Class, Race and Urban Renewal," *Land Economics*, XXXVI (Aug. 1960), 235–51; Mel J. Ravitz, "Effects of Urban Renewal on Community Racial Patterns," *Journal of Social Issues*, XIII, no. 4 (1957), 38–49; "Housing and Minorities," the Spring 1958 (vol. XIX) issue of *Phylon*; Lewis G. Watts, Howard E. Freeman, Helen M. Hughes, Robert Morris, and Thomas F. Pettigrew, *The Middle-Income Negro Family Faces Urban Renewal* (Waltham, Mass., 1964); and Elinor Richey, "Splitsville, U.S.A.: An Ironic Tale of Urban Renewal and Racial Segregation," *Reporter*, XXVIII (May 23, 1963), 35–38.

Beyond its base in generalized racial prejudice, private resistance to integrated housing has been firmly grounded in the belief that the entrance of blacks into white neighborhoods precipitates a decline in property values. Luigi Laurenti, *Property Values and Race: Studies in Seven Cities* (Berkeley and Los Angeles, 1960), finds instead that there is "no single or uniform pattern of non-white influence on property prices"; indeed, in the cases he examined, neighborhood integration was "much more often associated with price improvement or stability than with price weakening." Similar conclusions are reached by Chester Rapkin and William G. Grigsby, *The Demand for Housing in Racially Mixed Areas: A Study of the Nature of Neighborhood Change* (Berkeley and Los Angeles, 1960); Erdman Palmore and John Howe, "Residential Integration and Property Values," *Social Problems*, X (Summer 1962), 52–55; and Thomas L. Gillette, "A Study of the Effects of Negro Invasion on Real Estate Values," *American Journal of Economics and Sociology*, XVI (Jan. 1957), 151–62. A different approach to the problem, William M. Ladd, "The Effect of Integration on Property Values," *American Economic Review*, LII (Sept. 1962), 801–08, finds that it has no demonstrable effect at all. Nevertheless realtors have successfully used this specter to frighten white residents into selling before the market collapses; for one account of these tactics, see Norris Vitchek (as told to Alfred Balk), "Confessions of a Block-Buster," *Saturday Evening Post*, CCXXXV (July 14–21, 1962), 15–19. When white residents believe that the entrance of a few black families portends a change in the racial balance of their neighborhoods, their decision to move in effect precipitates the result they fear; see Eleanor P. Wolf, "The Invasion-Succession Sequence as a Self-Fulfilling Prophecy," *Journal of Social Issues*, XIII, no. 4 (1957), 7–20.

Whereas most residential integration has resulted when blacks enter formerly all-white neighborhoods, some privately financed housing developments have been planned at the outset for interracial occupancy. On the market for interracial housing, see three studies by Eunice and George Grier—*Buyers of Interracial Housing: A Study of the Market for Concord Park* (Philadelphia, 1957); "Market Characteristics in Interracial Housing," *Journal* *of Social Issues*, XIII, no. 4 (1957), 50–59; and *Privately Developed Interracial Housing: An Analysis of Experience* (Berkeley and Los Angeles, 1960)— as well as Morris Milgram, "Commercial Development of Integrated Housing," *Journal of Intergroup Relations*, I (Summer 1960), 54–60, and Chester Rapkin, *Market Experience and Occupancy Patterns in Interracial Housing Developments* (Philadelphia, 1957). Marvin Weisbrod, "Homes Without Hate," *Progressive*, XXV (Jan. 1961), 28–32, and U. S. Housing and Home Finance Agency, *Equal Opportunity in Housing: A Series of Case Studies* (Washington, 1964),* are accounts of the experiences of private developers operating on an open-occupancy basis. The practice of fixing racial quotas in open-occupancy housing developments in order to prevent them from becoming all black is explored in William E. Hellerstein, "The Benign Quota, Equal Protection, and 'The Rule in Shelley's Case,'" *Rutgers Law Review*, XVII (Spring 1963), 531–61. For a theoretical discussion of quotas as a tool for achieving racial equality, see Robert L. Carter, Dorothy Kenyon, Peter Marcuse, and Loren Miller, *Equality* (New York, 1965). William Goldner, *New Housing for Negroes: Recent Experiences* (Berkeley, 1958), examines 1955 data on new private housing developments designed for black occupancy. The roles of private realtors, both positive and negative, with respect to interracial housing are treated in *Report of the United States Commission on Civil Rights, 1959*, cited above, pp. 506–33. See also Margaret H. Bacon, "The White Noose of the Suburbs," *Progressive*, XXIV (Oct. 1960), 37–38.

During the last two decades, the improving economic status and increased mobility of some black Americans, together with the slow evolution of public policy in support of fair housing, have forced the issue of residential integration in previously all-white communities across the country, so that by the mid-1960s 19 per cent of the country's population lived in integrated neighborhoods; see Seymour Sudman, Norman M. Bradburn, and Galen Gockel, "The Extent and Characteristics of Racially Integrated Housing in the United States," *Journal of Business of the University of Chicago*, XLII (Jan. 1969), 50–92. At the same time, urban areas have been faced with white exodus to the suburbs, black migration from the South, and the spread of blight and decay in the available housing stock. There have been a number of studies of the different responses communities have made to changes or attempted changes in racial composition. L. K. Northwood and Ernest A. T. Barth, *Urban Desegregation: Negro Pioneers and Their White Neighbors* (Seattle, 1965), a study of integration in Seattle; Henry G. Stetler, *Racial Integration in Private Residential Neighborhoods in Connecticut* (Hartford, 1957);* and Chester L. Hunt, "Private Integrated Housing in a Medium Size Northern City," *Social Problems*, VII (Winter 1959–60), 196–209, all illustrate the process, the problems involved, and the results in terms of interracial relationships. Harvey Swados, "When Black and White Live Together," *New York Times Magazine*, Nov. 13, 1966, 47 ff., describes the consequences of integration in Rochdale Village, a white working-class community in Philadelphia. Joshua A. Fishman, "Some Social and Psychological Determinants of Intergroup Relations in Changing Neighborhoods: An Introduction to the Bridgeview Study," *SF*, XL (Oct. 1961), 42–51; Eleanor Leacock, Martin Deutsch, and Joshua A. Fishman, "The Bridgeview Study: A Preliminary Report," *Journal of Social Issues*, XV, no. 4 (1959), 30–37, and *Toward Integration in Suburban Housing: The Bridgeview Study* (New York, 1964); and Marvin Bressler, "The Myers' Case: An Instance of Successful Racial Integration," *Social Problems*, VIII (Fall 1960), 126–42, all deal with problems of suburban integration, while Harry M. Rosen and David H. Rosen, *But Not Next Door* (New York, 1962) is an account of the refusal of Deerfield, Illinois, to permit the construction of a housing development that would include black residents. See also Eleanor P. Wolf, "Racial Transition in a Middle-Class Area," *Journal of Intergroup Relations*, I (Summer 1960), 75–81.

The role of churches, neighborhood associations, and citizen fair housing agencies in helping blacks find housing in integrated communities is treated in Philip A. Johnson, *Call Me Neighbor, Call Me Friend: The Case History of the Integration of a Neighborhood on Chicago's South Side* (Garden City, N.Y., 1965); Henry Clark, *The Church and Residential Desegregation: A Case Study of an Open Housing Covenant Campaign* (New Haven, 1965); Marvin B. Sussman, "The Role of Neighborhood Associations in Private Housing for Racial Minorities," *Journal of Social Issues*, XIII, no. 4 (1957), 31–37; and two works by James A.

Tillman, Jr., "The Quest for Identity and Status: Facets of the Desegregation Process in the Upper Midwest," *Phylon*, XXII (4th Quarter 1961), 329–39, and *Not By Prayer Alone: A Report on the Greater Minneapolis Interfaith Housing Program* (Philadelphia, 1964).* Margaret Fisher and Charlotte Meacham, *Fair Housing Handbook*, published in 1964 by the National Committee Against Discrimination in Housing and the American Friends Service Committee, is a guide to techniques used in promoting open-housing opportunities in formerly all-white neighborhoods.

The experiences of urban areas that have organized private and public resources in campaigns to redress blight and create stable interracial communities are best illustrated in Chicago's Hyde Park-Kenwood. See Peter H. Rossi and Robert A. Dentler, *The Politics of Urban Renewal: The Chicago Findings* (New York, 1961), and Julia Abrahamson, *A Neighborhood Finds Itself* (New York, 1959). Two other studies that deal with combined private and public efforts toward conservation and rehabilitation of declining urban neighborhoods are Martin Millspaugh and Gurney Breckenfeld, *The Human Side of Urban Renewal: A Study of Attitude Changes Produced by Neighborhood Rehabilitation* (Baltimore, 1958),* and Office of Urban Renewal, District of Columbia, *Adams-Morgan: Democratic Action to Save a Neighborhood: A Demonstration of Neighborhood Conservation in the District of Columbia* (Washington, 1964).*

What is the impact of residential integration on the attitudes of whites toward their new black neighbors? Toward blacks in general? Of blacks toward their new white neighbors? For a variety of studies of public and private housing, see Bernard Meer and Edward Freedman, "The Impact of Negro Neighbors on White Home Owners," *SF*, XLV (Sept. 1966), 11–19; Daniel M. Wilner, Rosabelle Price Walkley, and Stuart W. Cook, *Human Relations in Interracial Housing: A Study of the Contact Hypothesis* (Minneapolis, 1955); Alvin E. Winder, "White Attitudes towards Negro-White Interaction in an Area of Changing Racial Composition," *American Psychologist*, VII (July 1952), 330–31 (abstract); Morton Deutsch and Mary Evans Collins, *Interracial Housing: A Psychological Evaluation of a Social Experiment* (Minneapolis, 1951); Stetler, *Racial Integration in Private Residential Neighborhoods in Connecticut*, cited above; Northwood and Barth, *Urban Desegregation*, cited above; Leacock, Deutsch, and Fishman, "The Bridgeview Study" and *Toward Integration in Suburban Housing*, both cited above; and Gordon W. Allport, *The Nature of Prejudice* (Cambridge, Mass., 1954),* ch. 16.

8. *The Black Family in Urban America*

Because of the family's central role in child-rearing, socialization, education, and transmission of values, family stability is an important index of the health of the society at large. In addition to these conventional processes of socialization, the black family historically has had a special function: teaching black children to adjust to a predominantly hostile white world. Until recently, most studies of the black family have been structured in terms of social disorganization. The significance of its distinctive features has been emphasized and perhaps exaggerated in analyzing the black man's "place" in American life and his attempts to secure his rights or expand his opportunities.

Black sociologist E. Franklin Frazier, for years the major writer on the black family, held that the moral standards and behavior patterns common to blacks were shaped by social conditions and not by race or African survivals. Under the impact of slavery, emancipation, and urbanization, he argued, some black families managed to develop stable, father-centered structures, but others fell into a pattern of matriarchy, illegitimacy, immorality, desertions, and casual family discipline, which, Frazier predicted, was likely to become increasingly prevalent. This is the thesis of his major study, *The Negro Family in the United States* (Chicago, 1939; rev. and abr. ed., Chicago, 1966),* but it is also elaborated in his other works: *The Negro Family in Chicago* (Chicago, 1932); *The Free Negro Family* (Nashville, 1932); "Traditions and Patterns of Negro Family Life in the United States," in E. B. Reuter, ed., *Race and Culture Contacts* (New York, 1934), ch. 12; and "The Impact of Urban Civilization upon Negro Family Life," *ASR*, II (Oct. 1937), 609–18.** For an early study whose findings in some respects prefigure Frazier's, see W. E. B. Du

Bois, *The Negro American Family* (Atlanta University Studies, #13, Atlanta, 1908, reprinted New York, 1968).

Frazier's works appeared amidst an upsurge of scholarly interest in blacks in the 1930s which produced a broad range of studies of black family life. The American Council on Education commissioned a series of books on black youth: Allison Davis and John Dollard, *Children of Bondage: The Personality Development of Negro Youth in the Urban South* (Washington, 1940);* E. Franklin Frazier, *Negro Youth at the Crossways: Their Personality Development in the Middle States* (Washington, 1940);* Charles S. Johnson, *Growing up in the Black Belt: Negro Youth in the Rural South* (Washington, 1941);* W. Lloyd Warner, Buford H. Junker, and Walter A. Adams, *Color and Human Nature: Negro Personality Development in a Northern City* (Washington, 1941);* and Ira De Augustine Reid, *In a Minor Key: Negro Youth in Story and Fact* (Washington, 1940). St. Clair Drake and Horace R. Cayton's work on the Chicago ghetto, *Black Metropolis: A Study of Negro Life in a Northern City* (New York, 1945),* contained considerable material on urban family life, while Charles S. Johnson's *Shadow of the Plantation* (Chicago, 1934)* illuminated rural conditions.

The indices of disorganization that Frazier set forth have governed much of the subsequent scholarship on the black family. Later studies—among them Gunnar Myrdal, *An American Dilemma: The Negro Problem and Modern Democracy* (New York, 1944),* pp. 927–35, app. 5; two articles by G. Franklin Edwards, "Marital Status and General Family Characteristics of the Non-white Population in the United States," *JNE,* XXII (Summer 1953), 280–96 (an interpretation of census data for the decade 1940–50), and "Marriage and Family Life Among Negroes," *ibid.,* XXXII (Fall 1963), 451–65 (on 1950–60); and Paul C. Glick, *American Families* (New York, 1957), a comparative analysis of white and non-white family patterns derived from the 1950 census data—confirmed the persistence of the traits Frazier singled out. The major recent study in the Frazier tradition is the "Moynihan Report"—officially, U. S. Department of Labor, Office of Policy Planning and Research, *The Negro Family: The Case for National Action* (Washington, 1965).* Finding what he evaluated as high rates of marital dissolution, illegitimacy, matriarchy, and welfare dependency in black families, the report's author, Daniel Patrick Moynihan, argued that the deterioration of the family structure was largely responsible for the social pathology of the black community. This thesis is also stated in his article, "Employment, Income, and the Ordeal of the Negro Family," *Daedalus*, XCIV (Fall 1965), 745–70,** which appears as pp. 134–59 of Talcott Parsons and Kenneth B. Clark, eds., *The Negro American* (Boston, 1966).*

The publication of the report inaugurated a fierce controversy among scholars, public officials, and black leaders. Moynihan has been widely criticized on many counts, especially for misusing statistical data and for neglecting the impact of poverty and discrimination by whites as factors deterring blacks from achieving full participation in American society. Lee Rainwater and William L. Yancey, *The Moynihan Report and the Politics of Controversy* (Cambridge, Mass., 1967),* which includes the text of the report, presents a full sampling of the reactions it provoked. For a brief summary, consult their article, "Black Families and the White House," *Trans-action*, III (July–Aug. 1966), 6–11, 48–53.** See also John Herbers, *The Lost Priority: What Happened to the Civil Rights Movement in America?* (New York, 1970), ch. 4, "The Moynihan Affair." Moynihan defends the report against his critics in "The President and the Negro: The Moment Lost," *Commentary*, XLIII (Feb. 1967), 31–45. For the results of a *Newsweek* survey confirming Moynihan's findings, see ch. 7 of William Brink and Louis Harris, *Black and White: A Study of U.S. Racial Attitudes Today* (New York, 1967).* C. Eric Lincoln, "The Absent Father Haunts the Negro Family," *New York Times Magazine*, Nov. 28, 1965, 60, 172–76, is an article by a black scholar that echoes Moynihan's themes.

Whereas Moynihan chose to emphasize the features of black family life that seemed to deviate from the white "norm," other scholars have noted that these traits are neither typical of the large majority of black families nor a characteristic black pattern. Important works that point to dangers inhering in the "myth" of family disorganization among blacks are Kenneth B. Clark, *Dark Ghetto: Dilemmas of Social Power* (New York, 1965);* Jessie Bernard, *Marriage and Family Among Negroes* (Englewood Cliffs, N.J., 1966);* and Andrew Billingsley, *Black Families in White*

America (Englewood Cliffs, N.J., 1968).* Billingsley's appendix, "The Treatment of Negro Families in American Scholarship," is especially noteworthy. Ulf Hannerz, *Soulside: Inquiries into Ghetto Culture and Community* (New York, 1969), ch. 4, traces the historiography and sociological schools of interpretation of black family structure in the United States and Latin America.

Some recent scholars have criticized the Frazier-Moynihan school for overgeneralizing in developing a single stereotype of urban black family life. Through intensive sociological investigations they have begun to reveal patterns of considerable diversity in styles of family living and child-rearing among urban blacks, both within and across class boundaries. See several studies by Hylan Lewis—"The Changing Negro Family," in Eli Ginzberg, ed., *The Nation's Children*, vol. I: *The Family and Social Change* (New York, 1960), pp. 108–37; "Culture, Class, and Family Life Among Low-Income Urban Negroes," in Arthur M. Ross and Herbert Hill, eds., *Employment, Race, and Poverty* (New York, 1967),* pp. 149–72; and "Child Rearing Practices Among Low-Income Families in the District of Columbia," in Marcel L. Goldschmid, *Black Americans and White Racism: Theory and Research* (New York, 1970),* pp. 107–13—as well as Elliott Liebow, *Tally's Corner: A Study of Negro Streetcorner Men* (Boston, 1967),* and his "Attitudes Toward Marriage and Family Among Black Males in Tally's Corner," *Milbank Memorial Fund Quarterly*, XLVIII (Apr. 1970), 151–80; Hannerz, *Soulside*, cited above, ch. 4; Carol B. Stack, "The Kindred of Viola Jackson: Residence and Family Organization of an Urban Black American Family," in Norman E. Whitten, Jr., and John F. Szwed, eds., *Afro-American Anthropology: Contemporary Perspectives* (New York, 1970), ch. 16; Joan Gordon, *The Poor of Harlem: Social Functioning in the Underclass* (New York, 1965); Lee Rainwater, *Behind Ghetto Walls: Black Family Life in a Federal Slum* (New York, 1970), and his "Crucible of Identity: The Negro Lower-Class Family," *Daedalus*, XCV (Winter 1966), 172–216,** which also appears as pp. 160–204 of Parsons and Clark, eds., *The Negro American*, cited above; and two works by David A. Schulz—"Variations in the Father Role in Complete Families of the Negro Lower Class," *SSQ*, XLIX (Dec. 1968), 651–59, which also appears as ch. 11 of Norval D. Glenn and Charles M. Bonjean, eds.,

Blacks in the United States (San Francisco, 1969), and *Coming up Black: Patterns of Ghetto Socialization* (Englewood Cliffs, N.J., 1969).* Another critique of the Moynihan Report, indicative of new scholarly hypotheses regarding black family structure and organization, is Warren TenHouten, "The Black Family: Myth and Reality," *Psychiatry*, XXXIII (May 1970), 145–73. See also Ludwig L. Geismar and Ursula C. Gerhart, "Social Class, Ethnicity, and Family Functioning: Exploring Some Issues Raised by the Moynihan Report," *Journal of Marriage and the Family*, XXX (Aug. 1968), 480–87; and Herbert H. Hyman and John Shelton Reed, " 'Black Matriarchy' Reconsidered: Evidence from Secondary Analysis of Sample Surveys," *Public Opinion Quarterly*, XXXIII (Fall 1969), 346–54. Charles A. Valentine, *Culture and Poverty: Critique and Counter-Proposals* (Chicago, 1968),* ch. 2, explores the deficiencies of the class-culture framework of analysis used by Frazier and Moynihan. For additional references on the role of the black family in the culture of the ghetto, see topic 14, below, "Black Life-Styles in the Ghetto."

Edward Wakin, *At the Edge of Harlem: Portrait of a Middle-Class Negro Family* (New York, 1965), is a perceptive word and picture essay on the life-style of one black family.

In addition to Davis and Dollard, *Children of Bondage*; Frazier, *Negro Youth at the Crossways*; and the works of Charles S. Johnson, all cited above, studies that focus especially on the South include Hylan Lewis, *Blackways of Kent* (Chapel Hill, 1955);* John H. Rohrer and Munro S. Edmondson, *The Eighth Generation Grows Up: Cultures and Personalities of New Orleans Negroes* (New York, 1960);* Lewis W. Jones, "Negro Youth in the South," in Eli Ginzberg, ed., *The Nation's Children*, vol. III: *Problems and Prospects* (New York, 1960), pp. 51–77; and Charles E. King, "The Negro Maternal Family: A Product of an Economic and a Culture System," *SF*, XXIV (Oct. 1945), 100–04.

For analyses of patterns of marital stability and instability in black families, consult several studies by Paul C. Glick—"Marriage and Marital Stability Among Blacks," *Milbank Memorial Fund Quarterly*, XLVIII (Apr. 1970), 99–125; "Marital Stability as a Social Indicator," *Social Biology*, XVI (Sept. 1969), 158–66; "Marriage Instability: Variations by Size of Place and Region,"

Milbank Memorial Fund Quarterly, XLI (Jan. 1963), 43–55; *Marriage and Divorce: A Social and Economic Study* (Cambridge, Mass., 1970), which he co-authored with Hugh Carter; "Trends and Current Patterns of Marital Status Among Nonwhite Persons," *Demography*, III, no. 1 (1966), 276–88, also co-authored by Carter; and "First-Marriage Decrement Tables by Color and Sex for the United States in 1958–60," *ibid.*, VI (Aug. 1969), 243–60, which he wrote with Walt Saveland—as well as Irene B. Taeuber, "Change and Transition in the Black Population of the United States," *Population Index*, XXXIV (Apr.–June 1968), 121–51; two research notes by J. Richard Udry, "Marital Instability by Race, Sex, Education, and Occupation Using 1960 Census Data," *AJS*, LXXII (Sept. 1966), 203–09, and "Marital Instability by Race and Income Based on 1960 Census Data," *ibid.* (May 1967), 673–74; Jessie Bernard, "Marital Stability and Patterns of Status Variables," *Journal of Marriage and the Family*, XXVIII (Nov. 1966), 421–39, with comments by Richard A. Schermerhorn, Lee Rainwater, and Catherine S. Chilman, 440–48; and Bernard's book, *Marriage and Family Among Negroes*, and the Moynihan Report, both cited above.

Studies of the impact of family structure on personality development among black children include Erik Erikson, "Memorandum on Identity and Negro Youth," *Journal of Social Issues*, XLII (Oct. 1964), 29–42; Joyce Ladner, *Tomorrow's Tomorrow: The Black Woman* (Garden City, N.Y., 1971), on adolescent girls; Eugene B. Brody, "Color and Identity Conflict in Young Boys: Observations of Negro Mothers and Sons in Urban Baltimore," *Psychiatry*, XXVI (May 1963), 188–201; R. V. Burton and J. W. M. Whiting, "The Absent Father and Cross-Sex Identity," *Merrill-Palmer Quarterly*, VII (Apr. 1961), 85–95; E. Mavis Hetherington, "Effects of Paternal Absence on Sex-Typed Behaviors in Negro and White Preadolescent Males," *Journal of Personality and Social Psychology*, IV (July 1966), 87–91; Ruth Shonle Cavan, "Negro Family Disorganization and Juvenile Delinquency," *JNE*, XXVIII (Summer 1959), 230–39; Charles J. Browning, "Differential Impact of Family Disorganization on Male Adolescents," *Social Problems*, VIII (Summer 1960), 37–44 (useful though not specifically about blacks); and Thomas F.

Pettigrew, A *Profile of the Negro American* (Princeton, 1964),*
pp. 15–24.

Studies of marital roles in the black family include Ladner, *Tomorrow's Tomorrow*, cited above; Joseph S. Himes, "The Interrelation of Occupational and Spousal Roles in a Middle Class Negro Neighborhood," *Marriage and Family Living*, XXII (Nov. 1960), 362–63; Russell Middleton and Snell Putney, "Dominance in Decisions in the Family: Race and Class Differences," *AJS*, LXV (May 1960), 605–09; Robert O. Blood, Jr., and Donald M. Wolfe, *Husbands and Wives: The Dynamics of Married Living* (New York, 1960);* Robert O. Blood, Jr., and Robert L. Hamblin, "The Effect of the Wife's Employment on the Family Power Structure," *SF*, XXXVI (May 1958), 347–52; Mollie Orshansky, "Children of the Poor," *Social Security Bulletin*, XXVI (July 1963), 3–13; two articles by Seymour Parker and Robert J. Kleiner, "Characteristics of Negro Mothers in Single-Headed Households," *Journal of Marriage and the Family*, XXVIII (Nov. 1966), 507–13, and "Social and Psychological Dimensions of the Family Role Performance of the Negro Male," *ibid.*, XXXI (Aug. 1969), 500–06; and the article by David A. Schulz, cited above. Mel Watkins and Jay David, eds., *To Be a Black Woman: Portraits in Fact and Fiction* (New York, 1971), includes some relevant material on the black woman as mother and wife. See also Josephine Carson, *Silent Voices: The Southern Negro Woman Today* (New York, 1969).

Allison Davis and Robert J. Havighurst, "Social Class and Color Differences in Child-Rearing," *ASR*, XI (Dec. 1946), 698–710,** which presents conclusions elaborated in their book, *The Father of the Man: How Your Child Gets His Personality* (Boston, 1947), finds relatively little difference in child-rearing among black and white mothers of comparable socioeconomic status. More recent studies have challenged these conclusions; see, for example, two articles by Zena Smith Blau, "Exposure to Child-Rearing Experts: A Structural Interpretation of Class-Color Differences," *AJS*, LXIX (May 1964), 596–608, and "Class Structure, Mobility, and Change in Child Rearing," *Sociometry*, XXVIII (June 1965), 210–19.

Other useful studies are Robert R. Bell, "Lower Class Negro

Mothers' Aspirations for Their Children," *SF*, XLIII (May 1965), 493–500;** Adelaide Cromwell Hill and Frederick S. Jaffe, "Negro Fertility and Family Size Preferences: Implications for Programming of Health and Social Services," in Parsons and Clark, eds., *The Negro American*, cited above, pp. 205–44; ch. 3, "Fertility and Family Planning," in Clyde V. Kiser, ed., "Demographic Aspects of the Black Community," *Milbank Memorial Fund Quarterly*, XLVIII (Apr. 1970), 183–307; James E. Teele and William M. Schmidt, "Illegitimacy and Race: National and Local Trends," *ibid.*, 127–50; and Joe R. Feagin, "The Kinship Ties of Negro Urbanites," *SSQ*, XLIX (Dec. 1968), 660–65, which appears as ch. 12 of Glenn and Bonjean, eds., *Blacks in the United States*, cited above. Jay David, ed., *Growing up Black* (New York, 1968),* includes selections on childhood experiences from the autobiographies of nineteen blacks.

The influence of family environment on the child's intellectual development—a matter of considerable consequence to framers of federal aid programs as well as to child psychologists and educational experts—is treated in Urie Bronfenbrenner, "The Psychological Costs of Quality and Equality in Education," *Child Development*, XXXVIII (Dec. 1967), 909–25; Nancy Bayley, "Comparisons of Mental and Motor Test Scores for Ages 1–15 Months By Sex, Birth Order, Race, Geographical Location, and Education of Parents," *ibid.*, XXXVI (June 1965), 379–411; Martin V. Covington, "Stimulus Discrimination as a Function of Social-Class Membership," *ibid.*, XXXVIII (June 1967), 607–13; Norman E. Freeberg and Donald T. Payne, "Parental Influence on Cognitive Development in Early Childhood: A Review," *ibid.*, XXXVIII (Mar. 1967), 65–87; Martin Deutsch and Bert Brown, "Social Influences in Negro-White Intelligence Differences," *Journal of Social Issues*, XX (Apr. 1964), 24–35; Robert D. Hess and Virginia C. Shipman, "Early Experience and the Socialization of Cognitive Modes in Children," *Child Development*, XXXVI (Dec. 1965), 869–86; Marjorie P. Honzik, "Mother-Child Interaction and the Socialization Process," *ibid.*, XXXVIII (June 1967), 337–64; Joseph McVicker Hunt, *Intelligence and Experience* (New York, 1961); Hilda Knobloch and Benjamin Pasamanick, "Further Observations on the Behavioral Development of Negro Children," *Journal of Genetic Psychology*, LXXXIII

(Sept. 1953), 137–57; Gerald S. Lesser, Gordon Fifer, and Donald H. Clark, "Mental Abilities of Children from Different Social-Class and Cultural Groups," *Monographs of the Society for Research in Child Development*, XXX, no. 4 (1965), 1–115; two articles by Benjamin A. Pasamanick, "A Comparative Study of the Behavioral Development of Negro Infants," *Journal of Genetic Psychology*, LXIX (Sept. 1946), 3–44, and "Tract for the Times: Some Sociological Aspects of Science, Race, and Racism," *American Journal of Orthopsychiatry*, XXXIX (Jan. 1969), 7–15; Maya Pines, *Revolution in Learning* (New York, 1967); and C. Etta Walters, "Comparative Development of Negro and White Infants," *Journal of Genetic Psychology*, CX (June 1967), 243–51.

9. Black Political Power

Since World War II blacks have become increasingly visible in American politics, both as voters and as officeholders. Voting rights legislation, intensive voter education and registration campaigns, legislative reapportionment, and continued urbanization have all contributed to the growing power of the black vote, North and South. Many black leaders consider the ballot the most important weapon for the future advancement of their race. Black politicians have risen to national prominence, and black voters hold the balance of power in several important states and major cities.

A. The North and the National Picture

For a brief overview of the subject, the best place to begin is James Q. Wilson, "The Negro in Politics," *Daedalus*, XCIV (Fall 1965), 949–73, which also appears as pp. 423–47 of Talcott Parsons and Kenneth B. Clark, eds., *The Negro American* (Boston, 1966).* Wilson's book *Negro Politics: The Search for Leadership* (Glencoe, Ill., 1960),* a comparative analysis of Chicago and New York, is still the best monograph in the field. Ch. 20 of *City Politics* (Cambridge, Mass., 1963),* the book Wilson co-authored with Edward C. Banfield, treats what they saw at that time as the anomaly of black numerical strength and political weakness. Harry A. Bailey, ed., *Negro Politics in America* (Columbus, Ohio, 1967),* is a fine compilation of articles on various facets of black politics in the 1950s and 1960s. Harold F. Gosnell and Robert E. Martin consider the progress since 1950 of "The Negro as Voter and Officeholder" in *JNE*, XXXII (Fall 1963), 415–25. Edward T. Clayton, *The Negro Politician, His Success and Failure* (Chicago, 1964), is a popular history that includes portraits of some major political figures and discussion of political tactics and voting behavior. Chuck Stone, *Black Political Power in America* (Indianapolis, 1968),* by a militant black journalist, is a study of major officeholders and of the uses of black political power. See also Richard P. Young, ed., *Roots of Rebellion: The Evolution of Black Politics and Protest Since World War II* (New York, 1970),* pts. 4–5.

Whether black political power is more effective as an independent force or in coalition with like-minded white political interests has been a matter of continuing debate among black leaders. Harry Holloway, "Negro Political Strategy: Coalition or Independent Power Politics?" *SSQ*, XLIX (Dec. 1968), 534–47,** is a succinct analysis of the alternatives. The best-known case against coalition with whites is made by Stokely Carmichael and Charles V. Hamilton, *Black Power: The Politics of Liberation in America* (New York, 1967),* esp. ch. 3, while Bayard Rustin, "From Protest to Politics: The Future of the Civil Rights Movement," *Commentary*, XXXIX (Feb. 1965), 25–31, is a classic argument for the other side.

The literature on black voting behavior is not especially satisfactory. Samuel Lubell, *White and Black: Test of a Nation* (New York, 1964),* is more sophisticated and more up-to-date than Henry Lee Moon's naïve *Balance of Power: The Negro Vote* (New York, 1948), but Moon still contains useful information. Oscar Glantz, "The Negro Voter in Northern Industrial Cities," *Western Political Quarterly*, XIII (Dec. 1960), 999–1010,** is a useful analysis concerning the 1960 election. The one significant exception to the pattern of overwhelming black allegiance to the national Democratic party which was established under President Franklin D. Roosevelt was the election of 1956, when President

Dwight D. Eisenhower won substantial black support. This development is analyzed in several articles: "Why the Negro Should Support the Republican Party," *Crisis*, LXIII (Oct. 1956), 454–59, in which the Republican National Committee makes the case for Eisenhower; Henry Lee Moon, "The Negro Break-away from the Democrats," *New Republic*, CXXXV (Dec. 3, 1956), 17, and his "The Negro Vote in the Presidential Election of 1956," *JNE*, XXVI (Summer 1957), 219–30. The election in which the presidential candidates posed the sharpest alternatives for black voters was probably the Johnson-Goldwater contest of 1964; the overwhelming black support for the Democrats is illuminated in "Official NAACP Position on the Presidential Election," *Crisis*, LXXI (Oct. 1964), 500–03; Samuel Lubell, "The Negro and the Democratic Coalition," *Commentary*, XXXVIII (Aug. 1964), 19–27; and Henry Lee Moon, "How We Voted and Why?" *Crisis*, LXXII (Jan. 1965), 26–31. Loren Miller treats "The Negro Voter in the Far West" in *JNE*, XXVI (Summer 1957), 262–72. Hanes Walton, Jr., *The Negro in Third Party Politics* (Philadelphia, 1969), is superficial.

Efforts to secure black voting rights through the courts and the Congress are treated in works listed in this Part, under topic 2, "The Supreme Court and Civil Rights," and topic 1, "Congress, the Executive, and Civil Rights."

B. The South

The black voter in the South has been handicapped by special disabilities imposed by legal and extralegal disfranchisement and intimidation. There have been many studies of the circumstances and problems peculiar to black politics in that region. The best of these are Harry Holloway, *The Politics of the Southern Negro: From Exclusion to Big City Organization* (New York, 1969), and Donald R. Matthews and James W. Prothro, *Negroes and the New Southern Politics* (New York, 1966).* Two articles in vol. LVII of the *APSR* by Matthews and Prothro, "Social and Economic Factors and Negro Voter Registration in the South" (Mar. 1963), 24–44,** and "Political Factors and Negro Voter Registration in the South" (June 1963), 355–67,** are also valuable. V. O. Key, Jr., *Southern Politics in State and Nation* (New York,

1949), is a classic study that assesses the historical importance of blacks in the one-party white supremacist southern political system. Samuel Du Bois Cook, "Political Movements and Organizations," *Journal of Politics*, XXVI (Feb. 1964), 130–53,** is a brief survey of southern politics in the 1950s.

Margaret Price, *The Negro Voter in the South* (Atlanta, 1957), and *The Negro and the Ballot in the South* (Atlanta, 1949); U. S. Commission on Civil Rights, *Report 1961*, Bk. I: *Voting* (Washington, 1961),* and its *Political Participation: A Study of the Participation by Negroes in the Electoral and Political Processes in 10 Southern States since Passage of the Voting Rights Act of 1965* (Washington, 1968), are all fine surveys of the problems and progress of black suffrage. The entire Summer 1957 (vol. XXVI) issue of the *JNE* is devoted to "The Negro Voter in the South." Frederick D. Ogden, *The Poll Tax in the South* (University, Ala., 1958), deals with one of the major obstacles to black voting in that region. Bernard Taper, *Gomillion versus Lightfoot: The Tuskegee Gerrymander Case* (New York, 1962), is an able case study of another favorite device employed by white southerners to negate potential black voting strength. Pat Watters and Reese Cleghorn, *Climbing Jacob's Ladder: The Arrival of Negroes in Southern Politics* (New York, 1967),* treats efforts to secure the vote in the 1960s and the impact of their success. Julian Bond, *Black Candidates: Southern Campaign Experiences* (Atlanta, 1968), benefits from the perspective of perhaps the most accomplished young black politician in the South.

Among the analyses of black voting and political organization in individual southern cities and states, the following are noteworthy: Everett Carll Ladd, Jr., *Negro Political Leadership in the South* (Ithaca, N.Y., 1966),* a study of Winston-Salem and Greenville, North Carolina; M. Elaine Burgess, *Negro Leadership in a Southern City* (Chapel Hill, 1962);* Hugh D. Price, *The Negro and Southern Politics: A Chapter of Florida History* (New York, 1957); Andrew Buni, *The Negro in Virginia Politics, 1902–1965* (Charlottesville, Va., 1967); Harry A. Holloway, "The Negro and the Vote: The Case of Texas," *Journal of Politics*, XXIII (Aug. 1961), 526–56; G. James Fleming, *An All-Negro Ticket in Baltimore* (New York, 1960); Charles V. Hamilton, *Politics in Black Belt Alabama* (New Brunswick, N.J., 1960), on Tuskegee;

William R. Keech, *The Impact of Negro Voting: The Role of the Vote in the Quest for Equality* (Chicago, 1968), a study of Durham, North Carolina, and Tuskegee; and Carmichael and Hamilton, *Black Power*, cited above, chs. 5–6, on Lowndes County and Tuskegee, Alabama.

The first major challenge to white monopoly of southern state political parties came with the formation in 1964 of the Mississippi Freedom Democratic Party. The MFDP failed to unseat the regular Mississippi delegation to that year's Democratic National Convention and to bar the seating of Mississippi's segregationist congressmen in 1965. But at the 1968 Democratic convention the Credentials Committee ruled in favor of the MFDP and a similar challenge to the all-white Georgia delegation. On the MFDP, see Jack Minnis, "The MFDP: A New Declaration of Independence," *Freedomways*, V (Spring 1965), 264–78; Carmichael and Hamilton, *Black Power*, cited above, ch. 4; Howard Zinn, *SNCC: The New Abolitionists* (Boston, 1964),* ch. 12; Holloway, *The Politics of the Southern Negro*, cited above, ch. 3; and the relevant portions of works cited under section D, "Mississippi Summer," in this Part, topic 3, "The Civil Rights Movement."

C. Officeholders

There is a growing literature on individual black politicians. Massachusetts Attorney General Edward W. Brooke in 1966 became the first black man to sit in the United States Senate since Reconstruction. Black membership in the House is not only on the increase—eleven black congressmen and one black congresswoman were elected in 1970—but the more recently elected representatives are notably more outspoken and race-conscious than those who were elected years ago. In September 1967 President Lyndon Johnson named Walter Washington mayor-commissioner of the reorganized District of Columbia government, making the nation's capital the first American city to have a black chief executive. That November, Carl Stokes and Richard Hatcher became the first elected black mayors, winning victories in Cleveland, Ohio, and in Gary, Indiana, respectively. In June 1970 Kenneth Gibson became the first black mayor of Newark. Charles Evers' election in 1969 as mayor of Fayette, Mississippi, is the best-known example of the increase in black political victories in the South. Most of these black officials are confronted by the problem of representing a biracial constituency, while at the same time serving as spokesmen for racial interests.

Among the many articles on the recently elected black political leaders, the following are the most useful: On Walter Washington, see "Two Firsts for Washington," *Time*, XC (Sept. 15, 1967), 23–24; Ragni Lantz, "D.C. Mayor Walter Washington," *Ebony*, XXIII (Mar. 1968), 72–74 ff.; and "First Mayor of the Nation's Capital," *NHB*, XXX (Nov. 1967), 4–5. On Richard Hatcher and Carl Stokes, consult Hal Higdon, "Dick Hatcher is Definitely a Soul Mayor," *New York Times Magazine*, Nov. 3, 1968, 32–33 ff., and "Gary's Next Mayor: White, Pink, or Black," *Reporter*, XXXVII (Nov. 2, 1967), 41–42; Phillip T. Drotning and Wesley W. South, *Up from the Ghetto* (New York, 1970),* ch. 6; James M. Naughton, "Cleveland: 'I Must Prove Their Fears Are Groundless'—Stokes," in "In Cleveland and Boston, the Issue is Race," *New York Times Magazine*, Nov. 5, 1967, 30 ff., and "Mayor Stokes: The First Hundred Days," *ibid.*, Feb. 25, 1968, 26–27 ff.; James F. Barnes, "Carl Stokes: Crisis, Challenge, and Dilemma," in William G. Shade and Roy C. Herrenkohl, eds., *Seven on Black: Reflections on the Negro Experience in America* (New York, 1969),* pp. 117–33; "Cleveland's Carl Stokes: Making It," *Newsweek*, LXXIII (May 26, 1969), 67–68, 73; Charles L. Sanders and Alex Poinsett, "Black Power at the Polls," *Ebony*, XXIII (Jan. 1968), 23–35; Jeffrey K. Hadden, Louis H. Masotti, Victor Thiessen, "The Making of the Negro Mayors 1967," *Transaction*, V (Jan.–Feb. 1968), 21–30; and "The Black Mayors," *Newsweek*, LXXVI (Aug. 3, 1970), 16–22, which also includes Kenneth Gibson. Charles Evers is the subject of Robert Canzoneri, "Charles Evers: Mississippi's Representative Man?" *Harper's*, CCXXXVII (July 1968), 67–74; Walter Rugaber, "'We Can't Cuss White People Any More. It's In Our Hands Now,'" *New York Times Magazine*, Aug. 4, 1968, 12–14 ff.; Joseph Lelyveld, "The Mayor of Fayette, Miss.," *ibid.*, Oct. 26, 1969, 54–55 ff.; and Charles Evers, *Evers*, ed. with intro. by Grace Halsell (New York and Cleveland, 1971).

Probably the best-known southern black politician is the young Georgia state legislator Julian Bond, who was barred from taking his seat because of his opposition to the Vietnam War and who was among the nominees for Vice President at the Democratic National Convention in 1968. See Herbert Shapiro, "Julian Bond: Georgia's 'Uppity' Legislator," *Nation*, CCII (Feb. 7, 1966), 145–48; Reese Cleghorn, "Here Comes Julian Bond—Quiet, But Angry, Rebel," *New York Times Magazine*, Oct. 20, 1968, 38–39 ff.; David Llorens, "Julian Bond," *Ebony*, XXIV (May 1969), 58–70; and John Neary, *Julian Bond: Black Rebel* (New York, 1971).

Senator Brooke is the subject of Allan Morrison, "Negro Political Progress in New England," *Ebony*, XVIII (Oct. 1963), 25–28 ff.; Simeon Booker, " 'I'm A Soul Brother—': Senator Edward Brooke," *ibid.*, XXII (Apr. 1967), 150–54; and George R. Metcalf, *Black Profiles* (rev. ed., New York, 1970), pp. 279–306. Adam Clayton Powell, *Marching Blacks* (New York, 1945); Neil Hickey and Ed Edwin, *Adam Clayton Powell and the Politics of Race* (New York, 1965); James Q. Wilson, "The Flamboyant Mr. Powell," *Commentary*, XLI (Jan. 1966), 31–35; and P. Allan Dionisopoulos, *Rebellion, Racism, and Representation: The Adam Clayton Powell Case and Its Antecedents* (De Kalb, Ill., 1970),* all treat the well-known former congressman from Harlem, while James Q. Wilson's "Two Negro Politicians: An Interpretation," *Midwest Journal of Political Science*, IV (Nov. 1960), 346–69,** compares him to his long-time (and more conservative) colleague from Chicago, the late William L. Dawson. On Dawson, see also "Negro America's Top Politician," *Ebony*, X (Jan. 1955), 17–20 ff. "Mr. Diggs Goes to Congress," *ibid.* (Apr. 1955), 104–09, is the story of the long-time black representative from Detroit. The "new breed" of black congressmen are treated in Stanley Friedman, "Successor to Adam Powell?" *New Republic*, CLVI (Feb. 4, 1967), 12–13, on John Conyers, Jr.; "New Faces in Congress," *Ebony*, XXIV (Feb. 1969), 56–65, on Shirley Chisholm, William Clay, and Louis Stokes; Susan Brownmiller, "As the 'First Black Woman Congressman' Herself Puts It, This Is Fighting Shirley Chisholm," *New York Times Magazine*, Apr. 13, 1969, 32–33 ff.; Shirley Chisholm, *Unbought and Unbossed* (Boston, 1970); Drotning and South, *Up from the Ghetto*, cited above, ch. 9; and, on the Congressional Black Caucus, "Black Politics: New Way to Overcome," *Newsweek*, LXXVII (June 7, 1971), 30–34, 39.

Harold M. Baron, "Black Powerlessness in Chicago," *Trans-action*, VI (Nov. 1968), 27–33,** is a provocative study of the underrepresentation of blacks in leadership positions in that city. On non-political black leadership, see also Harold W. Pfautz, "The Power Structure of the Negro Sub-Community: A Case Study and a Comparative View," *Phylon*, XXIII (2nd Quarter 1962), 156–66;** Lewis Bauman, "Racial Discrimination and Negro Leadership Problems: The Case of 'Northern Community,'" *SF*, XLIV (Dec. 1965), 173–86;** Jack L. Walker, "The Functions of Disunity: Negro Leadership in a Southern City," *JNE*, XXXII (Summer 1963), 227–36; and Lewis M. Killian and Charles U. Smith, "Negro Protest Leaders in a Southern Community," *SF*, XXXVIII (Mar. 1960), 253–57.

10. Black Nationalism Since World War II

Since the decline of Garveyism, the major mass-based black nationalist movement has been the Nation of Islam, or the Black Muslims. Founded in the 1930s, the Muslims peaked in strength and influence during the civil rights revolution of the 1950s and 1960s. The Muslim movement has appealed primarily to poorly educated, lower-class urban blacks upon whose condition civil rights advances have had little immediate impact. Preaching the foreordained destruction of white civilization and its replacement by a dominant black nation, the Muslims offer a spiritual and psychological basis for black pride and a promise of future black supremacy that makes it unnecessary to resort to violence. As a practical formula for short-run self-improvement, the Muslims insist upon a stringent moral code and a program of economic self-sufficiency based on thrift, hard work, and the establishment of separate black businesses.

A useful guide to literature on the Muslims is Daniel T. Williams and Carolyn L. Redden, *Black Muslims in the United States: A Selected Bibliography* (Tuskegee, Ala., 1964). Among the general studies, the two major works on contemporary black nationalism are E. U. Essien-Udom, *Black Nationalism: A Search for an Identity in America* (Chicago, 1962),* and C. Eric Lincoln, *The Black Muslims in America* (Boston, 1961).* Lincoln expands his views in *My Face Is Black* (Boston, 1964), in a brief essay—"The Black Muslims as a Protest Movement"—in Arnold M. Rose, ed., *Assuring Freedom to the Free: A Century of Emancipation in the USA* (Detroit, 1964), pp. 220–40, and in an article, "Extremist Attitudes in the Black Muslim Movement," *New South*, XVIII (Jan. 1963), 3–10. Articles that explore the Muslims' more conservative tendencies include Lawrence L. Tyler, "The Protestant Ethic Among the Black Muslims," *Phylon*, XXVII (1st Quarter 1966), 5–14, and Michael Parenti, "The Black Muslims: From Revolution to Institution," *Social Research*, XXXI (Summer 1964), 175–94. Chs. 5 and 6 (on the Muslims and Malcolm X) of Theodore Draper, *The Rediscovery of Black Nationalism* (New York, 1970),* are also important. Louis E. Lomax, *When the Word Is Given: A Report on Elijah Muhammad, Malcolm X, and the Black Muslim World* (Cleveland, 1963),* is a popular history of the movement and its leaders. Evaluations of the major nationalist groups and their objectives are John Henrik Clarke, "The New Afro-American Nationalism," *Freedomways*, I (Fall 1961), 285–95;** E. U. Essien-Udom, "Black Identity in the International Context," and John H. Bracey, Jr., "Black Nationalism since Garvey," in Nathan I. Huggins, Martin Kilson, and Daniel M. Fox, eds., *Key Issues in the Afro-American Experience*, 2 vols. (New York, 1971),* vol. II, pp. 233–79. Primary materials on post-World War II black nationalism can be found in pt. 5 of the excellent anthology by John H. Bracey, Jr., August Meier, and Elliott Rudwick, eds., *Black Nationalism in America* (Indianapolis, 1970).* For the influential works of the black psychiatrist Frantz Fanon, prophet of revolution in Algeria, see especially *Black Skins, White Masks* (New York, 1967),* which provides a psychological explanation of black nationalism, and *The Wretched of the Earth* (New York, 1965),* an examination of the necessity for violence in the liberation of colonial peoples.

Elijah Muhammad, the leader of the Nation of Islam, explains the theology and program of the Black Muslims in *Message to the Blackman in America* (Chicago, 1965). His best-known follower, Malcolm X, tells his own story in the extraordinarily powerful *Autobiography of Malcolm X* (New York, 1965),* compiled from taped interviews by Alex Haley. Malcolm X broke with the Muslims in March 1964, and the evolution of his philosophy after that time is best traced in the following works: Malcolm X, *Malcolm X on Afro-American History* (New York, 1967);* Archie Epps, ed., *The Speeches of Malcolm X at Harvard* (New York, 1968),* which includes a long biographical-analytical essay by Epps, a black Harvard dean; three books by the Trotskyite writer George Breitman, *Malcolm X Speaks: Selected Speeches and Statements* (New York, 1965),* *By Any Means Necessary: Speeches, Interviews and a Letter by Malcolm X* (New York, 1970),* both of which Breitman edited, and *The Last Year of Malcolm X: The Evolution of a Revolutionary* (New York, 1967); Benjamin Goodman, ed., *The End of White World Supremacy: Four Speeches by Malcolm X* (New York, 1971);* I. F. Stone, "The Pilgrimage of Malcolm X," *New York Review of Books,* V (Nov. 11, 1965), 3–5; and Gertrude Samuels, "Feud within the Black Muslims," *New York Times Magazine,* Mar. 22, 1964, 17 ff. John Henrik Clarke, ed., *Malcolm X: The Man and His Times* (New York, 1969),* is an anthology of essays by black writers which also includes some of Malcolm's speeches and writings.

For a case study of a special nationalist sect which illuminates the role black nationalism may play in alleviating black problems, see Howard Brotz, *The Black Jews of Harlem: Negro Nationalism and the Dilemmas of Negro Leadership* (New York, 1964).*

The relationship between black intellectuals and black nationalism is treated in Wilson Record, "The Negro Intellectual and Negro Nationalism," *SF,* XXXII (Oct. 1954), 10–18, and in Harold Cruse, *The Crisis of the Negro Intellectual* (New York, 1967),* pp. 337–44, 420–48, 544–65. Robert L. Allen, *Black Awakening in Capitalist America: An Analytic History* (Garden City, N.Y., 1969),* explores the revolutionary nationalism produced by the disillusionment of black intellectuals and ghetto dwellers with the irrelevance of civil rights gains to the black poor in northern cities. On the dichotomy between black nationalism and Marxist black radicalism, see Part VII, topic 14, "Blacks and Communism."

Several works focus specifically on the influence of Africa on the emergence of black nationalism in America and on the interrelationship between African and American nationalisms. A good place to start is Harold R. Isaacs, *The New World of Negro Americans* (Cambridge, Mass., 1963),* and for primary sources, see Adelaide Cromwell Hill and Martin Kilson, eds., *Apropos of Africa: Sentiments of Negro Leaders on Africa from the 1800s to the 1950s* (London, 1969). In addition, one should consult George Shepperson, "Notes on Negro American Influences on the Emergence of African Nationalism," *Journal of African History*, I (1960), 299–312,** for historical background; E. U. Essien-Udom, "The Relationship of Afro-Americans to African Nationalism," *Freedomways*, II (Fall 1962), 391–407; and Rupert Emerson and Martin Kilson, "The American Dilemma in a Changing World: The Rise of Africa and the Negro American," in Talcott Parsons and Kenneth B. Clark, eds., *The Negro American* (Boston, 1966),* pp. 626–55. Irene Tinker, "Nationalism in a Plural Society: The Case of the American Negro," *Western Political Quarterly*, XIX (Mar. 1966), 112–22, compares the problems of black nationalism in the United States with the constraints on the development of nationalism in other pluralistic nations.

Another form of black nationalism is a cultural nationalism founded on the premise that blacks in the United States comprise a cultural nation whose liberation depends on the development of black artistic and cultural forms. Cultural nationalists argue that cultural revolution must precede political and social revolution on the path to black liberation. A chief spokesman for this point of view is Ron Karenga, the leader of US, a cultural nationalist organization in Los Angeles. His ideas can be studied in Clyde Halisi and James Mtume, eds., *The Quotable Karenga* (Los Angeles, 1967), portions of which are excerpted in Floyd B. Barbour, ed., *The Black Power Revolt* (Boston, 1968),* pp. 190–200. Ray Rogers, "Black Guns on Campus," *Nation*, CCVIII (May 5, 1969), 558–60, deals with the conflict between US and the Black Panthers at UCLA. Another exponent of cultural nationalism is LeRoi Jones; see Part VIII, topic 2, "Black Poetry," and topic 6, "After Protest: Black Writers in the 1950s and 1960s." Robert L. Allen gives a brief discussion of cultural nationalism in *Black Awakening in Capitalist America*, cited above, esp. pp. 164–71. Allen also devotes considerable attention to other black nationalist groups, including the Muslims; his thesis is that black militant groups exploit the nationalist sentiments of the black masses "to advance the class interests of the black bourgeoisie."

For other expressions of postwar black nationalism, see topic 11, "Black Power," and topic 12, "The Black Panthers," following.

11. Black Power

The slogan "black power" was first popularized in 1966 in statements by Stokely Carmichael and Floyd McKissick, the new leaders respectively of the Student Nonviolent Coordinating Committee and the Congress of Racial Equality. The cry for black power grew out of a conviction that civil rights legislation and poverty programs were failing to wipe out inequality and poverty because they were products of the white power structure. In order to face that power structure from a viable bargaining position, black power spokesmen argued, it was essential to develop a strong political and economic power base within the black community itself. Black power meant black control of the major institutions directly affecting the lives of black Americans. It carried with it positive connotations of racial pride and ambiguous overtones of racial separatism; the latter in particular were responsible for the initial rejection of black power by moderate advocates of traditional goals of integration.

The major statements of the meaning of black power are Stokely Carmichael, "What We Want," *New York Review of Books*, VII (Sept. 22, 1966), 5–6, 8, and the important book by Carmichael and Charles V. Hamilton, *Black Power: The Politics of Liberation in America* (New York, 1967).* See also Carmichael, "Toward Black Liberation," *Massachusetts Review*, VII (Autumn 1966), 639–51; and Hamilton, "An Advocate of Black Power Defines It," *New York Times Magazine*, Apr. 14, 1968, 22–23 ff. For a sense of the ways in which other advocates of black power perceive the concept, the selections in Floyd B. Barbour, ed., *The Black Power Revolt: A Collection of Essays* (Boston, 1968);* August Meier, Elliott Rudwick, and Francis L. Broderick, eds., *Black Protest Thought in the Twentieth Century* (rev. ed., Indianapolis, 1971),* pt. 4; and Thomas Wagstaff, ed., *Black Power: The Radical Response to White America* (Beverly Hills, Calif., 1969),* are all especially useful. The 1967 National Conference on Black Power gave the term an extreme interpretation when it called for separate black and white nations in the United States; its resolutions are reprinted in *Ramparts,* VI (Dec. 1967), 46. Nathan Wright, Jr., an official of the Conference on Black Power, explores the utility of black power as a key to new approaches to urban problems in *Black Power and Urban Unrest: Creative Possibilities* (New York, 1967).* A variety of other black views are presented in Eldridge Cleaver, "On Meeting the Needs of the People," *Ramparts,* VIII (Sept. 1969), 34–35; Julius Lester, *Look Out Whitey! Black Power's Gon' Get Your Mama!* (New York, 1968);* James Boggs, "Black Power—A Scientific Concept Whose Time Has Come," *Liberator,* VII (Apr. 1967), 4–7, *ibid.* (May 1967), 8–10; Whitney M. Young, Jr., *Beyond Racism: Building an Open Society* (New York, 1969), pp. 236–55; two books by Sterling Tucker, *Beyond the Burning: Life and Death of the Ghetto* (New York, 1968),* pp. 50–52, ch. 5, and *Black Reflections on White Power* (Grand Rapids, Mich., 1969); Joseph R. Washington, Jr., *Black and White Power Subreption* (Boston, 1969); and C. T. Vivian, *Black Power and the American Myth* (Philadelphia, 1970). Arthur M. Brazier, *Black Self-Determination: The Story of the Woodlawn Organization* (Grand Rapids, Mich., 1969), is an argument for the organization of the black community in order to achieve self-determination.

For an indication of the spectrum of black criticisms of black power, see Martin Luther King, Jr., "Martin Luther King Defines 'Black Power,'" *New York Times Magazine,* June 11, 1967, 26–27 ff., which is adapted from his book, *Where Do We Go from Here: Chaos or Community?* (New York, 1967),* ch. 2; Bayard Rustin, "'Black Power' and Coalition Politics," *Commentary,* XLII (Sept. 1966), 35–40, and his "The Failure of Black Separatism," *Harper's,* CCXL (Jan. 1970), 25–34; two articles by Martin Kilson, "Black Power: Anatomy of a Paradox," *Harvard Journal of Negro Affairs,* II (1968), 30–34, and "Negro Militancy," *Saturday Review,* LII (Aug. 16, 1969), 28–31; Roy Wilkins, "Whither 'Black Power'?" *Crisis,* LXXIII (Aug.–Sept. 1966), 353–54; Robert L. Allen, *Black Awakening in Capitalist America: An Analytic His-*

tory (Garden City, N.Y., 1969),* chs. 2, 4; and Harold Cruse, "Behind the Black Power Slogan," in his *Rebellion or Revolution?* (New York, 1968),* ch. 13.

Scholarly studies and white analyses of the black power movement include Theodore Draper, *The Rediscovery of Black Nationalism* (New York, 1970),* ch. 8; Benjamin Muse, *The American Negro Revolution: From Nonviolence to Black Power, 1963–1967* (Bloomington, Ind., 1968),* ch. 16; Martin Duberman, "Black Power and the American Radical Tradition," *Partisan Review,* XXXV (Winter 1968), 34–68; Vincent Harding, "Black Radicalism: The Road from Montgomery," in Alfred F. Young, ed., *Dissent: Explorations in the History of American Radicalism* (De Kalb, Ill., 1968),* pp. 319–54; Joel D. Aberbach and Jack L. Walker, "The Meanings of Black Power: A Comparison of White and Black Interpretations of a Political Slogan," APSR, LXIV (June 1970), 367–88; Hugh D. Graham, "The Storm over Black Power," *Virginia Quarterly Review,* XLIII (Autumn 1967), 545–65; Edward Peeks, *The Long Struggle for Black Power* (New York, 1971); Charles E. Fager, *White Reflections on Black Power* (Grand Rapids, Mich., 1967); Raymond S. Franklin, "The Political Economy of Black Power," *Social Problems,* XVI (Winter 1969), 286–301; Dora Pantell and Edwin Greenidge, *If Not Now, When? The Many Meanings of Black Power* (New York, 1969); Christopher Lasch, "The Trouble with Black Power," *New York Review of Books,* X (Feb. 29, 1968), 4–14; Fred Powledge, *Black Power—White Resistance: Notes on the New Civil War* (Cleveland, 1967); Paul Feldman, "The Pathos of 'Black Power,'" *Dissent,* XIV (Jan.–Feb. 1967), 69–79; Harold C. Relyea, "Black Power as an Urban Ideology," *Social Studies,* LX (Oct. 1969), 243–50; Lewis M. Killian, *The Impossible Revolution? Black Power and the American Dream* (New York, 1968),* ch. 6; Robert L. Zangrando, "From Civil Rights to Black Liberation: The Unsettled 1960's," *Current History,* LVII (Nov. 1969), 281–86, 299; Joyce Ladner, "What 'Black Power' Means to Negroes in Mississippi," *Trans-action,* V (Nov. 1967), 7–15;** David Riesman, "Some Reservations About Black Power," *ibid.,* 20–22;** Jan E. Dizard, "Black Identity, Social Class, and Black Power," *Psychiatry,* XXXIII (May 1970), 195–207; Luther P. Gerlach and Virginia H. Hine, "The Social Organization of a Movement of

386 THE CIVIL RIGHTS REVOLUTION

Revolutionary Change: Case Study, Black Power," in Norman
E. Whitten, Jr., and John F. Szwed, eds., *Afro-American An-
thropology: Contemporary Perspectives* (New York, 1970), ch. 21;
Donald Canty, *A Single Society: Alternatives to Urban Apartheid*
(New York, 1969), ch. 4, "Black Pride"; John Herbers, *The Lost
Priority: What Happened to the Civil Rights Movement in
America?* (New York, 1970), ch. 5, "The Effects of Black Power";
and Richard P. Young, ed., *The Evolution of Black Politics and
Protest Since World War II* (New York, 1970),* pt. 3, on the
development of black pride. Robert L. Scott and Wayne Brockriede evaluate *The Rhetoric of Black Power* (New York, 1969).*
Attitudes of blacks toward black power, as revealed in a Gallup
opinion survey conducted in 1969 for *Newsweek*, are summarized
in Peter Goldman, *Report from Black America* (New York,
1970), ch. 6, app. C. For additional references, consult the excellent bibliography of periodical literature on black power in
Barbour, ed., *The Black Power Revolt*, cited above, pp. 323–28.

There are several studies of black power from the perspective of
the churches: Joseph C. Hough, Jr., *Black Power and White Protestants: A Christian Response to the New Negro Pluralism* (New
York, 1968);* James H. Cone, *Black Theology and Black Power*
(New York, 1969);* C. Freeman Sleeper, *Black Power and Christian Responsibility: Some Biblical Foundations for Social Ethics*
(Nashville, 1969); Joseph R. Barndt, *Why Black Power?* (New
York, 1968);* and Washington, *Black and White Power Subreption*, cited above, ch. 5. James Forman's 1969 demand that
white churches pay reparations to the black community is the subject of Robert S. Lecky and H. Elliott Wright, eds., *Black Manifesto: Religion, Racism, and Reparations* (New York, 1969).*

12. The Black Panthers

The Black Panther Party for Self-Defense (it has since dropped
"Self-Defense" from its title) was founded in 1966 in California
by two young black radicals, Huey P. Newton and Bobby Seale.
The Black Panthers are grass-roots black militants dedicated to us-

ing guerrilla tactics to achieve their goal of revolutionary change in American society. They see blacks as a colonial people oppressed by white institutions in general and police brutality in particular. Their program calls for an independent, self-governing black community organized according to socialist principles. One of the major Panther planks—armed self-defense for blacks in the ghetto—lies at the root of the on-going war between Panthers and the police. During the party's brief history there have been numerous violent clashes between its members and the police, resulting in fatalities on both sides. Many of the leading Panthers have died violently, and others are in jail or in self-exile, but the legal responsibility for the deaths remains in several instances unresolved. Panthers (and others) allege that there is a deliberate police-FBI conspiracy to wipe out the party, and there has been considerable public discussion about whether the Panthers could receive a fair trial anywhere in the United States. This well-publicized image of violence contrasts sharply with the less well-known program of important social services—for example, free breakfasts for ghetto children—that the Panther party has sponsored in several cities.

The writings of major figures among the Black Panthers provide the best introduction to the Panther movement. Panther Minister of Information Eldridge Cleaver's brilliant *Soul on Ice* (New York, 1968),* written during his imprisonment on charges of rape and assault with intent to kill, should be supplemented by his "Letter from Jail," *Ramparts*, VI (June 15, 1968), 17–21, "Requiem for Nonviolence," *ibid.* (May 1968), 48–49, and "The Fire Now: Field Nigger Power Takes over the Black Movement," *Commonweal*, LXXXVIII (June 14, 1968), 375–77, and later pieces in Robert Scheer, ed., *Eldridge Cleaver: Post-Prison Writings and Speeches* (New York, 1969), drawn largely from articles published during 1967 and 1968 in *Ramparts*. (*Ramparts* regularly publishes articles by or about Panthers and is a good, although certainly not unbiased, source of up-to-date information on their activities.) Kathleen Cleaver writes about her husband in "On Eldridge Cleaver," *Ramparts*, VII (June 1969), 4 ff. Lee Lockwood, *Conversation with Eldridge Cleaver: Algiers* (New York, 1970),* deals with Cleaver in exile. Bobby Seale, chairman of the Black Panther party, has written an impassioned autobiographical history, *Seize the Time: The Story of the Black Panther Party and Huey P. Newton* (New York, 1970).* Writing from prison, Newton himself explained the purpose and methods of the party in "The Black Panthers," *Ebony*, XXIV (Aug. 1969), 106–12. Earl Anthony's *Picking up the Gun: A Report on the Black Panthers* (New York, 1970), is the account of an erstwhile Panther disillusioned by the party's Marxist-Leninist orientation and its willingness to ally temporarily with white radicals. *I Was a Black Panther*, as told to Chuck Moore (Garden City, N.Y., 1970),* is the life story of a sixteen-year-old veteran of SNCC and the Panthers who also quit the party. The party's newspaper, *The Black Panther*, which first appeared in October 1968, is a useful source for continuing information on their activities. Philip S. Foner, ed., *The Black Panthers Speak* (Philadelphia, 1970),* is a fine anthology of Panther views.

Among non-Panther sources, the major analytical treatment of the party's ideology is Theodore Draper, *The Rediscovery of Black Nationalism* (New York, 1970),* ch. 7. *Ramparts* reporter Gene Marine's history, *The Black Panthers* (New York, 1969),* is highly partisan and emotional in tone. Don A. Schanche, *The Panther Paradox: A Liberal's Dilemma* (New York, 1970), provides a more balanced perspective, as do two articles in the *New York Times Magazine*—Sol Stern's "The Call of the Black Panthers," Aug. 6, 1967, 10–11 ff., and Harvey Swados' "Old Con, Black Panther, Brilliant Writer and Quintessential American," Sept. 7, 1969, 38–39 ff., a study of Cleaver. Reginald Major, *A Panther Is a Black Cat* (New York, 1971), is a sympathetic study of the party's ideological roots, historical development, and current policies and problems. Mary Ellen Leary, "The Uproar over Cleaver," *New Republic*, CLIX (Nov. 30, 1968), 21–24, is also useful. Edward Jay Epstein, "The Panthers and the Police," *New Yorker*, XLVII (Feb. 13, 1971), 45 ff., disputes the Panthers' allegation that the police have murdered nineteen or more party members in a deliberate attempt to decimate the group. Gilbert Moore, *A Special Rage* (New York, 1971), is a thoughtful study of the Panthers, focusing on the murder trial of Huey Newton. Gail Sheehy, *Panthermania: The Clash of Black Against Black in One American City* (New York, 1971), treats the Panthers in New Haven, with special attention to the murder of Alex Rackley.

During the early months of 1971 the Black Panther party appeared to be in a state of considerable internal turmoil. Earl Caldwell, "The Panthers: Dead or Regrouping," New York *Times*, Mar. 1, 1971, pp. 1, 16, is a thoughtful analysis of the party's changing fortunes. In late February and early March the party split into two factions, one headed by Chief of Staff David Hilliard and Defense Minister Huey P. Newton, with headquarters in Oakland, and the other, with headquarters in New York, under the leadership of Minister of Information Eldridge Cleaver, in self-exile in Algeria. The personal and ideological nature of the dispute between the two factions can be examined in Earl Caldwell, "Internal Dispute Rends Panthers," *ibid.*, Mar. 7, 1971, p. 26; "The Panthers: Their Decline—And Fall?" *Newsweek*, LXXVII (Mar. 22, 1971), 26–28; "Free Kathleen Cleaver," *The Black Panther*, VI (Mar. 6, 1971), supplement; and Phil Tracy, "Civil War within the Revolution?" *Village Voice*, Mar. 11, 1971, pp. 1, 71.

For further analysis of the status of blacks in the United States in terms of domestic colonialism, see Stokely Carmichael and Charles V. Hamilton, *Black Power: The Politics of Liberation in America* (New York, 1967),* ch. 1; Robert Blauner, "Internal Colonialism and Ghetto Revolt," *Social Problems*, XVI (Spring 1969), 393–408; and Robert L. Allen, *Black Awakening in Capitalist America: An Analytic History* (Garden City, N.Y., 1969).*

13. Urban Racial Violence: The 1960s

A decade of civil rights activity accomplished substantial change in the legal status of black men in America but very little change in the deep-rooted social and economic ills of the black ghetto. Long-simmering frustrations and grievances against slumlords, the police, exploitative white ghetto merchants—against the whole panoply of white institutional racism—exploded into a devastating cycle of looting, destruction, and death. Beginning with Harlem in 1964 and Watts in 1965, the "long, hot summer" of ghetto rioting became a characteristic feature of the 1960s.

The nationwide outbreak of racial violence following the assassination of Martin Luther King, Jr., in April 1968 prompted the appointment by President Lyndon Johnson of a National Advisory Commission on Civil Disorders, whose *Report* (New York, 1968),* known familiarly as the "Riot Commission Report," is a thorough analysis of race riots in the 1960s. For further detail, consult the important *Supplemental Studies for the National Advisory Commission on Civil Disorders* (Washington, 1968).* Commentaries on the *Report,* originally published as "The U.S. Riot Commission Report and the Social Sciences: A Symposium," *SSQ,* XLIX (Dec. 1968), 432–73, have been reprinted as chs. 35–42 of Norval D. Glenn and Charles M. Bonjean, eds., *Blacks in the United States* (San Francisco, 1969). See also Michael Lipsky and David J. Olson, "Riot Commission Politics," *Transaction,* VI (July–Aug. 1969), 8–21, and Gary T. Marx, "Two Cheers for the National Riot Commission," in John F. Szwed, ed., *Black America* (New York, 1970), ch. 7. Urban America, Inc., and the Urban Coalition register a discouraging progress report in *One Year Later: An Assessment of the Nation's Response to the Crisis Described by the National Advisory Commission on Civil Disorders* (New York, 1969).*

Arthur I. Waskow, *From Race Riot to Sit-In, 1919 and the 1960s: A Study in the Connections Between Conflict and Violence* (Garden City, N.Y., 1967),* and Elliott Rudwick and August Meier, "Negro Retaliatory Violence in the Twentieth Century," *New Politics,* V (Winter 1966), 41–51, place the upheavals of the 1960s in historical context. The Rudwick and Meier findings are also included in ch. 9 of Hugh Davis Graham and Ted Robert Gurr, eds., *Violence in America: Historical and Comparative Perspectives* (New York, 1969),* the official report to the National Commission on the Causes and Prevention of Violence. This volume is full of important background material for an understanding of contemporary race riots; among the more notable essays are ch. 2, "Historical Patterns of Violence in America," by Richard Maxwell Brown, and especially ch. 10, Morris Janowitz's "Patterns of Collective Racial Violence," which is probably the best brief anatomy of riots. The works of Allen D. Grimshaw provide essential background for a study of recent racial violence; see "Lawlessness and Violence in America and Their Special Manifestations in Changing Negro-White Relationships," *JNH*, XLIV (Jan. 1959), 52–72; "Urban Racial Violence in the United States: Changing Ecological Considerations," *AJS*, LXVI (Sept. 1960), 109–19;** "Relationships Among Prejudice, Discrimination, Social Tension and Social Violence," *Journal of Intergroup Relations*, II (Autumn 1961), 302–10; "Negro-White Relationships in the Urban North: Two Areas of High Conflict Potential," *ibid.*, III (Spring 1962), 146–58; "Factors Contributing to Colour Violence in the United States and Britain," *Race*, III (May 1962), 3–19; and "Actions of Police and the Military in American Race Riots," *Phylon*, XXIV (3rd Quarter 1963), 271–89. These articles are reprinted, together with other selections from Grimshaw's unpublished doctoral dissertation, in a volume he edited, *Racial Violence in the United States* (Chicago, 1969), an anthology of primary accounts and retrospective analyses of riots throughout American history. For a useful historical summary, see Joseph Boskin, "A History of Urban Racial Conflicts in the Twentieth Century," in Audrey Rawitscher, ed., *Riots in the City: An Addendum to the McCone Commission Report* (Los Angeles, 1967), pp. 1–24. Boskin has also edited a reader, *Urban Racial Violence in the Twentieth Century* (Beverly Hills, Calif., 1969).* For other source materials on riots over the period 1863–1968, see J. Paul Mitchell, ed., *Race Riots in Black and White* (Englewood Cliffs, N.J., 1970).*

There is already a voluminous literature analyzing the riot phenomenon and chronicling outbreaks in various cities. Harlem is treated in Fred C. Shapiro and James W. Sullivan, *Race Riots: New York, 1964* (New York, 1964). Lenora E. Berson, *Case Study of a Riot: The Philadelphia Story* (New York, 1966), is a pamphlet on the 1964 outbreak in that city. Among the individual riots, Watts has received the most intensive coverage to date. Robert E. Conot gives what is probably the best narrative account of Watts by an outsider in *Rivers of Blood, Years of Darkness* (Toronto, Ont., 1967),* but Jerry Cohen and William S. Murphy, *Burn, Baby, Burn! The Los Angeles Race Riot, August, 1965* (New York, 1966), and Spencer Crump, *Black Riot in Los Angeles: The Story of the Watts Tragedy* (Los Angeles, 1966), should also be consulted. Paul Bullock, ed., *Watts: The Aftermath; An Inside View of the Ghetto by the People of Watts* (New York,

1970),* affords an invaluable perspective on why and how Watts happened. Nathan Cohen, ed., *The Los Angeles Riots: A Socio-Psychological Study* (New York, 1970), is extremely thorough and informative. See also David O. Sears and T. M. Tomlinson, "Riot Ideology in Los Angeles: A Study of Negro Attitudes," *SSQ*, XLIX (Dec. 1968), 485–503, which also appears as ch. 30 of Glenn and Bonjean, eds., *Blacks in the United States*, cited above; Anthony Oberschall, "The Los Angeles Riot of August 1965," *Social Problems*, XV (Winter 1968), 322–41; H. Edward Ransford, "Isolation, Powerlessness, and Violence: A Study of Attitudes and Participation in the Watts Riot," *AJS*, LXXIII (Mar. 1968), 581–91;** and "Watts, 1965," in Richard Hofstadter and Michael Wallace, eds., *American Violence: A Documentary History* (New York, 1970),* pp. 263–66. The official report of the Governor's Commission on the Los Angeles Riots (the McCone Commission), *Violence in the City—An End or a Beginning?* (Los Angeles, 1965), has been the subject of much criticism; for a sample of views, see Paul Jacobs, *Prelude to Riot: A View of Urban America from the Bottom* (New York, 1967),* a detailed analysis of black grievances in Los Angeles; Robert M. Fogelson, "White on Black: A Critique of the McCone Commission Report on the Los Angeles Riots," *PSQ*, LXXXII (Sept. 1967), 337–67;** Bayard Rustin, "The Watts 'Manifesto' and the McCone Report," *Commentary*, XLI (Mar. 1966), 29–35; and Robert Blauner, "Whitewash over Watts," *Trans-action*, III (Mar.–Apr. 1966), 9.

There is an account of the 1967 riots in chs. 19–20 of Benjamin Muse, *The American Negro Revolution: From Nonviolence to Black Power, 1963–1967* (Bloomington, Ind., 1968).* Newark receives special attention in Tom Hayden, *Rebellion in Newark: Official Violence and Ghetto Response* (New York, 1967);* Nathan Wright, Jr., *Ready to Riot* (New York, 1968);* and the *Report for Action* (Trenton, 1968) of the Governor's Select Commission on Civil Disorders which investigated the New Jersey riots. The most useful study of Detroit is Hubert G. Locke, *The Detroit Riot of 1967* (Detroit, 1969); see also John Hersey, *The Algiers Motel Incident* (New York, 1968);* Van Gordon Sauter and Burleigh Hines, *Nightmare in Detroit: A Rebellion and Its Victims* (Chicago, 1968); Detroit Urban League, *A Survey of*

Attitudes of Detroit Negroes After the Riot of 1967 (Detroit, 1967); and "Detroit, 1967," in Hofstadter and Wallace, eds., *American Violence,* cited above, pp. 267–69. Henry Etzkowitz and Gerald M. Schaflander, *Ghetto Crisis: Riots or Reconciliation?* (Boston, 1969), chs. 16–17, deals with the eruption of racial tensions in the Bedford-Stuyvesant district of New York during the summer of 1967. One small phase of the conflagration following the King assassination is treated in the excellent book by Ben W. Gilbert and the staff of the Washington *Post, Ten Blocks from the White House: Anatomy of the Washington Riots of 1968* (New York, 1968).* On the Washington riot, see also Ulf Hannerz, *Soulside: Inquiries into Ghetto Culture and Community* (New York, 1969), ch. 8, which offers a sound analysis of the roots of riots in everyday frustrations and harassments of ghetto life. Garry Wills presents a frightening account of riot-control planning in police departments across the country in *The Second Civil War: Arming for Armageddon* (New York, 1968).*

During the summer of 1968, urban racial violence entered a new phase of armed guerrilla warfare with the gun battle in the streets of Cleveland between police and armed black militants led by black nationalist Fred Ahmed Evans. This episode and the riot it precipitated are the subject of Louis H. Masotti and Jerome R. Corsi, *Shoot-Out in Cleveland: Black Militants and the Police: July 23, 1968* (New York, 1969).* See also Terry Ann Knopf, "Sniping—A New Pattern of Violence?" *Trans-action,* VI (July–Aug. 1969), 22–29. Since that time, large-scale, unorganized rioting has generally faded from the scene, and armed confrontations between police and black militants, particularly the Black Panthers, have become the dominant pattern in urban racial violence. Martin Oppenheimer speculates on the "prospects for guerrilla warfare in the urban black ghetto" in ch. 5 of *The Urban Guerrilla* (Chicago, 1969). For accounts of the Panthers and the police, see the preceding topic, "The Black Panthers."

Sociologists, psychologists, and other investigators have already begun to study the riot phenomenon from a wide variety of perspectives, and the fruits of their research add up to an extensive and ever-growing literature. Two anthologies are especially useful: Robert H. Connery, ed., *Urban Riots: Violence and Social Change* (New York, 1968),* which originally appeared as vol.

XXIX, no. 1 (1968) of the *Proceedings of the Academy of Political Science;* and Louis H. Masotti and Don R. Bowen, eds., *Riots and Rebellion: Civil Violence in the Urban Community* (Beverly Hills, Calif., 1968).* Robert M. Fogelson, *Violence as Protest* (Garden City, N.Y., 1971), is an important monograph on the riots of the 1960s. Among other works, the following is necessarily only a partial listing (in alphabetical order) of the most worthwhile accounts: Saul Bernstein, *Alternatives to Violence: Alienated Youth and Riots, Race, and Poverty* (New York, 1967); Robert Blauner, "Internal Colonialism and Ghetto Revolt," *Social Problems,* XVI (Spring 1969), 393–408;** David Boesel, "The Liberal Society, Black Youths, and the Ghetto Riots," *Psychiatry,* XXXIII (May 1970), 265–81; Joseph Boskin, "Violence in the Ghettos (1968)," *New Mexico Quarterly,* XXVII (Winter 1968), 317–33; Richard A. Chikota and Michael C. Moran, *Riot in the Cities: An Analytical Symposium on the Causes and Effects* (Rutherford, N.J., 1970); Ralph W. Conant, *The Prospects of Revolution: A Study of Riots, Civil Disobedience and Insurrection in Contemporary America* (New York, 1971); Thomas J. Crawford and Murray Naditch, "Relative Deprivation, Powerlessness, and Militancy: The Psychology of Social Protest," *Psychiatry,* XXXIII (May 1970), 208–33; Harold Cruse, *The Crisis of the Negro Intellectual* (New York, 1967),* pp. 347–401, on the ideologies of violence in the black community; Charles U. Daly, ed., *Urban Violence* (Chicago, 1969);* Bryan T. Downes, "Social and Political Characteristics of Riot Cities: A Comparative Study," *SSQ,* XLIX (Dec. 1968), 504–20, which also appears as ch. 31 of Glenn and Bonjean, eds., *Blacks in the United States,* cited above; Russell Dynes and E. L. Quarantelli, "What Looting in Civil Disturbances Really Means," *Trans-action,* V (May 1968), 9–14;** Shalom Endelman, ed., *Violence in the Streets* (Chicago, 1968),* esp. pt. 4, "The Conflict of Race"; Joe R. Feagin, "Social Sources of Support for Violence and Nonviolence in a Negro Ghetto," *Social Problems,* XV (Spring 1968), 432–41; Joe R. Feagin and Paul B. Sheatsley, "Ghetto Resident Appraisals of a Riot," *Public Opinion Quarterly,* XXXII (Fall 1968), 352–62; Robert M. Fogelson, "From Resentment to Confrontation: The Police, the Negroes, and the Outbreak of the Nineteen-Sixties Riots," *PSQ,* LXXXIII (June 1968), 217–47;** James A. Geschwender, "Civil Rights Protest and Riots: A Disappearing Distinction," *SSQ*, XLIX (Dec. 1968), 474–84,** which also appears as ch. 29 of Glenn and Bonjean, eds., *Blacks in the United States*, cited above; "Ghetto Riots," the entire vol. XXVI (Winter 1970) of the *Journal of Social Issues*; Peter Goldman, *Report from Black America* (New York, 1970), ch. 4, app. C, which presents black attitudes toward riots as portrayed in a Gallup opinion survey conducted in 1969 for *Newsweek*; Charles V. Hamilton, "Riots, Revolts, and Relevant Response," in Floyd B. Barbour, ed., *The Black Power Revolt* (Boston, 1968),* pp. 201–10; Calvin C. Hernton, "Dynamite Growing Out of Their Skulls," in LeRoi Jones and Larry Neal, eds., *Black Fire: An Anthology of Afro-American Writing* (New York, 1968),* pp. 78–104; Joseph S. Himes, "The Functions of Racial Conflict," *SF*, XLV (Sept. 1966), 1–10;** Irwin Isenberg, ed., *The City in Crisis* (New York, 1968); Morris Janowitz, *Social Control of Escalated Riots* (Chicago, 1968);* Blair Justice, *Violence in the City* (Fort Worth, Tex., 1969); Stanley Lieberson and Arnold R. Silverman, "The Precipitants and Underlying Conditions of Race Riots," *ASR*, XXX (Dec. 1965), 887–98;** William McCord, John Howard, Bernard Friedberg, and Edwin Harwood, *Life Styles in the Black Ghetto* (New York, 1969),* chs. 2–3, 10–13; Raymond W. Mack, "Riot, Revolt, or Responsible Revolution: Of Reference Groups and Racism," *Sociological Quarterly*, X (Spring 1969), 147–56;** Louis H. Masotti, Jeffrey K. Hadden, Kenneth F. Seminatore, and Jerome R. Corsi, *A Time to Burn? An Evaluation of the Present Crisis in Race Relations* (Chicago, 1969); Eugene H. Methvin, *The Riot Makers: The Technology of Social Demolition* (New Rochelle, N.Y., 1970); Bayard Rustin, *Which Way Out? A Way out of the Exploding Ghetto* (New York, 1967); William F. Soskin, "Riots, Ghettos, and the 'Negro Revolt,'" in Arthur M. Ross and Herbert Hill, eds., *Employment, Race and Poverty* (New York, 1967),* pp. 205–33; Robert Samuelson, "Riots: The More There Are, the Less We Understand," *Science*, CLVII (Aug. 11, 1967), 663–65; two articles by T. M. Tomlinson, "The Development of a Riot Ideology Among Urban Negroes," *American Behavioral Scientist*, XI (Mar.–Apr. 1968), 27–31, and "Determinants of Black Politics: Riots and the Growth of Militancy," *Psychiatry*, XXXIII (May 1970), 247–64; Jules J. Wanderer, "1967 Riots: A Test of the Congruity of Events," *Social Problems,* XVI (Fall 1968), 191–98; Donald I. Warren, "Neighborhood Structure and Riot Behavior in Detroit: Some Exploratory Findings," *ibid.,* XVI (Spring 1969), 464–84; Aaron Wildavsky, "The Empty-Headed Blues: Black Rebellion and White Reaction," *Public Interest,* XI (Spring 1968), 3–16; and James Q. Wilson, *Varieties of Police Behavior: The Management of Law and Order in Eight Communities* (Cambridge, Mass., 1968).

14. Black Life-Styles in the Ghetto

Until recently, most sociologists discussed the lower-class culture of black urban ghettos as a pathological deviation from middle-class norms caused by poverty, oppression, and isolation from the mainstream of American life. Students of the ghetto tended to emphasize the themes of unemployment, delinquency, violence, crime, illegitimacy, family instability, and the widespread use of drugs. They saw the path to upward social mobility as blocked not only by discrimination, but also by a lack of commitment to such Protestant Ethic values as work, thrift, sobriety, rationality, and postponement of immediate gratifications for long-range goals. Sympathetic to the plight of the ghetto dweller, sociologists of both races (but mostly white) nevertheless expressed implicit or explicit negative value judgments on the ghetto subculture. Gunnar Myrdal entitled a subheading of ch. 43 of *An American Dilemma* (New York, 1944)* "The Negro Community as a Pathological Form of an American Community." Daniel P. Moynihan's *The Negro Family: The Case for National Action* (Washington, 1965)* viewed the ghetto as a "tangle of pathologies" that were both cause and effect of family instability. From this viewpoint, it followed that the ghetto subculture was not a genuine culture at all, but only an undesirable deviation from dominant American values. In his *The Negro in the United States* (rev. ed., New York, 1957), E. Franklin Frazier declared that "the Negro is not distinguished by culture from the dominant group," and in *Beyond the Melting Pot* (Cambridge, Mass., 1963),* Nathan

Glazer and Daniel P. Moynihan asserted that "the Negro is only an American and nothing else. He has no values and culture to guard and protect."

In the later 1960s, however, black separatists and intellectuals and an increasing number of sociologists and anthropologists began to proclaim that not only does a genuine and unique subculture exist in the ghettos, but that it also contains many positive values functional in the black struggle to survive in a hostile white world. Forms of music, dance, entertainment, sexual relations, dress, language, religious worship, humor, and food constitute what Lee Rainwater called an "expressive life-style" and what is now often designated by the single word "soul." Though difficult to define, the key features of soul seem to be an emphasis on emotion or feeling and an orientation to the vibrant present rather than the uncertain future; it is a ghetto version of existentialism. Champions of the soul life-style contrast its warmth and honesty with the presumed coldness, hypocrisy, and lack of emotion in white middle-class society. Erstwhile negative stereotypes of the black community are turned into self-proclaimed virtues: blacks *do* have more rhythm and sensuality and are proud of it. Soul music, soul food, the conviction that "black is beautiful," and the fraternal mystique between soul brothers are expressive of a culture whose values grow uniquely out of the black experience and cannot be fully shared by whites.

At the same time, some facets of the ghetto life-style have influenced white culture. Soul music appeals to white as well as black youth. Many expressions from the argot of "black English" have found their way into the American language: "square," "cool," "nitty-gritty," "jiving," "rapping," "hang-up," "put-on," "chicks," "cats," "bust," and "grass."

By 1970 a number of scholarly studies attempting to define and describe the black subculture had been published. Most of them were written by whites, but it appears that a major direction of black studies in the 1970s will be a growing effort by black writers, scholars, and artists to define and express their culture in their own terms. The existing studies are in some disagreement on such matters as whether the black subculture is similar to lower-class life-styles among other ethnic and racial groups or unique to the black experience in America and whether there is any evidence of

African cultural survivals among blacks in the United States. Future research in comparative anthropology and on the diffusion of African cultural patterns will, it is hoped, shed more light on these matters.

Some of the best subjective descriptions of the ghetto subculture are found in novels, autobiographies, and essays by black writers. Several participants in the Harlem renaissance of the 1920s glorified black lower-class life; an outstanding example was Claude McKay's *Home to Harlem* (New York, 1928).* For discussions of this theme, see Part VIII, topics 1 and 4, "The Harlem Renaissance" and "Fiction of the Renaissance: Jean Toomer and Claude McKay." Several white novelists in the 1920s also idealized black "primitivism"—see Part VIII, topic 3, "Exotic Primitivism in the White Novel." Claude Brown's classic *Manchild in the Promised Land* (New York, 1965),* though generally depressing in its portrait of the violence and ruined lives of black men in Harlem, contains also an appreciative account of the humor, music, and other forms of cultural adaptations that created a substructure of black pride and identity. See also Brown's "The Language of Soul," *Esquire*, LIX (Apr. 1958), 88 ff. The early chapters of *The Autobiography of Malcolm X* (New York, 1965)* show how the "hustler" became a folk hero in the ghetto. Similarly rewarding insights into the world of soul brothers are provided by Iceberg Slim, *Pimp, the Story of My Life* (Los Angeles, 1967).* Norman Mailer's *The White Negro* (San Francisco, 1959)* is a discussion of efforts by white "hipsters" to emulate black behavior patterns.

Several advocates of black nationalism or black power consider black cultural values a necessary basis for political action. Good examples of this viewpoint are several of the essays in LeRoi Jones, *Home: Social Essays* (New York, 1966);* Eldridge Cleaver, *Soul on Ice* (New York, 1968);* Julius Lester, *Look Out Whitey! Black Power's Gon' Get Your Mama!* (New York, 1968);* LeRoi Jones, "The Need for a Cultural Base to Civilrites & Bpower Mooments" and "Maulana Ron Karenga, from the Quotable Karenga," in Floyd B. Barbour, ed., *The Black Power Revolt* (Boston, 1968),* pp. 119–26 and 162–70; most of the essays in Douglas A. Hughes, ed., *From a Black Perspective: Contemporary Black Essays* (New York, 1970); Addison Gayle, Jr., *The Black Situation* (New York,

1970); and LeRoi Jones (Imamu Amiri Baraka) and Billy Abernathy (Fundi), *In Our Terribleness* (Indianapolis, 1971). Many of the items cited in this Part, topics 10 and 11, "Black Nationalism Since World War II" and "Black Power," and the sections on LeRoi Jones and on the "Black Aesthetic" in Part VIII, topics 2 and 6, "Black Poetry" and "After Protest: Black Writers in the 1950s and 1960s," also deal with this matter.

An early scholarly attempt to analyze patterns of lower-class ghetto behavior was St. Clair Drake and Horace R. Cayton, *Black Metropolis* (New York, 1945),* chs. 20–21. Kenneth B. Clark's penetrating studies of Harlem—*Dark Ghetto* (New York, 1965)* and *Youth in the Ghetto* (New York, 1964)—treat the black community partly in terms of social pathology, but contain sympathetic discussions of the creative responses of ghetto residents to their situation. The essays by St. Clair Drake ("The Social and Economic Status of the Negro in the United States") and G. Franklin Edwards ("Community and Class Realities: The Ordeal of Change") in Talcott Parsons and Kenneth B. Clark, eds., *The Negro American* (Boston, 1966),* pp. 3–46, 280–302, and Bonnie Bullough, "Alienation in the Ghetto," *AJS*, LXXII (Mar. 1967), 469–78, all provide a good introduction to the conditions of black communities in which distinctive mores and life-styles develop.

Some of the best systematic descriptions of the black ghetto subculture have been written by white sociologists and anthropologists. Perhaps the most influential book presenting the concept of a black soul culture to white readers was Charles Keil's *Urban Blues* (Chicago, 1966),* a study of male blues singers and their life-styles. "If we are ever to understand what urban Negro culture is all about," wrote Keil, "we had best view entertainers and hustlers as culture heroes, integral parts of the whole, rather than as deviants and shadow figures." Brief statements of variations on this theme are found in three articles by John F. Szwed: "Musical Style and Racial Conflict," *Phylon*, XXVII (4th Quarter 1966), 358–66; "Negro Music: Urban Renewal," in Tristram P. Coffin, ed., *Our Living Traditions: An Introduction to American Folklore* (New York, 1968), pp. 272–82; and "Afro-American Musical Adaptation," in Norman E. Whitten, Jr., and John F. Szwed, eds., *Afro-American Anthropology: Contemporary Per-*

spectives (New York, 1970),* pp. 219–28; and in Michael Haral-
ambos, "Soul Music and the Blues: Their Meaning and Relevance
in Northern United States Black Ghettos," *ibid.*, pp. 367–84.
Three black writers examine soul music as an expression of black
cultural values in Peter Labrie, "The New Breed," Lindsay Barrett, "The Tide Inside, It Rages!", and A. B. Spellman, "Not Just
Whistling Dixie," in LeRoi Jones and Larry Neal, eds., *Black
Fire: An Anthology of Afro-American Writing* (New York, 1968),
pp. 64–77, 149–68. See also Frank Kofsky, *Black Nationalism and
the Revolution in Music* (New York, 1970).* Many of the books
on black music cited in Part VIII, topic 11, "Soul Music: Blues,
Jazz, and Variations," develop the theme of music as an expres-
sion of black culture; see especially Nat Hentoff, *The Jazz Life*
(New York, 1961), and two books by LeRoi Jones—*Blues People*
(New York, 1963)* and *Black Music* (New York, 1967).* The
rise from rags to riches of "Soul Brother No. 1," the singer James
Brown, is chronicled by Phillip T. Drotning and Wesley W. South,
Up from the Ghetto (New York, 1970),* pp. 75–84, and Brown's
style is analyzed by Mel Watkins, "The Lyrics of James Brown,"
Amistad 2 (New York, 1971),* pp. 21–42.

Intensive investigations of black neighborhoods in Washington,
D.C., by two white scholars produced detailed and lucid analyses
of the urban folkways of black males. Elliot Liebow, *Tally's
Corner: A Study of Negro Streetcorner Men* (Boston, 1967),* is
a sensitive study of the rootless yet structured ghetto street life.
The descriptions of another black neighborhood in Washington
by Ulf Hannerz, a Swedish anthropologist, constitute the fullest
and most precise accounts of soul culture yet available. Hannerz
presented his findings and interpretations in one book and several
articles: *Soulside: Inquiries into Ghetto Culture and Community*
(New York, 1969); "Gossip, Networks and Culture in a Black
American Ghetto," *Ethnos*, XXXII, no. 1 (1967), 35–60; "The
Rhetoric of Soul: Identification in Negro Society," *Race*, IX (Apr.
1968), 453–65; "What Negroes Mean by 'Soul,'" *Trans-action*,
V (July–Aug. 1968), 57–61; and "Roots of Black Manhood: Sex,
Socialization and Culture in the Ghettos of American Cities,"
ibid., VI (Oct. 1969), 12–21.

Lower-class black culture is primarily oral rather than written.
Great emphasis is placed on verbal facility, and the "cat" who can

"signify" his way into a profitable situation or out of trouble enjoys a "rep" at least equal to that of the "gorilla" who is good with his fists or a switchblade. A ritualized game of obscene verbal insults variously called "playing the dozens," "sounding," or "joning" is a favorite pastime of teenage ghetto males and a training ground for adult verbal dexterity. This game was first described in sociological literature by John Dollard, "The Dozens: The Dialect of Insult," *American Imago*, I (Nov. 1939), 3–24. A white folklorist, Roger D. Abrahams, who lived and carried on research in a Philadelphia black neighborhood, has written the fullest accounts of ghetto folklore, humor, and argot as the basis of a genuine subculture in the following articles and books: "Playing the Dozens," *Journal of American Folklore*, LXXV (July–Sept. 1962), 209–20;** "The Changing Concept of the Negro Hero," in Mody C. Boatright, Wilson M. Hudson, and Allen Maxwell, eds., *The Golden Log* (Dallas, 1962), pp. 119–34;** *Deep Down in the Jungle: Negro Narrative Folklore from the Streets of Philadelphia* (rev. ed., Chicago, 1970);* and *Positively Black* (Englewood Cliffs, N.J., 1970).* In his autobiography Dick Gregory recounts his origins as a comedian in the verbal games of the ghetto: see Dick Gregory, with Robert Lipsyte, *Nigger: An Autobiography* (New York, 1964).* Muhammad Ali's verbal facility derives from a similar background: see Jack Olsen, *Black Is Best: The Riddle of Cassius Clay* (New York, 1967). Millicent R. Ayoub and Stephen A. Barnett, "Ritualized Verbal Insult in White High School Culture," *Journal of American Folklore*, LXXVIII (Oct.–Dec. 1965), 337–44, maintains that "sounding" exists among lower-class whites as well as blacks, but Bruce Jackson, in a critique of this article, "White Dozens and Bad Sociology," *ibid.*, LXXIX (Oct.–Dec. 1966), 374–77, asserts that the practice is far more common and elaborate among blacks. Russell Middleton and John Moland, "Humor in Negro and White Subcultures: A Story of Jokes Among University Students," *ASR*, XXIV (Feb. 1959), 61–69, compares the functional roles of black and white humor.

The distinct ghetto dialect is interpreted by Beryl L. Bailey, "Toward a New Perspective in Negro English Dialectology," *American Speech*, XL (Oct. 1965), 171–77; William A. Stewart, "Sociolinguistic Factors in the History of American Negro Dialects," *The Florida FL Reporter*, V (Fall 1967), 11 ff.; Thomas Kochman, "Toward an Ethnography of Black American Speech Behavior," *Trans-action*, VI (Feb. 1969), 26–34, revised version in Whitten and Szwed, eds., *Afro-American Anthropology*, cited above, pp. 145–62; and Clarence Major, *Dictionary of Afro-American Slang* (New York, 1970).*

Other facets of the expressive ghetto life-style are discussed in Harold Finestone, "Cats, Kicks, and Color," *Social Problems*, V (July 1957), 3–13; Bill R. Hampton, "On Identification and Negro Tricksters," *Southern Folklore Quarterly*, XXI (Mar. 1967), 55–65; John Horton, "Time and Cool People," *Trans-action*, IV (Apr. 1967), 5–12;** George J. McCall, "Symbiosis: The Case of Hoodoo and the Numbers Racket," *Social Problems*, X (Spring 1963), 361–71; and Earl Shorris, *Ofay* (New York, 1966).

Most of the studies cited in the foregoing paragraphs are based on the explicit or implicit assumption that there exists a definable black subculture separate from, though interrelated with, the dominant white culture. Liebow's *Talley's Corner*, cited above, is a partial exception; Liebow describes the ghetto dweller's behavior "not so much as a way of realizing the distinctive goals and values of his own subculture . . . but rather as his way of trying to achieve many of the goals and values of the larger society." J. Milton Yinger, "Contraculture and Subculture," *ASR*, XXV (Oct. 1960), 625–35, argues that ghetto life-styles are not a true subculture but a pathological "contraculture." Hyman Rodman, "The Lower-Class Value Stretch," *SF*, XLIII (Dec. 1963), 205–15, maintains that lower classes in all societies develop alternative value systems based on middle-class norms but accommodating or "stretching" them to fit the circumstances of poverty or deprivation. But Lester Singer, "Ethnogenesis and Negro-Americans Today," *Social Research*, XXIX (Winter 1962), 419–32, and Robert Blauner, "Black Culture: Myth or Reality?" in Whitten and Szwed, eds., *Afro-American Anthropology*, cited above, pp. 347–66, both argue that the unique experience of blacks in America, combined with the African heritage in music and language, have produced a distinctive subculture different in important ways from that of other racial or ethnic groups. Lee Rainwater, "Work and Identity in the Lower Class," in Sam Bass Warner, Jr., ed., *Planning for a Nation of Cities* (Cambridge,

Mass., 1966),* pp. 105–23, occupies a midposition in the debate between a class and ethnic interpretation. In a review of Keil's *Urban Blues*, cited above, Bennett M. Berger, "Soul-Searching," *Trans-action*, IV (June 1967), 54–57, criticizes the notion of a unique black culture.

Several scholars have attacked the concept pioneered by Oscar Lewis's studies of Mexican and Puerto Rican lower classes (especially *The Children of Sanchez* [New York, 1961]*) of a self-perpetuating "culture of poverty." These scholars see the behavior patterns of the poor as a series of pragmatic responses to situational constraints rather than as a genuine "culture" or even a subculture. See especially Jack L. Roach and Orville R. Gursslin, "An Evaluation of the Concept 'Culture of Poverty,'" *SF*, XLV (Mar. 1967), 383–92; Hylan Lewis, *Culture, Class, and Poverty* (Washington, 1967); and Charles A. Valentine, *Culture and Poverty: Critique and Counter Proposals* (Chicago, 1968).* Charles A. and Betty Lou Valentine, "Making the Scene, Digging the Action, and Telling It Like It Is: Anthropologists at Work in a Dark Ghetto," in Whitten and Szwed, eds., *Afro-American Anthropology*, cited above, pp. 403–18, expresses considerable skepticism toward the concept of a unique black subculture or even a system of lower-class values different from those of mainstream middle-class American society. The implications of these studies for the concept of a black subculture are not entirely clear; some of them accept the notion of distinctive ghetto behavior patterns, if not of a distinctive subculture. This problem plus other questions pertaining to the "soul" culture, including the persistence of African survivals, are taken up in four recent anthologies of reprinted and original articles: Elizabeth M. Eddy, ed., *Urban Anthropology: Research Perspectives and Strategies* (Athens, Ga., 1969); Lee Rainwater, ed., *Soul* (Chicago, 1970);* John F. Szwed, ed., *Black America* (New York, 1970); and Whitten and Szwed, eds., *Afro-American Anthropology*, cited above. See also Houston A. Baker, Jr., "Completely Well: One View of Black American Culture," in Nathan I. Huggins, Martin Kilson, and Daniel M. Fox, eds., *Key Issues in the Afro-American Experience*, 2 vols. (New York, 1971),* vol. I, 20–33. Other relevant studies are cited in Part I, topic 2, "Black and Negro as Image, Category, and Stereotype"; Part II, topic 4, "African Cultural Survivals Among Black Americans"; Part VII, topic 2, "The Development of the Ghetto"; and topic 6, above, "The Economic Status of Black Americans."

In reaction to Daniel P. Moynihan's controversial report on *The Negro Family*, cited above, some scholars emphasized the positive features of ghetto family life and the functional value of black institutions, including the family, for survival in a hostile environment. See Lee Rainwater and William L. Yancey, eds., *The Moynihan Report and the Politics of Controversy* (Cambridge, Mass., 1967),* and additional references in topic 8, above, "The Black Family in Urban America."

Other studies containing information helpful for an understanding of urban black folkways include John H. Rohrer and Munro Edmonson, *The Eighth Generation Grows Up: Cultures and Personalities of New Orleans Negroes* (New York, 1960);* Leonard Broom and Norval D. Glenn, *Transformation of the Negro American* (New York, 1965),* ch. 2; S. P. Fullinwider, *The Mind and Mood of Black America* (Homewood, Ill., 1969),* ch. 8; and David A. Schulz, *Coming up Black: Patterns of Ghetto Socialization* (Englewood Cliffs, N.J., 1969).* William McCord, John Howard, Bernard Friedberg, and Edwin Harwood, *Life Styles in the Black Ghetto* (New York, 1969),* deals primarily with the attitudes of ghetto dwellers toward civil rights, violence, and black power rather than with behavior patterns as such. William Moore, Jr., *The Vertical Ghetto: Everyday Life in an Urban Project* (New York, 1969),* describes a black housing project primarily in terms of social pathology and despair. Herb Goro, *The Block* (New York, 1970),* is a moving photographic essay on a black and Puerto Rican block in the Bronx where the expressiveness of a creative subculture is less apparent than poverty and misery. And Edward C. Banfield, *The Unheavenly City: The Nature and Future of Our Urban Crisis* (Boston, 1970),* argues that the ingrained habits and attitudes of the poor constitute a subculture (which he defines in class rather than racial terms) that will inhibit the success of antipoverty and urban rehabilitation efforts.

Index

Black nationalism (cont'd)
171; churches and, 154, 207, 331; civil rights movement and, 317, 318, 320, 321, 322, 379, 383; Communism and, 231, 233–34; cultural, 382, 398–99; decentralization issue and, 383–86; Harlem Renaissance and, 241–43, 263; music and, 290, 400; poetry and, 245–46, 247, 248, 249–50; politics and, 373; self-defense and, 386–89; slave revolt and, 60; social organizations and, 157; stereotypes and, 21–22
Black Panther, The (newspaper), 296, 388, 389
Black Panther party, 382, 386–89
Black Power movement, 107, 164, 266, 317, 321, 322, 349–50, 383–86, 398; churches and, 328, 329, 331, 386
Black Star Steamship Line, 203
Black studies, *ix–xi, xiii,* 3, 5, 7–9, 12; stereotypes and, 19–22
Blair, John L., 220
Blair Education Bill, 165
Bland, Edward, 245
Blascoer, Frances, 189
Blassingame, John W., 22
Blau, Peter M., 341
Blau, Zena Smith, 370
Blauner, Robert, 389, 392, 394, 402
Blaustein, Albert P., 12, 74, 312, 315, 333
Bleser, Carol K. Rothrock, 123
Blesh, Rudi, 275, 288
Bloch, Herman D., 169
Blood, Robert O., Jr., 370
Bloom, Allan D., 28
Bloomfield, Neil J., 323
Blossom, Virgil T., 306
Blotner, Joseph L., 268
Blues, 15, 17, 33, 286–90, 399
Blumenthal, Henry, 148
Blumrosen, Alfred W., 347, 358
Blyden, Edward Wilmot, 172
Boas, Franz, 143
Boatright, Mody C., 401
Bobbs-Merrill Reprint Series in Black Studies, *xiii,* 3, 12
Bock, E. Wilbur, 330
Bodo, John, 80
Boesel, David, 394
Bogart, Leo, 305
Boggs, James, 321, 384
Bogue, Donald J., 352
Bolling v. Sharpe (case), 332
Bond, Frederick W., 15, 274, 278, 279, 280
Bond, Horace Mann, 121, 163, 165, 214, 236
Bond, J. Max, 222
Bond, Julian, 375, 377–78
Bone, Robert A., 14, 104, 175, 243, 250, 252, 253–54, 255, 259, 260
Bonjean, Charles M., 11, 328, 342, 353, 367–68, 371, 390, 392, 394, 395
Bontemps, Arna, 9, 10, 16, 35, 51, 242, 244, 247, 252, 287, 298; fiction of, 253; on migration, 187; on slave revolts, 63
Booker, Simeon, 315, 378
Boon, James, 70
Boorstin, Daniel J., 48, 82, 85
Borgeson, Roger D., 345
Bornet, Vaughn D., 231
Boskin, Joseph, 196, 275, 391, 394
Boston, Massachusetts, 93, 97, 104, 146, 152, 161–62, 168, 189, 310, 377
Boston *Guardian* (newspaper), 152, 161–62, 294–95
Botkin, Benjamin A., 52, 82–83, 114, 118
Botume, Elizabeth Hyde, 118, 120
Boulding, Kenneth E., 20

Bouma, Donald, 338
Bourgeoisie, 69, 174, 209–12, 251, 252, 293, 294; churches and, 154, 206, 326, 330, 331
Bovill, Edward W., 26
Bowdoin exhibition, 181
Bowen, Don R., 394
Bowen, Louise De Koven, 189
Bowles, Frank, 335
Bowles, Samuel, 337
Boxer, Charles R., 66
Boxing, 297, 298–99
Boyar, Burt and Jane, 276
Boycotts, 210, 316–17, 319, 327
Boyd, Willis D., 89
Bracey, John H., Jr., 12, 94, 107, 171, 190, 203, 217, 380
Brackett, Jeffrey R., 43, 58
Bradburn, Norman M., 361
Braden, Anne, 322
Braden, Carl, 207
Bradford, Daniel, 269
Bradford, Perry, 287
Bradford, S. Sydney, 57
Bradley, A. C., 28
Bradley, David Henry, 84, 156
Bradley, Gerald, 281
Bradley, Phillips, 76
Bragg, George F., 79, 84, 156
Braithwaite, William S., 242
Brauer, Jerald C., 81, 154
Brawley, Benjamin G., 10, 14, 103, 175, 242, 248, 270, 291
Brazeal, Brailsford R., 229
Brazier, Arthur M., 384
Brazil, 66
Breckenfeld, Gurney, 363
Breitman, George, 381
Bressler, Marvin, 362
Brewer, J. Mason, 37
Brewer, James H., 43, 114
Brewer, William M., 94, 221
Breyfogle, William A., 95
Bridgman, Richard, 177
Briggs, Vernon M., Jr., 348
Bright, Jean M., 242, 270–71
Brink, William, 322, 366
Brisbane, Robert H., 202, 216
British West Indies, 188
Brock, William R., 112, 124
Brockriede, Wayne, 386
Broderick, Francis L., 13, 149–50, 153, 173, 197–98, 200, 319, 383
Brody, Eugene B., 369
Broek, Jacobus ten, 112, 124
Bronfenbrenner, Urie, 371
Bronz, Stephen H., 243, 246, 248, 252
Brooke, Edward W., 357, 376, 378
Brooklyn Dodgers, 297
Brooks, Charles H., 159
Brooks, Gwendolyn, 243, 249
Brooks, Maxwell, 294
Brooks, Van Wyck, 277
Brooks, Walter H., 83
Broom, Leonard, 341, 350, 404
Brophy, Ira N., 21
Brotherhood of Sleeping Car Porters, 229, 235
Brotz, Howard, 13, 150, 207, 381
Browder, Earl, 232
Brown, B. Katherine, 43
Brown, Bert, 371
Brown, Cecil, 265
Brown, Claude, 344, 398
Brown, Earl, 196, 236
Brown, Frank L., 249
Brown, H. Rap, 322

ST. LOUIS COMM. COL
AT FLORISSANT VALLEY

8/70 J
5-11

8678-7
5=17

CRITICAL
S-11

SUMMER 83

LIBRARY
ST. LOUIS COMMUNITY COLLEGE
AT FLORISSANT VALLEY